JavaServer™ Pages Illuminated

Prabhakar Metlapalli, PhD
University of Maryland University College
Javaonline.org

JONES AND BARTLETT PUBLISHERS

Sudbury, Massachusetts

BOSTON   TORONTO   LONDON   SINGAPORE

World Headquarters
Jones and Bartlett Publishers
40 Tall Pine Drive
Sudbury, MA 01776
978-443-5000
info@jbpub.com
www.jbpub.com

Jones and Bartlett Publishers
Canada
6339 Ormindale Way
Mississauga, Ontario L5V 1J2
CANADA

Jones and Bartlett Publishers
International
Barb House, Barb Mews
London W6 7PA
UK

Jones and Bartlett's books and products are available through most bookstores and online booksellers. To contact Jones and Bartlett Publishers directly, call 800-832-0034, fax 978-443-8000, or visit our website, www.jbpub.com.

Substantial discounts on bulk quantities of Jones and Bartlett's publications are available to corporations, professional associations, and other qualified organizations. For details and specific discount information, contact the special sales department at Jones and Bartlett via the above contact information or send an email to specialsales@jbpub.com.

Production Credits
Acquisitions Editor: Timothy Anderson
Production Director: Amy Rose
Marketing Manager: Andrea DeFronzo
Editorial Assistant: Laura Pagluica
V. P. Manufacturing and Inventory Control: Therese Connell
Composition: Northeast Compositors, Inc.
Cover Design: Kristin E. Ohlin
Cover Image: © sgame/ShutterStock, Inc.
Printing and Binding: Malloy, Inc.
Cover Printing: John Pow Company

Library of Congress Cataloging-in-Publication Data
Metlapalli, Prabhakar.
  JavaServer pages illuminated / Prabhakar Metlapalli.
     p. cm.
  Includes index.
  ISBN-13: 978-0-7637-3592-0
  ISBN-10: 0-7637-3592-2
  1. JavaServer pages. 2. Web sites--Design. 3. Web site development. I. Title.
  TK5105.8885.J38M42 2007
  006.7'6--dc22
                          2006026817

6048

Printed in the United States of America
11 10 09 08 07   10 9 8 7 6 5 4 3 2 1

To

My mother Saraswati who is no more, my father Krishnamurthy, my wife Sudha, my daughters Veena and Neha, my brother Rajendra, and my sister Madhuri

Preface

JavaServer Pages (JSP) has become extremely popular in the development of professional-looking and powerful web pages. This book is intended for use as either a textbook of JavaServer Pages for undergraduate-level courses or as a self-study guide for learning JSP. It includes background material on Java, HTML, CSS, Javascript, and SQL—it is *not* assumed that the reader is familiar with Java or HTML, although those who are can skip those topics as necessary.

The chapter-by-chapter content is summarized here, so you know what to expect:

- Chapters 1 and 2 provide a review of the Java programming language, and include all topics required for understanding JSP— except very elementary topics such as variables, arithmetic and logical operators and expressions, conditions, loops, etc., which I consider pretty straightforward and which one can get from a number of sources (you may want to consider the Java courses I offer on my website: http://javaonline.org).

- In addition to the Java review chapters, the book has a separate chapter (Chapter 3) on HTML, CSS, and Javascript that should get the reader up-to-speed on these topics.

- Chapter 4 deals with servlets, including installing and configuring the Apache Tomcat Web Server to have the basic set-up ready for the subsequent chapters.

- Chapter 5 teaches the fundamental "building blocks" of JSP, namely scriptlets, directives, and expressions.

- Chapter 6 goes on to show how to process HTML forms using the JSP tools learned in Chapter 5, and includes session management.

- Chapter 7 describes how to develop database-driven JSP web pages, including background material on JDBC and SQL. It also includes instructions on installing the free MySQL database and integrating with JSP's running on Tomcat.

- Chapter 8 explains the concepts of tag libraries, custom tags, and JavaBeans.

- Finally, Chapter 9 deals with the state-of-the-art Struts/Model-View-Controller (MVC) architecture.

Every topic is followed by comprehensive solved exercises that show how to write the code step-by-step, and includes actual screen shots at every stage. I assume you will try them out first on your own and then compare your solution with the one provided. Unsolved assignments are included at the end of every chapter; these can be assigned to students. The unsolved ones also include screen shots to help students get a feel of how it should look. Solutions to these unsolved assignments are provided to instructors. Every chapter also includes a comprehensive, multiple-choice quiz.

This is probably the only JSP book in the market that includes an exhaustive review of Java, HTML, and Javascript. The idea is to ensure that everyone is on the same page before beginning to learn JSP. I have seen many students fumble while learning JSP due to lack of sufficient Java background—especially topics such as packages. Those who feel fully confident of Java topics are free to skip them (Chapters 1–2) and go directly to Chapter 3. However, these chapters should still serve as a ready reference for them as well, in case they need to look up a specific topic down the road. The idea, again, is not to have to look at multiple books written by different authors and try to fit it all together. Instead, this single book is a one-stop guide that takes the novice reader all the way from HTML and Java to JSP and Struts.

Acknowledgments

I have worked in several companies in the USA over the past decade, and have been fortunate to come across some very talented individuals. Some of them laid the foundation for the concept of this text; others inspired me to delve into knowing more about JSP, and still others did both.

One of the jobs I held that helped build the background for this book was my 3 year stint at a start-up company called B2eMarkets, Inc. in Rockville, MD (which was later bought by Verticalnet, Inc.). I especially wish to express my sincere gratitude to a colleague of mine at B2eMarkets, **Mr. Keng Loh**, who currently works as a software consultant in the Washington D.C. metro area. Keng was there when I needed help the most. The foundation for some of the concepts in this book was laid during discussions with him.

I have been fortunate to have a very understanding wife, **Sudha**, and my two daughters, **Veena** and **Neha**, who have shown incredible patience while I was writing this book. During the project, I worked full-time at my day job and somehow extracted time on weekends and evenings to write the book. In the process, many other activities were sacrificed and my family took it with patience.

Last but not the least, I wish to thank the staff at Jones and Bartlett Publishers for all their efforts in releasing the book: Tim Anderson, Amy Rose, Diana Coe, Sarah Bayle, and Melissa Elmore. I also acknowledge the efforts of the reviewers who gave valuable feedback in drafting the manuscript:

Tim Downey, Florida International University

Jayantha Herath, St. Cloud State University

Michael J. Jajko, Pace University

Carol Lushbough, University of South Dakota

Joe Milukas, Pace University

Hong K. Sung, University of Central Oklahoma

Contents

CHAPTER 1

Java Review: Methods, Classes, Objects, and Packages

Chapter Objectives

- Review Java environment setup.

- Look at important options in `javac` and `java` commands.

- Learn about mixed arithmetic expressions and casting.

- Become familiar with escape character sequences.

- Study arrays and how to process them.

- Understand methods and how they work.

- Learn what a class is and how to instantiate an object from it.

- Become aware of the difference between instance and static class members.

- Learn how to create a package and add classes to it.

- Note the effect of access specifiers on class member access across packages.

So you want to learn JSP—one of the most useful applications of Java that has given tremendous power to several web sites and web-based applications in recent years. Before you begin learning JSP however, it is important to make sure that you are up-to-date with the required Java background. To this end, this book will include two review chapters focusing on Java topics that form an essential foundation for JSP. Due to space limitations, elementary material such as variables, operators, expressions, and control and looping statements (if, if-else, for, while, switch) will not be covered.[*] Those who already know the specific topics listed in Chapters 1 and 2 can go directly to Chapter 3; however the two explanatory chapters should serve as a ready reference for them as well. Since Java is a vast topic and students could have learned it from any of several "flavors" (or subsets) available out there, I wanted to make sure we are all on the same page before we begin our discussion of JSP.

This book will assume that you are using the Windows operating system. If you are using another system (such as Unix or Linux), the following adjustments should be made:

- Read the word "folder" as a "directory."
- Replace C: drive with your home directory (or /usr/local, as applicable).
- Replace a "command prompt window" with a "terminal window."
- For environment variables, replace %VAR_NAME% with $VAR_NAME.
- Use setenv instead of set.
- Replace backslashes in the command session and folder paths with forward slashes.

I assume that you have the JDK installed on your C drive, under C:\JDK, and that you have unzipped the JDK source files under C:\JDK\src. Make sure you follow the instructions for installing the JDK in Appendix A and set any required environment variables (PATH, CLASSPATH) as described in Appendix B. Let's begin by creating a new folder called JSP under the C drive that will be our working folder for the hands-on examples and exercises in this book. Under C:\JSP, we will be creating folders called Chapter1, Chapter2, etc.—one per chapter. Go ahead by creating the Chapter1 folder under C:\JSP.

1.0   Hello World

Let's begin with a review of the good old HelloWorld example. Type in the following program using any text editor of your choice (for example, Notepad) and save it as HelloWorld.java, say under C:\JSP\Chapter1.

```
class HelloWorld
```

---

[*](In case you are interested, I offer beginning Java courses that cover these, at http://javaonline.org.)

```
{
    public static void main(String[] args)
    {
        System.out.println("Hello, World!");
    }
}
```

Open a command prompt window using Start -> All Programs -> Accessories -> Command Prompt. Change to the C:\JSP\Chapter1 folder and compile the above program using the `javac` command, as follows:

```
C:\JSP\Chapter1>javac HelloWorld.java
```

This creates a new file, `HelloWorld.class` in the same directory. This is the `.class` file that corresponds to the `.java` file that you just compiled. Every time you compile a Java file, it creates a `.class` file with the same name as the class name in the Java file. In this example, the class name was `HelloWorld` above, so it created a file called `HelloWorld.class` in the same folder as the `HelloWorld.java` file, which is C:\JSP\Chapter1. The `.class` file is very important. You cannot run the `HelloWorld` program without having the `HelloWorld.class` file in that folder. (It will show an error if you try to do so.)

The next step is to run the `HelloWorld` example. For this, use the `java` command as shown below. (Here `java` is short for the executable file `java.exe` under C:\JDK\bin.)

```
C:\JSP\Chapter1>java HelloWorld
```

Hit Enter, and remember *not* to put any file name extension here. (Observe the difference between the compile and the run commands.)

This should show the output "`Hello, World!`" on your DOS prompt. The output session will look as shown here.

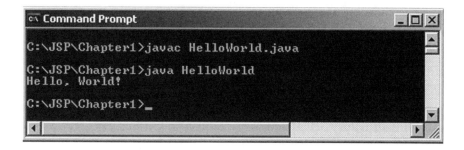

1.1 Directory Manipulation When Compiling/Running Java Programs

1.1.1 Running a Java Program from Another Folder Using CLASSPATH

You may have observed that for your first program to work, you need to have your HelloWorld.class file in the same folder (C:\JSP\Chapter1) where you execute the program (java HelloWorld). If you try going to some other folder (say, C:\Temp) and try running your program from there, it will not work unless you have HelloWorld.class in that folder. Try it out—with the HelloWorld.class file still under C:\JSP\Chapter1, go to C:\Temp and type in java HelloWorld as shown below:

C:\Temp>java HelloWorld

It will show an error as shown here:

```
Command Prompt                                                _ □ ×
C:\Temp>java HelloWorld
Exception in thread "main" java.lang.NoClassDefFoundError: HelloWorld

C:\Temp>
```

Java is saying that it is not able to find the .class file HelloWorld.class (it doesn't matter where you put your HelloWorld.java file—all that counts is the HelloWorld.class file.) To make it work from C:\Temp, you need to use the following slightly modified run command:

C:\Temp>java -classpath C:\JSP\Chapter1 HelloWorld

```
Command Prompt                                                _ □ ×
C:\Temp>java -classpath C:\JSP\Chapter1 HelloWorld
Hello, World!

C:\Temp>
```

Here, the part immediately to the right of -classpath, which is C:\JSP\Chapter1 in this example, tells Java where to search for a .class file when it tries to run the program. Here we are asking Java to find the HelloWorld.class file in C:\JSP\Chapter1. Instead of a single folder, the -classpath option may specify a series of several folder names separated by semicolons, and in this case, Java would search each of these folders, in sequence from left to right, for the .class file. For example, you could have

C:\Temp>java -classpath C:\JSP\Chapter1;C:\Windows HelloWorld

or even

```
C:\Temp>java -classpath .;C:\JSP\Chapter1;C:\Windows HelloWorld
```

Observe that in the last case, the period (.) immediately following the word -classpath refers to the *current* folder where one is running the java command (C:\Temp in this example). This means you are instructing Java to look for the HelloWorld.class file in the current folder (C:\Temp) first, then in C:\JSP\Chapter1, and finally in C:\Windows. If it does not find it in all three of these folders, it would give the same NoClassDefFoundError that you got earlier.

Once it finds the .class in a specific folder, it stops looking further and takes that .class file to run the program. So it is important to put the right sequence of folder names in the -classpath option.

As you can see, it would be quite cumbersome to keep typing the list of folders every time you try to run a program. A better alternative is to define an environment variable called CLASSPATH (just like the PATH variable) that contains a list of one or more folders that you want Java to look into for any .class files required. So next time when you say

```
java -classpath %CLASSPATH% filename
```

it knows where to look. Try it out:

Observe how I retain the period (.), meaning the current folder, as the first in the list of folders in CLASSPATH. The idea is to give the current folder precedence over other folders; if the .class file is not found there, then you want it to look in other folders. If the .class file with the same name exists in two or more folders listed in CLASSPATH, the one that appears first in the list would be taken. In that case, deciding the exact sequence of folder names in CLASSPATH is more a matter of developer judgment based on which version of the .class is to be used during execution. In this particular example, you could have put the period at the end (after C:\Windows) or even omitted it from CLASSPATH and it would still have worked, because the .class you want resides in C:\JSP\Chapter1, which is outside the current folder (C:\Temp).

Ok—you saw how to use the -classpath option in javac / java to specify where the .class files reside. You also saw how using a CLASSPATH environment variable makes the -classpath option more concise. There is one more advantage of defining the CLASSPATH environment variable: If you omit the -classpath option altogether, Java is preconfigured to use the current value of CLASSPATH environment variable as the list of folders to look for any `.class` files. So, you don't even have to type the `-classpath` option anymore (provided the current value of CLASSPATH variable is acceptable; otherwise you can change that value once and keep using `javac` / `java` multiple times without putting an explicit `-classpath`). So your session may look like this:

In the initial examples that we will be looking at, we compile all files in one folder—in other words, we will expect any `.class` files to reside in the folder where you execute the Java command from. So you won't encounter the issue of executing from a different folder (*except* when you deal with packages, described in Section 1.8). In order to ensure that Java is able to pick up the `.class` from the current folder, you need to make sure of the following:

- You have the period (.) in your CLASSPATH (in which case you don't have to use the `-classpath` option explicitly), or

- You use an explicit `-classpath .` option every time you use the `java` command.

To avoid using the `-classpath` option every time you use the `java` command, I recommend adding the period to the CLASSPATH environment variable (if is not already there), and making it a permanent change (by using Control Panel as described in Appendix B). After this, you simply say `java HelloWorld` and it will work.

1.1.2 Specifying the Output Folder When Compiling Java Programs

At this stage, you may be wondering why anyone would want to keep the `.class` files in a folder other than the one where the `java` execute command is run. To answer this, go back to the `javac` command we saw a little while ago:

```
C:\JSP\Chapter1>javac HelloWorld.java
```

Recall that this command creates a `.class` file in the same folder as the `.java` file. In a real-world corporate environment, you could have several folders, each with multiple Java files. When each of these is compiled as shown earlier, it would end up in several `.class` files spread across folders. To run a program that uses several `.class` files, you would have to be very careful to make a long list of folder names where each `.class` exists, and put them in the right sequence.

To avoid this, companies usually have a separate folder where all the .class files could be dumped and used when running Java programs. For example, let's say you create a separate folder called Output under C:\JSP\Chapter1, where you plan to dump all your .class files of this chapter. One way to dump the .class files into this folder after each compile would be to manually copy each .class file from the folder where it compiled, but that would be highly impractical! As a solution for this, the javac command has a nice option: the "-d" option, which allows you to specify where you want the .class files to go to, after every compile. In this example, you want the .class file to go to C:\JSP\Chapter1\Output. So when compiling HelloWorld.java, you would say

```
Command Prompt                                                    _ □ ×
C:\JSP\Chapter1>javac -d C:\JSP\Chapter1\Output HelloWorld.java
C:\JSP\Chapter1>_
```

or simply

```
Command Prompt                                                    _ □ ×
C:\JSP\Chapter1>javac -d Output HelloWorld.java
C:\JSP\Chapter1>
```

Here, Output is the *relative* path of the Output folder with respect to the *current* folder (C:\JSP\Chapter1).

This would create the HelloWorld.class file under C:\JSP\Chapter1\Output instead of the current folder (C:\JSP\Chapter1). To run this program from C:\JSP\Chapter1, you specify the Output folder in the -classpath option. You would thus say

```
Command Prompt                                                    _ □ ×
C:\JSP\Chapter1>java -classpath C:\JSP\Chapter1\Output HelloWorld
Hello, World!
C:\JSP\Chapter1>_
```

or simply

To run it from C:\Temp, you would use

or, using a relative path,

Here, .. ("dot-dot") means "one level up," so that would take it from C:\Temp to C:.

You can also use the CLASSPATH environment variable:

1.2   Mixed Arithmetic Expressions and Casting

An arithmetic expression consists of a combination of operands and arithmetic operators that can be evaluated to deduce a specific arithmetic value (or result). When constructing an arithmetic expression, there is no restriction on the data types of the operands involved. For example, although it is not the preferred way of doing things, you can very well add an int-type variable and a double-type variable, with no ensuing errors.

While evaluating such mixed arithmetic expressions, Java follows some rules behind the scenes to come up with the final answer. As a general rule, you are better off avoiding such mixed arithmetic expressions unless you are sure of the implications. In some situations, however, you might find it useful to use mixed data types in an expression. In these cases, you need to know what rules Java follows when evaluating such expressions, so that you know what result to expect.

To understand mixed data types, consider the integer division example shown here:

```
int i = 3 / 2;
```

This will give a truncated answer of 1 because both operands in the expression 3 / 2 are integers.

Now, consider a modified expression that defines i to be of type double instead of int:

```
double i = 3 / 2;
```

This still does not solve the problem of not getting the correct answer (1.5), because the right-hand side is evaluated first as an *integer* division with the integer operands 3 and 2. That would give a result of 1 (truncating the 0.5), which would then be converted to an equivalent double value of 1.0. So the final value of i would be 1.0. Although this is not what you want, this illustrates a very important concept of *data-type conversion*, which in technical parlance is called **casting**. In this example, the int value of 1 was cast into its double equivalent (1.0). Java relies heavily on such casting when dealing with mixed arithmetic expressions. One way to get the correct answer (1.5) is to make at least one of the operands on the right-hand side to be double, so that the division would be a normal division (as opposed to an integer division). Let's go ahead and do that:

```
double i = 3.0 / 2;
```

Notice the right-hand side operand of 3.0 (this time it is not just 3). In Java, there is a big difference between 3 and 3.0, although they actually represent the same value. Java would interpret 3.0 as a double value because it has a decimal (fractional) portion indicated by the decimal point (.), whereas the value 3 would be considered an int due to the absence of the decimal point. The way this instruction would be processed is described next.

Consider the right-hand side only; the operands are 3.0 (double) and 2 (int). Whenever Java encounters two operands of differing types, it automatically converts the one with the lower precision (int in this example) into the higher-precision type of the other operand (double in this example), so both would then be of the same precision. Java would thus convert the integer 2 into 2.0 (double). Divide 3.0 by 2.0 to give a double answer of 1.5, which would be the final answer stored in the variable i. Technically, the value 2 was cast into a double data type (with a value of 2.0), and then the division was carried out with two double operands. Since Java does the conversion for you, this type of casting is called *implicit casting.*

Rather than depend on Java to do the data-type conversion, there is a way to do the conversion at will—that is, when and where you want the conversion to occur. This is called *explicit casting.* In the preceding example, you would say this:

```
double i = (double) 3 / 2 ;
```

Observe the word double in parentheses preceding the integer 3 on the right-hand side. By putting an explicit data type in parentheses before a specific value, you are asking Java to explicitly cast the value into the requested data type and then proceed with the rest of the computation. In other words, the casting of 3 into the double equivalent 3.0 would occur first (see the precedence table in Appendix C to see that casting, denoted by (type), does have higher precedence than any arithmetic operator). The division would then be carried out between the converted 3.0 and the integer 2, which would result in 1.5 due to mixed-data-type arithmetic. Note that when you explicitly cast an operand to some data type, you must enclose the data type in parentheses; the operand itself may or may not be enclosed in parentheses.

To extend this further, you could also have explicitly cast both the operands to double before performing the division, and end up with the same result:

```
double i = (double) 3 / (double) 2;
```

Note that in either casting (implicit or explicit), you *cannot* cast a higher precision value into a lower precision one (for example, from double to int). If you try to do so, it will not compile. So a statement like

```
int k = 2.0;
```

will not compile and will give the following compile error:

```
------------------------------------
possible loss of precision
found: double
required: int
int k = 2.0;
    ^
1 error
------------------------------------
```

Exercise

Given:

Grade points in three courses are declared and initialized as follows:

```
int p1 = 3;
int p2 = 4;
int p3 = 2;
```

Write an instruction that computes the grade point average (GPA) as a double value.

Solution

```
double gpa = (double)( p1 + p2 + p3 ) / 3;
```

1.3 Escape Character Sequences

There are some special characters that can be used to instruct Java to perform certain actions. These special characters actually are a combination of two individual characters. Put together, however, they are treated as a single Java character with its own meaning. The two special characters must appear in exactly the specified sequence and be contiguous to each other. The two special characters form what is called an *escape character sequence.*

1.3.1 The New-Line Escape Character Sequence

As an example of escape character sequences, whenever you press the ENTER key at the end of typing a line, the text editor automatically inserts an invisible, new-line character at the end of the line. Let's say that you type the following statement and then press ENTER:

```
How are you?<Enter>
```

When this statement is saved in a file, it is saved with a terminal new-line character as follows:

```
How are you?[new-line character]
```

The new-line character in Java is represented by the escape character sequence \n (backslash character \ immediately followed by the character n). So the above line can be represented in a Java instruction as follows:

```
How are you?\n
```

For example, you can define a String variable that contains this value ("How are you?\n"), but if the String is printed out onto the computer's output console or a file, it would be printed as

```
How are you?
```

After this, the control would go to the next line, and it would start printing any subsequent text at the next line position. If the new-line character (\n) had *not* been present in the String variable (that is, if the value were simply "How are you?"), any subsequent text would be printed immediately to the right of this text, on the same line. Before we look at an example, recall that we can dump the contents of a String using the System.out.println instruction, passing it the String variable (or expression).

Now look at the following example using the new-line character:

```
String question = "How are you?\n";
String answer = "I am fine.";
System.out.println(question + answer);
```

You would see the following output:

```
How are you?
I am fine.
```

Observe how the new-line character (\n) is used only to bring the printing control to the next line but is not printed explicitly.

In contrast, consider the case where the new-line character (\n) is not present in the String question, as follows:

```
String question = "How are you?";
String answer = "I am fine.";
System.out.println(question + answer);
```

You would see the following output:

```
How are you?I am fine.
```

Observe how the content of answer is printed immediately to the right of the content of question (because there is no new-line character to instruct Java to print the next variable on a new line).

1.3.2   Escaping a Double-Quote

A double-quote is a valid String delimiter; so if you want to have the double-quote itself as part of a String, you need to use the backslash character preceding every double-quote that should be part of the String. For example:

```
String str = "This is a \"test\"";
```

would assign the value

```
This is a "test"
```

to the String str.

1.3.3 Escaping a Single-Quote

You don't need to escape a single-quote that is embedded in a String. For example, a valid String is

```
String str = "It's a good one";
```

Character variables are delimited by single-quotes; so if you want to define a character variable that consists of the single quote itself, you need to use the backslash character to escape it, as follows:

```
char c = '\";
```

This would assign the single-quote (') value to the variable 'c'.

1.3.4 Escaping the Backslash Itself

If you want the backslash itself as part of a String, you need to precede it with another backslash. For example:

```
String str = "The back-slash character, \\, is used for escaping special characters";
```

The resulting String that is actually stored in the str variable would contain only one backslash.

1.3.5 Other Escape Sequences

Some of the other (less commonly used) escape character sequences in Java are shown below:

Escape Character Sequence	Special Character Represented
\b	Backspace
\f	Form Feed
\r	Carriage Return
\t	Tab

1.4 Arrays

An array variable consists of a set of one or more values of the same data type. An array is useful when you want to represent several values of the same data type by using a single array variable. For example, let's say that a student enrolls in four courses, and obtains the following grades:

Course #	Grade	Grade Points
101	B	3
102	A	4
103	C	2
104	B	3

To find this student's GPA, you could write code as follows:

```
int points1 = 3;
int points2 = 4;
int points3 = 2;
int points4 = 3;
double sum = points1 + points2 + points3 + points4;
double gpa = sum / 4;
```

Note that points1, points2, points3, and points4 are four individual variables with no relationship to one another. This works, but it quickly becomes difficult to manage if the number of courses increases, because you have to define as many variables as the number of courses.

Instead, a cleaner solution would be to define a single array variable (let's call it points) that has four integer-type elements, and then use a for loop to compute the GPA as shown here:

```
int[] points = {3, 4, 2, 3};
double sum = 0.0;
for (int i = 0; i < points.length; i++)
{
    sum += points[i];
}
double gpa = sum / points.length;
System.out.println(" GPA = " + gpa);
```

Several points should be noted here:

- The length of the array is automatically set when all of its elements are initialized with specific values.

- Array initialization is a must before using it in any expression subsequently; otherwise, the code will not compile.

- Array elements are referred to by their index. You can think of an index as some number that identifies the position of each element in the array. In Java, arrays always begin with an index = 0, which is why they are said to be *zero-based*. So, use points[0] to refer to the first element of the points array, points[1] to refer to the second element,and so on.

- The index of the last array element is always one less than the length of the array. For example, if the array points has four elements (length = 4), the last array element would be points[3].

- Each of the elements of an array occupies some space in the computer's memory. The data type of an element determines how much space that element will occupy in memory. So, two elements of the same data type will each occupy the same amount of memory. The space that the entire array occupies would be the sum of the space occupied by the individual elements.

1.4.1 The new Keyword

Consider the statement you used for defining the points array:

```
int points[] = {3, 4, 2, 3};
```

You can declare and initialize the points array in an alternative way, as shown below, although it makes the code lengthier. However, these statements taken together would have an identical effect as the single statement above:

```
-----------------------
int[] points = new int[4];
points[0] = 3;
points[1] = 4;
points[2] = 2;
points[3] = 3;
-----------------------
```

Look at the use of the keyword new here. It is used to reserve memory space for the entire array, an essential step before individual elements can be assigned values. (You will learn more about the new keyword later.) The right-hand side (new int[4]) is asking the computer to reserve four spaces, with the size of each space equal to the size occupied by an int-type variable. An int-type variable always occupies a specific amount of space in the computer's memory. Similarly, a double-type variable always occupies a specific amount of space in the computer's memory, but this amount is more than that of an int-type variable because a double data type can hold higher precision numbers.

1.5 Methods

A *method* (also called *function*) is a set of instructions that can process data to produce the desired output. A method can process data but would not actually do so unless you explicitly call (or invoke) it.

A method has a name to identify it, just like a variable. You can name a method whatever you wish, but names must begin with a letter, an underscore(_), or a dollar sign ($)—the same as a variable name. Remember that Java is case-sensitive, so this applies to method names (just as it does to variable names).

As an example of writing methods, consider the GPA-calculation routine from Section 1.4. Rewrite the code, using a method called computeGPA. (You can name it whatever you want.) I am showing a complete working solution written as a Java class file (saved as GPA.java under C:\JSP\Chapter1). For now, concentrate on the computeGPA method and the way it is called from within the main method.

```
-------------------------------------
class GPA
{
    public static void main(String[] args)
    {
        int[] points = {3, 4, 2, 3};
        // 'gpa' is a method-level variable
        // (remains valid within the 'main' method only)
        double gpa = computeGPA(points);
        System.out.println(" GPA = " + gpa);
    }
    static double computeGPA(int[] gradePoints)
    {
        // 'sum' is a method-level variable
        // (remains valid within the 'computeGPA' method only)
        double sum = 0.0;
        for (int i = 0; i < gradePoints.length; i++)
        {
            sum += gradePoints[i];
        }
        double gpa = sum / gradePoints.length;
        return gpa;
    }
}
-------------------------------------
```

Let's look at how it works. Once you compile this .java file, Java creates a .class file in the same folder. You run the program using the java command as shown here:

```
C:\JSP\Chapter1>java GPA
```

Once you do this, Java automatically looks for the main() method, and executes the statements there, one by one.

In the main() method, it looks at the first statement:

```
int[] points = {3, 4, 2, 3};
```

This defines an array called points, containing four integers.

Next it looks at the statement:

```
double gpa = computeGPA(points);
```

Based on this statement, Java defines a double variable called gpa and assigns it whatever value is returned by the method computeGPA(). The points array is passed as an *argument* to the computeGPA method. An *argument* is a data variable that is passed to a method as input at the point where the method is called. Passing data to a method means supplying input data to the method for processing.

1.5.1 Method Definition

Notice that the computeGPA method starts with a definition as given here:

```
static double computeGPA(int[] gradePoints)
```

This has five distinct portions:

static	Defines the method to be static*
double	The data type of the data returned by the method.
computeGPA	The method name.
int[]	The data type of the method parameter (array of int).
gradePoints:	This is the method parameter.

This method definition should be read as follows:

"computeGPA is a method that takes in a single input parameter called gradePoints of data type int[], and returns data of data type double."

1.5.2 Method Parameters and Arguments

Recall that the primary objective of a method is to process incoming data, perform some action on it, and possibly return output data back to the caller. To do this, the method needs the input data to be specified (a name to identify the input data within the method, including the data type of the input). The incoming data is in the form of parameters to the method. A *parameter* is a data variable that represents the input to the method. A parameter's data type must precede its name.

Observe the difference between an *argument* and a *parameter*. An argument represents data at the point of invoking (calling) the method, whereas a parameter is input data that the method processes. In this example, the argument to the computeGPA method is the variable points, and the parameter is the variable gradePoints. The gradePoints parameter represents the argument points. In other words, when the argument points is passed to the computeGPA method, Java refers to it by the

---

*You will be learning about the static keyword in Section 1.7.7. You can ignore it for the moment, but you do need it here for the code to work. For the examples and exercises *until that section*, you can assume that you need the static keyword in front of every method.

name gradePoints within the computeGPA method body. Inside the method, the processing takes place using the parameter gradePoints. The data type of the argument must be the same as that of the parameter; otherwise, it will not compile (but the names could be the same or different).

If you need to send more than one input data variable to the method, you need to send them as a *parameter list*, which is a list of pairs of parameter data type and name, separated by commas. In this case, the data type of the arguments must match those of the parameters, one-for-one, from left to right. Java simply maps argument(s) to parameter(s) based on the data type and sequence.

For example, a call to the computeGPA() method with two arguments: points, remarks may look like this:

```
-------------------------------------
...
int[] points = {3, 2, 4, 3};
String remarks;
double gpa = computeGPA(points, remarks);
...
-------------------------------------
```

The corresponding method definition for computeGPA() may look like this:

```
static double computeGPA(int[] gradePoints, String rem)
{
    // some statements ...
}
```

The data type of points (an integer array) matches the first parameter, gradePoints. Similarly, the data type of the second argument, remarks (a String variable), matches that of the second parameter, rem. This will work fine. If the data type of one of the arguments does not match that of its corresponding parameter, the code will not compile.

It is not necessary that all methods have parameters. There are methods that do not have any; these are perfectly OK. Such methods do not need data in order to do the processing, or they may use class-level data ("class member variable") that is accessible throughout the class. The concept of a *class member variable* is explained briefly in Section 1.6.

In this example, there is only one parameter being sent in, called gradePoints, which is an array of integers (int[]). You cannot specify the length of the integer array at this point. For example, you cannot say

```
static double computeGPA (int[4] gradePoints) { ...
```

In the preceding example, I intentionally named the argument and the parameter with different names (points and gradePoints) to clearly distinguish them from one another. However, the argument and the parameter could very well have the same name (e.g., both named points). The code will still work fine because the points array argument will be a variable defined within the main method, whereas the points parameter would be a variable defined within the computeGPA method. The points parameter would still represent the points argument as before.

1.5.3 Return Data Type

The return data type for this method is double. It means the method will return data of data type double. It is *not* necessary that a method return something. You can have methods that process data and perform some operations but do not return any data. If a method does not return any data, you must specify the return data type as void.

1.5.4 Method Body

After the parameter list in parentheses comes the "method body"—the set of one or more instructions that perform the desired action on the inputs. The method body is always enclosed in curly braces ({}), and you must not use a semicolon at the end of the ending curly brace. In this example, the method body would be as follows:

```
{
    double sum = 0.0;
    for (int i = 0; i < gradePoints.length; i++)
    {
        sum += gradePoints[i];
    }
    double gpa = sum / gradePoints.length;
    return gpa;
}
```

1.5.5 Passing By Reference and Passing By Value

In Section 1.5.2, I stated that the parameter gradePoints represents the argument points. What if you make changes to the gradePoints array element(s) inside the computeGPA() method? For example, say that you change gradePoints[0] to 4 inside computeGPA(), as shown here:

```
static double compute GPA(int[] gradePoints)
{
    // 'sum' is a method-level variable
    // (remains valid within the 'computeGPA' method only)
    double sum = 0.0;
    gradePoints[0] = 4; // test only
    for (int I = 0; I < gradePoints.length; i++)
    {
        sum += gradePoints[i];
    }
    double gpa = sum / gradePoints.length;
    return gpa;
}
```

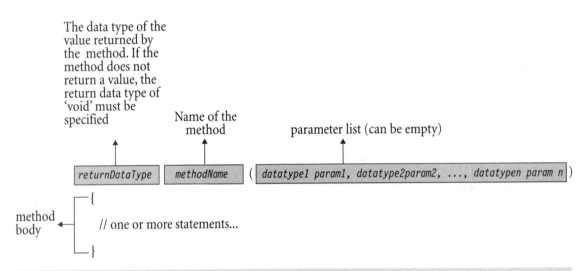

The data type of the value returned by the method. If the method does not return a value, the return data type of 'void' must be specified

Name of the method

parameter list (can be empty)

returnDataType   methodName   (datatype1 param1, datatype2param2, ..., datatypen param n)

method body

{
    // one or more statements...
}

Figure 1.1

General method structure.

The question is, would the change to gradePoints[0] get carried back to the argument points? The answer is yes—for arrays and any nonprimitive data (i.e., all "objects" *except* String type objects—we will get to classes and objects in just a moment), Java retains changes made to them inside the method. So points[0] would contain 4 inside main() after computeGPA() is called (instead of the original value of 3). This is called *passing by reference*. In other words, the points array is being passed by reference to the computeGPA() method.

For all primitive data types (int, double, float, char, boolean, etc.) and String objects, changes made to the parameter inside a method *do not* get carried back to the caller. Here, Java creates a copy of the argument, and the parameter points to the copy rather than to the original argument. So changes made to the parameter (i.e., the copy) inside the method make no difference to the original argument. This is called *passing by value*.

1.5.6   General Method Structure

Before proceeding further, let's generalize the structure of a method as shown in Figure 1.1

Solved Exercise 1.5

Objective: To learn how to process array elements using methods.

Steps:

- Create a folder called exer15 under C:\JSP\Chapter1 for holding files of this exercise.

- Define an array variable called sales that contains quarterly sales of a store for four consecutive quarters of a year, each of double data type. Initialize its elements with the following values: 1000.00, 1500.00, 2000.00, and 1800.00.

- Use this array to compute the annual sales of the store using a for loop, and display the result on the computer's console as follows. (Don't worry about the format; it's okay if column values are not perfectly aligned, but data should appear on different lines as shown.)

Quarter	Sales
1	1000.00
2	1500.00
3	2000.00
4	1800.00

- You must create two separate methods that process the array, as follows:

  - One called computeSum that computes and returns the total sales.

  - Another called displayResults that displays the output on the computer console.

- Write a main method that defines and initializes an array called sales, defines a double-type variable called sum, and then calls these two methods. Pass the sales array as an argument to the computeSum method. Enclose the entire code within a class called Sales saved in a file called Sales.java. Compile and run the program.

The command prompt session is shown here.

```
Command Prompt                                              _ □ ✕
Microsoft Windows XP [Version 5.1.2600]
(C) Copyright 1985-2001 Microsoft Corp.

C:\Documents and Settings\Prabhakar Metlapalli>cd \

C:\>cd JSP\Chapter1\exer15

C:\JSP\Chapter1\exer15>dir
 Volume in drive C has no label.
 Volume Serial Number is E879-70DC

 Directory of C:\JSP\Chapter1\exer15

05/28/2006  08:45 PM    <DIR>          .
05/28/2006  08:45 PM    <DIR>          ..
05/28/2006  08:45 PM               905 Sales.java
               1 File(s)            905 bytes
               2 Dir(s)  51,137,339,392 bytes free

C:\JSP\Chapter1\exer15>javac Sales.java

C:\JSP\Chapter1\exer15>java Sales
_____
Quarter Sales
_____
1 1000.0
2 1500.0
3 2000.0
4 1800.0
_____
Total 6300.0
_____

C:\JSP\Chapter1\exer15>_
```

Solution:

```java
//--- Begin: Sales.java ---------------
class Sales
{
    public static void main(String[] args)
    {
        double[] sales = {1000.0, 1500.0, 2000.0, 1800.0};
        double sum = computeSum(sales);
        displayResults(sales, sum);
    }

    static double computeSum(double[] inputSales)
    {
        double total = 0.0;
        for (int i = 0; i < inputSales.length; i++)
        {
            total += inputSales[i];
        }
        return total;
    }

    static void displayResults(double[] salesIn, double sumIn)
    {
        System.out.println("--------------------------------------- ");
        System.out.println(" Quarter Sales ");
        System.out.println("--------------------------------------- ");
        for (int j = 1; j <= salesIn.length; j++)
        {
            System.out.println(" " + j + " " + salesIn[j-1]);
        }
        System.out.println("--------------------------------------- ");
        System.out.println(" Total " + sumIn);
        System.out.println("--------------------------------------- ");
    }
}
//--- End: Sales.java ---------------
```

1.6   Variable Scope

Notice that all variables defined within the computeGPA method (sum, gpa, and gradePoints) remain defined only within that method, and they would cease to exist after the method call is over. If the method gets called again, these variables are born again but die at the end of executing the last statement in that method. They are temporary variables with a *local*, or *method-level scope*. If you try to refer to these variables outside of the methods where they are defined, the code will not compile.

In contrast to the local, "method-level" variables, there are also *class member* (or *global*, or *class-level*) *variables* (also called *class attributes*). Here the word "global" implies the entire class, but it is still not visible outside of the class. You will study what a class is in detail in the next section. For now, however, think of a class-member variable as one that is defined inside the curly braces ({}) that follow the class keyword but outside of any specific method in the class. These are *global* variables that are recognized throughout the class—that is, inside every method in the class.

For example, you can define an integer-type class-member variable j in the preceding GPA class as follows:

```
------------------------------------------------
class GPA
{
    int j = 0; // class-member variable
    public static void main(String[] args)
    {
    // .. rest of the code
------------------------------------------------
```

To understand class-member variables, let's go back to our GPA class and define a class-member array variable called points:

```
------------------------------------------------
class GPA
{
    // class-member variable
    static int[] points = {3, 4, 2, 3};

    public static void main(String[] args)
    {
        double gpa = computeGPA();
        System.out.println(" GPA = " + gpa);
    }
    static double computeGPA()
    {
        double sum = 0.0; // method-level (local) variable
                          // (remains valid within the 'computeGPA' method)
        for (int i = 0; i < points.length; i++)
        {
            sum += points[i];
        }
```

```
        double gpa = sum / points.length;
        return gpa;
    }
}
```

Notice that it is no longer necessary to pass the `points` array as an argument to the `computeGPA` method because it is now a class-member variable that is recognized throughout the class (inside all of its methods). This may look like a potential advantage for class-member variables, and you may be tempted to define every variable as a class member variable, but defining too many of such variables can make the code difficult to read and track how a variable is modified across methods.

The method-level (local) variables we saw earlier get created only when the method is invoked, and they die when exiting the method. That memory can then be used for other purposes. In contrast, global, class-member variables can be more memory-intensive because these need to be part of the class definition, and they need to be alive as long as the class object is alive. (We will come to classes and objects in just a moment.) Sometimes, however, defining a class-member variable can be important and more efficient than passing an argument across methods. For example, if you have two or more methods referring to the same data and using it in their processing instructions, you may define a class-member variable to store the common data rather than passing it around as an argument between the methods.

1.7   Classes and Objects

1.7.1   Introduction

You know how to use standard, predefined "primitive" data types such as `int`, `double`, `char`, and `boolean`. In this section, you will learn how to define and use your own custom data types, as well as how to use Java's predefined nonprimitive data types. Your custom data types will be more complex in the sense that they will have their own attributes and methods.

1.7.2   The Concept of a Class

Variables of simple (or "primitive") data types such as `int`, `double`, `char`, and `boolean`, contain a single data value. For example, an `int`-type variable `i` contains only a single data value of type `int`. It cannot hold, say two different pieces of data, nor can it perform operations on that data by itself. As coding requirements become more complex, we need data types that do much more than just hold a single data value. We need new data types that can store multiple, heterogeneous data values of various data types, and can process or perform operations on such data to give some result. For example, say that you need a new "composite" data type that can hold a customer's age and first and last names. Here age could be of type `int` whereas first and last names could be `String`—that makes it a set of heterogeneous data. Storing heterogeneous data is the first requirement; the other is being able to process that data to produce desired output, like concatenating the first and last names to come up with the customer's full name. So the new "composite" data type needs to have two features:

- the "attribute(s)" that would hold the heterogeneous data value(s), and/or
- the "method(s)" that can perform operations on the attribute(s) to give some useful result.

Such a composite data type could be considered as a collection of attributes and/or methods. The new data type would be much more powerful than the regular "primitive" data types and stand-alone methods because the data and methods always go together (hand-in-hand) and thus maintain consistency. The new data type can be referred to as one entity. We can organize data and related methods into new "composite" data types and this would make management of data attributes and methods more efficient.

In the example above, each customer has attributes of age and first and last names. Wouldn't it be convenient to represent customers by a single data type called Customer that contained all of these attributes? If that could be done, you could define variables of the new data type, each of which would represent one customer, and each would have the necessary attributes. Imagine how versatile this would be: If you have several customers, you could define an array of this new customer data type, which would hold data on several customers in a single array variable.

Sun Microsystems realized the utility of such complex data types, and went on to write ready-made, complex data types that they thought would be most commonly encountered. This is what forms the crux of the JDK, which you downloaded. There you will find hundreds of off-the-shelf, ready-to-use data types. These are extremely useful but are still not sufficient for real-world programming, because each business has its own needs. In other words, each corporation has business-specific data and its own way of processing the data. So it becomes necessary that a corporation define custom data types that meet its specific requirements. For example, one company may need to define a custom data type that represents a telephone, whereas another might need a custom data type that represents an automobile.

A data type with its own attributes and/or methods is technically called a *class* in Java. A class can either be a data type that Java "predefines" for you, or a data type that you create on your own, which would be a "custom class." A class is, by definition, a nonprimitive data type.

Java Predefined Classes

An example of a Java predefined class is the String data type. The JDK contains a collection of such Java predefined data types that you can freely use in your code. Each of the files in the JDK is a separate data type that is predefined for you, each with its own methods and attributes. By using such a common library of ready-made data types, you avoid writing code for commonly encountered data types.

Custom Classes

Writing your code means "writing your custom class." All Java code must belong to a class. You cannot simply write Java code without enclosing it within a specific class.

For example, you cannot just write instructions without an enclosing class structure, save it in a file, and then expect it to compile. Try it out: write the following code (exactly as shown below), save it in a file called Test.java, and try compiling it.

```
-------------------------------------
int i = 0;
i = i + 1;
System.out.println("i = " + i );
-------------------------------------
```

You will get the following error:

```
-------------------------------------
C:\JSP\Chapter1>javac Test.java
Test.java:1: Class or interface declaration expected.
int i = 0;
^
1 error
C:\JSP\Chapter1>
-------------------------------------
```

You always write code within your custom classes. This may sound a bit odd at first, but you will soon get used to it.

It is not necessary that a custom class contain both attributes and methods. A custom data type class may contain only methods with no attributes; similarly, it may contain only attributes but no methods, or it may contain single or multiple attributes and/or methods. All are legal.

In what situations do you define a class in order to use it as a new custom data type? Say that you are to write code to process data handled by a department store. The store has several customers every day, and each customer has a name and sales amount. To simplify the case, let's say that the store has a single customer and wants to print out the customer's name and sales amount for that customer. For example, a customer has a name "John Smith" and sales amount of 100.0, so you want the program to print out this customer's information as follows:

```
John Smith    100.0
```

You can make your code more robust and versatile by representing each customer using a new custom data type that contains the name and sales amount as class attributes. For simplicity, this new class does not contain any methods, but it is still a valid custom class. You would define the new data type called Customer as follows:

```
---------------------------------------
class Customer
{
    String name;
    double salesAmount;
}
---------------------------------------
```

1.7.3 Objects

Once you have defined your custom data type in the form of a custom class, the next logical step is to create a variable of that data type, so that it can hold data specific to a customer with name = "John Smith" and salesAmount = 100.0. You have been using the term *variable* in the case of primitive data types, but when talking about classes, the term *object* is more appropriate. An *object* is a variable of a nonprimitive data type (i.e., a class). In other words, an *object is an instance* of a class.

A class represents a data type, or a template, that defines general characteristics of that data type. You can create one or more objects, or instances, using the class template, each of which would contain exactly the same data structure as defined by the class template but could have different values. Returning to our example of the Customer class will make this clear. We begin by instantiating an object of type Customer (let's call it cst), and then we print out its name and salesAmount attribute values using System.out.println.

Let's consider a simple situation where you have one object of type Customer and you want to print out the concatenated name for that customer. To make the code cleaner, it is useful to create a separate "driver" class that would instantiate the customer object and have it print out the concatenated name. Say that "driver" class is called TestName, saved in a file called TestName.java in the same folder as Customer.java:

```
---------------------------------------
class TestName
{
    public static void main(String[] args)
    {
        Customer cst = new Customer();
        cst.name = "John Smith";
        cst.salesAmount = 100.0;
        System.out.println(cst.name + "   " + cst.salesAmount);
    }
}
---------------------------------------
```

Compile the Customer.java file, followed by the TestName.java file. Run the code; the output session should look like this:

```
----------------------------------------
C:\JSP\Chapter1>java TestName
John Smith    100.0
----------------------------------------
```

To extend this example a bit, let's say we want to be more specific about the name: We want the first name and last name to reside in separate attributes of the Customer class. We will need to change the Customer and TestName files as follows:

```
----------------------------------------
class Customer
{
    String firstName;
    String lastName;
    double salesAmount;
}

class TestName
{
    public static void main(String[] args)
    {
        Customer cst = new Customer();
        cst.firstName = "John";
        cst.lastName = "Smith";
        cst.salesAmount = 100.0;
        System.out.println(cst.firstName + " " + cst.lastName
                         + "    " + cst.salesAmount);
    }
}
----------------------------------------
```

Compile Customer.java, then TestName.java and run the program. It should display the same output as before.

Here we created a single object using our custom class, Customer. We can create multiple objects of Customer type, each having firstName, lastName, and salesAmount attributes but with different values. For example, customer1 could be an object of Customer type that has firstName = "John", lastName = "Smith" and salesAmount = 100.0. Another Customer type object may be called customer2 that has firstName = "Mike", lastName = "Brown", and salesAmount = 150.0.

With this design, if you want to add additional attributes to the Customer data type, you simply add them to the Customer class, and add corresponding statements in the TestName.java file to process the additional attributes.

Recall that for primitive data types, we use the term "variable definition" to describe the action of specifying a variable's name, its data type, and possibly an initial value. For example, "defining a variable called i of type int with initial value of 0" would look like

```
int i = 0;
```

When it comes to objects, you don't *define* an object; you *instantiate* it, although the concept is very similar. To instantiate an object means to create a new object of a nonprimitive data type (a class). The concept of instantiating objects applies to classes only: either Java predefined classes or your own custom classes.

For example, inside TestName.java, the line:

```
Customer cst = new Customer();
```

instantiates an object called cst of type Customer.

Here is another example of object instantiation, where we instantiate an object called str of type String, with a value of "hello":

```
String str = "hello";
```

Solved Exercise 1.7.3

Objective: To learn how to write a custom class and instantiate an object from it.

Steps:

- Create a folder called exer173 under C:\JSP\Chapter1 for holding files of this exercise.

- Write a custom class called Order that represents a customer's order. The class should have attributes for the Order ID (an integer), Item ID (an integer), Price Per Item (a double), and Quantity (an integer); call these as orderID, itemID, pricePerItem, and qty, respectively.

- Also write a test driver class called TestOrder that instantiates an object of type Order, setting its orderId = 100, itemId = 200, pricePerItem = 2.0, and qty = 12. The test driver class should compute the orderValue = pricePerItem X qty, and display the output line shown below. Don't worry about the format or columnar alignment, but values should at least appear on one line as shown.

Order ID	Item ID	Price Per Item	Qty	Order Value
100	200	2.0	12	24.0

A sample command prompt session is shown here.

Solution:

```
//--- Begin: Order.java ---------------
class Order
{
    int orderId;
    int itemId;
    double pricePerItem;
    int qty;
}
//--- End: Order.java --------------------

//--- Begin: TestOrder.java ---------------
class TestOrder
{
    public static void main(String[] args)
    {
        Order order = new Order();
        order.orderId = 100;
        order.itemId = 200;
        order.pricePerItem = 2.0;
        order.qty = 12;
        System.out.println("----------------------------------------------");
        System.out.println("Order ID Item ID Price per Item Qty Order Value");
        System.out.println("----------------------------------------------");
        System.out.println( order.orderId + " " + order.itemId + " " +
```

```
                    order.pricePerItem + " " + order.qty + " " +
                    order.pricePerItem * order.qty );
          System.out.println("-------------------------------------------");
      }
  }
  //--- End: TestOrder.java ----------------
```

1.7.4 Class Constructor

Let's go back to the way you initialize the value of an integer variable:

```
int i = 0;
```

Here, you defined an integer variable called i and initialized it with a value of 0.

If you want to instantiate an object of a specific class data type, you may need to similarly set initial values of the class attributes; otherwise those attributes may contain garbage or junk values to begin with. For this purpose, Java provides a special method within the class, which would set initial values of all of the class attributes and/or do some kind of "default" processing. This special method is called the *constructor* of the class. To distinguish the constructor from the other methods in the class, Java requires that the name of the constructor be the same as that of the class (case-sensitive); otherwise, it will not compile. Also, you cannot specify the return data type for the constructor. Other than these two requirements, a constructor looks and behaves exactly like any other method in a class. A constructor can thus optionally have a set of parameters and use those parameters to initialize class member data.

For example, consider the Customer class, this time with the following constructor:

```
-----------------------------------
class Customer
{
    String name;
    double salesAmount;
    // default constructor
    Customer()
    {
        name = "undefined";
        salesAmount = 0.0;
    }
}
-----------------------------------
```

Observe the following:

- The constructor has the name Customer, which is also the class name (case-sensitive). Having a constructor is optional, but if it is present, it must have the same name as the class name; otherwise, it will not compile.

- The constructor does not have any explicit return data type. The return type should never be present in any constructor; if it is, it will not compile.

- The constructor does not have any parameters—in this case only. You will see one with parameters in a moment.

- This constructor is called the *default constructor* because it does not take any arguments. By definition, a default constructor is one without any parameters; therefore, to identify a default constructor in any class, simply look for a constructor with no parameters.

Within the constructor, the class attributes name and salesAmount are initialized with the values "undefined" and 0.0 respectively. So, the next time you say new Customer(), this constructor gets called, and the class attributes get initialized with these values.

If you do not write an explicit default constructor in your class, Java will create one for you during compilation. This constructor may not initialize class attributes to the values you want. In other words, a constructor is optional in a class but important to define if you want specific initialization to occur every time an object is instantiated.

A more useful constructor would be one that allows you to supply arguments for the name and sales amount and initialize these attributes with the values sent in. This can coexist with the default constructor in your Customer class, so the rest of the code in the class remains intact. Remember that it is perfectly legal for a class to have multiple constructors, as long as each has a different set of parameters to keep it distinct.

Here's the constructor:

```
--------------------------------
Customer(String nameIn, double salesAmountIn)
{
    name = nameIn;
    salesAmount = salesAmountIn;
}
--------------------------------
```

Now, you can call this specific constructor from within the ComputeSales class. Follow along:

```
customer = new Customer("John", 100.0);
```

The single concise instruction above can now replace the following three lines in TestName.java we saw at the beginning of Section 1.7.3:

```
--------------------------------
customer = new Customer();
customer.name = "John";
customer.salesAmount = 100.0;
--------------------------------
```

You can repeat this for subsequent Customer type objects.

Isn't that neat? When Java sees the keyword new, it looks for a constructor that has a matching set of parameter types. In this case, you are sending in two arguments: a String and a double, in that sequence. Therefore, the only constructor that matches this sequence is the one you just added, which initializes the class attributes name and salesAmount to the ones sent in. If Java does not find a constructor in your class with parameters that exactly match the arguments, both in type and sequence, it will give a compile error.

Note that the physical sequence of placing the various constructors, methods, and attributes within your class does not matter. They need to be defined somewhere in the entire class, and you can safely interchange positions of these anywhere you like, within the curly braces for the whole class.

1.7.5   The this Keyword

I intentionally named the parameters different from the class attributes just to make the code look cleaner and easier to understand, but these two can have the same names. In that case, the this keyword must precede the class-member attribute in order to differentiate it from the parameter being sent in, as in the following example:

```
Customer(String name, double salesAmount)
{
    this.name = name;
    this.salesAmount = salesAmount;
}
```

The keyword this refers to the object of the *current* class data type that is being instantiated. Every time you use the keyword new for each customer, a separate object of the Customer data type gets instantiated, and the keyword this would mean the current customer object.

Solved Exercise 1.7.5

Objective: To learn how to write and use class constructors.

Steps:

- Create a new subfolder called exer175 under C:\JSP\Chapter1 and copy the Order.java and TestOrder.java files from Solved Exercise 1.7.3 into it. Modify the Order class so that it has a default constructor as well as another constructor that takes in the Order ID, Item ID, Price Per Item, and Quantity as input parameters.

- Modify TestOrder to instantiate an Order object using the new constructor, sending it the orderId, itemId, pricePerItem, and qty. Compile, and run your code, and verify that it produces the same output as in Solved Exercise 1.7.3.

Solution:

```
//--- Begin: Order.java ---------------
class Order
{
    int orderId;
    int itemId;
    double pricePerItem;
    int qty;

    // default constructor
    Order()
     {
          orderId = 0;
          itemId = 0;
          pricePerItem = 0.0;
          qty = 0;
     }
    Order( int orderId, int itemId, double pricePerItem, int qty )
     {
          this.orderId = orderId;
          this.itemId = itemId;
          this.pricePerItem = pricePerItem;
          this.qty = qty;
     }
}
//--- End: Order.java -----------------

//--- Begin: TestOrder.java -----------
class TestOrder
{
    public static void main(String[] args)
```

```
    {
        Order order = new Order(100, 200, 2.0, 12);
        System.out.println("---------------------------------------------");
        System.out.println("Order ID Item ID Price per Item Qty Order Value");
        System.out.println("---------------------------------------------");
        System.out.println( order.orderId + " " + order.itemId + " " +
                            order.pricePerItem + " " + order.qty + " " +
                            order.pricePerItem * order.qty );
        System.out.println("---------------------------------------------");
    }
}
//--- End: TestOrder.java -------------
```

1.7.6   Class Members: Attributes and Methods

You already looked at class-level or global, class-member attributes. Let's make it formal here, and extend it to methods as well. *Class member* is a technical term referring to either an attribute or a method in a class. You saw how you can specify attributes in a custom class. Your Customer class had the attributes name and salesAmount. You haven't written methods in your custom class, however. Let's do that to understand how methods can be useful in a class.

Go back to the earlier example in this chapter. Let's say that the store now wants to see the full name of each customer: last name, a comma, a space, and then the first name, followed by that customer's sales amount. For example, for a customer named "John Smith" whose sales amount is 100.0, you need to display the following:

```
Smith, John    100.0
```

The first name and the last name now need to be two different attributes of the Customer class. When the calling code loops through the different Customer objects, wouldn't it be convenient to have a method in the Customer class that performs the name concatenation for you and returns the result as the desired String?

Go ahead and do just that: add a method called concatName in your Customer class that concatenates the last name, comma, space, and the first name and then returns the result as a String. The Customer class would now look like this:

```
-------------------------------
class Customer
{
    String firstName;
    String lastName;
    double salesAmount;
    // default constructor
    Customer()
```

```
    {
        firstName = "undefined";
        lastName = "undefined";
        salesAmount = 0.0;
    }
    Customer(String firstName, String lastName, double salesAmount)
    {
        this.firstName = firstName;
        this.lastName = lastName;
        this.salesAmount = salesAmount;
    }
    String concatName()
    {
        String strName = lastName + ", " + firstName;
        return strName;
    }
}
```

Let's consider a simple situation where you have one object of type `Customer` and you want to print out the concatenated name for that customer. To do so, modify `TestName.java` at the end of Section 1.7.3 to instantiate the `Customer` object and call the `concatName()` on it as show below:

```
class TestName
{
    public static void main(String[] args)
    {
        Customer cst = new Customer("John", "Cox", 100.0);
        System.out.println(cst.concatName() + " " + cst.salesAmount);
    }
}
```

Compile the `Customer.java` file, followed by the `TestName.java` file. Run the code; the output session should look like this:

```
C:\JSP\Chapter1>java TestName
Cox, John 100.0
```

Observe how the `concatName()` method is called from within the `TestName` class. Notice the use of the dot operator (.) when invoking methods on objects; this resembles the procedure used to get the object's `salesAmount` attribute, when you said `cst.salesAmount`. So, the way you call a method on an object is identical to the way you refer to the object's attributes: You use the dot operator in both cases. The only difference is that the method call must always have a pair of parentheses following the method name, with or without arguments, as the case may be. Using the dot operator is fundamental to the concept of objects and object-oriented programming; so make sure you feel comfortable using it.

Solved Exercise 1.7.6

Objective: To learn how to write and call a new method in a custom class.

Steps:

- Create a new subfolder called `exer176` under `C:\JSP\Chapter1` and copy the `Order.java` and `TestOrder.java` files from Solved Exercise 1.7.5 into it. Modify the `Order` class to add a new method called `computeOrderValue` that computes the order value and returns it as a `double`. This method should multiply the `pricePerItem` by the `qty` to compute the order value.

- Modify `TestOrder` to call the new method when displaying the order value. Compile and run your code.

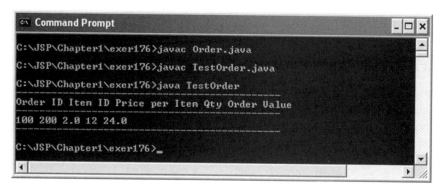

Solution:

```
//--- Begin: Order.java ---------------
class Order
{
    int orderId;
    int itemId;
    double pricePerItem;
    int qty;

    // default constructor
    Order()
    {
        orderId = 0;
        itemId = 0;
```

```
            pricePerItem = 0.0;
            qty = 0;
        }

    Order( int orderId, int itemId, double pricePerItem, int qty )
        {
            this.orderId = orderId;
            this.itemId = itemId;
            this.pricePerItem = pricePerItem;
            this.qty = qty;
        }
    double computeOrderValue()
        {
            return pricePerItem * qty;
        }
    }
//--- End: Order.java ----------------

//--- Begin: TestOrder.java -----------
class TestOrder
{
    public static void main(String[] args)
        {
            Order order = new Order(100, 200, 2.0, 12);
            System.out.println("----------------------------------------------");
            System.out.println("Order ID Item ID Price per Item Qty Order Value");
            System.out.println("----------------------------------------------");
            System.out.println( order.orderId + " " + order.itemId + " " +
                                order.pricePerItem + " " + order.qty + " " +
                                order.computeOrderValue() );
            System.out.println("----------------------------------------------");
        }
    }
//--- End: TestOrder.java -------------
```

1.7.7   Instance and Static Class Members

By now you are quite familiar with instantiating objects using class data types. You also know that custom classes can be used not only as custom data types but also as placeholders for your code.

If you do use it as a custom data type (as you did in the case of the Customer class), you can create instances of that class in the form of objects. Each object that you create from a class data type carries with it the same attributes and methods as the class data type. For example, you create a Customer type object called customer1 with attributes firstName="John", lastName="Smith", and salesAmount=100.0, and another Customer-type object called customer2 with attributes firstName="Jennifer", lastName="Taylor", and salesAmount=50.0. Here customer1 and customer2 are two distinct objects that have the same attributes (firstName, lastName, and salesAmount) but the attributes contain different values. The point is, Java recognizes these attributes in each customer object because you defined them in your Customer class. Similarly, Java recognizes that these objects can call the concatName method because this method is defined in your Customer class.

As discussed earlier, *class member* is a technical term for referring to either an attribute or a method in a class. For example, the attributes firstName, lastName, and salesAmount, and the method concatName are all class members of the Customer class. These members (more precisely, copies of these members) exist in each object or instance instantiated from the Customer class. These members are therefore called *instance members* of the Customer class. Copies of these members will exist in every instance of this class. It is also true that these members require the existence of an object of the Customer type before they can have any meaning. In other words, these members are relevant and make sense only in the context of a Customer object that is required to exist first. This implies that you must instantiate an object of the Customer type before you can refer to these attributes in the client code. (Note that the test driver TestName.java we saw earlier is considered client code.) By default, Java treats every class member as an instance member unless you explicitly use the keyword static in front of the member in your class.

Now consider a special case where you must use part of your class as a placeholder for your code. Suppose you want to write a method called concatName in a class such that it takes in the first name and last name, and returns the concatenated name as a result. The only purpose of this method is to take inputs for the first name and last name and concatenate them to give a result. This method would get every input that it needs in the form of arguments; therefore, it does not really depend on the rest of the class where it is written. It is a stand-alone piece of code in your class.

It still needs to be part of a class, because that is the Java requirement: Every piece of code must be enclosed within the class structure. To make the method effectively stand-alone, you use a special keyword static in front of the method name, as follows:

```
-------------------------------
class TestStatic
{
    static String concatName(String firstName, String lastName)
    {
        String strResult = lastName + ", " + firstName;
        return strResult;
    }
}
-------------------------------
```

Save this code in a separate file called `TestStatic.java`. To call a `static` method, you do not need to instantiate any object; you simply need to invoke the method on the class name itself, as in this example:

```
TestStatic.concatName(cst.firstName, cst.lastName);
```

Open the `TestName.java` file, and change it to call the `static` method above instead of the method from the `Customer` class, as shown here:

```
-------------------------------
class TestName
{
    public static void main(String[] args)
    {
        Customer cst = new Customer("John", "Cox", 100.0);
        System.out.println( TestStatic.concatName(
                        cst.firstName, cst.lastName)+ " " + cst.salesAmount );
    }
}
-------------------------------
```

Notice how you now call `concatName` directly on the `TestStatic` class, instead of an object `cst` of the `Customer` class. The other difference is that this time you send in arguments for first and last name to the `static` method, whereas earlier you did not need to because those were stored as class attributes, available as part of the object instantiated from the class.

Compile `TestStatic.java` first, followed by `TestName.java`. Run the `TestName` code; your output session should look like this (same as before):

```
C:\JSP\Chapter1>java TestName
Cox, John 100.0
```

The only difference here is that you are depending on a third-party class called `TestStatic` to get you the concatenated name, sending it the first and last names as arguments. By doing this, you conveniently segregated commonly used code and put it into a separate class called `TestStatic`, which other classes may want to use directly without instantiating objects. Notice that you did not instantiate any object from the `TestStatic` class; all you did was call the `concatName` method directly on the `TestStatic` class by writing `TestStatic.concatName(cst.firstName, cst.lastName)`.

You are free to add instance members to the `TestStatic` class for possible use when instantiating objects from the `TestStatic` class. In other words, just having a static method in your `TestStatic` class does not preclude the use of the class for instantiating objects. If you do add such instance members to `TestStatic` and you instantiate objects of that class, only the instance members would be recognized as part of those objects.

You could very well have made the concatName method in the Customer class itself as static rather than defining a separate class TestStatic to put stand-alone code for the concatenation. Again, the placement of static members is a matter of developer discretion and convenience; here, I was keeping it separate to avoid confusion and to help you understand the concept.

Ok—now imagine that you did make the concatName method in Customer class static, instead of creating the TestStatic class. The static method concatName of Customer cannot access instance members of the Customer class although the method is still a legitimate member of the class. In this regard, static members are treated differently when it comes to access to class members. They have to maintain a stand-alone or "outsider" type of identity within the class. Since the static method concatName cannot access the class members for first and last name, it must have parameters for these, and expect the caller to supply the values as arguments. Compare this with the original instance method concatName that did not take any parameters because it could access the class members firstName and lastName directly.

Try it out: Define the concatName method in the Customer class as static but without the parameters firstName and lastName, like this:

```
----------------------------------
static String concatName()
{
    String strResult = lastName + ", " + firstName;
    return strResult;
}
----------------------------------
```

You will get compile errors:

```
----------------------------------
C:\JSP\Chapter1>javac Customer.java
Customer.java:32: non-static variable lastName cannot be referenced from a static context
String strResult = lastName + ", " + firstName;
                   ^
Customer.java:32: non-static variable firstName cannot be referenced from a static context
String strResult = lastName + ", " + firstName;
                                     ^
2 errors
----------------------------------
```

As I mentioned earlier, static members do not recognize instance members of the class they belong to. This makes sense because static members are alive even when there is no object instantiated from the class. If a static member tries to access instance members that are tied to specific objects instantiated from this class, it would obviously give an error.

To fix this, add the parameters firstName and lastName to the parameter list of concatName; the static method concatName in the Customer class would now look like the following, which is identical to what it looks like in the TestStatic class:

```
--------------------------------
static String concatName(String firstName, String lastName)
{
    String strResult = lastName + ", " + firstName;
    return strResult;
}
--------------------------------
```

The parameters firstName and lastName here have no relation to the class instance members first-Name and lastName (although they have the same names). The parameters remain distinct local variables defined only within the scope of the method, and they die upon exiting it. In other words, they take precedence over any class attributes with the same names.

The calling code also needs to change, because it is a static method with no objects to call it on. In TestName.java, you would replace the line

```
System.out.println( TestStatic.concatName(cst.firstName, cst.lastName) + " " + cst.salesAmount );
```

with

```
System.out.println( Customer.concatName(cst.firstName, cst.lastName) + " " + cst.salesAmount);
```

This would work fine, and the results would be the same as before.

The static and the instance versions of concatName can coexist in the Customer class. Therefore, you can retain the instance version of concatName along with this static version if you wish.

You should now be able to understand why you had to use the static keyword in front of the computeGPA method in the GPA class of Section 1.5. It was because the computeGPA method was being called from within the main() method of the same class and not on an object of the GPA class.

Solved Exercise 1.7.7

Objective: To learn how to write and call a new static method in a custom class.

Steps:

- Create a subfolder called exer177 under C:\JSP\Chapter1 and copy Order.java and TestOrder.java from Solved Exercise 1.7.6 into it. Modify the Order class to make the computeOrderValue() method static, and call it directly from the TestOrder class.

- Alter TestOrder to make necessary changes. Compile and run your code.

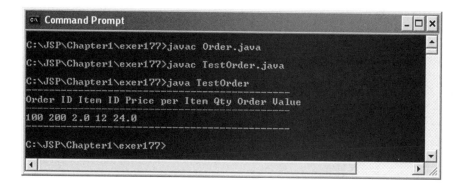

Solution:

```
//--- Begin: Order.java ---------------
class Order
{
    int orderId;
    int itemId;
    double pricePerItem;
    int qty;

    // default constructor
    Order()
    {
        orderId = 0;
        itemId = 0;
        pricePerItem = 0.0;
        qty = 0;
    }

    Order( int orderId, int itemId, double pricePerItem, int qty )
    {
        this.orderId = orderId;
        this.itemId = itemId;
        this.pricePerItem = pricePerItem;
        this.qty = qty;
    }
    static double computeOrderValue( double price, int quantity )
    {
        return price * quantity;
    }
}
//--- End: Order.java -----------------
```

```
//--- Begin: TestOrder.java -----------
class TestOrder
{
    public static void main(String[] args)
    {
        Order order = new Order(100, 200, 2.0, 12);
        System.out.println("-------------------------------------------");
        System.out.println("Order ID Item ID Price per Item Qty Order Value");
        System.out.println("-------------------------------------------");
        System.out.println( order.orderId + " " + order.itemId + " " +
                        order.pricePerItem + " " + order.qty + " " +
                        Order.computeOrderValue(order.pricePerItem,
                                        order.qty) );
        System.out.println("-------------------------------------------");
    }
}
//--- End: TestOrder.java -------------
```

1.7.8   Using an Array of Objects

Let's take up a more complex example. Say that the store has three customers on a particular day and wants to print out the list of customer names, along with their sales amount, and show a nice total at the end, as the following table shows:

Customer Name	Sales Amount
Cox, John	100.0
Long, Mike	200.0
Smith, Nancy	150.0
Total Sales:	450.0

This would consist of repeatedly instantiating three Customer type objects in a loop, and printing out the data from each object. Alternatively, you can store all three objects in an array of type Customer, and loop through the array to print the results. The following driver code will do this:

```
-----------------------------------------------
class ComputeSales
{
    public static void main(String[] args)
    {
        double totalSales = 0.0;
        Customer[] customers = new Customer[3]; // array of 'Customer'
        customers[0] = new Customer("John", "Cox", 100.0);
```

```
        customers[1] = new Customer("Mike", "Long", 200.0);
        customers[2] = new Customer("Nancy", "Smith", 150.0);
        System.out.println("-----------------------------------");
        System.out.println("Customer Name Sales Amount");
        System.out.println("-----------------------------------");
        for (int i = 0; i < 3; i++)
        {
            System.out.println(customers[i].concatName() + " " + customers[i].salesAmount);
            totalSales += customers[i].salesAmount;
        }
        System.out.println("-----------------------------------");
        System.out.println(" Total Sales: " + totalSales);
        System.out.println("-----------------------------------");
    }
}
---------------------------------------------------------
```

In the line

```
Customer[] customers = new Customer[3]; // array of 'Customer' data type
```

you are instantiating an object called customers of data type *array of* Customer. At the same time, you are also allocating memory space equal to three times the space occupied by a single Customer data type object. Notice that customers is an array of Customer, so each element is itself an object of type Customer.

Look at the following expression:

```
customers[i].concatName()
```

In it, customers[i] represents the ith element in the customers array (where i has the current loop index value), so that element is a valid Customer type object. When you say customers[i].concat-Name(), you are invoking the concatName() method on that object.

Solved Exercise 1.7.8

Objective: To learn how to write, create, and use an array of custom class objects.

Steps:

- Create a folder exer178 under C:\JSP\Chapter1, and copy the Order.java and TestOrder.java files from Solved Exercise 1.7.7 into it. Rename TestOrder.java to TestOrderList.java, also modify the class inside it (call it TestOrderList instead of TestOrder). It should define an array of Order objects, each an instance of the Order class (use the values shown below), and display the output as follows. Don't worry about the format or columnar alignment, but the values need to appear on separate lines as shown.

Order ID	Item ID	Price Per Item	Qty	Order Value
100	200	2.0	12	24.0
101	201	3.0	5	15.0
102	202	2.5	3	7.5
Total				46.5

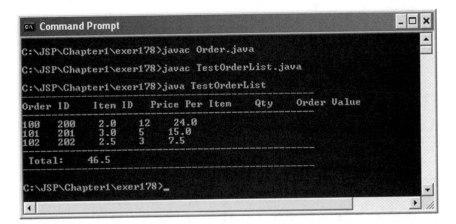

Solution:

```
//--- Begin: TestOrderList.java -----------
class TestOrderList
{
    public static void main(String[] args)
    {
        double totalOrderValue = 0.0;
        int totalQty = 0;
        Order[] orders = new Order[3];    // array of Order data type
        orders[0] = new Order(100, 200, 2.0, 12);
        orders[1] = new Order(101, 201, 3.0, 5);
        orders[2] = new Order(102, 202, 2.5, 3);
        System.out.println("---------------------------------------------------");
        System.out.println("Order ID   Item ID   Price Per Item   Qty   Order Value");
        System.out.println("---------------------------------------------------");
        for (int i = 0; i < 3; i++)
        {
            double orderVal = Order.computeOrderValue( orders[i].pricePerItem,
                                                       orders[i].qty);
            System.out.println( orders[i].orderId + "   " + orders[i].itemId
                          + "   " + orders[i].pricePerItem + "   "
                          + orders[i].qty + "   " + orderVal );
```

```
            totalOrderValue += orderVal;
        }
        System.out.println("--------------------------------------------------");
        System.out.println(" Total: " + "     " + totalOrderValue);
        System.out.println("--------------------------------------------------");
    }
}
//--- End: TestOrderList.java -------------
```

1.8 Packages

1.8.1 The Need for Packaging a Class

In Section 1.7, you wrote individual classes that did not interact much with the outside world; they were almost self-contained, except that some of them referred to Java classes from the java.lang package (such as String). In the real world, several developers write code in the form of Java classes, but all such code must eventually be brought together to work as one application. Corporate applications frequently have scores or even hundreds of classes spread out as Java files sitting in various folders. As coding requirements become more complex, it becomes important for your custom Java classes to be able to satisfy two requirements:

- They need to be able to use or refer to other Java classes sitting in various folders, in an effective manner.

- Their ability to refer to other classes should be independent of the machine used to execute the code. In other words, the custom classes could be spread out across folders, but as long as such files maintain a fixed "relative path"—relative to some "root" or "reference" folder—the code should be able to compile and run well. With this requirement, such code becomes truly machine-independent, as long as you refer everything relative to the "reference folder," which you can specify just before running the program, or as a permanent environment variable.

Until now, the code you wrote involved a maximum of two or three interdependent classes; you could thus very well keep all your .class files in a single folder and refer to each class without explicitly stating where to find it.

For example, when you compiled the Customer.java file, Java created a Customer.class file in the same folder (C:\JSP\Chapter1). Your TestName.java file referred to the Customer class by saying this:

```
Customer cst = new Customer("John", "Cox", 100.0);
```

When compiling TestName.java, Java looked at this statement and immediately recognized that there is an unfamiliar data type called Customer that is being referred to. So, using the list of folder names in the -classpath option, Java searched for a file named Customer.class in each folder in the list, one after the other, until it found the required file.

When -classpath is not explicitly used, Java uses "-classpath %CLASSPATH%" implicitly, behind-the-scenes. Since currently your CLASSPATH has the period (.) in the list of folder names, Java has not been complaining until now as long as you referred to classes sitting in the same folder. Java was then able to interpret the preceding statement, using the definition of the Customer class in your Customer.class file. Next, it compiled the rest of the code in the TestName.java file, looking for any unfamiliar data types in subsequent statements, until all such references were resolved.

To consider a more realistic example, let's say that you are asked to organize your Java files into various folders so that they are easier to maintain. Say that all of your custom data type classes (e.g., Customer.java and Order.java) need to be put under one folder (C:\JSP\Chapter1\MySource), and that all of the test-driver classes (e.g., TestName and ComputeSales) need to be put under another folder (C:\JSP\Chapter1\TestDrivers). In other words, you are asked to organize the files as follows:

```
------------------------------------
C:
+ JSP\
    + Chapter1\
      + MySource\
         -- Customer.java
      + TestDrivers\
         -- TestName.java
------------------------------------
```

This looks like a small change at first sight, but this can completely mess up the ability to run your code!

Try it out: Copy Customer.java from Section 1.7.6 into a new folder: C:\JSP\Chapter1\MySource, and copy TestName.java from Section 1.7.6 into another new folder: C:\JSP\Chapter1\TestDrivers. Remove the default constructor from the Customer class, so that you can focus on the relevant part. Compile Customer.java first, and then try compiling TestName.java. You will see the following compile errors:

```
------------------------------
C:\JSP\Chapter1\TestDrivers>javac TestName.java
TestName.java:5: cannot resolve symbol
symbol : class Customer
location: class TestName
Customer cst = new Customer("John", "Cox", 100.0);
    ^
TestName.java:5: cannot resolve symbol
symbol : class Customer
location: class TestName
```

```
Customer cst = new Customer("John", "Cox", 100.0);
             ^
2 errors
--------------------------------
```

The error showed up because Java could not locate the `Customer.class` file in the current folder (`C:\JSP\Chapter1\TestDrivers`). From what we learned in Section 1.1.1, you can use the `-classpath` option in `javac` when your class needs to refer to classes outside the current folder.

For example, in the preceding case, one option would be to redefine your `CLASSPATH` as follows:

`C:\JSP\Chapter1\TestDrivers>set CLASSPATH=.;C:\JSP\Chapter1\MySource`

Instead of manipulating the `CLASSPATH` every time, another approach is to use the `-classpath` option as follows:

`C:\JSP\Chapter1\TestDrivers>javac -classpath C:\JSP\Chapter1\MySource;%CLASSPATH% TestName.java`

Your code should compile and run now without any errors. You did achieve your objective in this particular case, but it soon becomes impractical to keep adding folder names to the `-classpath` option as your code refers to more and more classes spread out in several folders. To get an idea of what a corporate folder structure may look like, just go to your `C:\JDK\src\java` folder to look at the JDK API. There you will find hundreds of Java classes spread out in several folders and subfolders. If your code wanted to refer to some of these classes, imagine adding a different list of folder-path names every time you need to compile a specific Java class!

As a solution to this, Sun came up with the idea of a single, fixed "reference folder." In other words, you specify only the "reference folder" path as part of the `-classpath` option. This would work, provided all `.class` files reside directly under the "reference folder" (irrespective of the source file structure).

Again, the concept of having all `.class` files of a web application directly under the reference folder would work in theory, but it would cause maintenance headaches if you have several hundred `.class` files as part of an application. So it becomes necessary to organize them into subfolders under the reference folder, with the exact "relative" folder path to traverse to the required `.class` file configurable by the developer (to make it truly flexible). In other words, the first thing a developer needs to do is to organize the `.class` files into separate subfolders under the reference folder—i.e., to decide names of the subfolders under the reference folder, and also what `.class` file(s) will go under each subfolder.

Usually this folder structure is kept the same as that of the source files, for easier maintenance, but it is not required that these be the same. At this point, let me keep aside our `Customer/TestName` example for a moment, and digress a little bit on the folder/file structures. Say that you have two `.class` files, `Customer.class` and `Order.class` that need to go under a folder called `mypackage` under the reference folder, and another called `Address.class` that needs to go under a folder called `mypackagecommon` under the reference folder. Let's say you want to have the reference folder as `C:\JSP\Chapter1\Output`. So the structure you want the `.class` files to adhere to would be as follows:

```
------------------------------------------------------------
C:
+ JSP\
    + Chapter1\
        + Output\
            + mypackage\
                -- Customer.class
                -- Order.class
            + mypackagecommon\
                -- Address.class
------------------------------------------------------------
```

(Note that the + in front means it is a folder or directory, whereas the -- means it is a file.)

As I just stated, you are free to choose a completely different path structure for `.class` files, than the corresponding source files (`.java`). So your source files could be spread as follows:

```
------------------------------------------------------------
C:
+ JSP\
    + Chapter1\
        + MySource\
            + salesdept\
                -- Customer.java
                -- Order.java
            + common\
                -- Address.java
------------------------------------------------------------
```

As you can see, the folder structure for `.java` files is different than that for `.class` files. Java is concerned mainly with where to look for the `.class` files (not `.java`). Note that the "relative path" (folder path relative to the reference folder) to the `Customer.class` file is `mypackage`, and that for the `Address.class` file is `mypackagecommon`. To extend the concept, you could have a `.class` file sitting several folders deep under the reference folder, such as the following:

```
------------------------------------------------------------
C:
+ JSP\
    + Chapter1\
        + Output\
            + mypackage\
```

```
      -- Customer.class
      -- Order.class
      + sales\
        + northamerica\
          + usa\
            -- Summary.class
      + mypackagecommon\
        -- Address.class
-------------------------------------------------------------
```

Here, the relative path for the Summary.class file would be "mypackage\sales\northamerica\usa".

Let's now go back to our original Customer/TestName example. Say that all .class files (for MySource .java source code) need to be created relative to C:\JSP\Chapter1\Output, which would be our "reference folder." Specifically, say that you want Customer.class file to get created in a subfolder called mypackage under this reference folder. Also, say that test drivers are treated differently in that their .class files can be created directly under the source folder. (Usually test drivers are considered "client code," so it would be safe to assume that organizing files is limited to source code that may run into scores or hundreds of files—such as Customer.java.) In other words, at the end of the compile process, you want the files/folders to look like this:

```
-----------------------------------
C:
+ JSP\
    + Chapter1\
      + MySource\
        -- Customer.java
      + TestDrivers\
        -- TestName.java
        -- TestName.class
      + Output\
        + mypackage\
          -- Customer.class
-----------------------------------
```

To ensure that Customer.class does get created this way, we could do one of two things:

- Manually create a new subfolder called mypackage under C:\JSP\Chapter1\Output and then use -d C:\JSP\Chapter1\Output\mypackage when compiling Customer.java.

- Use a "package statement" inside the Customer.java file, and use -d C:\JSP\Chapter1\Output when compiling it, so that the compiler creates a new mypackage subfolder for you, under C:\JSP\Chapter1\Output.

The first option is obviously impractical; when you have several source files spread out in several folders and you want their `.class` files to be created in similar folder structures, you cannot keep creating new subfolders manually every time.

We will look at the second option in more detail in the next section.

1.8.2   The package Statement

Instead of manually creating the output folders/subfolders, Java provides a more efficient way of automating the process via the source code itself. That way the exact *relative* output folder structure is guaranteed to be fixed, no matter where the source code is compiled. In other words, if you "somehow" specify the desired *relative* output folder path in the source file itself, Java can interpret that to create the subfolder(s) for you, relative to some reference folder. It leaves the exact reference folder to be specified at compile time, via the -d option in `javac`. With this, the reference folder is allowed to change at each compile, but the relative folder path under it remains fixed, dictated by the source code. The concept is similar to a zip file, where the relative path of each constituent file in the zip is fixed, but you are free to extract all of those files under any "root" folder you wish. That folder becomes your reference folder, and the constituent files get extracted to subfolders under that reference folder, based on each file's relative path.

You can have multiple `.class` files sharing the same relative folder path, in which case all such files are considered a "named set of classes," technically called a **package**. So a package consists of one or more `.class` files with the same relative folder path. Here, the word "named" means you assign a name to the set or group of classes. Again Java enforces standardization by requiring that the name of the package be the same as the concatenation of subfolder names taken from the relative path for that package (separating the subfolder names by periods (.) if more than one subfolder is involved). That way Java can deduce the relative folder path from the package name (and conversely, you deduce the package name from the desired relative folder path). In effect, the "package name" and "relative folder path" become interchangeable and mean more or less the same thing.

In the example discussed in Section 1.8.1, the "relative path" for `Customer.class` and `Order.class` is `mypackage`, relative to the `Output` folder. So, the package consisting of `Customer.class` and `Order.class` would need to be named `mypackage`. Similarly, the relative path of `Summary.class` is `mypackage\sales\northamerica\usa`, so its package needs to be called `mypackage.sales.northamerica.usa`.

To specify the desired relative output folder path in the source file itself, you need to use a *package statement* as the first line in the source code. In other words, you specify the name of a package and its constituent class(es) by using a package statement in each class that needs to be part of that package. A package statement consists of the word `package` followed by the package name (no double-quotes), ending in a semicolon. Note that the package statement MUST be the first statement in the source code file.

For example, in the case of the Customer class in Section 1.8.1, you would have

```
--------------------------------------------------------
package mypackage;
class Customer
{
    String firstName;
    String lastName;
    double salesAmount;
    Customer(String firstName, String lastName, double salesAmount)
    {
        this.firstName = firstName;
        this.lastName = lastName;
        this.salesAmount = salesAmount;
    }
    String concatName()
    {
        String strName = lastName + ", " + firstName;
        return strName;
    }
}
--------------------------------------------------------
```

In effect, you are specifying that the relative folder path of the Customer.class file is mypackage. In other words, you are creating a package called mypackage and specifying that Customer class belongs to it.

The files we have been compiling until now were being created as part of a *default package*—a package with no name that Java provides for all classes without an explicit package statement. Classes within the default package can refer to one another without any problems. However, Java has a restriction that classes belonging to a named package (i.e., other than the default package) cannot refer to classes in the default package. For classes of a named package to refer to your class, your class must belong to the same named package as the one referring it, or belong to another named package (but not the default package).

To ensure that your class is part of a named package, you need to add the package statement *and* use the -d option in javac. Adding the package statement resolves part of the problem but is not sufficient by itself. In order for it to work, you must use the -d option in javac, *in addition to* using the package statement. So, even after adding the package statement in Customer.java as shown earlier, if you compile it using your usual javac command without the -d option, you would end up with the

`Customer.class` file getting generated in the same folder where `Customer.java` exists—no new sub-folder called `mypackage` would get created. Although it will not be part of the default package (because you used a package statement), it still will not be part of the legitimate `mypackage` package because it does not reside under a `mypackage` folder (recall that package name and folder name go hand-in-hand). So in effect, the `Customer.class` cannot be referred to by classes of other named packages, nor by those in the default package (since it belongs to neither). To fix this, you must use the `-d` option in `javac`.

In this example, for classes of other named packages to be able to refer to it, `Customer` class must reside in a named package (other than the default package). We want `Customer.class` to reside in the `mypackage` package; in other words, we want `Customer.class` to get created in a folder called `mypackage` under the reference folder specified at compile time via the `-d` option in `javac`.

The JSP_OUT Environment Variable

Since we will be frequently using the "reference folder" in this book, let's create an environment variable `JSP_OUT` that contains its path:

`C:\JSP\Chapter1>set JSP_OUT=C:\JSP\Chapter1\Output`

(I am calling it `JSP_OUT` since this book is on JSP. It will be used in later chapters, although we will be changing its value as we move from one chapter to the next.) You still need to use the `-d` option to specify the reference folder, but you can now use `-d %JSP_OUT%` instead of `-d C:\JSP\Chapter1\Output`. Similarly, you will now say `-classpath %JSP_OUT%` instead of: `-classpath C:\JSP\Chapter1\Output`.

Note that the package statement only specifies the relative folder path for the generated `.class` file, but not the reference folder itself. To specify the reference folder to which this path needs to be relative to, you need to use the `-d` option in `javac`. Whatever follows immediately to the right of `-d` would be taken as the reference folder by `javac`. In this example, we want the reference folder to be `C:\JSP\Chapter1\Output`, which is now the same as `%JSP_OUT%`, so you will be using `-d %JSP_OUT%` in your `javac`, as follows:

`C:\JSP\Chapter1\MySource>javac -d %JSP_OUT% Customer.java`

This should create the `Customer.class` file under a new subfolder called `mypackage` under `C:\JSP\Chapter1\Output`.

You can add other classes to this package later if you wish, by adding the same package statement at the beginning of those classes. For example, you can add this package statement (package mypackage;) at the beginning of your Order.java file, and compile it, so that the Order class is also a part of the mypackage package.

As stated earlier, the source file containing the package statement can be located in any folder; the package statement specifies only the destination folder name where the compiled .class file will reside. The new destination folder is always created relative to the reference folder path specified immediately following the -d option in your javac command. If the destination folder with that name and path already exists, no new folder would be created; the .class file would be put in that existing folder.

1.8.3 Importing Classes from Other Packages

Now that Customer.class resides in C:\JSP\Chapter1\Output\mypackage, we need to convey this information to TestName.java when it looks at the unfamiliar data type Customer. So, we want to communicate to TestName.java something like "Customer is a new data type I created, but its .class file resides in C:\JSP\Chapter1\Output\mypackage." You do this as a two-step process:

1. Use an *import statement* for Customer class in your TestName.java file.

2. While compiling TestName.java, use the -classpath option (or set the CLASSPATH environment variable) such that Java would look for the Customer.class file under the reference folder (%JSP_OUT%).

Let's now look at both steps, one after the other.

1. An import statement consists of the word import (lowercase) followed by the fully qualified name of the class (Customer) you want the current class (TestName) to use. The *fully qualified name of the class* is the full package name preceding the name of the class, with a period (.) separating the two. For example, the fully qualified name for the Customer class is now mypackage.Customer. So, you would change TestName.java to look like this:

```
--------------------------------------------------
import mypackage.Customer;

class TestName
{
    public static void main(String[] args)
    {
        Customer cst = new Customer("John", "Cox", 100.0);
        System.out.println(cst.concatName() + " " + cst.salesAmount);
    }
}
--------------------------------------------------
```

2.   While compiling `TestName.java`, you need to communicate to Java that the imported class (`mypackage.Customer`) resides under the `C:\JSP\Chapter1\Output` "reference folder" (`%JSP_OUT%`). To do so, you use `-classpath %JSP_OUT%` as follows:

```
C:\JSP\Chapter1\TestDrivers>javac -classpath %JSP_OUT% TestName.java
```

Notice how you specify only the reference folder; Java can figure out the subfolders under it, based on the import statement's fully qualified path for the `Customer` class (`mypackage.Customer`). In other words, when you say the reference folder is `C:\JSP\Chapter1\Output` and the import statement says `mypackage.Customer`, Java knows that you mean `Customer.class` resides under `C:\JSP\Chapter1\Output\mypackage`.

Instead of using `-classpath %JSP_OUT%` here, you could achieve the same effect by setting the value of the `CLASSPATH` environment variable to contain `%JSP_OUT%` and then omitting `-classpath` in `javac`.

```
C:\JSP\Chapter1\TestDrivers>SET CLASSPATH=%JSP_OUT%
C:\JSP\Chapter1\TestDrivers>javac TestName.java
```

Either way, you will find that `TestName.java` still does not compile; it gives the following compile errors:

Let's look at the reasons why. When you compile any file without an explicit package statement, Java puts it in a *default package* that does not have a name. When you compile `TestName.java`, which does not have a package statement, it becomes part of the default package, whereas your `Customer` class is now part of the `mypackage` package as you specified. You now have two files in two separate packages: the `TestName` class in the default package trying to refer to the `Customer` class in the `mypackage` package.

This is what gives rise to error: Classes have a scope limited to the package they belong to. Every class belonging to a specific package can freely refer to every other class in the same package without qualifying it or specifying the package it resides in. For example, assume you put the same package statement (`package mypackage;`) in both of your `Customer.java` and `Order.java` files. Each of these can freely refer to one another without using any import statement or the fully qualified class name.

However, a class outside of the mypackage package cannot freely refer to the Customer or Order classes or their attributes or methods.

If it should, you need to do the following:

1. The outsider class (TestName in this example) needs to use the import statement with a fully qualified name for the class it is seeking to use (Customer in this example).

2. The class it is seeking needs to have public access, not just package-level access. Until now, you have been defining classes by simply using the word "class" followed by the class name, with no access specifiers in front of class. This would generate a class with a default, package-level access. To change a class from a default, package-level access to one with public access, you must use the public keyword explicitly in front of the word class in the source file.

3. If the class it is seeking has a constructor, it must be declared public by using a public keyword in front of the constructor's name.

4. Even after these changes, the outsider class can only access public attributes or methods from the class it is seeking. Unspecified access means package-level access by default.

Go ahead and perform Steps 2 through 4: Add the public keyword in front of the Customer class in the Customer.java file, the constructor, the salesAmount attribute (because TestName accesses it directly), and the concatName method. The Customer.java file now looks like this:

```
-------------------------------------
package mypackage;

public class Customer
{
    String firstName;
    String lastName;
    public double salesAmount;
    public Customer(String firstName, String lastName, double salesAmount)
    {
        this.firstName = firstName;
        this.lastName = lastName;
        this.salesAmount = salesAmount;
    }
    public String concatName()
    {
        String strName = lastName + ", " + firstName;
        return strName;
    }
}
-------------------------------------
```

Compile `Customer.java` again, and then try compiling `TestName.java`; it should work fine now. At the end of compile, verify that the files/folders do look the way you wanted:

```
-----------------------------------
C:
+ JSP\
    + Chapter1\
      + MySource\
          -- Customer.java
      + TestDrivers\
          -- TestName.java
          -- TestName.class
      + Output\
          + mypackage\
              -- Customer.class
-----------------------------------
```

To run `TestName`, you need to use `-classpath .;%JSP_OUT%`, because `TestName.class` resides in the current folder, whereas `Customer.class` resides under `%JSP_OUT%`. Somehow it needs both files' paths during execution although `TestName.class` was created using them. So your command would look like this:

```
C:\JSP\Chapter1\TestDrivers>java -classpath .;%JSP_OUT% TestName
Cox, John 100.0
```

To recap, you fixed your reference folder to `C:\JSP\Chapter1\Output` and created an environment variable called `JSP_OUT` to store this reference folder:

```
SET JSP_OUT=C:\JSP\Chapter1\Output
```

Next, your command session looked like this:

```
C:\JSP\Chapter1\MySource>javac -d %JSP_OUT% Customer.java
```

You verified that it created a new subfolder called `mypackage` under `C:\JSP\Chapter1\Output`, and put `Customer.class` in it. Next you compiled `TestName.java` using the following `-classpath` option:

```
C:\JSP\Chapter1\TestDrivers>javac -classpath %JSP_OUT% TestName.java
```

Finally, you ran the program using `-classpath .;%JSP_OUT%`:

```
C:\JSP\Chapter1\TestDrivers>java -classpath .;%JSP_OUT% TestName
Cox, John 100.0
```

You may notice that a corollary of this is that you must use the package statement in your class if you want to refer to your class in other classes that belong to packages other than the default package. This is because if you do not use the package statement in your class, it would belong to the default package. This means that there is no way other classes outside of the default package can refer to your class, since there is no explicit import statement that allows you to import classes belonging to the default package.

To simplify the preceding example and to reinforce the concept, I will now take up the case where you want the reference folder to be the same as the current folder—i.e., the one holding Customer.java. Create a new subfolder called sec183 under C:\JSP\Chapter1, copy Customer.java from C:\JSP\Chapter1\MySource into it, and also TestName.java from C:\JSP\Chapter1\TestDrivers into it. The objective is to compile Customer.java with the package statement, and then get TestName.java to refer to Customer class. To put the reference folder same as the current folder (C:\JSP\Chapter1\sec183), you will need to use -d . in javac when compiling Customer.java. This will create a mypackage folder under the current folder, which is C:\JSP\Chapter1\sec183. In other words, the mypackage folder is created directly under the current folder (C:\JSP\Chapter1\sec183). The compile command would look like this:

```
C:\JSP\Chapter1\sec183>javac -d . Customer.java
```

This creates a subfolder called mypackage under the current folder (C:\JSP\Chapter1\sec183), and puts Customer.class under it.

Now compile TestName.java using -classpath . as shown here:

```
C:\JSP\Chapter1\sec183>javac -classpath . TestName.java
```

Finally, run the program (your CLASSPATH already has the period in it, so you do not need -classpath .):

```
C:\JSP\Chapter1\sec183>java TestName
Cox, John 100.0
```

The command prompt window is shown here:

The folder/file structure at the end of this would look as follows:

```
------------------------------------
C:
+ JSP\
    + Chapter1\
      + sec183\
         -- Customer.java
         -- TestName.java
         -- TestName.class
         + mypackage\
            -- Customer.class
------------------------------------
```

Finally, you can always add other classes to a package by simply using the same package name. For example, say you want Order.class to belong to the mypackage package, then Order.java needs to say

```
-------------------------
package mypackage;
class Order
{
  // rest of Order class . . . .
}
-------------------------
```

Observe that whenever Java encounters a package statement in a class, it first looks if a package folder with that name was already created by other classes. If so, it simply adds the current class to that folder; otherwise, it creates a new package folder for that class.

Order.java can reside anywhere, but for the sake of simplicity, say that it resides in the same folder as Customer.java. So the output file structure you want is

```
------------------------------------
C:
+ JSP\
    + Chapter1\
      + MySource\
         -- Customer.java
         -- Order.java
      + TestDrivers\
         -- TestName.java
         -- TestName.class
      + Output\
         + mypackage\
            -- Customer.class
            -- Order.class
------------------------------------
```

You have two ways to import `Customer` and `Order` classes inside `TestName`. One way is to add individual `import` statements for each class you need, as shown here:

```
--------------------------
import mypackage.Customer;
import mypackage.Order;
class TestName
{
   // rest of TestName class (as before)...
}
--------------------------
```

A more concise way is to use the wildcard character (*) to import all classes of a package. You would thus say

```
--------------------------
import mypackage.*;
class TestName
{
   // rest of TestName class (as before)...
}
--------------------------
```

This would import both `Customer` and `Order` classes (and any others) that belong to `mypackage` package. It is preferable to go for the wildcard character if several classes of a package need to be imported; otherwise picking specific classes you need and using individual imports should be good enough.

Solved Exercise 1.8.3

Objective: To practice how to package a class.

Steps:

- Copy the `Customer.java` file from the end of Section 1.8.3, and save it under a new folder, `C:\JSP\Chapter1\exer183`. Make it part of a new package called `exer183pkg` (instead of `mypackage`).

- Write a new test-driver class called `TestReport` in the same folder, and do *not* make it part of a named package (in other words, let it become part of the default package). In `TestReport`, define an array of three `Customer`-type objects, with the first name, last name, and sales amount as follows:

1. First Name = Judy, Last Name = Miller, Sales Amount = 150.0

2. First Name = Jane, Last Name = Armstrong, Sales Amount = 300.0

3. First Name = Mike, Last Name = Johnson, Sales Amount = 200.0

- Show the output as follows. Don't worry about the format or columnar alignment.

#	Name	Amount
1	Miller, Judy	150.0
2	.Armstrong, Jane	100.0
3	Johnson, Mike	200.0
Total		450.0

Note: For this exercise, set environment variable JSP_OUT as

```
SET JSP_OUT=C:\JSP\Chapter1\Output
```

Then use this JSP_OUT in the -d option of javac for compiling the Customer class.

Also, when compiling TestReport, use the -classpath option with a value of %JSP_OUT%, but do not use the -d option since it needs to belong to the default package. Verify that a new folder called exer183pkg is created under C:\JSP\Chapter1\Output and Customer.class is created there. To execute TestReport, use the -classpath .;%JSP_OUT% option.

You need to have the following file structure at the end of this exercise:

```
----------------------------------
C:
+ JSP\
    + Chapter1\
      + exer183\
          -- Customer.java
          -- TestReport.java
          -- TestReport.class
      + Output\
          + exer183pkg\
            -- Customer.class
----------------------------------
```

The command session is shown here.

```
Command Prompt                                                        _ □ ×

C:\JSP\Chapter1\exer183>SET JSP_OUT=C:\JSP\Chapter1\Output

C:\JSP\Chapter1\exer183>javac -d %JSP_OUT% Customer.java

C:\JSP\Chapter1\exer183>javac -classpath %JSP_OUT% TestReport.java

C:\JSP\Chapter1\exer183>java -classpath .;%JSP_OUT% TestReport

 # Name Sales Amount
-------------------------------------------------------------
1 Miller, Judy 150.0
2 Armstrong, Jane 100.0
3 Johnson, Mike 200.0
-------------------------------------------------------------
 Total 450.0
-------------------------------------------------------------

C:\JSP\Chapter1\exer183>
```

Solution:

```java
// ----------Begin: Customer.java ----------
package exer183pkg;
public class Customer
{
    String firstName;
    String lastName;
    public double salesAmount;

    public Customer(String firstName, String lastName, double salesAmount)
    {
        this.firstName = firstName;
        this.lastName = lastName;
        this.salesAmount = salesAmount;
    }

    public String concatName()
    {
        String strName = lastName + ", " + firstName;
        return strName;
    }
}
// ----------End: Customer.java ----------


// ----------Begin: TestReport.java ----------
import exer183pkg.Customer;
class TestReport
```

```
{
    public static void main(String[] args)
    {
        Customer[] cst = new Customer[3];
        cst [0] = new Customer("Judy", "Miller", 150.0);
        cst [1] = new Customer("Jane", "Armstrong", 100.0);
        cst [2] = new Customer("Mike", "Johnson", 200.0);

        double totSales = 0.0;
        System.out.println("------------------------------------------------");
        System.out.println(" # Name Sales Amount ");
        System.out.println("------------------------------------------------");

        for (int i = 0; i < cst.length; i++)
        {
            double salesAmt = cst[i].salesAmount;
            totSales += salesAmt;
            System.out.println( (i+1) + " " + cst[i].concatName() + " " + salesAmt);
        }
        System.out.println("------------------------------------------------");
        System.out.println(" Total " + totSales );
        System.out.println("------------------------------------------------");
    }
}
// -----------End: TestReport.java ----------
```

1.8.4 Packages Using Several Folders

Package names are not restricted to single folder or subfolder names. A single package name can consist of names of several folders or subfolders concatenated with each other; in this case, the folder names must be separated by periods. For example, the package mypackage could have been named mypackage.salesdept for the Customer data type. Having a period in the package name has its own meaning though. If you used the package name mypackage.salesdept, Java would create two new subfolders: one named mypackage and another named salesdept under the mypackage subfolder just created. The mypackage subfolder would sit under the folder specified by the path following the -d option in your javac command. With the reference folder still fixed at %JSP_OUT%= C:\JSP\Chapter1\Output, this would mean that you want the folder structure to look like this:

```
------------------------------------
C:
+ JSP\
    + Chapter1\
      + MySource\
        -- Customer.java
```

```
        + TestDrivers\
           -- TestName.java
           -- TestName.class
        + Output\
           + mypackage\
              + salesdept\
                 -- Customer.class
----------------------------------
```

Customer.java would now look like:

```
------------------------------
package mypackage.salesdept;
public class Customer
{
    // rest of the Customer class (as before)
}
------------------------------
```

To compile it, you would use -d %JSP_OUT% as before:

```
C:\JSP\Chapter1\MySource>SET JSP_OUT=C:\JSP\Chapter1\Output
C:\JSP\Chapter1\MySource>javac -d %JSP_OUT% Customer.java
```

This would create Customer.class under a new subfolder called salesdept under
C:\JSP\Chapter1\Output\mypackage.

The calling class (TestName) also needs to be changed accordingly for the code to work. The TestName
class would now use a different import statement:

```
------------------------------
import mypackage.salesdept.Customer;
class TestName
{
    // rest of the TestName class (as before)
}
------------------------------
```

To compile TestName, you use the same line as before:

```
C:\JSP\Chapter1\TestDrivers>javac -classpath %JSP_OUT% TestName.java
```

Finally, to run TestName, you use the same java command as before:

```
C:\JSP\Chapter1\TestDrivers>java -classpath .;%JSP_OUT% TestName
Cox, John 100.0
```

As you can see, using a fixed reference folder is useful: You define a single environment variable
(JSP_OUT) and reuse it no matter how the output folder structure changes. The only thing is that you
need to use the appropriate package and import statements in the source code for it to work. In

other words, once you ship out the source code, the relative position of the `.class` files is fixed, and the build process is portable and machine-independent (as long as you set the reference folder appropriately). The set of `.class` files now behave just like a zip file.

When the package consists of multiple subfolders, other issues arise. What if you have `.class` files directly under one subfolder, and some others under its subfolder(s)? For example, say that you have `Address.class` directly under the `mypackage` folder, and `Customer.class` continues under the `mypackage/salesdept` subfolder. The `Address.java` file would have the following package statement:

```
package mypackage;
public class Address
{
    // some code here ..
}
```

The `Address.class` file directly under the `mypackage` folder would then be part of a package called `mypackage`, whereas the `Customer.class` file under the subfolder `\mypackage\salesdept` would be part of a separate package called `mypackage.salesdept`. These two packages are independent of each other. So, inside client code (say `TestName.java`), if you import all files under the `mypackage` package using

```
import mypackage.*;
```

only the `.class` file(s) *directly* under the `mypackage` folder would be imported but *not* the ones under any subfolders below it. Recall that the asterisk (`*`) used here is a wild-card character, which means you want to import *all* classes of that package. If you do want the `Customer` class file under the `\mypackage\salesdept` subfolder, you must also use another `import` statement:

```
import mypackage.salesdept.Customer;
```

So the lines in `TestName.java` would look like this:

```
import mypackage.*;
import mypackage.salesdept.Customer;
class TestName
{
    // rest of the TestName class (as before)
}
```

Suppose you want to use both `Customer` and `Address` classes in your `TestName.java` code. Your Test-Name.java may look like this:

```
import mypackage.salesdept.Customer;
import mypackage.Address;
```

```
class TestName
{
    // rest of the code (as before)
}
```

If you have multiple .class files under a package (e.g., Customer.class and Order.class under the mypackage.salesdept package), and you need *all* the files in that package, you can use multiple import statements, one for each class, as follows:

```
import mypackage.salesdept.Customer;
import mypackage.salesdept.Order;
```

Or, more concisely, you can use a wildcard character * after the package name to get all the .class files in that package:

```
import mypackage.salesdept.*;
```

The wildcard-character method still gets the .class files directly under that folder, not the ones under its subfolders. Suppose you say the following:

```
import mypackage.*;
```

Doing so would get you only Address.class, not Customer.class and Order.class under the \mypackage\salesdept subfolder. So, if you want all three classes, your imports would look like this:

```
import mypackage.*;
import mypackage.salesdept.*;
```

Solved Exercise 1.8.4

Objective: To learn how to create a multifolder package and also how to use the private access specifier.

Steps:

- Copy the Customer class from Solved Exercise 1.8.3, and save it under a new folder: C:\JSP\Chapter1\exer184\MySource\SalesDept.
  Make it part of a new package called exer184pkg.mypackage.salesdept that represents multiple folders.

- Make the salesAmount attribute private by using the private keyword, and write a public getter method called getSalesAmount() that returns the salesAmount as a double value.

- Open a new command prompt window, cd to C:\JSP\Chapter1\exer184\MySource\SalesDept. Compile Customer.java using -d %JSP_OUT%. (JSP_OUT=C:\JSP\Chapter1\Output, as done in Solved Exercise 1.8.3). Verify that it created Customer.class under C:\JSP\Chapter1\Output.

- Copy the test driver `TestReport.java` from Solved Exercise 1.8.3 into a new folder `C:\JSP\Chapter1\exer184\TestDrivers`, and do not make it part of any named package (in other words, let it become part of the default package). Make changes to it to import the necessary `Customer` file from the other package `exer184pkg.mypackage.salesdept`, and to call the new getter method for `salesAmount`.

- Compile `TestReport` from `C:\JSP\Chapter1\exer184\TestDrivers` using `-classpath %JSP_OUT%`. Verify that it created `TestReport.class` under `C:\JSP\Chapter1\exer184\TestDrivers`.

- Execute `TestReport` from `C:\JSP\Chapter1\exer184\TestDrivers`, using `-classpath .;%JSP_OUT%`:

  `C:\JSP\Chapter1\exer184\TestDrivers>java -classpath .;%JSP_OUT% TestReport`

```
C:\JSP\Chapter1\exer184\MySource\SalesDept>javac -d %JSP_OUT% Customer.java

C:\JSP\Chapter1\exer184\MySource\SalesDept>cd ..\..\TestDrivers

C:\JSP\Chapter1\exer184\TestDrivers>javac -classpath %JSP_OUT% TestReport.java

C:\JSP\Chapter1\exer184\TestDrivers>java -classpath .;%JSP_OUT% TestReport
# Name Sales Amount
------------------------------------
1 Miller, Judy 150.0
2 Armstrong, Jane 100.0
3 Johnson, Mike 200.0

Total 450.0
------------------------------------
C:\JSP\Chapter1\exer184\TestDrivers>_
```

- The output should look the same as in Solved Exercise 1.8.3. Verify that the new folder `exer184pkg` and its subfolders are created under `C:\JSP\Chapter1\Output`.

- You need to have the following file structure at the end of this exercise:

```
-----------------------------------
C:
+ JSP\
  + Chapter1\
    + exer184\
      + MySource\
        + SalesDept\
          -- Customer.java
      + TestDrivers\
          -- TestReport.java
          -- TestReport.class
    + Output\
      + exer184pkg\
```

```
                        + mypackage\
                          + salesdept\
                             -- Customer.class
         ----------------------------------
```

Solution:

```java
// -----------Begin: Customer.java ----------
package exer184pkg.mypackage.salesdept;
public class Customer
{
    String firstName;
    String lastName;
    private double salesAmount;
    public double getSalesAmount() { return salesAmount;}

    public Customer(String firstName, String lastName, double salesAmount)
    {
        this.firstName = firstName;
        this.lastName = lastName;
        this.salesAmount = salesAmount;
    }

    public String concatName()
    {
        String strName = lastName + ", " + firstName;
        return strName;
    }
}
// -----------End: Customer.java ----------

// -----------Begin: TestReport.java ----------
import exer184pkg.mypackage.salesdept.Customer;
class TestReport
{
    public static void main(String[] args)
    {
        Customer[] cst = new Customer[3];
        cst [0] = new Customer("Judy", "Miller", 150.0);
        cst [1] = new Customer("Jane", "Armstrong", 100.0);
        cst [2] = new Customer("Mike", "Johnson", 200.0);

        double totSales = 0.0;
        System.out.println("-------------------------------------------------");
```

```
        System.out.println(" # Name     Sales     Amount ");
        System.out.println("-------------------------------------------------");

        for (int i = 0; i < cst.length; i++)
        {
            double salesAmt = cst[i].getSalesAmount();
            totSales += salesAmt;
            System.out.println( (i+1) + " " + cst[i].concatName()
                            + " " + salesAmt);
        }
        System.out.println("-------------------------------------------------");
        System.out.println(" Total " + totSales );
        System.out.println("-------------------------------------------------");
    }
}
// -----------End: TestReport.java ----------
```

1.8.5　The JDK Package Structure

Every predefined class under the JDK exists as part of specific packages defined by Sun. If you look at the `C:\JDK\src\java` folder, you will find several subfolders, many of which have their own subfolders. All of these folders/subfolders represent individual packages. For example, the subfolder `applet` under the `java` folder represents a package called `java.applet`, which contains four classes. Similarly, the subfolder `awt` represents a package called `java.awt`, which has 92 classes directly under it, and 10 subfolders (or sub-packages) under it. Subfolder `event` under the `awt` folder represents a package called `java.awt.event`, which has 39 classes under it.

If you need any of these predefined Java classes, use the corresponding import statement in your code. For example, if your code needs to use the classes `Applet` under `\java\applet` and `ActionListener` under `\java\applet\event`, use the following two import statements:

```
import java.applet.Applet;
import java.applet.event.ActionListener;
```

Or, if you need multiple files under the `\java\applet` and `\java\applet\event` folders, you would say this:

```
import java.applet.*;
import java.applet.event.*;
```

Note that you do *not* need to change your CLASSPATH to include the `C:\JDK` folder for this to work. Java knows to look in your JDK install folder for its own classes.

There is one exception to the use of explicit `import` statements for Java predefined classes. The classes under the `java.lang` package under the `\java\lang` folder do not need an explicit `import` statement in your code; these get imported into every class by default because they are the ones most commonly used. If you look at the classes under the \java\lang folder, you will find classes such as String and System there. These are the ones you have been using until now in your code, without using an explicit import statement. When you said

```
System.out.println("Hello World");
```

you were invoking the public method called println on a public, static attribute called out, of data type PrintStream class defined under the \java\io folder, in a class called System under the \java\lang folder. You were passing to the println method a String object with no name but with a value of "Hello World" as an argument.

To see how the System class looks, open the System.java file in Notepad and search for the word out. You will notice it is of type PrintStream. The System.java file recognizes the PrintStream data type because there is an import statement (import java.io.*;) at the beginning of the file that imports the PrintStream class belonging to the java.io package.

To see the definition of the println method, you will have to open the PrintStream.java class under the \java\io folder in Notepad, and search for the word println. You will find ten different versions of println there, each taking a parameter of a different data type. The one that you invoked is the one that has a String object parameter.

Solved Exercise 1.8.5

Objective: To learn how to import "non-java.lang" JDK classes into your code.

Steps:

- Copy Customer.java and TestReport.java of Solved Exercise 1.8.4 to a new folder C:\JSP\Chapter1\exer185. Modify Customer.java to remove the package statement. Modify TestReport.java to add import statements for the following Java predefined classes:

  1. BigDecimal under java.math package

  2. BufferedReader, InputStreamReader, and PrintWriter classes under java.io package

  3. ActionListener under java.awt.event package and change the import statement to get the Customer class.

- Modify Customer.java to add an import statement for the BigDecimal class under java.math package.

- Compile and run your code to confirm that you get that same output shown in Solved Exercise 1.8.4.

  The command session would look like this.

Solution:

```
// -----------Begin: Customer.java ----------
import java.math.BigDecimal;  // OR: import java.math.*;
                             // -> will also work but not preferred
public class Customer
{
    String firstName;
    String lastName;
    private double salesAmount;
    public double getSalesAmount() { return salesAmount;}

    public Customer(String firstName, String lastName, double salesAmount)
    {
        this.firstName = firstName;
        this.lastName = lastName;
        this.salesAmount = salesAmount;
    }

    public String concatName()
    {
        String strName = lastName + ", " + firstName;
        return strName;
    }
}
// -----------End: Customer.java ----------

// -----------Begin: TestReport.java ----------
// OR: import exer185pkg.mypackage.salesdept.*;
import java.math.BigDecimal;  // OR:  import java.math.*;
```

```
import java.io.*;   // Using * may be a good idea here,
                    // since 3 classes of io package are imported,
                    // otherwise you can use 3 individual import statements
import java.awt.event.ActionListener; // OR: import java.awt.event.*;
                                      // (but the first one is preferred way
                                      // of doing it; only import the classes
                                      // you need)
class TestReport
{
    public static void main(String[] args)
    {
        Customer[] cst = new Customer[3];
        cst [0] = new Customer("Judy", "Miller", 150.0);
        cst [1] = new Customer("Jane", "Armstrong", 100.0);
        cst [2] = new Customer("Mike", "Johnson", 200.0);

        double totSales = 0.0;
        System.out.println("------------------------------------------------------");
        System.out.println(" # Name Sales Amount ");
        System.out.println("------------------------------------------------------");

        for (int i = 0; i < cst.length; i++)
        {
            double salesAmt = cst[i].getSalesAmount();
            totSales += salesAmt;
            System.out.println( (i+1) + " " + cst[i].concatName() + " " + salesAmt );
        }
        System.out.println("------------------------------------------------------");
        System.out.println(" Total " + totSales );
        System.out.println("------------------------------------------------------");
    }
}
// -----------End: TestReport.java ----------
```

1.8.6 Wrapper Classes for Primitive Data Types

If you look under the C:\JDK\src\java\lang folder, you will find four special classes of interest to you: Integer.java, Double.java, Character.java, and Boolean.java. These are not the same as the primitive data types you used earlier (int, double, char, and boolean), although they sound similar. Notice how these classes begin with an uppercase letter, as opposed to the primitive data types that begin with a lowercase letter.

These represent the class-equivalent data types for the primitive data types. They not only store the primitive data values but also have some additional attributes and methods to make them more useful when writing code. These classes are called *wrapper classes* for primitive data types.

To understand how they differ from their primitive equivalents, open `Integer.java` in Notepad, and search for the words

```
private int value
```

The `value` attribute in the `Integer` class is a `private` attribute of type `int` that contains the primitive equivalent data. In addition, you will find constructors and other methods in the `Integer` class that make it useful. To instantiate an integer-type object using an integer value of 1, you would say this:

```
Integer i = new Integer(1);
```

The `Integer` class has a method called `toString()` that returns the `String` equivalent of the integer value it contains. For example, if an integer object contains the `int` value 123, the `toString()` method would return the `String` "123."

It also has a method called `intValue()` that returns the `int` value of the `Integer` class. You can either use an `Integer` object directly in arithmetic expressions, or invoke the `intValue()` method on the `Integer` object and use that in the expression. For example, if you instantiate an `Integer` object i as shown above, you can use it in an arithmetic expression as follows:

```
int x = i.intValue() + 2;
```

Here, `i.intValue()` would get replaced with 1, which is the value of i. So the statement would assign the value 3 to x.

The `Integer` class has other useful, utility methods, such as a `static` method `parseInt` that takes a `String` object representing an integer. This method returns an `int` value from the `String` object passed in. For example, if you send in a `String` with a value "123" to the `parseInt` method using `Integer.parseInt("123")`, it will return the `int` value of 123.

The `Integer` class has other useful methods as well. Similar methods exist in the other classes: `Double`, `Character`, and `Boolean`.

Solved Exercise 1.8.6

Objective: To learn how to use JDK Wrapper classes instead of primitive data types.

Steps:

- Copy the `Customer.java` and `TestReport.java` files from Solved Exercise 1.8.4 to a new folder: `C:\JSP\Chapter1\exer186`. Modify the `Customer` class to remove the package statement.

- Change the `salesAmount` to be of type `Double` (instead of `double`).

- Make all necessary modifications to `Customer.java` and `TestReport.java` to accommodate these changes.

■ Compile and run your code. Verify that the output looks the same as in Solved Exercise 1.8.4. The command session is shown here.

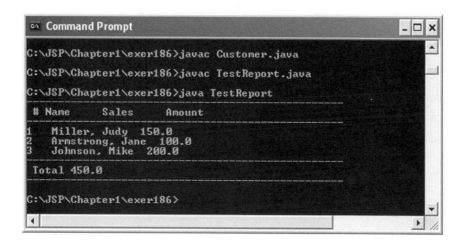

Solution:

```
// -----------Begin: Customer.java ----------
public class Customer
{
    String firstName;
    String lastName;
    private Double salesAmount;

    public Double getSalesAmount() { return salesAmount;}

    public Customer(String firstName, String lastName, Double salesAmount)
    {
        this.firstName = firstName;
        this.lastName = lastName;
        this.salesAmount = salesAmount;
    }

    public String concatName()
    {
        String strName = lastName + ", " + firstName;
        return strName;
    }
}
// -----------End: Customer.java ----------
```

```java
// ----------Begin: TestReport.java ----------
class TestReport
{
    public static void main(String[] args)
    {
        Customer[] cst = new Customer[3];
        cst [0] = new Customer("Judy", "Miller", new Double(150.0));
        cst [1] = new Customer("Jane", "Armstrong", new Double(100.0));
        cst [2] = new Customer("Mike", "Johnson", new Double(200.0));

        double totSales = 0.0;
        System.out.println("---------------------------------------------------");
        System.out.println(" # Name      Sales      Amount ");
        System.out.println("---------------------------------------------------");

        for (int i = 0; i < cst.length; i++)
        {
            Double salesAmt = cst[i].getSalesAmount();
            totSales += salesAmt.doubleValue();
            System.out.println( (i+1) + "    " + cst[i].concatName() + "    " + salesAmt);
        }
        System.out.println("---------------------------------------------------");
        System.out.println(" Total " + totSales );
        System.out.println("---------------------------------------------------");
    }
}
// ----------End: TestReport.java ----------
```

1.8.7   The null Object

Another advantage of having a full-fledged class to represent an integer is that you can set objects to an undefined, null object value rather than 0. There are situations when you do not want an integer object to initialize to 0 but instead want to initialize it to some undefined state. In these cases, the value of null comes in handy. The instruction would look like this:

Integer i = null;

Later in the code, you could set a specific value of, say, 1 for i as follows:

i = new Integer(1);

Note that null is a valid Java-reserved word; it represents an object that is undefined. An object of any class (custom or Java predefined) can be assigned a value of null. It is a useful way of initializing an object to an undefined state. In a real-world programming environment, you will find the null object being used extensively to initialize objects with undefined values.

You need to be careful when using null objects in expressions or other instructions. If you try accessing methods on a null object, you will get an error at run time. Suppose you try to run the following lines of code:

```
class Test
{
    public static void main(String[] args)
    {
        Integer i = null;
        System.out.println(" Value of i = " + i.intValue());
    }
}
```

Here you are trying to invoke the intValue() method on i, which is a null object. Although the code will compile, you will get a run-time error as shown here:

```
C:\JSP\Chapter1>java Test
Exception in thread "main" java.lang.NullPointerException
at Test.main(Test.java:6)
```

Now insert an additional instruction just before the System.out as shown here:

```
Integer i = null;
i = new Integer(1);
System.out.println(" Value of i = " + i.intValue());
```

This will work fine, because i is not null at the time of invoking the intValue() method on it. It is useful to check if an object is not null before invoking methods on it or using it in expressions, as shown here:

```
if (i != null)
{
    System.out.println(" Value of i = " + i.intValue());
    int j = i.intValue();
}
```

That way, you can ensure that your code will not blow up at run time.

As discussed before, you can use the null object as a legitimate value for an object of any class. For a String object, use it as follows:

```
String str = null;
```

1.8.8   Packages and Access Specifiers

Access specifiers provide different levels of encapsulation, or data hiding, from inadvertent use by outsiders. The three access specifiers based on what we learned until now are: private, *unspecified*, and public (protected will be discussed in Chapter 2). These differ in the extent of access they provide to outsiders in that sequence—with private access meaning no access to outsiders, and public access meaning access to everybody. Let's briefly recap the effects of these access levels:

- private: Gives access to that class only—not to any outsider, including objects instantiated from that class, or subclasses inheriting from it. (We will see subclasses and inheritance in Chapter 2.)

- *unspecified:* Gives access to every class in that package and to objects instantiated from it or its subclasses in that package. This is like a package-level access; it allows access to everyone in that package.

- public: Gives access to every class or subclass in every package and to all objects anywhere.

A full picture of the effect of access specifiers on classes spread out in different packages is shown in Figure 1.2.

As you can see, classes within the same package can access each other's attributes and methods that are public, protected, or have unspecified access. The private members still remain private to the class; therefore objects instantiated from that class or other classes in the same package cannot access them.

To access attributes hidden by access specifiers, you need to have separate *getter* methods that return the attribute value to outside callers. If the outsider needs to be able to change the value of such attributes, you also need to provide setter methods that set the value of the attribute.

Solved Exercise 1.8.8

Objective: To learn how to use the private and public access specifiers and to write getter and setter methods.

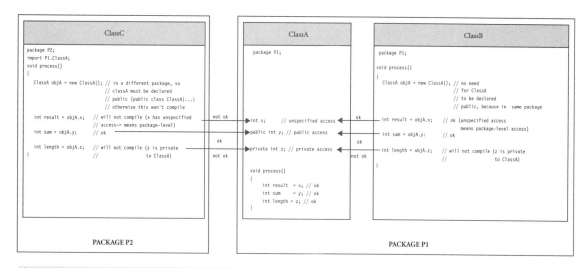

Figure 1.2

The effect of access specifiers on class member access across packages.

Steps:

- Create a new subfolder called exer188 under C:\JSP\Chapter1 and copy the Order.java and TestOrder.java files from Solved Exercise 1.7.6 into it. Modify the Order class to make the computeOrderValue() method public by using the public keyword in front of it.

- Make all attributes in the Order class private to the class. Write public getter and private setter methods that get/set the values of these attributes for outsiders.

- Make changes to TestOrder to call the new getter methods in the Order class. Compile and run your code.

- The output session may look like this.

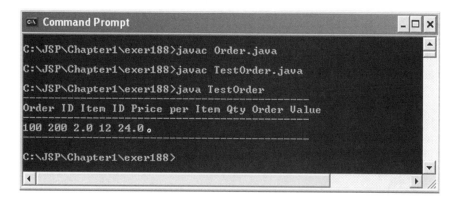

Solution:

```java
// -----------Begin: Order.java ----------
class Order
{
    private int orderId;
    private int itemId;
    private double pricePerItem;
    private int qty;

    // default constructor
    Order()
    {
        orderId = 0;          // OR: setOrderId(0);
        itemId = 0;           // OR: setItemId(0);
        pricePerItem = 0.0;   // OR: setPricePerItem(0.0);
        qty = 0;              // OR: setQty(0);
    }

    Order(int orderId, int itemId, double pricePerItem, int qty)
    {
        this.orderId = orderId;             // OR: setOrderId(orderId);
        this.itemId = itemId;               // OR: setItemId(itemId);
        this.pricePerItem = pricePerItem;   // OR: setPricePerItem(pricePerItem);
        this.qty = qty;                     // OR: setQty(qty);
    }

    public double computeOrderValue()
    {
        return pricePerItem * qty;
    }

    // getters
    public int getOrderId() { return orderId; }
    public int getItemId() { return itemId; }
    public double getPricePerItem () { return pricePerItem; }
    public int getQty() { return qty; }

    // setters
    private void setOrderId(int orderId) { this.orderId = orderId; }
    private void setItemId(int itemId) { this.itemId = itemId; }
    private void setPricePerItem(double pricePerItem)
```

```
        {
            this.pricePerItem = pricePerItem;
        }
        private void setQty(int qty) { this.qty = qty; }
    }


// -----------End: Order.java ----------------


// ----------Begin: TestOrder.java ----------
class TestOrder
{
    public static void main(String[] args)
    {
        Order order = new Order(100, 200, 2.0, 12);
        System.out.println("----------------------------------------------");
        System.out.println("Order ID Item ID Price per Item Qty Order Value");
        System.out.println("----------------------------------------------");
        System.out.println( order.getOrderId() + " " + order.getItemId()
                            + " " + order.getPricePerItem() + " "
                            + order.getQty() + " "
                            + order.computeOrderValue() );
        System.out.println("----------------------------------------------");
    }
}
// ----------End: TestOrder.java ------------
```

1.9   Summary

In this chapter, you reviewed Java environment setup, and also looked at important options in javac and java commands. You learned about mixed arithmetic expressions and how to cast values to a different data type. You became familiar with the use of escape character sequences. You studied arrays and how to process them. You understood what methods are, including how they work, how to supply input to them, and how to call them from elsewhere in the code. You now know what a class is, and how to instantiate an object from it. You are aware of the difference between instance and static class members. You practiced the use of access specifiers and understood their implications in member access. Finally you noted the use of packages, including how to create one, add classes to it, and the effect of access specifiers on class member access across packages.

1.10   Chapter Quiz

1. Which of the following is true? (Select all that apply.)

    i. By definition, a class is a nonprimitive data type.

    ii. A class is a data type that has its own attributes and/or methods.

    iii. A class can be a Java predefined class or your own custom class.

    iv. A class can have multiple attributes, each of a different data type.

    v. A class can process or perform operations on its data to give results.

    a. All of the above

    b. (i), (ii), (iii), and (v) only

    c. (ii) and (iv) only

    d. (i), (ii), (iii), and (iv) only

2. Which of the following is true? (Select all that apply.)

    i. A class is a template that can be used to create objects.

    ii. An object is an instance of a class.

    iii. Instantiating an object of a class always invokes the default constructor of that class.

    iv. In order to instantiate an object of a class, you must use the new keyword.

    v. Use of the new keyword always bypasses the default constructor.

    vi. Multiple constructors can coexist in a class, but each must have a distinct set of parameters (in both data type and sequence) to distinguish it from the others.

    a. (i), (ii), and (vi) only

    b. (i), (ii), (iii), (iv), and (vi) only

    c. (i), (ii), (iv), and (v) only

    d. All of the above

3. Which of the following is true? (Select all that apply.)

    i. You can position your class members anywhere within the enclosing class.

    ii. Having a constructor in your class is optional; if there isn't one, Java defines a default constructor for you implicitly.

    iii. A constructor must have the same name as the class (case-sensitive).

iv. A default constructor is simply one that does not have any parameters.

v. A class member is a term used to refer to either class attributes or class methods.

vi. If an access specifier is absent, class members are accessible from only within that class but not from outside.

a. All of the above

b. (i), (ii), (iii), (iv), and (v) only

c. (ii), (iii), (iv), and (v) only

d. (i), (ii), (iii), (v), and (vi) only

4. What would the output of the following code be? (Assume that you save the `Customer` and `TestName` classes in separate files and attempt compiling the `Customer` class followed by the `TestName` class.)

```
class Customer
{
    String firstName;
    String lastName;
    static String concatName()
    {
        String strResult = lastName + ", " + firstName;
        return strResult;
    }
}
class TestName
{
    public static void main(String[] args)
    {
        Customer cst = new Customer();
        cst.firstName = "John";
        cst.lastName = "Cox";
        System.out.println( Customer.concatName(cst.firstName, cst.lastName) );
    }
}
```

a. The `Customer` class would not compile.

b. The `Customer` class would compile, but the `TestName` class would not compile.

c. The code would run fine and show an output as `Cox, John`.

d. Both `Customer` and `TestName` classes would compile but it would give a run-time error.

5. What would the output of the following code be? (Assume that you save the Customer and TestName classes in separate files and attempt compiling the Customer class followed by the TestName class.)

```java
class Customer
{
        private String firstName;
        private String lastName;
        public String concatName()
        {
                String strResult = lastName + ", " + firstName;
                return strResult;
        }
}
class TestName
{
        public static void main(String[] args)
        {
                Customer cst = new Customer();
                cst.firstName = "John";
                cst.lastName = "Cox";
                System.out.println(cst.concatName());
        }
}
```

   a. The Customer class would not compile.

   b. The Customer class would compile but the TestName class would not compile.

   c. Both classes would compile but would give a run-time error.

   d. Both classes would compile and run fine, and show an output as Cox, John.

6. Which of the following are true? (Select all that apply.)

   i. A package is a named set of classes.

   ii. You must use the -d option in javac in order for it to properly create a new folder representing your package.

   iii. A package represents a physical folder name, relative to the reference folder path you use after the -d option in javac.

   iv. If you do not use an explicit package statement in your class, that class is not part of any package.

   v. You must use the public keyword in front of the class definition if you want outsiders to the package containing that class to access it.

vi. Once you use the `public` keyword in front of your class definition, you can either use the `public` keyword or *not* use an access specifier (unspecified access specifier) in front of attributes/methods in a class in order that outsiders to that package are able to access those attributes/methods.

a. All of the above

b. (i), (ii), and (iii) only

c. (i), (ii), (iii), (iv), and (v) only

d. (i), (ii), (iii), and (v) only

7. What would happen if you try to compile and run the following code?

```
class Test
{
    public static void main(String[] args)
    {
        String str = "Hello";
        str = null;
        System.out.println(" Value of str is " + str);
    }
}
```

a. It will give a compile error.

b. It will give a run-time error (`NullPointerException`).

c. It will run fine with no errors.

d. Can't say; it depends on the compiler.

8. What will happen if you try to compile and run the following code?

```
class Test
{
    public static void main(String[] args)
    {
        Integer i = new Integer(1);
        int j = i + 2;
    }
}
```

a. It will give a compile error.

b. It will give a run-time error.

c. It will run fine with no errors.

d. Can't say; it depends on the compiler.

9. Assume that ClassA and ClassB are classes in two different packages. If you want ClassB to be able to freely refer to ClassA and some of its attributes/methods, which of the following do you need to ensure (select all that apply.)

   i. ClassB needs to use an import statement with a fully qualified name for ClassA

   ii. ClassA must use the public keyword explicitly in front of the word class

   iii. If ClassA has a constructor, it must be declared public by using the public keyword in front of the constructor's name.

   iv. Attributes/methods in ClassA that ClassB wants to directly access must have the public keyword in front of them.

   a. All of the above

   b. (i), (ii), and (iii) only

   c. (ii), (iii), and (iv) only

   d. (i), (iii), and (iv) only

10. Say that ClassA is in package p1 and ClassB is in package p1.sub. If ClassC belongs to a third package p2 and needs to use both ClassA and ClassB in its code, then which import statement sets are acceptable for use in ClassC?

    i.
    ```
    import p1.ClassA;
    import p1.sub.ClassB;
    import p1.*;
    import p1.sub.*;
    ```

    ii.
    ```
    import p1.ClassA;
    import p1.sub.ClassB;
    ```

    iii.
    ```
    import p1.*;
    ```

    iv.
    ```
    import p1.*;
    import p1.sub.*;
    ```

    v.
    ```
    import p1.*;
    import p1.sub.ClassB;
    ```

    a. (i) and (ii) only

    b. (iii) only

    c. (ii) and (iv) only

    d. (i), (ii), (iv), and (v) only

1.11   Answers to Chapter Quiz

1. The correct answer is (a). All statements are true.

2. The correct answer is (a). Options (i), (ii), and (vi) are true but (iii), (iv), and (v) are not true. Option (iii) is not true because you can define your own constructor with parameters and use it to instantiate an object, in which case the default constructor would not be called. Option (iv) is not true because it is not necessary to use the new keyword to instantiate an object. For example, you can instantiate a String object str by saying String str = "Hello", which is a valid instantiation of a String object without using the new keyword. Option (v) is not true because use of the new keyword may or may not call the default constructor. The calling of the default constructor depends only on whether you supply arguments during object instantiation; if no arguments are supplied, the default constructor is called, and if specific arguments are supplied, Java looks for a constructor that has a matching parameter list (in both data type and sequence).

3. The correct answer is (b). All statements except (vi) are true. Option (vi) is not true because if an access specifier is absent, class members are accessible from within the class as well as by outsiders in the same package.

4. The correct answer is (a). The Customer class will not compile. The static method concatName cannot access instance members firstName and lastName.

5. The correct answer is (b). The TestName class will not compile since it is trying to set values of private members, firstName and lastName, of the Customer class. The Customer class would compile without errors because the non-static method concatName is accessing private members of the same class.

6. The correct answer is (d). All statements except (iv) and (vi) are true. Option (iv) is false because if you do not use an explicit package statement in your class, it becomes part of a default package. Option (vi) is false because you must explicitly use the public keyword in front of attributes and methods in a class in order to allow outsiders to that package to access those attributes and methods, even if you already used the public keyword in front of your class definition. Remember that unspecified access means package-level access only; so outsiders to that package cannot access those members.

7. The correct answer is (c). The code will run without any errors. Although str is null, you can still use it as part of a string concatenation expression, but you cannot invoke methods on a null object—for example, str.length().

8. The correct answer is (c). You can use an object of type Integer directly in an arithmetic expression, or use the value returned by intvalue() method in the expression. Earlier versions of JDK would give rise to a compile error:

```
C:\JSP\Chapter1>javac Test.java
Test.java:6: operator + cannot be applied to java.lang.Integer,int
int j = i + 2;
        ^
1 error
```

9. The correct answer is (a). You need to ensure that all of these requirements are met.

10. The correct answer is (d). All of the options are acceptable sets except (iii). Option (iii) is not acceptable because the given import statement would import ClassA, which is directly under package p1, but would not import ClassB, which is in a subfolder under the p1 folder.

1.12   Unsolved Assignments

Assignment 1.1

Objective: To practice instantiating an object using a class constructor.

Steps:

- Create a new folder called assign11 under C:\JSP\Chapter1.

- Copy the Order and TestOrder classes of Solved Exercise 1.7.5 into this folder. Modify TestOrder class to instantiate two separate Order objects (instead of one), sending the orderId, itemId, pricePerItem, and qty to the constructor, as follows:

- 1st Order object: orderId = 201, itemId = 101, pricePerItem = 2.0, and qty = 3

- 2nd Order object: orderId = 202, itemId = 102, pricePerItem = 3.5, and qty = 4

- Compile and run your code. The command session is shown here. I'm assuming your CLASSPATH has the period in it. If it doesn't, use -classpath . in javac and java below.

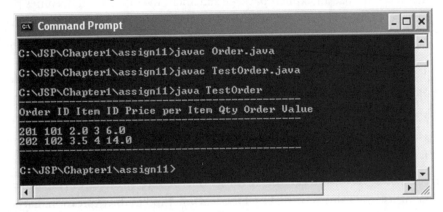

- Submit TestOrder.java.

Assignment 1.2

Objective: To learn how to instantiate and process an array of objects.

Steps:

- Create a new folder called `assign12` under `C:\JSP\Chapter1`.
- Define a new class called `Course` (save in a file called `Course.java`), with class attributes as follows:

  ### Attributes:
  - `courseId (String)`
  - `courseTitle (String)`
  - `creditHours (int)`

  ### Constructors:
  - The default constructor (should set `courseId = ""`, `courseTitle = ""`, `creditHours = 0`)
  - The "init" constructor (input parameters: `courseId, courseTitle, creditHours`)

- Write a test driver called `TestCourse.java` that instantiates an array of `Course` objects with the following details:

  1st element: `courseId = "CS101"`, `courseTitle = "Introductory Computer Science,"` `creditHours = 3`

  2nd element: `courseId = "CS102"`, `courseTitle = "Data Structures,"` `creditHours = 3`

  3rd element: `courseId = "CS103"`, `courseTitle = "C++ Programming,"` `creditHours = 4`

- The test driver should then display the list of courses offered as follows. (Don't worry about the formatting and columnar alignment.)

```
************************************************************
           Courses Offered
************************************************************
Course ID   Course Title                   Credit Hrs
-----------------------------------------------------------
CS101       Introductory Computer Science    3
CS102       Data Structures                  3
CS103       C++ Programming                  4
************************************************************
```

- A sample command session is shown here.

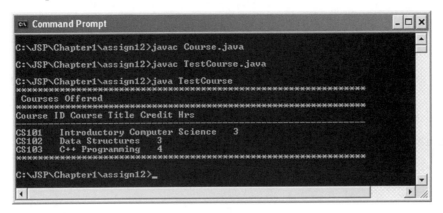

- Submit Course.java and TestCourse.java.

Assignment 1.3

Objective: To learn how to write a class that has an array as a class attribute, and to pass an array to a method.

Steps:

- Create a new folder called assign13 under C:\JSP\Chapter1, for putting all files of this assignment. Copy Course.java from Assignment 1.2 into this folder.

- Define a new class called Student (save in a file called Student.java), with class members as follows:

Attributes:

- firstName (String)

- lastName (String)

- studentID (int)

- courseIDsEnrolled (array of String)

Constructors:

- The default constructor (should set firstName = "", lastName = "", studentID = 0)

- The "init" constructor (input parameters: studentID, firstName, lastName, coursesEnrolled)

Methods:

- concatName (should return name as: "firstName lastName")

- getStudentID (should return studentID as an int)

- setStudentID (should take an int parameter representing studentID, and set studentID to the parameter)

- getLastName (should return firstName as a String)

- setLastName (should take a String parameter representing lastName, and set lastName to the parameter)

- getFirstName (should return firstName as a String)

- setFirstName (should take a String parameter representing firstName, and set firstName to the parameter)

- getCourseIDsEnrolled (should return the courseIDsEnrolled array)

- setCourseIDsEnrolled (should take an array parameter representing courseIDsEnrolled, and set courseIDsEnrolled to the parameter)

- Using Course.java and Student.java, write a test driver called TestStudent.java that instantiates a Student object with the following details:

  - firstName = "John"

  - lastName = "Smith"

  - studentID = 100

  - courseIDsEnrolled: array with two elements each of type String: "CS101," "CS103"

- Define an array called coursesOffered with three elements, each of type Course, as follows:

  1st element: courseId = "CS101," courseTitle = "Introductory Computer Science," creditHours = 3

  2nd element: courseId = "CS102", courseTitle = "Data Structures", creditHours = 3

  3rd element: courseId = "CS103", courseTitle = "C++ Programming", creditHours = 4

- For each element of the courseIDsEnrolled array of the Student object, find the matching element of coursesOffered array, and display the course title and credit hours from the matching course element, using the appropriate getter method. Repeat for all elements of courseIDsEnrolled array in the Student object. At the end, display the sum of credit hours enrolled for that student.

■ The test driver should display the output as follows. (Don't worry about the formatting and columnar alignment.)

```
***************************************************
                Student Report
***************************************************
Name:        John Smith
Student ID: 100

Courses Enrolled
------------------------------------------------------
Course ID     Course Title              Credit Hrs
------------------------------------------------------
  CS1013      Introductory Computer Science   3
  CS1034      C++ Programming                 4
------------------------------------------------------
```

A sample command session is shown here.

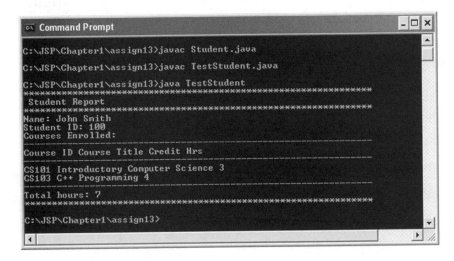

■ Submit Student.java and TestStudent.java.

Assignment 1.4

Objective: To learn how to create and process an array of objects of a class that has an array as a class attribute.

Steps:

- Create a new folder called assign14 under C:/JSP/Chapter1, for putting all files of this assign- ment. Copy Course.java, Student.java, and TestStudent.java from Assignment 1.3 into this folder.

- Modify TestStudent.java of Assignment 1.3 such that it instantiates an array of three Stu- dent objects, with the following elements.

1st Student object:

- firstName = "John"

- lastName = "Smith"

- studentID = 100

- courseIDsEnrolled: array with two elements each of type String: "CS101," "CS103."

2nd Student object:

- firstName = "Michael"

- lastName = "Armstrong"

- studentID = 101

- courseIDsEnrolled: array with two elements each of type String: "CS101," "CS102."

3rd Student object:

- firstName = "Judy"

- lastName = "Miller"

- studentID = 102

- courseIDsEnrolled: array with three elements each of type String: "CS101," "CS102," "CS103."

Loop through the elements of the Student array, and for each Student object, display the student report, which should show the list of courses in which the student is enrolled, and the total credit hours. Repeat the process for all three students.

TestStudent.java should display the output as follows. (Don't worry about the formatting and columnar alignment.)

```
****************************************************
            Student Report for: John Smith
****************************************************
  Student ID:     100
  Courses Enrolled:
  ----------------------------------------------------
  Course ID    Course Title                 Credit Hrs
  ----------------------------------------------------
  CS101        Introductory Computer Science    3
  CS103        C++ Programming                  4
  ----------------------------------------------------
               Total hours:                     7
  ----------------------------------------------------


****************************************************
            Student Report for: Michael Armstrong
****************************************************
  Student ID:     101
  Courses Enrolled:
  ----------------------------------------------------
  Course ID    Course Title                 Credit Hrs
  ----------------------------------------------------
  CS101        Introductory Computer Science    3
  CS102        Data Structures                  3
  ----------------------------------------------------
               Total hours:                     6
  ----------------------------------------------------


****************************************************
            Student Report for: Judy Miller
****************************************************
  Student ID:     102
  Courses Enrolled:
  ----------------------------------------------------
  Course ID    Course Title                 Credit Hrs
  ----------------------------------------------------
  CS101        Introductory Computer Science    3
  CS102        Data Structures                  3
  CS103        C++ Programming                  4
  ----------------------------------------------------
               Total hours:                    10
  ----------------------------------------------------
```

- A sample command session is shown here.

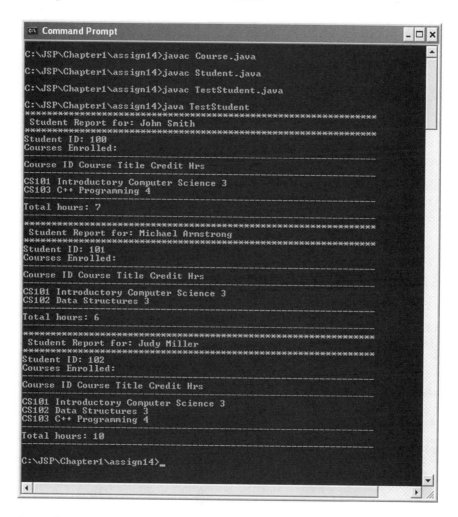

- Compile Course.java, Student.java, then TestStudent.java, and run the code for TestStudent. Submit TestStudent.java only.

Assignment 1.5

Objective: To practice creating a new package with a single class in it, and referring to it from a class in the default package.

Steps:

- Create a new folder: C:\JSP\Chapter1\assign15. Copy the Course.java file from Assignment 1.2 into this folder. Modify it so that it belongs to a new package called computerscience.

- Copy the `TestCourse.java` file from Assignment 1.2 into this folder. DO NOT use any package statement in it (in other words, let it belong to the default package). Compile `Course.java`, then `TestCourse.java`, and run the code for `TestCourse` to confirm that you get the same output as Assignment 1.2.

- *Note:* For this assignment, direct your output `Course.class` file to the `C:\JSP\Chapter1\Output` (`%JSP_OUT%`) folder by using the "`-d %JSP_OUT%`" option in `javac`.

- You need to have the following file structure at the end of this assignment:

```
------------------------------------
C:
+ JSP\
   + Chapter1\
      + assign15\
         -- Course.java
         -- TestCourse.java
         -- TestCourse.class
      + Output\
         + computerscience\
            -- Customer.class
------------------------------------
```

- The command session for this assignment may look like this:

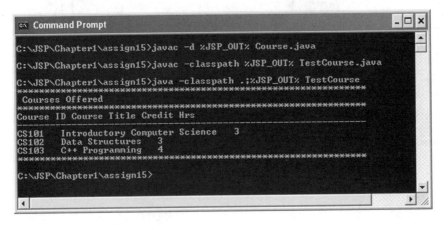

- Note that after the command

  `javac -d %JSP_OUT% Course.java`

  you should confirm that it created a new folder called `computerscience` under `C:\JSP\Chapter1\Output` and put `Course.class` in that folder. Similarly, after the command

  `javac TestCourse.java`
  confirm that it created `TestCourse.java` directly under `C:\JSP\Chapter1\assign15`

- Submit `Course.java` and `TestCourse.java`.

Assignment 1.6

Objective: **To learn how to create new "multifolder" packages and to refer to classes spread across multiple packages.**

Steps:

- Create a new folder: `C:\JSP\Chapter1\assign16`. Copy the `Course.java` file from Assignment 1.5 into this folder, and change the package name to `myschool.departments.computerscience`. The class members remain the same as before (no changes).

- Copy the `Student.java` file from Assignment 1.3 into this folder. Add a `package` statement so that the `Student` class becomes part of a new package called `myschool.admissions` package. Make appropriate changes to the class access specifiers so that they can be referred to from outside this package.

- Copy the `TestStudent.java` file from Assignment 1.3 into this folder. Make the `TestStudent` class part of a new package called `myschool.testdrivers`. Compile `Course.java`, then `Student.java`, and finally `TestStudent.java`, then run the code for `TestStudent`, and confirm that you get the same output as in Assignment 1.3. Use the same `JSP_OUT` environment variable as before.

- To compile TestStudent.java, you will need to use both `-d` and `-classpath` options, as follows:

  ```
  javac -d %JSP_OUT% -classpath %JSP_OUT% TestStudent.java
  ```

* *Note:* To run the code from `C:\JSP\Chapter1\assign16` folder, you need to use

  ```
  java -classpath %JSP_OUT% myschool.testdrivers.TestStudent
  ```

  and NOT

  ```
  java -classpath .;%JSP_OUT% TestStudent
  ```

  because `TestStudent` now belongs to the `myschool.testdrivers` package.

- You need to have the following file structure at the end of this assignment:

  ```
  -----------------------------------
  C:
  + JSP\
     + Chapter1\
        + assign16\
           -- Course.java
  ```

```
        -- Student.java
        -- TestCourse.java
        -- TestCourse.class
   + Output\
      + myschool\
         + departments\
            + computerscience\
               -- Course.class
         + admissions\
            -- Student.class
         + testdrivers\
            -- TestStudent.class
-----------------------------------
```

- Your command session for this assignment may look like this:

- Submit Course.java, Student.java and TestStudent.java.

## CHAPTER 2

Java Review: Inheritance and Exceptions

Chapter Objectives

- Learn how to create new classes based on existing ones using the concept of inheritance

- Understand how objects of a parent class can dynamically point to instances of their subclasses and how to cast objects to the appropriate type

- See how using the `protected` keyword allows member access to subclasses, and get the big picture of effect of access specifiers on class member access across packages

- Analyze the difference between overloading and overriding a method

- Become familiar with `abstract` classes and `interfaces` and how to use them

- Study the available utility classes: `ArrayList`, `Hashtable`, and `HashMap` and the interfaces: `List`, `Map`, and `Iterator`

- Note the various kinds of exceptions that can be thrown and how to code for catching them and providing a graceful exit when error occurs.

2.1   Inheritance

2.1.1   The Concept of Inheritance

You've achieved a lot using classes and objects, and I suppose you're feeling confident with your knowledge. Although you now have a good foundation for using classes and objects, there are still areas that they would not be able to address efficiently in the state you know them now. As I mentioned in the previous chapter, Sun Microsystems realized the utility of writing commonly used code in the form of ready-to-use, off-the-shelf classes so that others do not have to repeat writing the same code. There are situations in the corporate world also where new custom classes could utilize attributes and methods in existing custom classes or other Java predefined classes instead of repeating them.

For example, consider the `Customer` class of Solved Exercise 1.8.3 that has attributes of first name, last name, and sales amount. Suppose you need to write another custom class called `Employee` that also has the attributes of a first name and last name, but has an additional attribute of salary. Both classes share common attributes of `firstName` and `lastName`, but each has its own extra attribute: The `Customer` class has a `salesAmount` attribute, whereas the `Employee` class has a `salary` attribute. One way to write the `Employee` class would be as follows:

```
public class Employee
{
    String firstName;
    String lastName;
    double salary;
    public Employee(String firstName, String lastName, double salary)
    {
        this.firstName = firstName;
        this.lastName = lastName;
        this.salary = salary;
    }
    public String concatName() { return lastName + ", " + firstName; }
}
```

This works fine, but notice how the attributes `firstName` and `lastName` and the method `concatName` are common between the `Employee` class and the `Customer` class. In a real-world corporate environment, you encounter scores of custom classes, many of which share attributes and/or methods. Wouldn't it be more efficient to define a common custom class from which both classes could somehow inherit the common attributes and methods?

This is possible in Java through a concept called *class inheritance*. A class can inherit attributes and methods from another, existing class by using the keyword `extends` followed by the class name from which it wants to inherit. The class from which attributes and methods are inherited is called the *base class* (or *parent class* or even *super class*), and the class that inherits from it is called the *subclass* (or *child class* or *derived class*). It is similar to a parent-child relationship in the sense that the attributes and methods are inherited by the child classes from parent classes.

For example, you could define a new custom class called Person that contains the common attributes firstName and lastName and the method concatName. Your Customer and Employee classes would then extend the Person class, so that they automatically inherit these common attributes and methods without a need to redefine them. Here, the Person class is the base class, and the Customer and Employee classes are its two subclasses. To focus on the concept of inheritance, let's not use the package statements, so that all three files sit in the same folder and belong to the default package. The code would look like this:

```java
// ---- Begin Person.java --------
public class Person
{
    String firstName;
    String lastName;
    public Person(String firstName, String lastName)
    {
        this.firstName = firstName;
        this.lastName = lastName;
    }
    public String concatName() { return lastName + ", " + firstName; }
}
// ---- End Person.java --------
```

The Customer and Employee classes need to change if they want to use the Person class. They would look like this:

```java
// --------- Begin Employee.java -------------------
public class Employee extends Person
{
    double salary;
    public Employee(String firstName, String lastName, double salary)
    {
        super(firstName, lastName);
        this.salary = salary;
    }
}
// --------- End Employee.java -------------------
```

```
// --------- Begin Customer.java -------------------
public class Customer extends Person
{
    double salesAmount;
    public Customer (String firstName, String lastName, double salesAmount)
    {
        super(firstName, lastName);
        this.salesAmount = salesAmount;
    }
}
// --------- End Customer.java -------------------
```

Observe how neat it is now. The Customer and Employee classes look much smaller, because they contain only the additional code specific to those classes. All the common code is now moved to a separate class called Person. Code becomes easier to maintain this way. For example, if there is a change in the way the concatName method returns the concatenated name, all you need to do is make the change in the Person class, and the code in the Customer and Employee classes remains intact.

2.1.2   How a Subclass Differs from Other Classes

Look at the Customer class as an example of a subclass of Person. There are two main differences between this and the earlier version of Customer in Solved Exercise 1.8.3.

The first is the way the Customer class definition begins. The line now looks like this

```
public class Customer extends Person
```

instead of

```
public class Customer
```

The additional words

```
extends Person
```

declare the Customer class to be a subclass of Person. Therefore Customer inherits all the attributes and methods of Person, except those that are explicitly declared as private in Person. To ensure that your Customer class inherits from the Person class, you must use the extends keyword in the class definition.

The second difference is related to the instructions within the constructor. This is the first instruction in the constructor:

```
super(firstName, lastName);
```

The keyword super refers to the constructor of the "parent class" (also called a "super class"). This instruction invokes the constructor of the parent Person class, passing it the arguments firstName and lastName. You can think of this statement as roughly equivalent to instantiating a new Person object with the firstName and lastName supplied, and somehow storing it as part of the current Customer object. In other words, a certain portion of the Customer object stores its parent Person class's attributes and methods, and this instruction constructs, or populates, that part of the Customer object.

Notice that you are forcibly invoking the constructor in Person that takes firstName and lastName arguments by using two matching arguments in the call to super. If you intentionally did not want that constructor to be invoked, and wanted the default constructor in Person to be invoked instead, you could have said this:

super();

However, this may not initialize values of firstName and lastName attributes the way you want, so it may not be as useful. But I wanted to show that you have the freedom to invoke a specific constructor of the parent class by sending in matching arguments to the super() method accordingly.

The rest of the instructions in the constructor initialize the attributes specific to the Customer class.

You are not required to call the super class's constructor using the super keyword or to call the parent class's constructor from the child class's constructor. You could have omitted this line completely from the constructor, but then the default constructor in the parent class would be invoked, so it would not be the one that takes the firstName and lastName attributes.

Recall that Java automatically defines a default constructor with no parameters in any class if you do not explicitly define it. In this case, the attributes of firstName and lastName in Customer would contain default values as assigned by Java. It is thus useful to call the specific constructor of the parent class using the super keyword in order to have initial values of these attributes set the way you want.

The concatName() method is defined in the Person class and it is inherited by the Customer and Employee classes. Every object instantiated from the Customer or Employee classes would have the attributes firstName and lastName and also the method concatName() defined.

Java actually creates copies of the firstName and lastName attributes and the concatName() method of the parent in each child object instantiated. You can directly refer to the attributes on such objects or invoke the method on these objects to get the concatenated name just like you did before, although the Customer/Employee classes do not have an explicit definition of the concatName() method. Therefore the TestName class would remain the same.

Solved Exercise 2.1.2

Objective: To learn how default and specific constructors get called for a subclass object.

Steps:

- Save three java files: Parent.java, Child.java, and TestParentChild.java (as defined below) under a new folder: C:\JSP\Chapter2\exer212:

```java
// -------- Parent.java ---------------
class Parent
{
    // default constructor in Parent
    Parent()
    {
        System.out.println(" in parent: default constructor");
    }
    Parent(String name)
    {
        System.out.println(" in parent: specific constructor");
    }
}


// -------- Child.java ---------------
class Child extends Parent
{
    String name;
    // default constructor in Child
    public Child()
    {
        System.out.println(" in child: default constructor");
    }
    // specific constructor in Child
    public Child(String name)
    {
        System.out.println(" in child: specific constructor");
        this.name = name;
    }
}


// -------- TestParentChild.java ---------------
class TestParentChild
{
    public static void main(String[] args)
    {
        System.out.println(
```

```
            " Instantiating Child1 using Default Constructor:");
        Child child1 = new Child();
        System.out.println(
            " Instantiating Child2 using Specific Constructor:");
        Child child2 = new Child("John");
    }
}
```

- Compile `Parent.java`, then `Child.java`, and finally `TestParentChild.java`.

- Run `TestParentChild`, and confirm that the output you see is as follows. Note the sequence in which Java calls the default/specific constructors in the child/parent classes, depending on which constructor you invoke in the child.

2.1.3   Creating Dynamic Objects That Point to Objects of Different Data Types

You can use the `Person` class as a data type for objects of any of its subclasses. This makes Java very powerful, because you can now dynamically point to objects of different data types at run time. For example, you could define an object called `prs` of type `Person` as follows:

```
Person prs = new Person("John", "Smith");
```

The `prs` object can actually contain objects of any of its child classes (`Customer` or `Employee`). For example, the next instruction could be as follows:

```
prs = new Customer("John", "Cox", 150.0);
```

After some processing, you may want to point `prs` to an `Employee`-type object. The next instruction could be as follows:

```
prs = new Employee("Mike", "Smith", 1000.0);
```

The contents of `prs` now get replaced with a new `Employee` object. Remember that `prs` can now point dynamically to objects of any of its subclasses, each a different data type; therefore, you need to be careful when using it.

The `instanceof` Keyword

If you want to ascertain the actual data type of the object during run time, you can use the `instanceof` expression, which consists of two operands and the `instanceof` keyword. The left-hand operand is the object being tested; as a right-hand operand, you need to supply the name of the class of which the object could be an instance of. The expression returns a `boolean` result if the left-hand object is an instance of the right-hand class.

For example, after you say

```
Person prs;
prs = new Customer("John", "Cox", 150.0);
```

you can ascertain whether or not `prs` is currently an instance of the `Customer` class by saying this:

```
if (prs instanceof Customer)
{
    // .. do something ..
}
```

As a beginner, you may feel more comfortable declaring objects of the subclass type rather than the parent class, and then dynamically pointing to different subclass types. You can more safely say this:

```
Customer cst = new Customer("John", "Cox", 150.0);
```

For `Employee`, you can say this:

```
Employee empl = new Employee("Mike", "Smith", 1000.0);
```

However, the concept of dynamically pointing to subclass types is used extensively by many Java predefined classes, so it is important to understand it before you create custom classes that inherit from them.

2.1.4   Casting Objects

You saw how you can dynamically point to different class-type objects at run time. This has its own associated issues. Suppose you declare `prs` to be of `Person` type, and then make it point to an object that is `Customer` type. Although the `Customer` class has an attribute called `salesAmount`, you cannot directly access it from the `prs` object, even if it is pointing to a `Customer`-type object. You cannot write code as shown here:

```
class TestReport
{
    public static void main(String[] args)
    {
        Person prs;
        prs = new Customer("Judy", "Miller", 150.0);
```

```
        double salesAmt = prs.salesAmount;
    }
}
```

This will not compile. You will get the following error:

```
C:\JSP\Chapter2>javac TestReport.java
TestReport.java:7: cannot resolve symbol
symbol : variable salesAmount
location: class Person
double salesAmt = prs.salesAmount;
                  ^
1 error
```

Here, salesAmount belongs strictly to the child class (Customer), not to the parent class (Person). Remember that a child class has attributes of the parent, but not vice versa. So in this example, prs is an object of the Person class that continues to behave like a Person object even when it temporarily points to a Customer object. You have to explicitly convert it to a Customer type before referring to any Customer class specific attributes and methods on it.

You learned about such explicit conversion in Section 1.2; it is called *casting*. The concept applies to objects as well. In this case, you need to change the last line as follows:

```
double salesAmt = ((Customer)prs).salesAmount;
```

Observe that two pairs of parentheses were used here. As shown in the operator-precedence table of Appendix C, the dot operator (.) has higher precedence than the casting (type) operator. Therefore, if you want to access an attribute of the Customer class, you need an additional pair of parentheses enclosing the converted object. You cannot say this:

```
double salesAmt = (Customer)prs.salesAmount;
```

Doing so would first evaluate the dot operator on prs; therefore it would still try to access the salesAmount attribute on prs (a Person-type object); this would not compile. Try it out: Confirm that you get the errors shown here:

```
-------------------------------------------
C:\JSP\Chapter2>javac TestReport.java
TestReport.java:7: cannot resolve symbol
symbol : variable salesAmount
location: class Person
double salesAmt = (Customer)prs.salesAmount;
                  ^
TestReport.java:7: incompatible types
found : Customer
required: double
```

```
double salesAmt = (Customer)prs.salesAmount;
                 ^
2 errors
-------------------------------------------
```

Casting objects from one type to another has its repercussions. If prs currently points to an Employee object and you cast it to a Customer object, it will give a run-time error in the form of ClassCastException. Furthermore, you cannot expect to access attributes specific to the Customer class when prs points to an Employee object. You can do so only if prs currently points to a Customer object.

For example, suppose the following statement has prs pointing to an Employee-type object:

```
prs = new Employee("John", "Smith", 1000.0);
```

Now, you cannot access the salesAmount attribute on it, because salesAmount is not part of either the Person class or the Employee class.

If you try to cast prs to a Customer-type object, you will get a run-time error in the form of ClassCastException. Try it out: modify TestReport as shown here:

```
class TestReport
{
    public static void main(String[] args)
    {
        Person prs;
        prs = new Customer("Judy", "Miller", 150.0);
        double salesAmt = ((Customer)prs).salesAmount;
        prs = new Employee("John", "Smith", 1000.0);
        salesAmt = ((Customer)prs).salesAmount;
    }
}
```

This will compile, but when you try to run it, you see the following run-time error:

```
C:\JSP\Chapter2>java TestReport
Exception in thread "main" java.lang.ClassCastException: Employee
at TestReport.main(TestReport.java:9)
```

This emphasizes the fact that you cannot cast objects from one type to another without being aware of the consequences. This also requires care on the part of the developer, who should never cast objects into a sibling type (e.g., Customer to Employee, or vice versa, or to a completely unrelated type, such as Address).

Solved Exercise 2.1.4

Objective: To practice how to dynamically point an object to one of its subclass types and to cast it appropriately.

Steps:

- Copy the Person, Customer, and Employee.java files at the end of Section 2.1.1 and save them in a new folder: C:\JSP\Chapter2\exer214.

- Write a new test-driver class called `TestReport` in this folder, instantiating five objects: one of `Person`, two of `Customer`, and two of `Employee` classes, sending the first name, last name, sales amount, and salary as follows:

  `Person`: First Name = Jonathan, Last Name = Smith

  `Customer`: First Name = Judy, Last Name = Miller, Sales Amount = 145.0

  `Customer`: First Name = Jane, Last Name = Armstrong, Sales Amount = 300.0

  `Employee`: First Name = Mike, Last Name = Johnson, Salary = 1000.0

  `Employee`: First Name = Jennifer, Last Name = Peterson, Salary = 1200.0

- Use an array of `Person` data type that contains all five objects.

- Loop through this array to show the output as follows. (This need not be as formatted, although you can use the tab escape character sequence, \t, to do some basic formatting.)

```
------------------------------------------------------------
#    Name                 Sales Amount       Salary
------------------------------------------------------------
1.   Smith, Jonathan
2.   Miller, Judy             145.0
3.   Armstrong, Jane          300.0
4.   Johnson, Mike                           1000.0
5.   Taylor, Jane                            1200.0
------------------------------------------------------------
```

A sample output session is shown here.

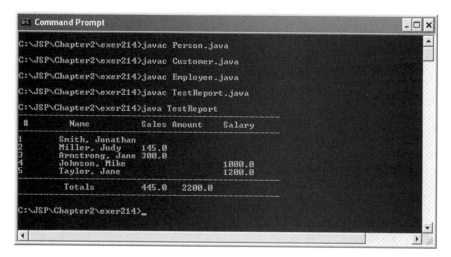

- Submit `TestReport.java`.

Solution:

```java
// -----------Begin: TestReport.java ----------
class TestReport
{
    public static void main(String[] args)
    {
        Person[] prs = new Person[5];
        prs[0] = new Person("Jonathan", "Smith");
        prs[1] = new Customer("Judy", "Miller", 145.0);
        prs[2] = new Customer("Jane", "Armstrong", 300.0);
        prs[3] = new Employee("Mike", "Johnson", 1000.0);
        prs[4] = new Employee("Jane", "Taylor", 1200.0);
        double totSales = 0.0, totSalary = 0.0;
        System.out.println("----------------------------------------------------");
        System.out.println(" # \t  Name \t\tSales Amount\tSalary");
        System.out.println("----------------------------------------------------");
        for (int i = 0; i < prs.length; i++)
        {
            if (prs[i] instanceof Customer)
            {
                double salesAmt = ((Customer)prs[i]).salesAmount;
                totSales += salesAmt;
                System.out.println((i+1) + "\t" + prs[i].concatName() + "\t" + salesAmt);
            }
            else if (prs[i] instanceof Employee)
            {
                double sal = ((Employee)prs[i]).salary;
                totSalary += sal;
                System.out.println((i+1) + "\t" + prs[i].concatName() + "\t\t\t" + sal);
            }
            else
                System.out.println((i+1) + "\t" + prs[i].concatName());
        }
        System.out.println("----------------------------------------------------");
        System.out.println("\t Totals\t\t" + totSales + "\t" + totSalary );
        System.out.println("----------------------------------------------------");
    }
}
// -----------End: TestReport.java ----------
```

2.1.5 How Every Class Inherits from the Object Class

If you do not use an explicit extends clause in your class definition, Java automatically assumes that your class is inheriting from a global parent class called Object, defined under Object.java in the java.lang package. Even if you do use the extends clause, the parent class will be inheriting from the Object class at some point. For example, Customer extends from Person, and Person does not have an explicit extends clause, so Person inherits from Object, which implies that Customer inherits indirectly from Object as well. Therefore you could say that eventually every class in Java—either your own custom class or a predefined class in JDK—inherits from the Object class. The Object class has some useful methods, such as toString(), which returns a String equivalent of any object, as far as possible.

2.1.6 Controlling Access to Class Members: The protected Keyword

Earlier you saw the utility of encapsulating attributes and methods by using the private access specifier. You could prevent outsiders from accessing or manipulating certain attributes by using the private keyword in front of them. In the example of the Person class in Section 2.1.1, you defined the attributes firstName and lastName with unspecified access. You could not use the private keyword for these, because doing so would prohibit every outsider—including subclasses such as Customer and Employee—from accessing these attributes directly.

There is an access specifier that is slightly more liberal than private designed specifically for inheritance: the protected access specifier. It gives access that is not as restricted as private but not as liberal as the *unspecified* access either; it is somewhere between the two. Attributes that use the protected access specifier can be directly accessed by subclasses but not by any other outsider, including objects instantiated from either the parent or the subclass. If you use the protected specifier for the firstName and lastName attributes, your Person class will look like this:

```
public class Person
{
    protected String firstName;
    protected String lastName;
    // rest of the Person class (as before) ...
}
```

The Customer and Employee classes remain unchanged, but now only these two subclasses can access the firstName and lastName attributes directly.

2.1.7 The Full Picture for Access Specifiers

You have now been introduced to all four kinds of access specifiers: private, protected, *unspecified*, and public. These differ in the extent of access they provide to outsiders in that sequence—with private access meaning no access to outsiders and public access meaning access to everybody. It is useful to quickly recap the effects of these access levels:

- private   Gives access to that class only—not to any outsider, including objects instantiated from it or subclasses extending from it.

- protected   Gives access to that class and its subclasses only—not to any other outsider, including objects instantiated from either the parent or the subclasses. Note that it does not matter whether the subclass belongs to the same package as the parent class or to some other package; in both cases the protected members are accessible in the subclass.

- *unspecified* Gives access to every class in that package and to objects instantiated from it or its subclasses in that package. This is like a package-level access; it allows access to everyone in that package.

- public   Gives access to every class/subclass in every package and to all objects anywhere.

Figure 2.1 illustrates the effect of access specifiers and inheritance on the ability to access class members across packages.

2.1.8   Overloading a Method

Go back to the Person class of Section 2.1.1. The concatName() method was defined as:

```
public String concatName()
{
    return lastName + ", " + firstName;
}
```

This method has a rather rigid way of concatenating the first name and last name of Customer: it always concatenates the last name followed by the first name. Suppose you were asked to write a method in the Person class, one that is flexible enough to display the name in two different ways:

- Last name, followed by a comma, followed by the first name
- First name, followed by the last name, with a space in between

The method should return the concatenated name in one of these two ways, depending on a boolean argument passed to it specifying which way the name should be displayed. This would need a different version of the concatName method that has a boolean parameter. The method would look like this:

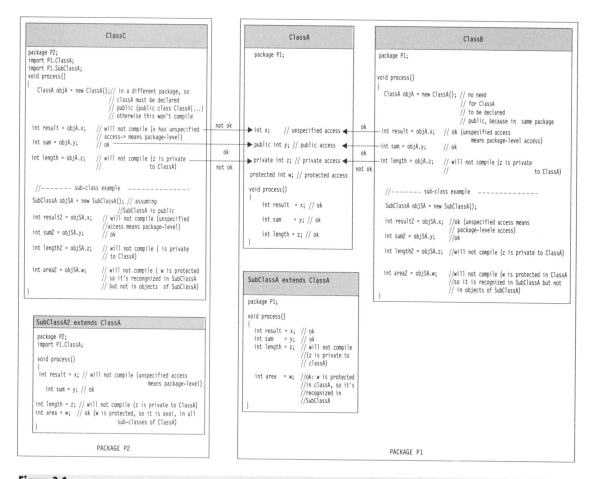

Figure 2.1

The effect of access specifiers on class member access across packages and subclasses.

```
public String concatName(boolean bLastFirst)
{
    if (bLastFirst)
        return lastName + ", " + firstName;
    else
        return firstName + " " + lastName;
}
```

The old concatName() method would still be useful. If someone calls concatName without any arguments, the name would be displayed in the default way: last name, followed by a comma, followed by the first name. Therefore, you would want to retain the old concatName method also in your Person class.

You now have two different versions of the same method, concatName, in the same class, Person. The only difference between the two versions is the method signature, or the number and data type of the parameters in parentheses. One of them has no parameters; the other has a single parameter of type boolean.

Java would not allow two methods with the same name and parameters (in number and data type)—which may or may not have the same return data type—to coexist in the same class because the compiler would not be able to differentiate between the two. Methods that have the same name with a different return data type but the same parameters would still not be considered distinct.

However, Java does allow two methods with the same name but different parameters—which may or may not have the same return data type—because this clearly differentiates one method from another, based on the number of parameters and their data type. In this case, the two versions of the concatName method can coexist because they have a different parameter list. When a method has two or more versions with different parameter lists coexisting in the same class, the method is said to be **overloaded**. In this example, the concatName method is overloaded in the Person class.

Solved Exercise 2.1.8

Objective: To practice overloading a method and use of the private access specifier.

Steps:

- Copy the Person, Customer, Employee, and TestReport.java files from Solved Exercise 2.1.4 into a new folder: C:\JSP\Chapter2\exer218. Modify the code so that the output now shows a dollar sign ($) in front of sales amounts of Customer objects.

- Make the salesAmount attribute private by using the private keyword, and write a getter method called getSalesAmount() that returns the salesAmount as a double value.

- Write an overloaded public getter method, getSalesAmount(), that takes in a String prefix parameter for the currency sign (e.g., "$"), prepends it in front of the sales amount, and returns the result as a String. The overloaded method should be flexible enough to take in any String prefix value and then prepend that to the sales amount.

- Modify TestReport.java so that it calls this overloaded version of the getSalesAmount() method (the one that prepends the dollar sign) for Customer objects when displaying the sales amount. Also prepend the dollar sign in front of the total sales amount. The output should look like this:

```
-----------------------------------------------------------
#    Name                    Sales Amount         Salary
-----------------------------------------------------------
1.   Smith, Jonathan
2.   Miller, Judy               $145.0
3.   Armstrong, Jane            $300.0
4.   Johnson, Mike                               1000.0
5.   Taylor, Jane                                1200.0
-----------------------------------------------------------
          Totals                $445.0          2200.0
```

A sample session is shown here:

- Submit `Customer.java` and `TestReport.java`.

Solution:

Note: Highlighted portion shows the part that is different for this exercise.

```java
// ------------- Begin: Customer.java ----------
public class Customer extends Person
{
    private double salesAmount;
    public Customer (String firstName, String lastName, double salesAmount)
    {
        super(firstName, lastName);
        this.salesAmount = salesAmount;
    }
    public double getSalesAmount () { return salesAmount; }
    public String getSalesAmount (String prefix)
    {
```

```java
            return prefix + salesAmount;
    }
}
// -------------End: Customer.java ----------


// -----------Begin: TestReport.java ----------
class TestReport
{
    public static void main(String[] args)
    {
        Person[] prs = new Person[5];
        prs[0] = new Person("Jonathan", "Smith");
        prs[1] = new Customer("Judy", "Miller", 145.0);
        prs[2] = new Customer("Jane", "Armstrong", 300.0);
        prs[3] = new Employee("Mike", "Johnson", 1000.0);
        prs[4] = new Employee("Jane", "Taylor", 1200.0);
        double totSales = 0.0, totSalary = 0.0;
        System.out.println("--------------------------------------------------");
        System.out.println(" #  \t  Name \t\tSales Amount\tSalary");
        System.out.println("--------------------------------------------------");
        for (int i = 0; i < prs.length; i++)
        {
            if (prs[i] instanceof Customer)
            {
                double salesAmt = ((Customer)prs[i]).getSalesAmount();
                totSales += salesAmt;
                String strSalesAmt = ((Customer)prs[i]).getSalesAmount("$");
                System.out.println( (i+1) + "\t" + prs[i].concatName()
                                    + "\t" + strSalesAmt);
            }
            else if (prs[i] instanceof Employee)
            {
                double sal = ((Employee)prs[i]).salary;
                totSalary += sal;
                System.out.println((i+1) + "\t" + prs[i].concatName()
                                    + "\t\t\t" + sal);
            }
            else
                System.out.println((i+1) + "\t" + prs[i].concatName());
        }
        System.out.println("--------------------------------------------------");
        System.out.println("\t Totals\t\t$" + totSales + "\t" + totSalary );
```

```
        System.out.println("-------------------------------------------------");
    }
  }
}
// -----------End: TestReport.java ----------
```

2.1.9 Overriding a Method

As you know, a subclass inherits methods from its parent class. For example, the Customer class inherits the concatName() method from the Person class. If you invoke the concatName() method on an object instantiated from the Customer class, the returned String would be the last name, followed by a comma, followed by the first name (assuming concatName() is not overloaded as in Section 2.1.8). Suppose you were asked to display the names of employees differently than the names of customers. Suppose employee names needed to be displayed with the String (EMPL) in parentheses at the end of the name so that it became easy to differentiate between employees and customers.

If you went ahead and changed the concatName() method in the Person class, it would change the output String for all inheriting classes; therefore, all objects instantiated from either the Customer or Employee class would have the String (EMPL) at the end of the displayed name. You don't want this. You want objects instantiated from only the Employee class to show the additional String in parentheses. For this, you need some way to override the processing done by the parent class's concat-Name() method from within the Employee class. To do so, you need to redefine or override the concatName() method in the Employee class as follows:

```
public String concatName()
{
    String strName = super.concatName();
    strName += "(EMPL)";
    return strName;
}
```

The concatName() method in the Person class remains intact. However, now you have another version of the concatName() method in the child class, Employee, with the same parameter list and return data type. When that happens, Java picks the one in the child and completely ignores the one in the parent. So the only way the parent version could be invoked is if the child version explicitly calls the parent version (using the super keyword). Note that Java would *not* allow a method in the child class and another method with the same name in the parent class to have the same parameters (in number and data type) with *different* return data types.

The first instruction in the child class's concatName() method calls the super class's concatName() by saying super.concatName(). The value returned by the *super-class* (parent) method is assigned to a String object, and the String *(EMPL)* is appended to this before returning the result to the caller. Now when you call the `concatName()` method on an object of the `Employee` class, the method in the child class (`Employee`) is invoked, instead of the one in the parent class (`Person`).

Remember that attributes and methods in the child take precedence over the ones in the parent if the name of the attribute or method is the same in both parent and child. Notice that the `concatName()` method in the child class is free to call whatever instructions it needs; it might not even invoke the `concatName()` of the parent class at all—this is legal.

Overloading a method applies to *any* Java class and is not specifically related to the concept of inheritance. However, the concept of *overriding* applies solely to subclasses that inherit from other classes. I put these two side by side to give a contrasting picture of two terms that students commonly confuse.

Solved Exercise 2.1.9

Objective: To practice overriding a method and use of JDK wrapper classes.

Steps:

- Copy files from Solved Exercise 2.1.8 into a new folder: `C:\JSP\Chapter2\exer219`.
- Modify the code so that the output now shows "n/a" for values that are not applicable (e.g., sales amount for `Employee` objects, or salary for `Customer` objects). *Do not* use the `instanceof` keyword to check what class-type each object one is. Instead, use the return value from get-SalesAmount() / getSalary() (described below) to decide what to display.
- Change the `salary` attribute in the `Employee` class to be of type `Double`, and make it `private`. Write a getter method `getSalary()` in the `Person` class, so that it returns a `Double` value of `null` as a default.
- Override the `getSalary()` method in the `Employee` class, so that it returns the value of the `salary` attribute as a `Double`.
- Change the `salesAmount` attribute in the `Customer` class to be of type `Double`, and make it `private`. Write a method `getSalesAmount()` in the `Person` class, so that it returns a `Double` value of `null` as a default.
- Remove the overloaded `getSalesAmount()` method in `Customer` that returns a `String`. Override the `getSalesAmount()` method in the `Customer` class, so that it returns the value of the `salesAmount` attribute as a `Double`.
- Use the `getSalary` and `getSalesAmount` methods on elements of the `Person` array when displaying the sales amount and salary values. *Do not* use the `instanceof` method to check what class-type each object is.

- The output should look like this. (*Hint:* Use the tab escape character sequence, \t, to align the values in the columns.):

```
-----------------------------------------------------------
#    Name                       Sales Amount        Salary
-----------------------------------------------------------
1.   Smith, Jonathan                n/a              n/a
2.   Miller, Judy                 145.0              n/a
3.   Armstrong, Jane              300.0              n/a
4.   Johnson, Mike                  n/a           1000.0
5.   Taylor, Jane                   n/a           1200.0
-----------------------------------------------------------
            Totals                445.0           2200.0
```

A sample command session is shown here.

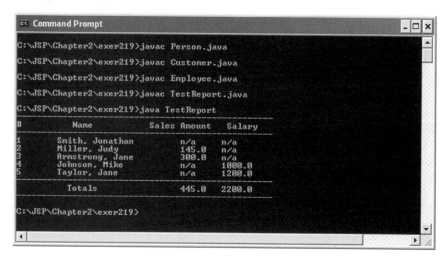

- Submit Person.java, Customer.java, Employee.java, and TestReport.java.

Solution:

```
// ------------- Begin: Person.java ----------
public class Person
{
    String firstName;
    String lastName;
    public Person(String firstName, String lastName)
    {
        this.firstName = firstName;
```

```java
            this.lastName = lastName;
        }
    public String concatName() { return lastName + ", " + firstName; }
    public Double getSalesAmount() { return null; }
    public Double getSalary() { return null; }
}
// ------------- End: Person.java ----------


// ------------- Begin: Customer.java ----------
public class Customer extends Person
{
    private Double salesAmount;
    public Customer (String firstName, String lastName, Double salesAmount)
    {
        super(firstName, lastName);
        this.salesAmount = salesAmount;
    }
    public Double getSalesAmount() { return salesAmount; }
}
// -------------End: Customer.java ----------


// ------------- Begin: Employee.java ----------
public class Employee extends Person
{
    private Double salary;
    public Employee(String firstName, String lastName, Double salary)
    {
        super(firstName, lastName);
        this.salary = salary;
    }
    public Double getSalary() { return salary; }
}
// -------------End: Employee.java ----------


// -----------Begin: TestReport.java ----------
class TestReport
{
    public static void main(String[] args)
    {
        Person[] prs = new Person[5];
        prs[0] = new Person("Jonathan", "Smith");
        prs[1] = new Customer("Judy", "Miller", new Double(145.0));
        prs[2] = new Customer("Jane", "Armstrong", new Double(300.0));
```

```
    prs[3] = new Employee("Mike", "Johnson", new Double(1000.0));
    prs[4] = new Employee("Jane", "Taylor", new Double(1200.0));
    double totSales = 0.0, totSalary = 0.0;
    System.out.println("----------------------------------------------------");
    System.out.println("# \t    Name \t  Sales Amount \t Salary");
    System.out.println("----------------------------------------------------");
    for (int i = 0; i < prs.length; i++)
    {
        String strSalesAmt = "n/a";
        Double salesAmt = prs[i].getSalesAmount();
        if (salesAmt != null)
        {
            strSalesAmt = salesAmt.toString();
            totSales += salesAmt.doubleValue();
        }
        String strSalary = "n/a";
        Double salary = prs[i].getSalary();
        if (salary != null)
        {
            strSalary = salary.toString();
            totSalary += salary.doubleValue();
        }
        System.out.println( (i+1) + "\t" + prs[i].concatName() +  "\t\t"
                            + strSalesAmt +  "\t"  +  strSalary);
    }
    System.out.println("----------------------------------------------------");
    System.out.println("\t  Totals  \t\t" + totSales + "\t"  +  totSalary);
    System.out.println("----------------------------------------------------");
    }
}
// ------End: TestReport.java ----------
```

2.1.10 Abstract Methods and Abstract Classes

Let's extend the idea of overriding the concatName() method a bit. Say that you were to append the String "(EMPL)" to the name for all objects instantiated from the Employee class, and you were also asked to append the String "(CUST)" to all objects instantiated from the Customer class. This would require you to override the concatName() method in both classes, each with its own appended String at the end of the name.

The concatName() method in the Person class now does not really make sense because you are sure that every subclass of the Person class will definitely override the concatName() method. You might as well keep the entire content of the concatName() method in the Customer and Employee classes, and append the desired String locally. The concatName() method in the Person class is now merely a dummy method that simply dictates the method signature and the return data type; the contents of the method will always be found in the child classes. Such a dummy method without a body in the parent class is called an **abstract method**.

If you want every subclass from the Person class to override the concatName() method, you can conveniently define the concatName() method in the Person class as abstract by using the abstract keyword in front of it and having no method body. The concatName() method in Person would now look like this:

```
public abstract String concatName();
```

Notice that this has no method body. This is actually a requirement; if you declare a method as abstract, you cannot have the method body in that class. The abstract keyword must be placed before the return data type, but it can be before or after any access specifier. Therefore, you can say either

```
public abstract ..
```

or

```
abstract public ..
```

By declaring the method as abstract, every class that inherits from Person *must* have a complete method definition for the concatName() method. Otherwise, those classes will not compile. That way, you ensure that every subclass of Person—present or future—implements the concatName() method with a full method definition.

The Person class now has an abstract method called concatName() that has no body. Any class that has one or more abstract methods is called an **abstract class**, and you must use the abstract keyword in front of the class definition statement as well. In other words, an abstract class can have non-abstract methods in addition to abstract ones. The class members of an abstract class get inherited into its subclass just like they do from a normal parent class. The only difference is that the subclass must implement every abstract method of the parent abstract class; otherwise the code for the subclass will not compile. So the Person class definition must look like this:

```
public abstract class Person
{
    String firstName;
    String lastName;
    public Person(String firstName, String lastName)
    {
        this.firstName = firstName;
        this.lastName = lastName;
    }
    public abstract String concatName();
}
```

You cannot instantiate objects from an abstract class, although you can declare objects of the abstract class type. In this case, the Person class is abstract, so you can declare an object of the Person type as follows:

```
Person prs;
```

But you cannot instantiate objects of the Person class, because it is now abstract. Therefore, you cannot say this:

```
prs = new Person("John", "Smith");
```

However, as before, the prs object can still hold objects of any of its child classes (Customer or Employee). Therefore, this could be the next statement:

```
prs = new Employee("Mike", "Smith", 1000.0);
```

The next instruction could point prs to a Customer-type object:

```
prs = new Customer("John", "Cox", 150.0);
```

Notice that although you cannot instantiate objects of an abstract class (e.g., Person), you can always instantiate objects of its subclasses (e.g., Customer or Employee). The concatName() method in Employee and Customer would now contain the complete method body. This method would look like the following in the Employee class:

```
public String concatName()
{
    String strName = lastName + "," + firstName;
    strName += "(EMPL)";
    return strName;
}
```

Observe how the return data type and the parameter list match for the abstract method in the parent class and its implementation in the child class. The concatName() method would also have to be defined in the Customer class and would look similar, with the String "(CUST)" appended, instead of "(EMPL)."

Solved Exercise 2.1.10

Objective: To practice creating and using an abstract class / abstract methods

Steps:

- Copy the files Person.java, Customer.java, Employee.java, and TestReport.java from Solved Exercise 2.1.9 and put them in a new folder: C:\JSP\Chapter2\exer2110.

- Modify the code so that the displayed name is followed by the four-character code in parentheses: (EMPL) for Employee objects and (CUST) for Customer objects. *Do not* use the instanceof keyword to check what class-type each object is. Instead, use the return value from getSalesAmount() / getSalary() (described below) to decide what to display.

- Modify the Person class to make it abstract and to make its concatName() method also abstract. Modify its subclasses (Customer, Employee) to implement the concatName() method such that it returns the concatenated name and the four-character code in parentheses.

- Assume that you do not need the Person object (John Smith), which means that the array of Person objects would now contain only four elements instead of five. (*Reason:* Since Person is now abstract, you cannot instantiate Person object anymore.) Use an array of Person data type that contains all four objects. The output should look like this:

```
-----------------------------------------------------------
 #   Name                  Sales Amount    Salary
-----------------------------------------------------------
 1.  Miller, Judy (CUST)       145.0        n/a
 2.  Armstrong, Jane (CUST)    300.0        n/a
 3.  Johnson, Mike (EMPL)      n/a         1000.0
 4.  Taylor, Jane (EMPL)       n/a         1200.0
-----------------------------------------------------------
        Totals                 445.0       2200.0
-----------------------------------------------------------
```

A sample command session is shown here:

- Submit Person.java, Customer.java, Employee.java, and TestReport.java.

Solution:

```java
// ------------- Begin: Person.java ----------
public abstract class Person
{
    String firstName;
    String lastName;
    public Person(String firstName, String lastName)
    {
        this.firstName = firstName;
        this.lastName = lastName;
    }
    public abstract String concatName();
    public Double getSalesAmount() { return null; }
    public Double getSalary() { return null; }
}
// ------------- End: Person.java ----------


// ------------- Begin: Customer.java ----------
public class Customer extends Person
{
    private Double salesAmount;
    public Customer (String firstName, String lastName, Double salesAmount)
    {
        super(firstName, lastName);
        this.salesAmount = salesAmount;
    }
    public Double getSalesAmount() { return salesAmount; }
    public String concatName(){ return lastName + ", " + firstName + " (CUST)"; }
}
// -------------End: Customer.java ----------


// ------------- Begin: Employee.java ----------
public class Employee extends Person
{
    private Double salary;
    public Employee(String firstName, String lastName, Double salary)
    {
        super(firstName, lastName);
        this.salary = salary;
    }
    public Double getSalary() { return salary; }
    public String concatName(){ return lastName + ", " + firstName + " (EMPL)"; }
}
// -------------End: Employee.java ----------
```

```java
// ------ Begin: TestReport.java ----------
class TestReport
{
    public static void main(String[] args)
    {
        Person[] prs = new Person[4];
        prs[0] = new Customer("Judy", "Miller", new Double(145.0));
        prs[1] = new Customer("Jane", "Armstrong", new Double(300.0));
        prs[2] = new Employee("Mike", "Johnson", new Double(1000.0));
        prs[3] = new Employee("Jane", "Taylor", new Double(1200.0));
        double totSales = 0.0, totSalary = 0.0;
        System.out.println("--------------------------------------------------");
        System.out.println("# \t   Name \t  Sales Amount\t Salary");
        System.out.println("--------------------------------------------------");
        for (int i = 0; i < prs.length; i++)
        {
            String strSalesAmt = "n/a";
            Double salesAmt = prs[i].getSalesAmount();
            if (salesAmt != null)
            {
                strSalesAmt = salesAmt.toString();
                totSales += salesAmt.doubleValue();
            }
            String strSalary = "n/a";
            Double salary = prs[i].getSalary();
            if (salary != null)
            {
                strSalary = salary.toString();
                totSalary += salary.doubleValue();
            }
            System.out.println((i+1) + "\t" + prs[i].concatName() +  "\t"
                               + strSalesAmt + "\t" + strSalary);
        }
        System.out.println("--------------------------------------------------");
        System.out.println("\t Totals \t\t"  + totSales + "\t" + totSalary);
        System.out.println("--------------------------------------------------");
    }
}
// ------End: TestReport.java ----------
```

2.1.11 Interfaces

An interface is a class consisting solely of constants and abstract methods. Every method in an interface must be abstract. You can think of an interface class as some kind of template for defining subclasses. All methods in an interface are public and abstract by default; therefore, you do not need to explicitly use the public or abstract keyword in front of each method. Similarly, every constant in an interface is public, static, and final by default; therefore, you do not have to explicitly use these keywords in front of constants either.

Classes can inherit from an interface class just like they do from a parent class. The only difference is that you need to use the keyword implements followed by the interface class name—instead of extends followed by the parent class name—in the class definition. The constants/abstract methods of an interface get inherited into the subclass just like they do from a normal parent class. Java allows only a single parent class to extend from. However, a class is free to implement multiple interface classes while also extending from the single parent class, if necessary. In that sense, you can get the benefits of multiple inheritance: the child class now has the attributes and methods of the parent class, plus all the attributes and methods of each of the interfaces it implements. It is not necessary for the class to extend from another class while implementing the interface(s). You can have a class that only implements the interface(s) but does not extend from any class. Note that all methods in an interface are abstract; therefore, a class that implements that interface must have a full method definition for every method in the interface, or else it will not compile.

As with abstract classes, you can declare objects of the interface class type, but you cannot instantiate objects from it. Again, as with abstract classes, although you cannot instantiate objects of an interface class, you can always instantiate objects of classes that implement that interface. Go back to the example where you had to concatenate the String "(EMPL)" for employees, and "(CUST)" for customers. These values will not change in your code; they are fixed. Therefore, they are good candidates to be declared as constants that are final. Either the Customer or Employee subclasses will use these. You could define these as part of the Person class. However, it is cleaner to define a separate interface class that possibly holds other constants and abstract methods as well. You can also move the concatName() method from the Person class to this interface, because you want every subclass to implement this method.

The Person class now no longer needs to be abstract because all abstract content has now been moved to a separate interface class. That way, you are also free to instantiate objects of the Person class if need be. So go ahead and remove the abstract keywords from the Person class, so that it is back to the state it was at the beginning of Section 2.1.1. Call the new interface class Person-Interface. It should look like this:

```
public interface PersonInterface
{
    String EMPLOYEE_CODE = "(EMPL)";
    String CUSTOMER_CODE = "(CUST)";
    String concatName();
}
```

For simplicity, save this file under the same folder as your Person, Customer, and Employee files. The concatName() method is an abstract method that you want every subclass to implement with a full method definition. The concatenated name that this method returns should include the code "(EMPL)" or "(CUST)" at the end. The Customer and Employee classes now implement the PersonInter-face in addition to extending the Person class. These classes would therefore look like this:

```
// --------- Begin Employee.java -------------------
public class Employee extends Person implements PersonInterface
{
    double salary;
    public Employee(String firstName, String lastName, double salary)
    {
        super(firstName, lastName);
        this.salary = salary;
    }
    public String concatName()
    {
        String strName = lastName + "," + firstName;
        strName += EMPLOYEE_CODE;
        return strName;
    }
}
// --------- End Employee.java -------------------

// --------- Begin Customer.java -------------------
public class Customer extends Person implements PersonInterface
{
    double salesAmount;
    public Customer (String firstName, String lastName, double salesAmount)
    {
        super(firstName, lastName);
        this.salesAmount = salesAmount;
    }
    public String concatName()
    {
        String strName = lastName + "," + firstName;
```

```
            strName += CUSTOMER_CODE;
            return strName;
        }
    }
}
// --------- End Customer.java -------------------
```

Solved Exercise 2.1.11

Objective: To practice use of interface classes.

Steps:

- Start with the source files of Section 2.1.11, and copy them into a new folder called exer2111 under C:\JSP\Chapter2.

- This time use all five objects (including Person: John Smith), since Person is no longer abstract, you can now instantiate Person object as well. For "pure" Person objects (those that are NOT Customer or Employee), the displayed name need NOT show the four-character code after the name.

- The interface class should contain the necessary constants (Strings "(EMPL)," "(CUST)"), and the abstract method concatName().

- The Person class should now implement the interface PersonInterface and fully define the concatName() method. The concatName() method in Customer and Employee should call their parent's concatName() first, append the appropriate code from the PersonInterface class, and return the resulting String.

- Use an array of Person data type that contains all five objects. Run the code again to get the output shown here.

```
-----------------------------------------------------------------
#   Name                      Sales Amount          Salary
-----------------------------------------------------------------
1.  Smith, Jonathan              n/a                 n/a
2.  Miller, Judy (CUST)          145.0               n/a
3.  Armstrong, Jane (CUST)       300.0               n/a
4.  Johnson, Mike (EMPL)         n/a                 1000.0
5.  Taylor, Jane (EMPL)          n/a                 1200.0
-----------------------------------------------------------------
    Totals                       445.0               2200.0
-----------------------------------------------------------------
```

A sample command prompt session is shown here.

- Submit `PersonInterface.java`, `Person.java`, `Customer.java`, `Employee.java` and `TestReport.java`.

Solution:

```java
// ---------Begin: PersonInterface.java --------
public interface PersonInterface
{
    String EMPLOYEE_CODE = "(EMPL)";
    String CUSTOMER_CODE = "(CUST)";
    String concatName();
}
// --------- End: PersonInterface.java --------


// ------------- Begin: Person.java ----------
public class Person implements PersonInterface
{
    String firstName;
    String lastName;
    public Person(String firstName, String lastName)
    {
        this.firstName = firstName;
        this.lastName = lastName;
    }
    public String concatName() { return lastName + ", " + firstName; }
    public Double getSalesAmount() { return null; }
    public Double getSalary() { return null; }
}
// ------------- End: Person.java ----------
```

```java
// ------------- Begin: Customer.java ----------
public class Customer extends Person
{
    private Double salesAmount;
    public Customer (String firstName, String lastName, Double salesAmount)
    {
        super(firstName, lastName);
        this.salesAmount = salesAmount;
    }
    public Double getSalesAmount() { return salesAmount; }
    public String concatName() { return super.concatName() + " "
                                + CUSTOMER_CODE; }
}
// -------------End: Customer.java ----------

// ------------- Begin: Employee.java ----------
public class Employee extends Person
{
    private Double salary;
    public Employee(String firstName, String lastName, Double salary)
    {
        super(firstName, lastName);
        this.salary = salary;
    }
    public Double getSalary() { return salary; }
    public String concatName() { return super.concatName() + " "
                                + EMPLOYEE_CODE; }
}
// -------------End: Employee.java ----------

// ------ Begin: TestReport.java ----------
class TestReport
{
    public static void main(String[] args)
    {
        Person[] prs = new Person[5];
        prs[0] = new Person("Jonathan", "Smith");
        prs[1] = new Customer("Judy", "Miller", new Double(145.0));
        prs[2] = new Customer("Jane", "Armstrong", new Double(300.0));
        prs[3] = new Employee("Mike", "Johnson", new Double(1000.0));
        prs[4] = new Employee("Jane", "Taylor", new Double(1200.0));

        double totSales = 0.0, totSalary = 0.0;
```

```
System.out.println("-------------------------------------------------");
System.out.println("# \t   Name \t  Sales Amount\t Salary");
System.out.println("-------------------------------------------------");
for (int i = 0; i < prs.length; i++)
{
    String strSalesAmt = "n/a";
    Double salesAmt = prs[i].getSalesAmount();
    if (salesAmt != null)
    {
        strSalesAmt = salesAmt.toString();
        totSales += salesAmt.doubleValue();
    }
    String strSalary = "n/a";
    Double salary = prs[i].getSalary();
    if (salary != null)
    {
        strSalary = salary.toString();
        totSalary += salary.doubleValue();
    }
    System.out.println( (i+1) + "\t" + prs[i].concatName() +  "\t"
                      + strSalesAmt  +  "\t"  +  strSalary );

}
System.out.println("------------------------------------------------");
System.out.println("\t  Totals  \t\t" + totSales + "\t" + totSalary);
System.out.println("------------------------------------------------");
    }
  }
}
// ------End: TestReport.java ----------
```

2.2   List, ArrayList, Map, Hashtable / HashMap **Classes of** java.util **Package**

In this section, we will look at two important java.util interfaces: List and Map and their implementing classes: ArrayList and Hashtable/HashMap respectively, that we will later use in our JSP hands-on exercises. These classes are widely used in a real-world programming environment, especially for processing database data in JSPs.

2.2.1   List **interface and** ArrayList **class of** java.util **package**

List is an interface that represents a collection or set of objects. When I say "objects" here, I literally mean objects deriving from the Object superclass (which every Java class does inherit from). So this means that although you can use primitive data such as int, char, double, etc. to form a List, Java creates corresponding wrapper-class objects (Integer, Character, Double, etc.) and adds those objects to the List. A List behaves exactly like an array, with the only difference being that you do not have to declare or know the exact size of the List beforehand (as you do in the case of an array). Since List is an interface, you cannot instantiate objects of the List type, although you can declare objects of the List type.

Several classes implement the List interface, the most important and common of them being the ArrayList class, which is one you can instantiate. Each element of the ArrayList is of type Object, but it can dynamically point to any valid subclass of Object. Java requires you to declare upfront, the exact subclass you plan to use for elements of the ArrayList (and for any other implementation of the List interface). That way it ensures that you do not inadvertently create a List with two or more elements of different data types. The subclass type needs to be specified as a template parameter enclosed in angle brackets < > following the word List or ArrayList. As an example, you may want to create an ArrayList of Customer, so you declare and instantiate it as follows:

```
List<Customer> cstList = new ArrayList<Customer>();
```

To add an object to a List, you use the add() method, passing it the object to be added. To retrieve an element of the List, you use either the get() method passing it the element index (or use the next() method on an Iterator object that iterates over the list).

Note that the List maintains the elements in the order in which they were added.

In Section 1.7.8, we used an array of Customer type objects. Instead, we could have also used an ArrayList of Customer objects, giving identical results.

To see sample code that would create an ArrayList of Customer, assume that Customer class is as shown here:

```
----------------------------------------------------------------
//--- Begin: Customer.java ---------------
public class Customer
{
    private String firstName;
    private String lastName;
    private int age;
    private double salesAmount;
    public Customer( String firstName, String lastName,
                     int age, double  salesAmount )
    {
        this.firstName = firstName;
        this.lastName = lastName;
        this.age = age;
        this.salesAmount = salesAmount;
    }
    public String concatName() { return firstName + " " + lastName; }
    public int getAge() { return age; }
```

```
    public double getSalesAmount() { return salesAmount; }
}
//--- End: Customer.java ---------------
```

You would now declare an ArrayList object called cstList of type List and add Customer type objects
as follows:

```
//--- Begin: TestCustomer.java ---------------
import java.util.List;
import java.util.ArrayList;
import java.util.Iterator;

class TestCustomer
{
    public static void main(String[] args)
    {
        List<Customer> cstList = new ArrayList<Customer>();
        cstList.add(new Customer("John", "Smith", 30, 100.0));
        cstList.add(new Customer("Judy", "Miller", 25, 150.0));
        cstList.add(new Customer("Neil", "Armstrong", 27, 200.0));
        System.out.println("----------------------------------------------");
        System.out.println(" Name Age Sales Amount");
        System.out.println("----------------------------------------------");
        for (int i = 0; i < cstList.size(); i++)
        {
            Customer cst = cstList.get(i);
            System.out.println( cst.concatName() + "    " + cst.getAge()
                              + "    " + cst.getSalesAmount() );

        }
        // OR, alternatively, you can use a while loop
        // with an 'Iterator' object as follows:
        // java.util.Iterator<Customer> it = cstList.iterator();
        // while (it.hasNext())
        // {
        //    Customer cst = it.next();
        //    System.out.println( cst.concatName() + "    " + cst.getAge()
        //                      + "    " + cst.getSalesAmount() );
        // }
        System.out.println("----------------------------------------------");
    }
}
//--- End: TestCustomer.java ---------------
```

Compile and run your program. Your output will look like this:

```
------------------------------------------
Name              Age    Sales Amount
------------------------------------------
John Smith         30        100.0
Judy Miller        25        150.0
Neil Armstrong     27        200.0
------------------------------------------
```

The code shows two ways to loop through a List–a for loop and a while loop (commented out). To use a while loop, you need to use an Iterator object that represents the current element in the List. Iterator is an interface in the java.util package; its specification is available at the JDK API documentation site in Appendix D.

Try out the Iterator part of the TestCustomer code and verify that you get the same output as before.

2.2.2   Map Interface and Hashtable / HashMap Classes of java.util Package

A List is a one-dimensional collection of objects, but many times you encounter "two-dimensional" situations where you need to associate an object (or a value) to a particular "key," so that later you can retrieve the value by its key. In other words, you need to store "key-value" pairs, with a unique value (or even a whole object) associated with a given key. To make it truly versatile, the key and value could each be of type Object, so that any custom or predefined class data type could be used to actually create the key and the value. So in a general case, the key could be any object that inherits from Object, but usually it is of type String. The value can be any object that inherits from Object (not necessarily String).

For example, say that your customers can log on to a Web site by entering their username and password. To verify if the username-password combination is valid, you need to first store all valid username-password combinations so that you can look it up for any given username-password. For simplicity, let's say that you only have three customers in all, so you need to store three possible username-password combinations, as follows:

```
--------------------
Key (Username)   Value (Password)
--------------------

 "John"           "bluesky"

 "Mike"           "greentree"

 "Judy"           "clearwater"
--------------------
```

Such a table is technically called a Map, something that maps "keys" to their corresponding "values." The key and the value must each be an instance of the superclass Object. In this case, the key and the value is each a String, which inherits from Object by definition, so this is a valid candidate for a Map. In this example, your Map consists of three key-value pairs. Map is an interface in the java.util package, with important classes that implement this interface being Hashtable and HashMap. The main difference between Hashtable and HashMap is that Hashtable does not allow you to have a value of null (for a given key) whereas HashMap allows that. In that sense, HashMap is more flexible and is therefore more widely used in the real world.

To place an object into a Map, you use the put() method, passing it the key and the value. To retrieve the object by a key, you use the get() method, passing it the key. An example follows:

```
// -------------- Begin: TestMap.java ----------------------
import java.util.Map;
import java.util.HashMap;

class TestMap
{
    public static void main(String[] args)
    {
        Map<String,String> map = new HashMap<String,String>();
        map.put("John", "bluesky");
        map.put("Mike", "greentree");
        map.put("Judy", "clearwater");

        String password = map.get("John");
        System.out.println("The password for username of John is " + password);
    }
}
// -------------- End: TestMap.java ----------------------
```

Compile and run the code. It should look like this:

```
-------------------------------------------------------------
C:\JSP\Chapter2>javac TestMap.java
C:\JSP\Chapter2>java TestMap
The password for username of John is bluesky
-------------------------------------------------------------
```

How to Loop Through a HashMap

To determine if a given username-password combination exists in your HashMap, you need to loop through all the name-value pairs of the username-password HashMap. Note that the "names" in a HashMap represent a set of "keys," with each key having an associated value to it. So, to loop through the HashMap, you need to first get the set of keys. The keys of a HashMap can be obtained by calling the keySet() method on a HashMap object; this method returns a Set type object. Set is an interface defined in java.util package. (Details on this interface are available at the JDK/API documentation site in Appendix D.)

In the example of username-password pairs, you can get the set of the HashMap's "username keys" by saying

```
Set usernames = map.keySet();
```

Next, using an Iterator type object, loop through this Set. To instantiate an Iterator object called it on a Set called usernames you would say

```
Iterator<String> it = usernames.iterator();
```

To loop through the Set using this Iterator object, and to determine if a username John and password bluesky is valid, you would say

```
--------------------------------------------------------
boolean found = false;
String uname, password;
while (it.hasNext())
{
    uname = it.next();
    password = map.get(uname);
    if ( uname.isEqual("John") and password.isEqual("bluesky") )
    {
        found = true;
        System.out.println("Found username of John and password of bluesky");
        break;
    }
}
--------------------------------------------------------
```

2.3 Exceptions

2.3.1 Introduction

This section will explain how Java handles errors that arise during the execution of code. Examples of such errors could be division by zero, trying to find the square root of a negative number, or trying to parse a numeric value from a String that has non-numeric characters.

In these situations, it is critical that the application properly handle the error so that execution continues with the rest of the program. Sometimes you may be calling a method in a class without knowing its limitations. In such cases, the method needs to be able to gracefully handle the error, or to transmit the error to the caller, who may be better equipped to handle that kind of error.

Java provides a very powerful way of either handling errors or transmitting them to the caller. For this, it uses a special kind of predefined class called `Exception`, defined in the file `Exception.java` under `java.lang` package. An *exception* is an object that is created when an erroneous situation arises from your code during run time. It is an object of the `Exception` class or one of its subclasses that gets instantiated. In technical terms, this is called *throwing an exception.*

There are two issues you need to be aware of when handling the error:

- What data type (subclass of `Exception`) the exception object is or could be
- How to catch the exception object and use it to display a useful message to the user

Let's talk about the data type of the exception object first. The `Exception` class under the `java.lang` package provides attributes and methods for properly handling such erroneous situations. The data type of the exception object that gets instantiated is `Exception` or one of its subclasses. Exception classes are either Java predefined—most of them under the `java.lang` package—or custom ones that you define yourself.

2.3.2   Predefined Exception Classes

There are various kinds of predefined exception classes in Java, each meant to handle a specific kind of erroneous situation. Each of these exception classes directly or indirectly inherits from the `Exception` class defined under the `java.lang` package. The `Exception` class has a constructor that allows you to set a specific error message that you can communicate to the user in case an exception is thrown.

Consider the following code for finding the square root of an integer `n`, where `n` is supplied at the command prompt:

```
class TestRoot
{
    public static void main(String[] args)
    {
        int n = Integer.parseInt(args[0]);
        double root = Math.sqrt(n);
        System.out.println("Square root of " + n + " is: " + root);
    }
}
```

The function used is a `static` method called `sqrt` defined in `Math.java` under the `java.lang` package. Save this file as `TestRoot.java` under `C:\JSP\Chapter2`, and compile it. Then run it to find the square root of 9. For this, at the command line, supply an argument value of 9; the output session should look like this:

```
C:\JSP\Chapter2>java TestRoot 9
Square root of 9 is: 3
```

This worked fine. Now run it by supplying an argument value of abc, and see what happens:

```
C:\JSP\Chapter2>java TestRoot abc
Exception in thread "main" java.lang.NumberFormatException: abc
at java.lang.Integer.parseInt(Integer.java:405)
at java.lang.Integer.parseInt(Integer.java:454)
at TestRoot.main(TestRoot.java:5)
```

Java threw an error in the form of NumberFormatException.

Solved Exercise 2.3.2

Objective: To learn how a NullPointerException is generated due to faulty code.

Steps:

- Create a new folder exer232 under C:\JSP\Chapter2.

- Write a class called TestNull, and save it in a file called TestNull.java in the new folder.

- Inside TestNull, declare str as a String variable, and assign it a value of null (null object). Then write an instruction that displays the length of str, using the length() method on the String object.

- Compile the code, and then run the code to verify that you get a run-time exception (NullPointerException).

- The output session should look something like this:

Solution:

```java
class TestNull
{
    public static void main(String[] args)
    {
        String str = null;
        System.out.println("Length of str is: " + str.length());
    }
}
```

2.3.3 Catching the Exception

I'm sure you'll agree that this wasn't exactly a graceful way of exiting the erroneous situation. Instead of letting the exception go its own way after it is thrown, you can actually *catch* the exception by using a Java statement construct called the *try-catch block*. The try-catch block consists of two portions:

- The try portion, where you put all your code that you think might give rise to an exception; and

- The catch part, where you catch the exception if it is thrown, and put instructions that you think should be executed in that scenario.

There are exactly two scenarios here: Either an exception is thrown, or no exception is thrown when executing instructions in the try block. The action taken in each scenario would be as follows:

- If an exception is thrown at a specific instruction in the try block, the rest of the instructions in the try block are skipped, and control goes directly to a catch block that has an exception type matching that of the exception object thrown.

- If no exception is thrown in the try block, all of your code in the try block is executed, and control goes to the first statement after the catch block. (The instructions in the catch block are not executed.)

In the TestRoot example of the previous section, you can use a try-catch statement as follows:

```java
class TestRoot
{
    public static void main(String[] args)
    {
        try
        {
            int n = Integer.parseInt(args[0]);
            double root = Math.sqrt(n);
            System.out.println("Square root of " + n + " is: " + root);
        }
        catch ( NumberFormatException e )
        {
            System.out.println("Please enter a numeric value as input.");
            System.exit(0);
        }
    }
}
```

Observe how you enclose all the statements in the try block in curly braces ({}) and follow it up with a catch block. In the catch block, you specify an exception object named e to be of type Number-FormatException, because you want to catch an exception of that type.

You are free to name the exception object whatever you wish at this stage. For example, you could have named it ex or something else, instead of e. Also, the exception object e would have a scope limited to its catch block only; therefore it is not recognized outside of its catch block.

Now if you run the program supplying an input value of abc, you will get the following output:

```
C:\JSP\Chapter2>java TestRoot abc
Please enter a numeric value as input.
C:\JSP\Chapter2>
```

This looks much better.

Solved Exercise 2.3.3

Objective: To practice writing a try-catch block.

Steps:

- Create a new folder called exer233 under C:\JSP\Chapter2. Copy the TestNull class of Solved Exercise 2.3.2 into this folder.

- Modify it to use a try-catch statement that catches the NullPointerException and displays a suitable error message.

- The output session should look like this:

Solution:

```
class TestNull
{
    public static void main(String[] args)
    {
        try
        {
            String str = null;
            System.out.println("Length of str is: " + str.length());
        }
        catch ( NullPointerException e )
```

```
        {
            System.out.println("The string is a null object.");
        }
    }
}
```

2.3.4   Handling Different Kinds of Exceptions Using Multiple catch Blocks

As mentioned before, Java has several different exception classes, each meant to handle a specific kind of error. The NumberFormatException is one that is specific to errors due to bad, non-numeric data when a numeric value is expected. Another exception data type is called ArrayIndexOutOfBounds-Exception, which is specific to errors from referring to an array element that is beyond its maximum limits. For example, if an array has three elements and you try to process an undefined, fourth element, you will get an ArrayIndexOutOfBoundsException.

Try it out: run TestRoot by not providing any input arguments, as shown here:

```
C:\JSP\Chapter2>java TestRoot
Exception in thread "main" java.lang.ArrayIndexOutOfBoundsException
at TestRoot.main(TestRoot.java:7)
```

Because you did not supply any input arguments, the array args has no elements. Here you refer to an undefined, first element (args[0]) of args in the instruction:

```
int n = Integer.parseInt(args[0]);
```

When you do so, Java throws an ArrayIndexOutOfBoundsException. You did not explicitly catch an ArrayIndexOutOfBoundsException type of exception in your catch block; therefore the output displays the way Java configured it.

You added a catch block for a NumberFormatException type of exception only. That would take care of all exceptions of NumberFormatException type or its subclasses but not an ArrayIndexOutOfBoundsException type, which is a sibling class. Recall that NumberFormatException and ArrayIndexOutOfBoundsException both inherit from the Exception class. To make a cleaner exit in this new scenario, you need to put another catch block for the ArrayIndexOutOfBoundsException type, as follows:

```
class TestRoot
{
    public static void main(String[] args)
    {
        try
        {
            int n = Integer.parseInt(args[0]);
            double root = Math.sqrt(n);
            System.out.println(" Square root of " + n + " is: " + root);
        }
```

```
        catch ( NumberFormatException e )
        {
            System.out.println("Please enter a numeric value as input.");
            System.exit(0);
        }
        catch ( ArrayIndexOutOfBoundsException e )
        {
            System.out.println( "Please specify number to find root of" );
            System.exit(0);
        }
    }
}
```

Note that you need to retain the old NumberFormatException catch block intact because your code can now throw either a NumberFormatException type or an ArrayIndexOutOfBoundsException type of exception. Also notice how you have control of each kind of exception that could be thrown, with a specific error message in each case.

After this change, if your code throws a NumberFormatException type of exception, the first catch block would be invoked, and the second catch block would be skipped. Remember that Java invokes one and only one catch block for each try clause, even if you have multiple catch blocks associated with it. If an ArrayIndexOutOfBoundsException type of exception is thrown, the first catch block would be skipped and the second catch block would be invoked. If the exception object is not of NumberFormatException or ArrayIndexOutOfBoundsException type, then Java would handle it in its own default way, and you would not be exiting that exception gracefully.

Solved Exercise 2.3.4

Objective: To learn how to write multiple catch blocks for a given try block.

Steps:

- Create a new class called DivideByZero in a new folder: C:\JSP\Chapter2\exer234. Declare two double variables d1 and d2, and assign them the double value parsed from the first two command-line arguments (d1 should have the first argument, and d2 should have the second). (*Hint:* Use the parseDouble method in the Double class.)

- Display the values of d1 and d2, and also the result of dividing d1 by d2, using System.out.println. Add catch blocks for NumberFormatException and ArrayIndexOutOfBounds-Exception types of exception objects, with an appropriate error message in each.

- Compile and run the code for three test cases:

  1. By providing input values 5 and 2 (verify that the right output is displayed),

2. By providing input values 5 and 'xyz' (verify that the right `catch` block is invoked), and

3. With no input arguments (verify that the right `catch` block is invoked)

- The output session should look like this:

Solution:

```
// ------- Begin: DivideByZero.java -------------
class DivideByZero
{
    public static void main(String[] args)
    {
        try
        {
            double d1 = Double.parseDouble(args[0]);
            double d2 = Double.parseDouble(args[1]);
            System.out.println( "Input values are: d1 = " + d1 + ", d2 = " + d2
                          + " and d1 / d2 = " + d1/d2 );
        }
        catch ( NumberFormatException e )
        {
            System.out.println("Please provide a numeric value input");
        }
        catch ( ArrayIndexOutOfBoundsException e )
        {
            System.out.println("Please provide input; usage is: java DivideByZero num den");
        }
    }
}
// -------End: DivideByZero.java -------------
```

2.3.5 Some Special Exception Classes

In general, if your method can potentially throw an exception, it *must* include a `throws` clause for that type of exception, or `catch` it explicitly, otherwise the code won't compile. However, this rule does *not* apply if the exception that could be thrown belongs to a small set of exception classes that inherit from the `RuntimeException` class (which itself inherits from the `Exception` class) under the `java.lang` package. `RuntimeException` is the superclass of those exceptions that can be thrown during normal operation, and it is *not* necessary for you to `catch` these exceptions or to `rethrow` them from your methods, although you can if you want to. If you do not `catch` or `rethrow` these exceptions, your code will compile. However, if one of these exceptions is thrown at run time, it shows up as an ugly error message, similar to what you saw in Section 2.3.2. The eleven special exception classes that inherit from the `RuntimeException` class are as follows:

- `ArithmeticException`
- `IndexOutOfBoundsException` (including its subclass, `ArrayIndexOutOfBoundsException`)
- `NegativeArraySizeException`
- `NullPointerException`
- `ArrayStoreException`
- `ClassCastException`
- `IllegalArgumentException`
- `SecurityException`
- `IllegalMonitorStateException`
- `IllegalStateException`
- `UnsupportedOperationException`

2.4 Summary

In this chapter, you learned how to create new classes based on existing ones using the concept of inheritance. You understood how objects of a parent class can dynamically point to instances of their subclasses and how to cast objects to the appropriate type. You saw how using the `protected` keyword allows member access to subclasses, and got the big picture of effect of the access specifiers on class member access across packages. You analyzed the difference between overloading and overriding a method. You became familiar with `abstract` classes and `interfaces` and how to use them. You studied the available utility classes: `ArrayList`, `Hashtable` and `HashMap` and the interfaces: `List`, `Map` and `Iterator`. Finally, you noted the various kinds of exceptions that can be thrown and how to code for catching them and providing a graceful exit when error occurs.

2.5   Chapter Quiz

1. Which of the following are true? (Select all that apply.)

    i. A subclass inherits every attribute and method of its parent class.

    ii. A subclass must belong to the same package as its parent class.

    iii. Class members that have unspecified access can be accessed by all other classes whether inside or outside of the package that the class belongs to.

    iv. Public members of a class can be accessed by all other classes whether inside or outside of the package that the class belongs to.

    v. Private members of a class can be accessed by objects instantiated from it but not by its subclasses or objects instantiated from subclasses.

    a.   All of the above

    b.   (i), (ii), (iv), and (v) only

    c.   (i), (ii), and (iv) only

    d.   (iv) only

2. Say that you define three classes (`Parent`, `Child`, and `TestParentChild`) as follows in the same folder, and run `TestParentChild`.

```
class Parent
{
    // default constructor in Parent
    Parent() { }
    // Matching constructor in Parent
    Parent(String name) { }
}

class Child extends Parent
{
    String name;
    // default constructor in Child
    public Child(){ }
    // specific constructor in Child
    public Child(String name) {this.name = name; }
}

class TestParentChild
```

```
{
    public static void main(String[] args)
    {
        Child child = new Child("John");
    }
}
```

Which of the following statements is true?

a. The default constructor of Parent is always called first, followed by the specific constructor of Child. The matching constructor in Parent never gets called.

b. Child class's default constructor is called first, followed by the specific constructor of Child, and finally the Parent class's default constructor.

c. The Child class's specific constructor is called first, followed by the Parent class's matching constructor, followed by the Parent class's default constructor.

d. The Parent class's matching constructor is called first, followed by the Child class's specific constructor. The default constructors in Parent and Child are never called.

3. Assume that the Person, Customer, and Employee classes are defined as in Section 2.1.1. If prs is an object of type Person, and it currently points to a Customer type object, which of the following are true? (Select all that apply.)

i. If you cast prs to an Employee type object; it will compile fine but you will get a run-time error.

ii. If you cast prs to a Person type object, you will not get compile or run-time errors.

iii. If you cast prs to a Customer type object, you will not get compile or run-time errors.

iv. On the prs object, you can invoke public methods that are specifically defined in the Person class, even if you cast prs to Customer type and then invoke those methods on the resulting object.

v. On the prs object, you can invoke public methods that are specifically defined in the Customer class, provided you cast prs to Customer type first, and then invoke those methods on the resulting object.

vi. On the prs object, you can invoke public methods that are specifically defined in the Employee class, provided you cast prs to Employee type first, and then invoke those methods on the resulting object.

   a. All of the above

   b. (iii) and (v) only

   c. (i), (ii), (iii), (iv), and (v) only

   d. (ii), (iii), and (v) only

4. Assume that Person, Customer, and Employee classes are as defined in Section 2.1.1. What would you expect if you try to compile and run the following program?

```
class TestReport
{
    public static void main(String[] args)
    {
        Person prs;
        prs = new Customer("Judy", "Miller", 150.0);
        double salesAmt = (Customer)prs.salesAmount;
    }
}
```

   a. This will give a compile error.

   b. This will give a run-time error.

   c. This will run fine with no errors.

   d. Can't say—depends on the compiler.

5. Which of the following is true? (Select all that apply.)

   i. The toString() method is defined in Object.java under java.lang package.

   ii. You can invoke the toString() method on an object of any class, custom or Java pre-defined, with no compile or run-time errors.

   iii. Every class, whether custom or Java predefined, directly or indirectly inherits from the Object class, even if its immediate parent class is other than Object class.

   a. All of the above

   b. (i) and (iii) only

   c. (ii) and (iii) only

   d. (i) and (ii) only

6. For a method to be overloaded, two or more versions of the same method in the same class must have

   a. different parameters lists and different return data types.

   b. different parameters lists but can have the same or different return data types.

   c. the same parameters lists but must have different return data types.

   d. the same parameters lists but can have the same or different return data types.

7. For a method to be overridden, two versions of the same method must exist: one in the parent class and one in the child class. These must have

   a. the same parameters lists and the same return data types.

   b. different parameters lists, but they can have the same or different return data types.

   c. the same parameters lists, but they can have the same or different return data types.

   d. different parameters lists, but they must have the same return data types.

8. Which of the following statements are true? (Select all that apply.)

   i. You can have a method that is overloaded and also overridden at the same time.

   ii. If you invoke an overridden method on an object of the child class, the method in the parent always gets called first followed by the one in the child.

   iii. If you invoke an overridden method on an object of the child class, the method in the child always gets called first; the parent class's method then gets called only if you explicitly invoke it from within the child class's method using the super keyword.

   a. All of the above

   b. (i) and (iii) only

   c. (i) and (ii) only

   d. (ii) and (iii) only

9. Which of the following statements are true? (Select all that apply.)

   i. An abstract method is one that has no method body.

   ii. An abstract class is one that contains one or more abstract methods, but it can contain non-abstract methods as well.

   iii. An abstract class is one that contains only abstract methods.

   iv. You can instantiate objects of an abstract class type.

   v. You can declare objects of an abstract class type.

   a. (i), (ii), (iv), and (v) only

   b. (i), (iii), and (v) only

    c. (i), (iii), (iv), and (v) only

    d. (i), (ii), and (v) only

10. Which of the following statements are true? (Select all that apply.)

    i. An `interface` class is one that contains one or more constants and one or more `abstract` methods, but it can also contain non-constant attributes and non-abstract methods.

    ii. An `interface` class is one that contains only constants and `abstract` methods.

    iii. All the methods in an `interface` class are `public` and `abstract` by default.

    iv. All the constants in an `interface` class are `public`, `static`, and `final` by default.

    a. All of the above

    b. (ii), (iii), and (iv) only

    c. (ii) and (iv) only

    d. (i), (iii), and (iv) only

11. Which of the following is true? (Select all that apply.)

    i. A `List` cannot directly hold values of primitive data types—it uses wrapper classes to convert such data into objects before adding to the `List`.

    ii. Every element of a `List` must be an object.

    iii. The most important and common implementation of the `List` interface is the `ArrayList` class.

    iv. The `List` interface has a "max size" attribute that specifies the maximum number of elements the list can hold.

    v. To add an element to a `List`, you use the `add()` method passing it the object you want to add.

    a. All of the above

    b. (i), (ii), (iii), and (v) only

    c. (i), (ii), (iii), and (iv) only

    d. (ii), (iii), and (v) only

12. Which of the following is true? (Select all that apply.)

    i. `ArrayList` implements `List` interface and `List` implements `Map` interface.

ii. Hashtable inherits from HashMap.

iii. A Map is a collection of key-value pairs.

iv. The main difference between Hashtable and HashMap is that Hashtable doesn't allow you to have a value of null (for a given key) whereas HashMap allows that.

v. When creating a List or ArrayList, using a template data type guarantees that all elements are of the same data type.

a. All of the above

b. (i), (ii), (iii), and (iv) only

c. (i), (ii), and (v) only

d. (iii), (iv), and (v) only

13. Which of the following is true? (Select all that apply.)

i. An Iterator is an interface in java.util package that you can use to iterate over a collection.

ii. The iterator() function on a List object returns an Iterator type object.

iii. The next() function in the Iterator class returns the next Iterator object in the List (or collection) over which it is iterating.

iv. The hasNext() function in the Iterator class returns true if the collection over which it is iterating has more elements (beyond the current cursor position).

v. Map is an interface in java.util package and is implemented by HashMap and Hashtable classes.

a. All of the above

b. (i), (ii), (iii), and (v) only

c. (i), (iii), and (iv) only

d. (i), (ii), (iii), and (iv) only

14. Say that ParentExceptionClass and ChildExceptionClass are two exception classes, with ChildExceptionClass a subclass of ParentExceptionClass. Assume that you have a try block

that can potentially throw an exception of either `ParentExceptionClass` type or `ChildExcep-tionClass` type. The code is as follows:

```
try
{
    // some code that can throw an exception of
    // either ParentExceptionClass or ChildExceptionClass type
}
catch ( ParentExceptionClass e )
{
    System.out.println("Caught parent");
}
```

What output would you expect if an exception of type `ChildExceptionClass` is thrown by the try block?

a. `Caught parent`

b. Will show an `UncaughtException` error

c. Will show a different error message as configured by Java

d. Will not show any message in the output

15. Say that `SiblingExceptionClass1` and `SiblingExceptionClass2` are two exception classes that inherit from the `Exception` class, and neither of these two classes is a subclass of the other. Assume that you have a try block that can potentially throw an exception of either `SiblingExceptionClass1` type or `SiblingExceptionClass2` type. The code is as follows:

```
try
{
    // some code that can throw an exception of
    // either SiblingExceptionClass1 or SiblingExceptionClass2 type
}
catch ( SiblingExceptionClass1 e ) { System.out.println("Caught sibling 1"); }
catch ( SiblingExceptionClass2 e ) { System.out.println("Caught sibling 2"); }
catch ( Exception e ) { System.out.println("Caught parent"); }
```

What output would you expect if an exception of type `SiblingExceptionClass2` is thrown by the try block?

a. `Caught sibling 1`

b. `Caught sibling 2`

   c. Caught sibling 1
       Caught parent

   d. Caught sibling 2
       Caught parent

2.6   Answers to Quiz

1. The correct answer is (d). All statements except (iv) are false. Option (i) is false because a subclass does not inherit `private` attributes and methods of its parent class. Option (ii) is false because a subclass may belong to a different package than that of its parent. Option (iii) is false because class members that have unspecified access can be accessed only by other classes that are inside of the package that class belongs to. Option (v) is false because `private` members of a class can be accessed only within that class; they cannot be accessed by objects instantiated from it nor by its subclasses or objects instantiated from subclasses.

2. The correct answer is (a). The default constructor of the parent class is always called first, followed by the specific constructor of the subclass that you use to instantiate the object; the matching constructor in the parent, if present, never gets called. Even if you instantiate a `Child` object using the default constructor in `Child`, the `Parent` class's default constructor is called first, followed by the default constructor in `Child`.

3. The correct answer is (c). All statements except (vi) are true. Option (vi) is false because `prs` is currently pointing to a `Customer` object, so you cannot cast it to `Employee` type and invoke `public` methods that are specifically defined in the `Employee` class. You need to use the `new` keyword (for example, `prs = new Employee("John","Smith", 1000.0);`) before attempting to cast `prs` to an `Employee` object.

4. The correct answer is (a). This will give a compile error as follows:

```
TestReport.java:7: cannot resolve symbol

symbol : variable salesAmount
location: class Person
double salesAmt = (Customer)prs.salesAmount;
                 ^
TestReport.java:7: incompatible types
found : Customer
required: double
double salesAmt = (Customer)prs.salesAmount;
                 ^
2 errors
```

5. The correct answer is (a). All statements are true.

6. The correct answer is (b). For a method to be overloaded, two or more versions of the same method in the same class must have different parameters lists, but they can have the same or different return data types.

7. The correct answer is (a). The methods must have the same parameters lists and the same return data types.

8. The correct answer is (b). Option (ii) is false because if you invoke an overridden method on an object of the child class, the method in the child always gets called first; the parent class's method then gets called only if you explicitly invoke it from within the child class's method using the super keyword.

9. The correct answer is (d). All statements except (iii) and (iv) are true. Option (iii) is false because an abstract class is one that contains one or more abstract methods but can contain nonabstract methods as well. Option (iv) is false because you cannot instantiate objects of an abstract class type, although you can declare objects of the abstract class type.

10. The correct answer is (b). All statements except (i) are true. Option (i) is false because an interface class is one that contains only constants and abstract methods; it cannot contain nonconstant attributes or nonabstract methods.

11. The correct answer is (b). Option (iv) is false because the List interface does NOT have any "max size" attribute that specifies the maximum number of elements the list can hold. A List can hold any number of elements.

12. The correct answer is (d). Option (i) is false because List does not implement Map interface. Option (ii) is false because Hashtable does not inherit from HashMap.

13. The correct answer is (a). All statements are true.

14. The correct answer is (a). The first catch block has an exception type (ParentExceptionClass) that is a legitimate parent of type of the exception object being thrown (ChildExceptionClass).

15. The correct answer is (b). The second catch block (for SiblingExceptionClass2) will be invoked and the other catch blocks will not be executed.

2.7   Unsolved Assignments

Assignment 2.1

Objective: To learn and practice the use of inheritance.

Steps:

- Create a new folder called `assign21` under `C:\JSP\Chapter2`, for putting all files of this assignment. Copy `Person.java`, `Employee.java`, and `TestReport.java` from Solved Exercise 2.1.4 into this folder.

- Modify `Employee.java` to make the `salary` attribute `private`, and also to add the following class members:

Attributes (`private`):

- `emplId` (`int`)

- `emplType` (`String`) (should contain "`MGR`" for Manager, "`SALESASSOC`" for SalesAssociate)

- `emplTypeDescr` (`String`) (should contain "`Sales Manager`" if `emplType` = "`MGR`", and "`Sales Assoc`" if `emplType` = "`SALESASSOC`".)

Constructor:

- Change the constructor in `Employee.java` to take additional parameters for the new attributes (`emplId`, `emplType`). The constructor should set `emplTypeDescr` appropriately, depending on the value of `emplType`.

Methods:

- Add getter and setter methods for the new attributes `emplId`, `emplType`, and `emplTypeDescr`, and for `salary` (follow naming convention: all getters and setters should begin with lowercase letters (`get` or `set`), followed by the attribute name with first character in uppercase and rest in lowercase. (For example: `getEmplId()`, `setEmplId()`, and so on.) To prevent outsiders from accidentally changing the `emplTypeDescr` to be out of sync with the `emplType` value, make the `setEmplTypeDescr()` method `private`.

Note: The `setEmplType()` method should set the value of `emplType`; in addition, it should also set `emplTypeDescr` appropriately. (Set `emplTypeDescr` to "`Sales Manager`" if `emplType` = "`MGR`", and "`Sales Assoc`" if `emplType` = "`SALESASSOC`".)

- Define a new class called `Manager` (save it in `Manager.java`) that extends from the `Employee` class and has additional members of its own, as follows:

Attributes (`private`):

- `salesAssociateEmplIds` (array of `int`; represents employee id's of this manager's subordinates.)

Constructor:

- Specific constructor that takes `salesAssociateEmplIds` (array of `int`), in addition to `emplId`, `firstName`, `lastName`, and `salary`. The constructor should call `setEmplType()` on its parent, passing it the `String` "MGR".

Methods:

- Getter and setter methods for `salesAssociateEmplIds`. (Follow naming convention as in `Employee` class.)
- Define a new class called `SalesAssociate` (save it in `SalesAssociate.java`) that extends from the `Employee` class, and has additional members of its own, as follows:

Attributes (`private`):

- `amountSold` (double)
- `commissionRate` (double)

Constructor:

- Specific constructor that takes `amountSold` (double), and `commissionRate` (double), in addition to `emplId`, `firstName`, `lastName`, and `salary`. The constructor should call `setEmplType()` on its parent, passing it the `String` "SALESASSOC".

Methods:

- Getter, setter methods for `amountSold`, `commissionRate`
- Remove all code inside the `main()` method of `TestReport.java`. Inside the `main()` method, instantiate an array of four `Employee` type objects (call it `empl`), and instantiate each element as either a `Manager` or `SalesAssciate` object, as follows:

1st `Employee` object (type `Manager`):

`emplId=100`, `firstName=`"John", `lastName=`"Smith", `salary=5000.00`, `salesAssociateEmplIds = {101,102,103}`

2nd `Employee` object (type `SalesAssociate`):

emplId=101, firstName="Judy", lastName="Miller", salary=1000.00, amountSold=200.00, commissionRate=0.05

3rd Employee object (type SalesAssociate):

emplId=102, firstName="Mike", lastName="Johnson", salary=1500.00, amountSold=500.00, commissionRate=0.07

4th Employee object (type SalesAssociate):

emplId=103, firstName="Steve", lastName="Armstrong", salary=900.00, amountSold=300.00, commissionRate=0.05

- Loop through the empl array twice; generate a salary report followed by a sales report as follows. (Don't worry about formatting and columnar alignment; use tabs for basic formatting.)

```
******************************************************************************
                              Salary Report
******************************************************************************
------------------------------------------------------------------------------
Employee ID      Name              Employee Type            Salary
------------------------------------------------------------------------------
   100        Smith, John          Sales Manager           5000.00
   101        Miller, Judy         Sales Assoc             1000.00
   102        Johnson, Mike        Sales Assoc             1500.00
   103        Armstrong, Steve     Sales Assoc              900.00
------------------------------------------------------------------------------
                 Totals:                                   8400.00
------------------------------------------------------------------------------


******************************************************************************
                              Sales Report
******************************************************************************
------------------------------------------------------------------------------
Employee ID      Name           Amount Sold           Commission
------------------------------------------------------------------------------
   101        Miller, Judy       200.00                  10.00
   102        Johnson, Mike      500.00                  35.00
   103        Armstrong, Steve   300.00                  15.00
------------------------------------------------------------------------------


------------------------------------------------------------------------------
                 Totals:         1000.00                  60.00
------------------------------------------------------------------------------
```

A sample session is shown here:

- Submit `Employee.java`, `Manager.java`, `SalesAssociate.java`, and `TestReport.java`.

Assignment 2.2

Objective: To practice the use of abstract classes and overloading a method.

Steps:

- Create a new folder called `assign22` under `C:\JSP\Chapter2`, for putting all files of this assignment. Copy `Person.java`, `Employee.java`, `Manager.java`, `SalesAssociate.java`, and `TestReport.java` from Assignment 2.1 into this folder.

- Modify the Employee class as follows:
  - Make the Employee class abstract, and also make the getEmplTypeDescr() and getEmplType() methods abstract (so child classes of Employee must implement these two methods).
  - Remove the emplType and emplTypeDescr attributes from the Employee class (since these are no longer required).
  - Remove the setEmplTypeDescr() and setEmplType() methods from Employee.
  - Make emplId protected.
- Modify the Manager class as follows:
  - Implement the getEmplType() method so that it returns the String "MGR".
  - Implement the getEmplTypeDescr() method so that it returns the String "Sales Manager".
  - Don't call the setEmplType() method anymore in the constructor.
- Modify the SalesAssociate class as follows:
  - Implement the getEmplType() method so that it returns the String "SALESASSOC".
  - Implement the getEmplTypeDescr() method so that it returns the String "Sales Assoc".
  - Don't call the setEmplType() method anymore in the constructor.
  - Overload the getCommissionRate() method with one that takes a boolean parameter addBonus. If addBonus is true, the method should multiply commissionRate by 1.2 and return the result; otherwise, it should return commissionRate as is.
- Modify TestReport.java to call the overloaded getCommissionRate() method, sending it true.
- Compile and run the code to verify that it gives the same output as in Assignment 2.1 (with the only difference being in the commission for the sales associate, since a bonus is now being added).

A sample session is shown here:

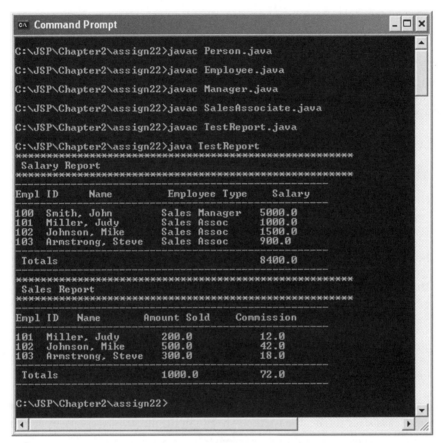

- Submit `Employee.java`, `Manager.java`, `SalesAssociate.java`, and `TestReport.java`.

Assignment 2.3

Objective: **To practice the use of interface classes.**

Steps:

- Create a new folder called `assign23` under `C:\JSP\Chapter2`, for putting all files of this assignment. Copy `Person.java`, `Employee.java`, `Manager.java`, `SalesAssociate.java`, and `TestReport.java` from Assignment 2.2 into this folder.

- Create a new interface class called `EmployeeInterface` (save it in `EmployeeInterface.java`) with the following `String` constants:

  - `EMPL_TYPE_MGR = "MGR"`

- ■ EMPL_TYPE_SA = "SALESASSOC"

- ■ EMPL_TYPE_DESCR_MGR = "Sales Manager"

- ■ EMPL_TYPE_DESCR_SA = "Sales Assoc"

- ■ Modify the Manager and SalesAssociate classes as follows:

  - ■ These should now implement the EmployeeInterface class (in addition to extending from Employee).

  - ■ The getEmplTypeDescr() and getEmplType() methods should return the appropriate String constant from EmployeeInterface.

- ■ Compile and run the code to verify that it gives the same output as in Assignment 2.2.

  A sample session is shown here:

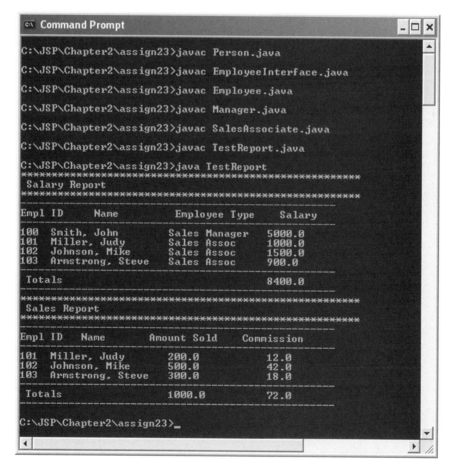

- ■ Submit EmployeeInterface.java, Manager.java, and SalesAssociate.java.

CHAPTER 3

HTML and Javascript Overview

Chapter Objectives

- Understand how the Internet works.

- Learn how to write HTML pages.

- Study how to format Web page content using HTML tables and style sheets.

- Become familiar with passing values from one HTML page to another using HTML forms.

- Learn how to validate form data using JavaScript.

3.1   How the Internet Works

Before we go on to learn JSP, we need to understand how the Internet works. The internet is a network of computers communicating with each other over telephone or cable lines. Each computer in the network has a unique identifying address called the IP address (IP stands for Internet Protocol).

To understand how Internet communication works, take a look at Figure 3.1.

The Internet browser allows you to communicate with other computers in the network and to look at files on those computers in a browser-palatable, HTML format. The computer on which the browser runs is called the *client computer*, and the computer with which it is communicating is the *server computer*. To begin the communication, the client needs to specify which computer it wants to communicate with. To do this, it needs the unique "address" of the server computer.

3.1.1   Communicating Using the IP Address

As mentioned earlier, every computer in the network has an IP address—an address by which it can be uniquely identified. To know the IP address of your computer, you can open a command prompt window and type in `ipconfig` and it will spit out its IP address (which may look something like `150.10.200.30`). The IP address of a computer in the network is unique, which means no two computers in the entire worldwide network can have the same IP address.

To specify the "server computer" that the client wants to communicate with, you can specify the server's IP address in the "Web address" box of your browser. For example, if the IP address of the server computer is `150.10.200.30`, you would type in `http://150.10.200.30`, and hit the `Go` button. Once you do this, the browser begins a communication with that computer.

The browser allows you to look at one file only at a time, so just specifying the IP address of the destination is not sufficient; you still need to specify which directory on the server, and which file in that directory to get. In other words, the communication consists of requesting a *file* on the server,

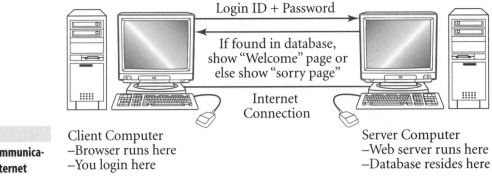

Figure 3.1

Client-server communication over the Internet

Client Computer
–Browser runs here
–You login here

Server Computer
–Web server runs here
–Database resides here

which could be a file ending with .html, .asp, .jsp or other extensions. Notice how the "request" from the client consists of three parts:

- machine (server's IP address)
- directory
- file name (with extension)

The directory and the file name are optional and take default values when unspecified.

3.1.2 Web Root Directory

The default directory is called the **Web root directory**, one that the administrator on the server computer can specify when setting it up. The default file is index.html is expected to reside in the Web root directory (we will later see how the default file could even be index.jsp for a JSP-based server). So when you specify the Web address as http://150.10.200.30, you are actually requesting a file called index.html on the Web root directory of a server computer with an IP address of 150.10.200.30.

There is a specific reason why we need a Web root directory. It obviously does not make sense to allow access to all files and directories on the computer to outsiders due to security reasons. So the server computer will have a certain folder (or directory) that is accessible to the outside world—the *Web root directory*. Directories other than the "Web root" remain invisible to outsiders. When you type in the Web address of the computer and the file, you are, in effect, requesting the server computer for showing the content of a file in that "Web root" directory, or its subdirectories. The server computer can be configured to set the "Web root directory" to a specific folder. For example, the Web root directory could be C:\www, in which case it will look for a file index.html under C:\www of the server computer.

3.1.3 Request and Response

The server computer, in turn, responds by sending the content of the requested file (index.html in this example) via the network to the client. In technical parlance, every time you type in a Web site address in your browser, you send a "request" for a file to some server computer in the network, which sends back a "response" in a special format or language that the browser can interpret. This "special format" is HTML, or Hyper Text Markup Language. In sum, the client sends a request, and the server sends a response back to the client. *The final response from the server to the client (browser) is almost always plain HTML (unless of course, if you are requesting a Word/PDF document or an image file).* Next time you enter another Web address or click on another hyperlink, the browser sends another request and gets a response back that is displayed in your browser. This process is repeated as you browse through different Web pages on the Internet. Notice that typing in the Web address of a site in the browser and clicking on a hyperlink that contains a Web address have exactly the same effect and are equivalent.

3.1.4   Protocol

The request itself follows certain rules, which are embodied in the form of a "protocol"; the most common one is Hyper Text Transfer Protocol (HTTP). You will notice the "http://" part in front of Web addresses, which means that the request is based on the HTTP protocol and is thus an "HTTP request." Similarly, the response is called an "HTTP response."

3.1.5   Communicating Using Domain Names

Using IP addresses seems to be fine in theory, but we usually type in a Web address as plain text, such as "www.microsoft.com," and not as an IP address. The plain text address, technically called a **domain name**, is basically a more user-friendly equivalent of the IP address. Behind the scenes, a domain name is converted to its equivalent IP address before the browser begins the communication with the server. So, how does the browser know which IP address the domain name represents? The answer is, behind the scenes, the text address maps to the actual IP address, so the browser looks up the domain name to determine which specific IP address it represents. The mapping between IP addresses and domain names is maintained by a third party, known as the Domain Name Server (DNS).

For example, when you type in the Web address as http://www.microsoft.com, you are requesting a file called index.html on the Web root directory of a server computer that has the domain name "microsoft.com" (actually, its equivalent IP address). To recap, the address of the server computer can either be an IP address or a more user-friendly domain name.

3.1.6   Web Server

We already saw an example of the default file being requested from the server. Let's consider the case when you request a file other than the default. In this case, you need to specify the directory and/or file name (with extension). Again, the directory is optional; if unspecified, it defaults to the Web root directory.

So if you type in "http://www.microsoft.com/abc.html," you are requesting a file named "abc.html" on the Web root directory of the server that has a domain name of "microsoft.com." Instead, if you say "http://www.microsoft.com/explorer/abc.html," you are requesting a file named "abc.html" in a subdirectory called "explorer" under the Web root directory of the server with domain name "microsoft.com." Notice how the part "/explorer" following the domain name means a directory relative to the Web root directory. The directory name is always relative to the Web root directory on the server.

The file requested by the client may not always be an HTML file. For example, the client may request a file ending with ".asp" or ".jsp." Note that the final response that goes to the client must be HTML (in most cases), otherwise the browser will not be able to interpret and display it. So, when the request is for a non-HTML file, the server needs some software that can parse the non-HTML file (such as `.asp` or `.jsp`), convert it to equivalent HTML, and then send it to the client. This piece of software on the server computer is called the **Web server**—a piece of software that runs on the destination computer and receives requests for specific files, processes the requests, and sends HTML content back to the client. There are a variety of Web servers available in the market, each capable of processing certain kinds of files. For example, a JSP Web server (*Apache Tomcat* is a popular one, which we will see later) can process requests for files ending with `.jsp`, and an ASP Web server can process requests for files ending with `.asp`. Another Web server may be able to process requests for files ending with the `.html` extension only.

If you are using Windows, a Web server that comes with it is the Microsoft Personal Web Server, which can handle file extensions of `.html` and `.asp`.

3.2   HTML Basics

An HTML (HyperText Markup Language) page (or a file with a `.html` extension) consists of normal text enclosed in **markers** or **tags**—predefined characters in angle brackets (< and >) that tell the browser how the enclosed text needs to be displayed in the browser window. So a simple text file that you create in Notepad would contain plain text only, but an HTML file is slightly more than a text file in that it has tags around portions of the text. The browser knows how to interpret these predefined tags and to display any enclosed text in a particular way in the browser. A tag is one or more characters enclosed in angle brackets (< >). For example, the tag, `<FONT>` .. `</FONT>` would allow you to specify what font the enclosed text (represented by ..) should appear in. Similarly, a `<BR>` tag denotes a line break, so the browser would display the text following it on a new line. There are hundreds of other predefined tags, each with its own meaning. See `http://www.htmlref.com/` for a comprehensive listing of all HTML tags along with their meaning. In this chapter, we will be looking at tags that are important from the perspective of learning JSP.

Most HTML tags require that you have an ending tag as well, so that the browser can easily identify the enclosed text that needs to be displayed in a particular way. Let's create an HTML page to get a feel for what I am talking about.

3.2.1   Your First HTML Page

Say that you want to display the simple text "Hello, World!" on your browser. You need to create a file that ends with `.html` so that the browser can display its contents. Let's call the file `HelloWorld.html`. Create a new subfolder called `Chapter3` under the `C:\JSP` folder, and another subfolder called `sec321` inside the `Chapter3` subfolder. From now on, I will assume you will similarly create a new subfolder for a section as necessary, and put all files of that section in that subfolder. Note that I use chapter folder names that begin with an uppercase letter, whereas section subfolder names begin with a lowercase letter. The names of the files themselves begin with an uppercase letter, and follow a title-case—for example: `HelloWorld.html`. We will be following this rule throughout this book to be consistent. This makes it more organized and easy to retrieve in the future.

Open Notepad (or other text editor) and type the following HTML into it:

```
-------------------------------
<HTML>
    Hello, World!
</HTML>
-------------------------------
```

Save the file as `HelloWorld.html` under `C:\JSP\Chapter3\sec321`. That's it—you have written your first HTML page! Open Windows Explorer, and double-click on `HelloWorld.html`; it should show the text "`Hello, World`" in a new browser window:

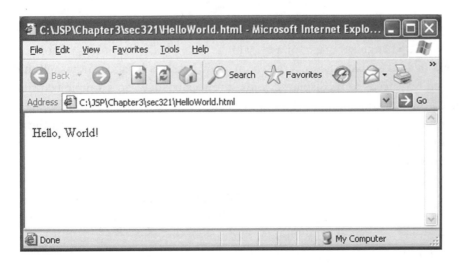

In this simple case, the "client" was the browser on your machine, and the "server" was also your machine. Your page contains an `<HTML>` tag followed by the words `Hello, World!` and ending with an `</HTML>` tag. Notice how you have an ending tag (`</HTML>`) that is identical to the starting tag (`<HTML>`), except that the ending tag has a forward-slash (`/`) just before the tag name. Your browser understands these tags to mean the beginning and end of an HTML page. Note that HTML is case-insensitive; you could as well have used `<html>` instead of `<HTML>`, with the same end result. The `<HTML>` tag is one of several hundred predefined tags that the browser understands and knows how to interpret.

HTML consists of a rich collection of such predefined tags that you can use to make your HTML page look and feel better. This chapter will be reviewing important tags that we will need to use later when writing JSP pages.

To consider an example of another HTML tag, let's extend our first HTML page to show the text in bold-face. For this, you have another tag that must start with <B> and end with </B>. Text that is enclosed within these two tags would show up in boldface. So your HTML page would now contain the following:

```
--------------------------------
<HTML>
    <B>Hello, World!</B>
</HTML>
--------------------------------
```

Open Windows Explorer, double-click on this file, and notice how the text Hello, World! now shows up in boldface font:

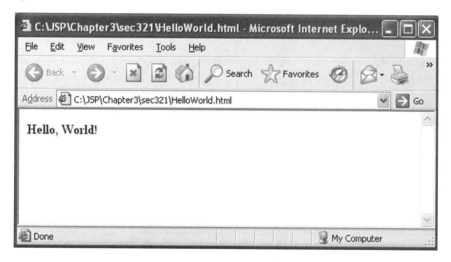

In the real world, HTML pages are much more involved than the simple ones we just created. Such pages usually contain a certain portion that we want to display on the browser and another portion that we do not want to display but do want to use as a placeholder for functions and other information that the displayable portion would use if necessary. The displayable portion in an HTML page needs to be enclosed in a <BODY> tag, and the nondisplayable portion needs to be enclosed in a <HEAD> tag. Both tags need to sit within the overall <HTML> tags, which mark the beginning and end of an HTML page. Your simple HTML page currently has only the HTML tags, so let's go ahead and enclose the Hello, World! text in a pair of <BODY> tags, so that we can later add a <HEAD> tag if necessary. Your HTML page would now look like this:

```
--------------------------------
<HTML>
    <BODY>
        <B>Hello, World!</B>
    </BODY>
</HTML>
--------------------------------
```

If you double-click on HelloWorld.html, you will see the same content as before. We will look at the <HEAD> tag shortly, when we look at JavaScript.

Notice how you need to use both a begin and an end BODY tag. This is true of most HTML tags, which must have both a begin and end tag so that the browser can interpret the enclosed text to display in a particular way.

Solved Exercise 3.2.1

Objective: To learn how to nest HTML tags and the use of the italic <I> tag.

Steps:

- Create a new folder called exer321 under C:\JSP\Chapter3. Copy HelloWorld.html from Section 3.2.1 into this folder.

- Modify it so that the words Hello World show up in bold and italic font. (*Hint:* For italic font, you can use the <I> .. </I> tags. Nest the <I> .. </I> tags within the <B> .. </B> tags.)

Solution:

```
<HTML>
    <BODY>
        <B><I>Hello, World!</I></B>
    </BODY>
</HTML>
```

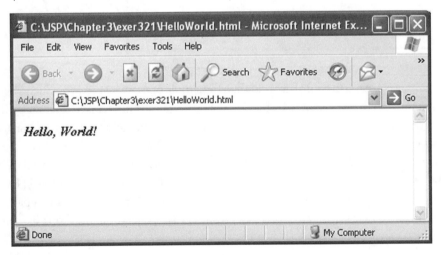

3.2.2   URL

The Web address that you type in a browser's address box is technically called a Uniform Resource Locator (URL). The word "resource" refers to a file on the Web server, like an HTML file. You can also embed URLs inside your HTML page, so that when you click on any of those URLs, the browser goes to the selected URL. This has the same effect as typing in the destination Web address in your browser's address box.

3.2.3 Using the Anchor Tag

The basic purpose of browsing the Internet is to network—in other words, to navigate from a file on one computer to another file on some other computer in the Internet's network of computers. This is achieved by **hyperlinks**—underlined text that shows a hand sign as you move your mouse over it, and then takes you to some other Web address when you click on it. Hyperlinks are created inside your HTML page using an anchor tag (<A> .. </A>), which displays the enclosed text as a hyperlink. Inside the anchor tag, you specify a destination URL by specifying a value for its "HREF" attribute. So, when someone clicks on the hypertext, the Web address is automatically changed to the one specified under the HREF value.

Let's go ahead and put a hyperlink in your HTML page, which will take you to Sun's Java page:

```
-------------------------------
<HTML>
    <BODY>
        <B>Hello, World!</B>
        <A HREF="http://java.sun.com">Click here to go to Sun's Java site:</A>
    </BODY>
</HTML>
-------------------------------
```

The page now looks like this:

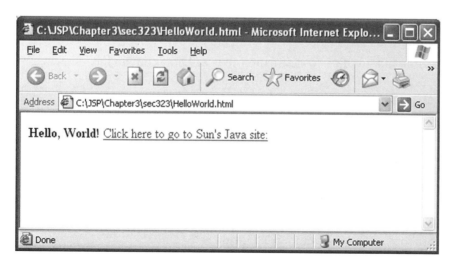

You must have an anchor tag in order to display text as a hyperlink. The anchor tag begins with <A ..> but must end with </A>.

3.2.4   Optional End Tags

Notice how the begin and end tags (<A> and </A>) for the anchor tag must have the same abbreviation ('A'), and that the end tag is preceded by a forward slash (</A>). For some tags, the end tag is optional—the browser knows how to interpret them as such. For example, the <BR> tag does not need an end tag such as </BR>, since it simply denotes a line break at the place where it appears.

3.2.5   Absolute and Relative File Paths as URLs

A URL could also be a path to a file—a file that resides on the destination (server) machine. The file path in the URL could be either an *absolute* or a *relative* path. An **absolute file path** begins with the root directory (for example, C:\) and includes the full list of folders that help locate the file. For example, C:\JSP\Chapter3\HelloWorld.html is an absolute URL.

Let's look at an example that will help you understand absolute URLs. Say that you have two HTML files: HelloWorld.html under C:\JSP\Chapter3\sec325 and another called Page2.html in a new subfolder misc under C:\JSP\Chapter3\sec325. You want to put a hyperlink in HelloWorld.html that takes the user to Page2.html. For this, first create a folder called sec325 under C:\JSP\Chapter3 and then copy the HelloWorld.html file from Section 3.2.3. Create a subfolder called misc under C:\JSP\Chapter3\sec325 and create a new file called Page2.html in it, with the following content:

```
---------------------------------
<HTML>
    <BODY>
        You have reached the second page!
    </BODY>
</HTML>
---------------------------------
```

Now change HelloWorld.html to link to this new destination so it will now contain the following:

```
---------------------------------
<HTML>
    <BODY>
        <B>Hello, World!</B>
        <A HREF="C:/JSP/Chapter3/sec325/misc/Page2.html">
          Click here to go to the second page
      </A>
      </BODY>
</HTML>
---------------------------------
```

Note that we use forward slashes (/) in URL's embedded inside HTML files.

Save changes to `HelloWorld.html`, then double-click on it in Windows Explorer. If you click on the hyperlink, it should take you to `Page2.html`.

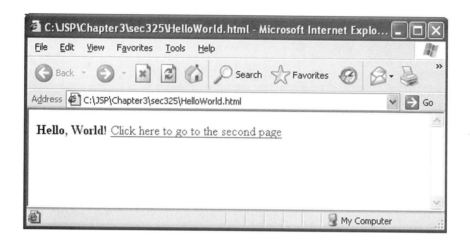

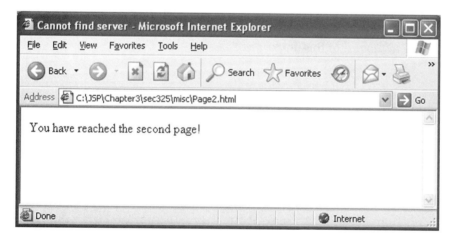

A **relative file path** is a path that is relative to the location of the current file in which it appears. So in the folder structure we saw above, the absolute path of the `misc` folder would be `C:\JSP\Chapter3\sec325\misc`, but its path relative to `sec325` would simply be `misc`. Conversely, if you are currently in the `misc` folder, the relative path of the `sec325` folder relative to the current (`misc`) would be "`..`", where the `..` means "one folder level above the current one" (which is the same as in a simple command prompt window).

To understand relative URLs, change `HelloWorld.html` to use `HREF="misc/Page2.html"` instead of `HREF="C:/JSP/Chapter3/sec325/misc/Page2.html"`, which would still work the same as before, because you have now specified a relative folder path, a path that is relative to where `HelloWorld.html` currently resides.

So your new `HelloWorld.html` would look as follows:

```
--------------------------------
<HTML>
    <BODY>
        <B>Hello, World!</B>
        <A HREF="misc/Page2.html">Click here to go to the second page</A>
    </BODY>
</HTML>
--------------------------------
```

To sum it up, to put a link to `Page2.html` inside `HelloWorld.html`, you could either have a fully qualified (absolute) URL, such as `C:/JSP/Chapter3/sec325/misc/Page2.html`, or more conveniently, you could specify a relative URL as `misc/Page2.html`. By using a relative path, the HTML files would become independent of whichever machine they run on; they would work fine as long as you make sure the same relative folder structure is available. So in this example, it would work on any machine as long as there is a subfolder called `misc` under the folder that contains `HelloWorld.html`, and that subfolder contains a file called `Page2.html`. The use of a relative folder path is the preferred way to go and will be followed in the rest of this book.

Solved Exercise 3.2.5

Objective: To understand relative URLs.

Steps:

- Create a new folder called `exer325` under `C:\JSP\Chapter3`. Create two subfolders under `C:\JSP\Chapter3\exer325`; call them `folder1` and `folder2` respectively. Create a subfolder called `subfolder1` under `C:\JSP\Chapter3\exer325\folder1`.

- Copy `HelloWorld.html` from Section 3.2.5 into `C:\JSP\Chapter3\exer325\folder1\subfolder1`. Copy `Page2.html` from `C:\JSP\Chapter3\sec325` into `C:\JSP\Chapter3\exer325\folder2`.

- Change `HelloWorld.html` to use a *relative* file path in its `HREF`, to invoke the link to go to `Page2.html`.

- Submit `HelloWorld.html`.

Solution:

```
<!-- Begin HelloWorld.html -->
<HTML>
    <BODY>
        <B>Hello, World!</B>
        <A HREF="../../folder2/Page2.html">
```

```
        Click here to go to the second page
     </A>
     </BODY>
</HTML>
<!-- End HelloWorld.html -->
```

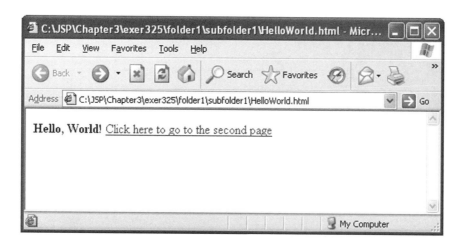

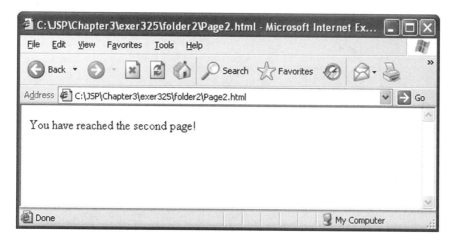

3.2.6   HTML Comments

HTML comments are very useful in making your HTML readable. Comments begin with <!-- and end with -->. Anything in between these two would be considered a comment and will not be processed. If you have the <!-- and --> on separate lines, that would still count as a valid, multiline comment. Some examples of HTML comments follow:

Single-line HTML comment

```
-------------------------------
<!-- Begin: HelloWorld.html -->
<HTML>
    <BODY>
        <!-- <B>Hello, World!</B> -->
        <B>Hello, Bob!</B>
    </BODY>
</HTML>
<!-- End: HelloWorld.html -->
-------------------------------
```

Multiline HTML comment

```
-------------------------------
<!-- Begin: HelloWorld.html -->
<HTML>
    <BODY>
        <!-- <B>Hello, World!</B>
        <B>Hello, Bob!</B>
        -->
        <B>Hello, John!</B>
    </BODY>
</HTML>
<!-- End: HelloWorld.html -->
-------------------------------
```

Solved Exercise 3.2.6

Objective: To learn the use of HTML comments.

Steps:

- Create a new folder called exer326 under C:\JSP\Chapter3. Copy HelloWorld.html from the end of Section 3.2.6 (the one with the multiline HTML comment) into this folder.

- Modify this file so that the part: Hello, John! is also commented out. (*Hint:* Use the <!-- --> around the part you want commented.) Add a new line below it, that would display the words Hello, Mike! in bold font.

Solution:

```
<!-- Begin: HelloWorld.html -->
<HTML>
    <BODY>
        <!-- <B>Hello, World!</B>
        <B>Hello, Bob!</B>
        -->
```

```
            <!-- <B>Hello, John!</B> -->
                  <B>Hello, Mike!</B>
          </BODY>
    </HTML>
    <!-- End: HelloWorld.html -->
```

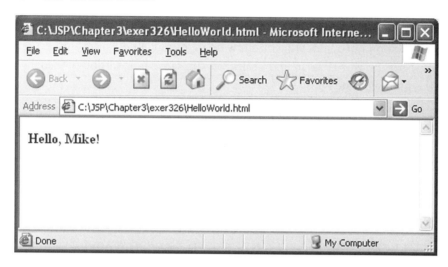

3.2.7 The
 Tag and

In an HTML page, if you use a plain TAB character, it will not translate into indentation on the actual Web page content when it is displayed. Similarly, if you want to put more space between the words "Hello" and "World!," you cannot just insert multiple spaces using the spacebar between these two words in your editor and expect the words to show up wide apart. Try it out:

```
--------------------------------
<HTML>
    <BODY>
        Hello   World!
    </BODY>
</HTML>
--------------------------------
```

This contains additional spaces between the words Hello and World!. If you display this page, you will notice that the words Hello and World! still show up as before—in other words, with no additional spaces between them. To insert a space so that it shows up as a real "space" character, you must use an HTML equivalent, . So to induce two consecutive blank spaces between the words Hello and World!, your HTML needs to look like this:

```
--------------------------------
<HTML>
    <BODY>
```

```
        Hello  World!
    </BODY>
</HTML>
```

This is a bit odd at first, but you will soon get used to it.

Similarly, to break a line onto a new line, you cannot just press the Enter key and start typing on the next line; if you do so, the text on both lines will still show up in a single line. For example, the following HTML will still show the words Hello and World! on the same line, although visually the HTML seems to have them on separate lines:

```
<HTML>
    <BODY>
        Hello
        World!
    </BODY>
</HTML>
```

HTML does not recognize special characters such as space, tab, new line, etc. You need to tell it explicitly that you want a space ( ) or a new line(<BR>). Let's look at an example of breaking lines. Say that you want to show the words Hello and World! on two separate lines one below the other. You need to use the following HTML:

```
<HTML>
    <BODY>
        Hello<BR>World!
    </BODY>
</HTML>
```

The <BR> tag between the words Hello and World! instructs the browser to display the two words on separate lines.

3.3   HTML Tables

As Web pages become more complex, it becomes important to be able to organize the content displayed in the browser. HTML tables provide a very useful way of organizing and formatting data displayed to the user. A table consists of rows and columns, and if you have multiple columns, each row consists of multiple "cells." In HTML, the <TR> tag represents a row and the <TD> tag represents a cell in the row. So you would need a TR tag with one or more TD tags embedded in it to represent a single row. Each TD tag would have text or data to be displayed for a row-column intersection. Let's go ahead and add an HTML table to the Web page we created earlier:

```
-------------------------------
<HTML>
    <BODY>
        <TABLE BORDER=1>
            <TR>
                <TD>Hello</TD><TD>World!</TD>
            </TR>
        </TABLE>
    </BODY>
</HTML>
-------------------------------
```

Note that the BORDER attribute in a TABLE tag allows you to specify whether you want to see the lines demarcating the cells of the table. The default is BORDER=0, which means no borders. I put BORDER=1 to show the concept of a table and how its cells look. Note that most HTML tags have one or more attributes whose values you can specify. Here, we have a <TABLE> tag that has an attribute called BORDER, to which I specified a value of 1. The value may or may not be enclosed in double quotes—both are identical. So I could have used BORDER="1" instead of BORDER=1 with the exact same result. Also, note that HTML tags are case-insensitive, so a <TABLE> tag could be written as <table>; similarly, BORDER=1 could be written as border=1. The choice of using double quotes for values and lowercase tag names is left to the developer.

Save your changes and open the file in your browser. You will notice how the text is now better organized into nice cells.

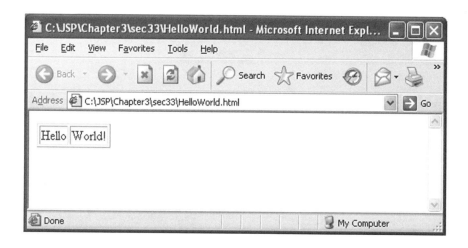

To add additional rows, you would add corresponding <TR> .. </TR> to the table. For example, if you want an extra row below the Hello World! to show the words Welcome home! (with each word in a different table cell), then your file would look like this:

```
--------------------------------
<HTML>
    <BODY>
        <TABLE BORDER=1>
            <TR>
                <TD>Hello</TD><TD>World!</TD>
            </TR>
            <TR>
                <TD>Welcome</TD><TD>home!</TD>
            </TR>
        </TABLE>
    </BODY>
</HTML>
--------------------------------
```

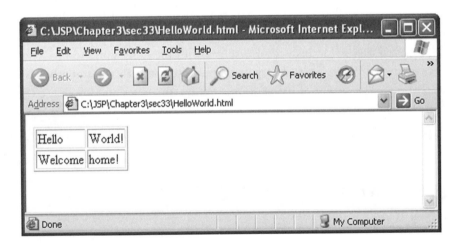

In this example, there were exactly two words in Hello World! and also in Welcome home!, so you have two TD cells in each TR row, making the columns perfectly aligned. But what if the second row had more than two words, such as: Welcome to this site! which would be four words? Try it out to see what happens:

```
--------------------------------
<HTML>
    <BODY>
        <TABLE BORDER=1>
            <TR>
                <TD>Hello</TD><TD>World!</TD>
```

```
                </TR>
                <TR>
                    <TD>Welcome</TD><TD>to</TD><TD>this</TD><TD>site!</TD>
                </TR>
            </TABLE>
        </BODY>
</HTML>
```

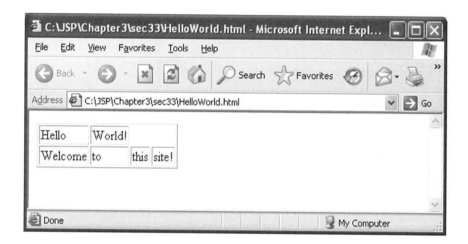

The first row seems to have messed up at the end. To align the cells in the first and second rows, there is a COLSPAN attribute that allows you to specify how many columns your TD cell spans (the default is 1). Using this attribute, you can force the TD cells in the first row to each span two columns (instead of the default of one column), so that the two cells together would span the four columns generated by the second row. The HTML would look like this:

```
<HTML>
    <BODY>
        <TABLE BORDER=1>
            <TR>
                <TD COLSPAN=2>Hello</TD><TD COLSPAN=2>World!</TD>
            </TR>
            <TR>
                <TD>Welcome</TD><TD>to</TD><TD>this</TD><TD>site!</TD>
            </TR>
        </TABLE>
    </BODY>
</HTML>
```

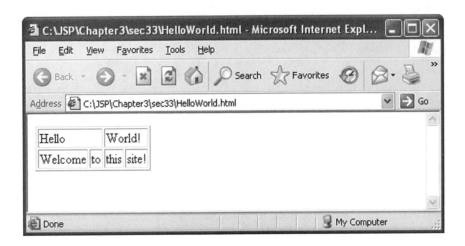

Notice that the text "Hello" is left-justified in its TD cell—that is the default. You can specify centered or right-justified, using an ALIGN attribute in the TD tag, as follows:

```
<TD COLSPAN=2 ALIGN=CENTER>Hello</TD>
```

The page would look like this.

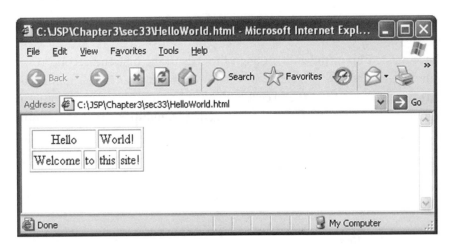

Note that in HTML, it does not make a difference whether you enclose the value of an attribute in double quotes (both behave same). You could thus say ALIGN="CENTER" or ALIGN=CENTER with the same result.

The previous tables show the border just to see the demarcation of the cells. The BORDER attribute defaults to 0, which means no borders, but the text is still aligned within the table cells as before. Try omitting the BORDER attribute (or use BORDER=0) and it should look like this:

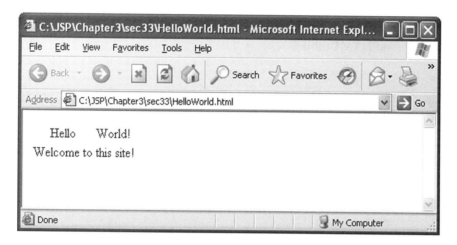

Instead of using the COLSPAN attribute to align the columns, you could club all words in each row into a single TD, as follows:

```
------------------------------
<HTML>
    <BODY>
        <TABLE BORDER=1>
            <TR>
                <TD>Hello World!</TD>
            </TR>
            <TR>
            <TD>Welcome to this site!</TD>
            </TR>
        </TABLE>
    </BODY>
</HTML>
------------------------------
```

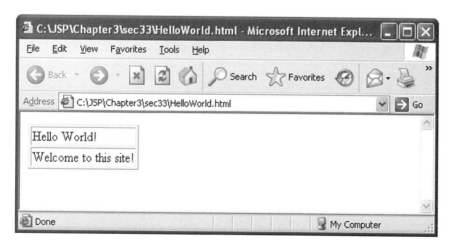

Solved Exercise 3.3

Objective: To practice the use of HTML tables.

Steps:

- Create a new folder called exer33 under C:\JSP\Chapter3. Copy HelloWorld.html from the end of Section 3.3 into this folder, and rename it CustomerReport.html.

- Modify this file so that it displays the following tabular information (instead of what it did earlier). Each cell or row/column intersection below should appear in a separate TD. Don't worry about the alignment of the values in the cells for now. (*Hint:* For displaying a horizontal line, enclose the <HR> tag in a TD tag.)

```
-------------------------------------------------------
                    Customer Report
-------------------------------------------------------
 #   Name                 Age      Sales Amount ($)
-------------------------------------------------------
 1.  Smith, Jonathan      35            150.00
 2.  Armstrong, John      30             50.00
 3.  Miller, Judy         25            175.00
-------------------------------------------------------
        Total                           375.00
-------------------------------------------------------
```

Solution:

```html
<!-- Begin: CustomerReport.html -->
<HTML>
    <BODY>
        <TABLE>
            <TR><TD COLSPAN=4><HR></TD></TR>
            <TR><TD COLSPAN=4 ALIGN="CENTER"><B>Customer Report</B></TD>
            <TR><TD COLSPAN=4><HR></TD></TR>
            <TR><TD>#</TD><TD>Name</TD><TD>Age</TD><TD>Sales Amount ($)</TD></TR>
            <TR><TD COLSPAN=4><HR></TD></TR>
            <TR>
                <TD>1.</TD>
                <TD>Smith, Jonathan</TD>
                <TD>35</TD>
                <TD ALIGN="RIGHT">150.00</TD>
            </TR>
            <TR>
                <TD>2.</TD>
```

```
          <TD>Armstrong, John</TD>
          <TD>30</TD>
          <TD ALIGN="RIGHT">50.00</TD>
        </TR>
        <TR>
          <TD>3.</TD>
          <TD>Miller, Judy</TD>
          <TD>25</TD>
          <TD ALIGN="RIGHT">175.00</TD>
        </TR>
        <TR><TD COLSPAN=4><HR></TD></TR>
        <TR>
          <TD COLSPAN=2 ALIGN="RIGHT">Total:</TD>
          <TD> </TD>
          <TD ALIGN="RIGHT">375.00</TD>
        </TR>
        <TR><TD COLSPAN=4><HR></TD></TR>
      </TABLE>
    </BODY>
</HTML>
<!-- End: CustomerReport.html -->
```

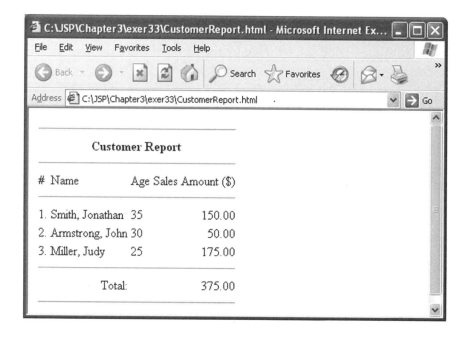

3.4   Cascading Style Sheets

You may have noticed that the words Hello and World! appear in a default, Times Roman font of a fixed size. Also, the letters appear in black color with a white background. These are the defaults for HTML. If you want your text to appear in any other font and/or different font size and/or different background color, a convenient and powerful way of doing it is to use "style sheets." A "style" represents a named set of properties that defines how text should look. It is similar to a Java object instantiated from a class that has attributes for font name, font size, font color, background color, etc. In the previous HTML table example, say that you want the text to appear in Arial Helvetica font of size 10 with a pink background. The set of properties we are talking about here is as follows:

```
--------------------------------
Font family: Arial, Helvetica
Font size: 10 pt
Font color: Black
Font Background color: PINK
--------------------------------
```

Let's go ahead and define a style that has these four properties—call it whatever you wish. I am calling it myStyle. A style needs to be defined before it can be used. All style definitions need to be enclosed in a <STYLE> tag inside the <HEAD> tag we talked about earlier. If you recall, the <HEAD> tag allows you to put all definitions and other functions that the rest of the HTML can use as necessary. A style definition must begin with the period (.), followed by the name of the style. Your HTML would now look like this:

```
-------------------------------------------------------------
<HTML>
    <HEAD>
        <STYLE>
            .myStyle { font-family:Helvetica,Arial; font-size:10pt; color:black;
                    background-color:PINK }
        </STYLE>
    </HEAD>
    <BODY>
        <TABLE BORDER=1>
            <TR CLASS="myStyle">
                <TD>Hello</TD><TD>World!</TD>
            </TR>
        </TABLE>
    </BODY>
</HTML>
-------------------------------------------------------------
```

Notice how the TR tag now has the word CLASS followed by the style name (myStyle). The word CLASS makes sense; a style represents some kind of "class" (set of attributes) that we are all familiar with in Java. By specifying the CLASS parameter for the TR tag, we are asking the browser to display the entire content of the row in the specified style. In other words, we are asking the browser to display all text in that TR in Arial Helvetica font (10 pt font size) in black with a pink background.

Note that the CLASS is a valid attribute of the TD tag as well, so you could use a different CLASS in each TD if you wish (that would override the CLASS in its parent TR tag). Note also that the background color (PINK) must be either a hexadecimal value or certain standard values (such as BLUE, RED, GREEN, etc.).

Save your changes, and double-click the HTML file to see it in the browser. You will see how the page looks much better with the font and style characteristics that you want.

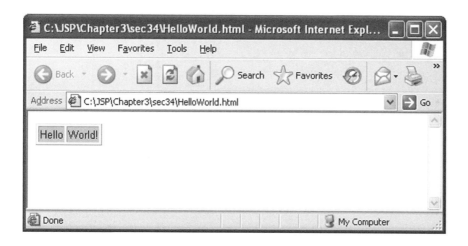

You can have a different style for each row, which means that you can create two styles for the two rows in our example of Section 3.3:

```
------------------------------------------------------------
<HTML>
    <HEAD>
        <STYLE>
            .myStyle1 { font-family:Helvetica,Arial; font-size:10pt; color:black;
                        background-color:PINK }
            .myStyle2 { font-family:Book,Antiqua; font-size:11pt; color:black;
                        font-weight:bold; background-color:CYAN }
        </STYLE>
    </HEAD>
    <BODY>
```

```
        <TABLE BORDER=1>
            <TR CLASS="myStyle1">
                <TD>Hello</TD><TD>World!</TD>
            </TR>
            <TR CLASS="myStyle2">
                <TD>Welcome</TD><TD>home!</TD>
            </TR>
        </TABLE>
    </BODY>
</HTML>
-----------------------------------------------------------
```

The page would now look like:

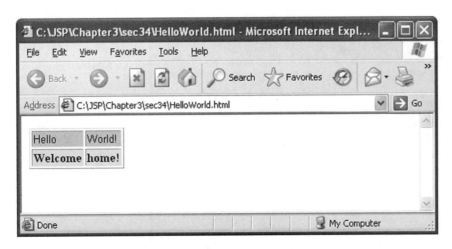

Instead of limiting yourself to a few standard colors (such as PINK, CYAN, BLUE, etc.), you can use more subtle color combinations specified in the hexadecimal color specification for Red, Green, and Blue. To get the hexadecimal spec for a color you want, you can either use software such as Paint, or go to some Web sites (such as http://www.yvg.com/twrs/RGBConverter.html) that convert it for you. For example, a hexadecimal spec for a color may look like: #FFEBFF, so to use this color in myStyle1, you would simply replace PINK with #FFEBFF as follows:

```
.myStyle1 { font-family:Helvetica,Arial; font-size:10pt; color:black;
            background-color:#FFEBFF }
```

The page would now look like this:

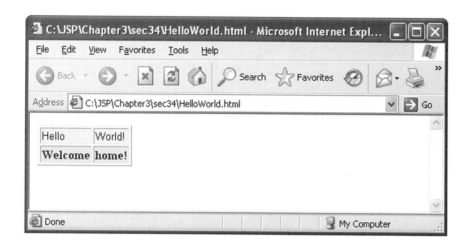

As you add more styles under the <STYLE> tag, the HTML file tends to get cluttered. One way to avoid this is to use the <LINK> tag. You move the individual styles into a separate file with a .css extension and then replace the <STYLE> tag in HelloWorld.html with the <LINK> tag. Say that you move the styles into a file called styles.css in the same folder as HelloWorld.html. The contents of styles.css would be as follows:

```
--------------------------------------
.myStyle1 { font-family:Helvetica,Arial; font-size:10pt; color:black;
            background-color:PINK }
.myStyle2 { font-family:Book,Antiqua; font-size:11pt; color:black;
            font-weight:bold; background-color:CYAN }
--------------------------------------
```

The <LINK> tag in HelloWorld.html would then look like this:

```
<LINK REL="stylesheet" TYPE="text/css" HREF="styles.css" />
```

which needs to be nested under the <HEAD> tag. You refer to the styles in the TR tags the same as before; the final result would look exactly same, but the HTML is cleaner. Also, all styles are stored in one place, so there is no need to repeat them in every HTML file and changes to styles are easier to maintain.

3.4.1 The SPAN tag

CSS can be applied to stand-alone text as well, not just to text in a table cell. To do this, you need to use the SPAN tag, which also has a CLASS attribute. For example, you can have a style called default-Text and the SPAN tag used as follows:

```
-----------------------------------------------------------------------
<HTML>
    <HEAD>
        <STYLE>
            .defaultText { font-family:Helvetica,Arial; font-size:10pt; color:black;
                           font-weight:bold; font-style:italic }
        </STYLE>
    </HEAD>
    <BODY>
      <SPAN CLASS="defaultText">This is bold text using SPAN tag!</SPAN>
    </BODY>
</HTML>
-----------------------------------------------------------------------
```

Save the file as `TestSpan.html`; it will appear as shown here.

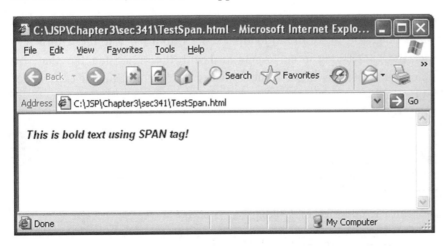

Contrast this with using the `<B>` and `<I>` tags. (Isn't this neat and powerful?) The HTML reference site I gave in Section 3.2 provides a full list of CSS attributes as well.

3.5   HTML Forms

Whatever HTML we have discussed so far only allows you to display text to the user. But in a real Web page, you may want to accept input from the user (such as name and address), and possibly store or process that kind of data. HTML forms allow you to do just that—to accept input from the user and pass it on to your server so that it can store or process it as necessary.

An HTML form represents the HTML equivalent of the physical "form" you so often see in real life—for example, filling out a new patient form at a doctor's office or an application for admission to a university. In other words, an HTML form consists of one or more input fields in which the user enters the necessary information. For example, you could have an input field for first name and another for last name.

The input field in a form is defined using the <INPUT> tag. This tag has several attributes, as do other HTML tags. The <INPUT> tag has the following important attributes:

NAME: Specifies a name to identify this input field.

TYPE: Specifies the type of the input field, such as text (for a text field), checkbox (for checkbox).

VALUE: Specifies an initial value for this input field (optional).

Let's go ahead and see how a form with input fields looks. Say that you have only two fields: First Name and Last Name. Call the file Login.html, which would have the following HTML:

```
------------------------------------------------------------
<!-- Begin: Login.html -->
<HTML>
    <BODY>
        <FORM>
            First name:<INPUT TYPE="text" NAME="firstName"></INPUT><BR>
            Last name:<INPUT TYPE="text" NAME="lastName"></INPUT>
        </FORM>
    </BODY>
</HTML>
<!-- End: Login.html -->
------------------------------------------------------------
```

You will notice that you now have a form with two input fields, named firstName and lastName. You can name the form as well, for which you need to use the NAME attribute on the <FORM> tag. It is useful to name your form in order to distinguish it from other forms that may be in your HTML page. Let's say you named your form main. So your HTML line would be:

```
<FORM NAME="main">
```

instead of

```
<FORM>
```

Double-click this file in Windows Explorer; you will see two input text fields that allow you to enter first and last name, as shown here.

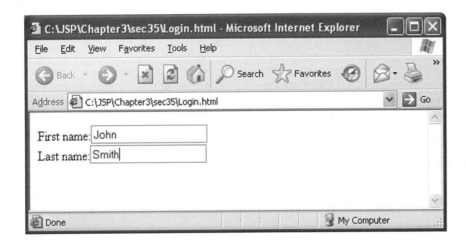

Note that the <INPUT> tag can be of different types. When you say: TYPE=text, you mean a text input field—one that allows you to enter text such as first name or last name. Other types of <INPUT> tags could be checkboxes (TYPE="checkbox"), radio buttons (TYPE="radio"), and submit buttons (TYPE="submit").

3.5.1   Submitting an HTML Form

As we noted earlier, an HTML form allows you to collect input from the user (from the client's browser) and send it to the server, where you can process that data or store it in a database for future retrieval. The form we just saw simply does the first part—namely, it accepts data inputs from the user for fields named firstName and lastName, but does not really submit any data to the server. In other words, we have not seen how and where that data is sent to. This is the second part, for which we need two additional changes to our HTML form:

- Add the INPUT button with TYPE="submit".
- Add the ACTION attribute in the FORM tag.

Let's look at each aspect separately.

A submit button is the one that enables you to actually send the input information from the form to the server. Clicking on the Submit button generates a sequence of instructions to the browser to take all the information from the form and transmit it to the form's destination URL, which is contained in its ACTION attribute.

If your form is to display a submit button that users can click to provide their information, you need to add an INPUT tag with TYPE="submit". The following line should be added after the two INPUT fields for first and last name:

```
<INPUT TYPE="submit" value="Submit"></INPUT>
```

Note that the part VALUE="Submit" inside the submit INPUT tag is optional; it only allows you to change the text label that shows up on the Submit button. (If you do not have the VALUE attribute in your submit INPUT tag, the default text: Submit Query would show up as the label on the submit button.)

After adding the submit button, Login.html would look like this:

```
---------------------------------------------------------------
<!-- Begin: Login.html -->
<HTML>
    <BODY>
        <FORM NAME="main">
            First name:<INPUT TYPE="text" NAME="firstName"></INPUT><BR>
            Last name:<INPUT TYPE="text" NAME="lastName"></INPUT><BR>
            <INPUT TYPE="submit" value="Submit"></INPUT>
        </FORM>
    </BODY>
</HTML>
<!-- End: Login.html -->
---------------------------------------------------------------
```

Open this file in the browser. Notice that it now shows a submit button at the bottom. Enter some values in the first and last name fields, and hit the Submit button. It will not do anything useful; it simply stays on the same page.

The reason is that your FORM tag is missing an important attribute called the ACTION attribute, which should contain the URL you want it to go to, after the form is submitted. That URL should be such that it can take the input from the form on the original page, process that information, and return back an appropriate response. Such a URL is usually a JSP page, or ASP, or a servlet that can process the input data from the request. (We will see how that is done in Chapter 4.) For now, we will consider a simple case where the ACTION URL is another HTML page (welcome.html) that will not process the input data but will simply display a static message: Welcome, you have reached the second page! no matter what the input first and last names are. Welcome.html will reside in the same folder as Login.html and will contain the following HTML:

```
---------------------------------------------------------------
<!-- Begin: Welcome.html -->
<HTML>
    <BODY>
        Welcome, you have reached the second page!
    </BODY>
</HTML>
<!-- End: Welcome.html -->
---------------------------------------------------------------
```

Now that you want your form on Login.html to go to Welcome.html, you need to modify the form tag on Login.html to add the ACTION attribute as follows:

```
<FORM NAME="main" ACTION="Welcome.html">
```

So your Login.html would now look like this:

```
---------------------------------------------------------------
<!-- Begin: Login.html -->
<HTML>
    <BODY>
        <FORM NAME="main" ACTION="Welcome.html">
            First name:<INPUT TYPE="text" NAME="firstName"></INPUT><BR>
            Last name:<INPUT TYPE="text" NAME="lastName"></INPUT><BR>
            <INPUT TYPE="submit" value="Submit"></INPUT>
        </FORM>
    </BODY>
</HTML>
<!-- End: Login.html -->
---------------------------------------------------------------
```

Try it out with these changes: Double-click on Login.html, so it opens in your browser, showing the first and last name fields. Enter some values in these fields, then hit the Submit button. It should take you to Welcome.html that displays the static text: Welcome, you have reached the second page!

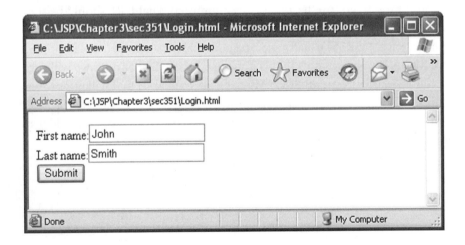

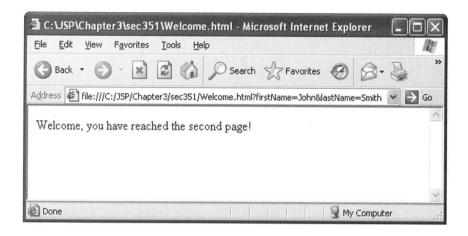

Solved Exercise 3.5.1

Objective: To practice the use of HTML forms and INPUT fields.

Steps:

- Copy Login.html and Welcome.html from Section 3.5.1 into a new folder exer351 under C:\JSP\Chapter3.

- Modify Login.html so that it shows two INPUT fields called username and password (instead of firstName and lastName). For the username field, use TYPE="text", but for the password field, use TYPE="password" (so when the user types in the password, it does not display the actual characters typed in).

Solution:

```
<!-- Begin: Login.html -->
<HTML>
    <BODY>
        <FORM NAME="main" ACTION="Welcome.html">
            User name:<INPUT TYPE="text" NAME="username"></INPUT><BR>
            Password:<INPUT TYPE="password" NAME="password"></INPUT><BR>
            <INPUT TYPE="submit" value="Submit"></INPUT>
        </FORM>
    </BODY>
</HTML>
<!-- End: Login.html -->
```

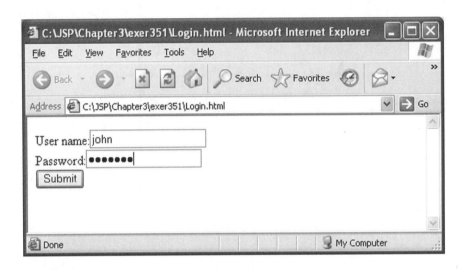

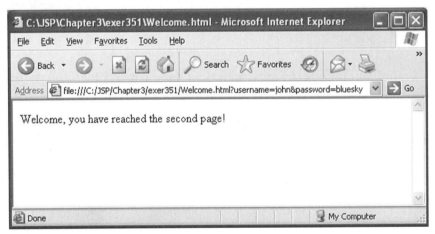

3.5.2   GET and POST

The HTTP request can be of two types: GET and POST. By default, it is a GET, which means that the requester is asking for a file on the server and that input parameters, if any, need to be appended at the end of the URL itself. We will see what input parameters are, and how to append them to the URL in Section 3.5.3. All requests we have seen so far are GETs. We will discuss POST toward the end of Section 3.5.3.

3.5.3   Request Parameters and Request Type

When the HTML form is submitted, we want the input supplied by the user on the form to be transmitted to the server so that it can process that information and return an appropriate response. This information can be sent as additional name-value pairs attached to the requested URL (Welcome.html in the previous example). A name-value pair consists of the parameter name, followed by an equal (=) sign, followed by the value of that parameter. For example, a first name of "John" entered by the user could be sent in a name-value pair as firstName=John. A URL for Welcome.html that has this name-value pair attached to its end should put the name-value pair after a question mark (?) at the end of the original URL, so it would look like this:

```
C:/JSP/Chapter3/Welcome.html?firstName=John
```

Similarly, a name-value pair for a last name of "Smith" would look like lastName=Smith. Both of these name-value pairs can be sent at the same time by separating them by the ampersand (&) sign, as follows:

```
C:/JSP/Chapter3/Welcome.html?firstName=John&lastName=Smith
```

In the case of the Login.html file in Section 3.5.1, notice that when you are on the second page Welcome.html, the address box of the browser shows

```
file:///C:/JSP/Chapter3/sec351/Welcome.html?firstName=John&lastName=Smith
```

(where John and Smith would be replaced with the exact values you entered in the first and last name fields of Login.html). The request type is still a GET, but now we have parameters appended to the end of the URL.

Sending the input parameters is useful in those situations where the response should depend on what those parameters are. For example, you may want to send a response that changes based on what the first and last names entered by the user are. So if the input first name is "John" and the last name is "Smith," you would want the response to be: Welcome, John Smith, you have reached the second page! If the input first name is "Mike" and the last name is "Taylor," you want the response to change, and say: Welcome, Mike Taylor, you have reached the second page! Here the response is *dynamic*—that is, it changes based on whatever input is supplied on the previous page.

Also notice how the parameters are sent from the immediately preceding HTML page. You cannot send parameters for user input entered more than one page in the past. Let's say the user enters input on page1.html, submits it, which takes him to page2.html, where he enters some more information and submits it, which takes him to page3.html. In this case, the request for page3.html can only have attached to it the parameters entered on page2.html, and not from page1.html. HTTP is therefore called "stateless"—it has a very short-term memory consisting of only the immediately preceding page. The server does not know that these two requests came from the same client because every request-response pair is treated as a separate transaction.

Processing the user input sent to the server consists of two parts:

A: the client needs to send the input information to the server.

B: the server needs to use that information to create a dynamic response.

We will only look at part (A) here; part (B) requires the use of a .jsp or servlet (or .asp) file that we will look at later.

The way the input information is sent to the server depends on the request type:

- In case of a GET, this is done by appending the parameters to the end of the URL requested.
- In case of a POST, all INPUT type fields on HTML form(s) on the immediately preceding page are automatically sent hidden in the request.

When a GET occurs, user input is appended as name-value pairs at the end of the URL. In our example, Welcome.html receives the parameters firstName and lastName as parameters at the end of the URL, but since it is a plain HTML file, it cannot use or process that information in any way. You need a .jsp or .asp file to be able to process such information. This is part (B), mentioned earlier. We will see how it is done when we look at form processing using JSPs.

As mentioned earlier, the request sent to the server can be of two types—GET and POST. The request type is a GET by default. A GET requires that any parameters be appended to the end of the URL, but there is a limit to the number of characters that may be appended in this way. For example, you may have a huge description type field that exceeds the limits and would get truncated if appended to the end of the URL. Also, the parameters are visible as part of the URL itself, so it is very insecure when you want to send parameters such as a password. Finally, you may have special characters in the values being sent; for example, the value itself may contain an ampersand (&) or question mark (?), in which case they need to be properly encoded before appending to the URL, a process that can give rise to errors if not done properly.

As a solution to these problems, a second type, called a POST, is available. In a POST, the name-value pairs are not appended to the end of the URL; instead, all INPUT field values on HTML form(s) get sent as parameters hidden in the request. To make the request a POST, you must explicitly set the METHOD attribute of the FORM tag to POST. Copy Login.html and Welcome.html from Section 3.5.1 into a new folder sec353. Modify Login.html so that it looks as follows:

```
------------------------------------------------------------
<!-- Begin: Login.html -->
<HTML>
    <BODY>
        <FORM NAME="main" ACTION="Welcome.html" METHOD=POST>
            First name:<INPUT TYPE="text" NAME="firstName"></INPUT><BR>
            Last name:<INPUT TYPE="text" NAME="lastName"></INPUT><BR>
            <INPUT TYPE="submit" value="Submit"></INPUT>
        </FORM>
    </BODY>
</HTML>
<!-- End: Login.html -->
------------------------------------------------------------
```

Open this file in your browser, enter values in the first and last name fields, and hit the submit button. You will notice that the Web address for Welcome.html no longer has the parameters appended at the end of the URL.

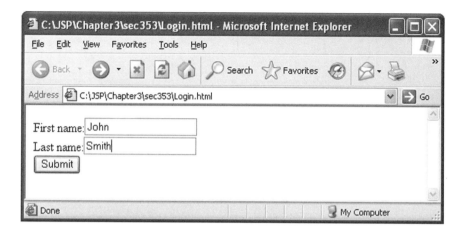

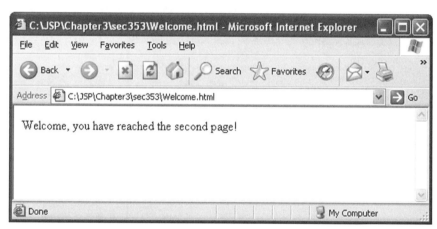

With a POST, the request still contains the firstName and lastName attributes hidden in it, although these are not appended to the end of the URL. Since the destination URL is HTML (Welcome.html), it cannot extract that information from the request.

Solved Exercise 3.5.3

Objective: To learn how to send parameters from an HTML form as a POST.

Steps:

- Copy Login.html and Welcome.html from Solved Exercise 3.5.1 into a new folder exer353 under C:\JSP\Chapter3.

- Modify Login.html so that it submits the form as a POST instead of a GET.

- Verify that the browser does not append the input parameters at the end of the form's destination URL (Welcome.html).

Solution:

```
<!-- Begin: Login.html -->
<HTML>
    <BODY>
        <FORM NAME="main" ACTION="Welcome.html" METHOD="POST">
            User name:<INPUT TYPE="text" NAME="username"></INPUT><BR>
            Password:<INPUT TYPE="password" NAME="password"></INPUT><BR>
            <INPUT TYPE="submit" value="Submit"></INPUT>
        </FORM>
    </BODY>
</HTML>
<!-- End: Login.html -->
```

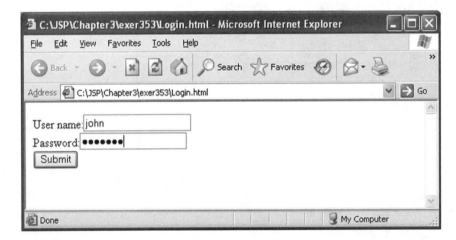

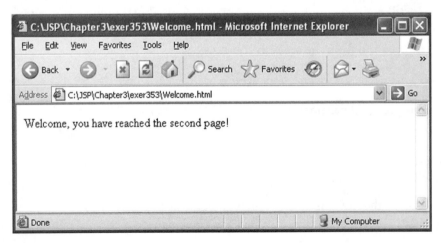

3.5.4 Using HTML Tables with HTML Forms

The first and last name fields may not be exactly aligned in this example. You could use the `<TABLE>` tag in conjunction with the `<FORM>` tag to achieve alignment of the fields, as follows:

```
-----------------------------------------------------------------------------------------
<!-- Begin: Login.html -->
<HTML>
    <HEAD>
        <STYLE>
            .defaultText { font-family:Helvetica,Arial; font-size:10pt; }
        </STYLE>
    </HEAD>
    <BODY>
        <FORM NAME="main" ACTION="Welcome.html" METHOD=POST>
            <TABLE>
                <TR CLASS="defaultText">
                    <TD>First name:</TD>
                    <TD><INPUT TYPE="text" NAME="firstName"></INPUT></TD>
                </TR>
                <TR CLASS="defaultText">
                    <TD>Last name:</TD>
                    <TD><INPUT TYPE="text" NAME="lastName"></INPUT></TD>
                </TR>
                <TR>
                    <TD colspan=2><INPUT TYPE="submit" VALUE="Submit"></INPUT></TD>
                </TR>
            </TABLE>
        </FORM>
    </BODY>
</HTML>
<!-- End: Login.html -->
-----------------------------------------------------------------------------------------
```

The login page would now look as shown here (notice how the fields are more aligned and the label text is better formatted than before):

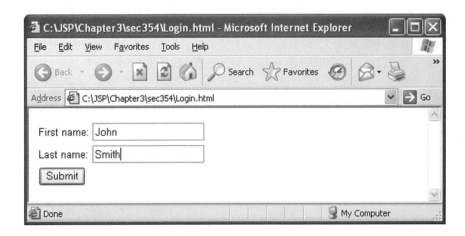

Also notice how you embed <INPUT> fields inside <TD> tags. So <TD> tags can contain either plain text or other tags, such as <INPUT>, or even other <TABLE> or <FORM> tags (in which case you would have nested <TABLE> or <FORM> tags respectively).

3.5.5   The Checkbox Type Form Element

We will look at the checkbox as an example of form controls—INPUT elements that you can click on to change their values, instead of typing in the text. Note that these "clickable" INPUT elements represent input data that also needs to get transmitted to the server. For creating a checkbox type input, you simply need to say TYPE="checkbox" instead of TYPE="text" in your <INPUT> tag. By default, a checkbox has a value of "on" when selected (or checked), but you can change this default to whatever you wish using its VALUE attribute.

For example, say that you have an HTML form that has three input fields, each a checkbox, that represent three products being offered: a pen, a pencil, and an eraser. We will also allow the user to input the quantities required for each item in text boxes. The quantities should default to 1 when the page comes up the first time. This is achieved by using VALUE=1 inside the INPUT TYPE="text" quantity fields. The use of a few more (optional) attributes of the checkbox type INPUT field is as follows:

- The SIZE attribute in an INPUT element limits the field width to the specified number of characters. So if you say SIZE=3 for the quantity INPUT field, the user cannot enter more than 999 as the quantity.

- The VALUE attribute in an INPUT element sets its default value.

Save the following HTML in a file called ShowAllItems.html under C:\JSP\Chapter3\sec355 and double-click it to see the form in your browser.

```
-------------------------------------------------------------------------------------------------
<!-- Begin: ShowAllItems.html -->
<HTML>
    <HEAD>
        <STYLE TYPE="text/css">
            .defaultText { font-family:Helvetica,Arial; font-size:10pt; }
            .tableEvenRow { font-family:Helvetica,Arial; font-size:9pt;
                            background-color:#E6E6E6; }
            .tableOddRow { font-family:Helvetica,Arial; font-size:9pt; }
        </STYLE>
    </HEAD>
    <BODY>
        <FORM NAME="main" ACTION="ThankYou.html" METHOD="POST">
            <TABLE ALIGN="center">
                <TR CLASS="tableEvenRow">
                    <TD></TD> <TD>Item #</TD>
                    <TD>Item Name</TD>
                    <TD>Price</TD>
                    <TD>Quantity</TD>
                </TR>
                <TR CLASS="tableOddRow">
                    <TD><INPUT TYPE="checkbox" NAME="penSelect"</INPUT></TD>
                    <TD>101</TD>
                    <TD>Pen</TD>
                    <TD>$2.00</TD>
                    <TD>
                        <INPUT TYPE="text" NAME="penQty" size="3" value="1"></INPUT>
                    </TD>
                </TR>
                <TR CLASS="tableEvenRow">
                    <TD><INPUT TYPE="checkbox" NAME="pencilSelect"</INPUT></TD>
                    <TD>102</TD>
                    <TD>Pencil</TD>
                    <TD>$1.00</TD>
                    <TD>
                        <INPUT  TYPE="text" NAME="pencilQty" size="3" value="1"></INPUT>
                    </TD>
                </TR>
                <TR CLASS="tableOddRow">
                    <TD><INPUT TYPE="checkbox" NAME="eraserSelect"</INPUT></TD>
                    <TD>103</TD>
                    <TD>Eraser</TD>
```

```
                    <TD>$0.50</TD>
                    <TD>
                        <INPUT TYPE="text" NAME="eraserQty" size="3" value="1"></INPUT>
                    </TD>
                </TR>
                <TR>
                    <TD ALIGN="center" COLSPAN=5>
                        <INPUT TYPE="submit" VALUE="Submit"></INPUT>
                    </TD>
                </TR>
            </TABLE>
        </FORM>
    </BODY>
</HTML>
<!-- End: ShowAllItems.html -->
```

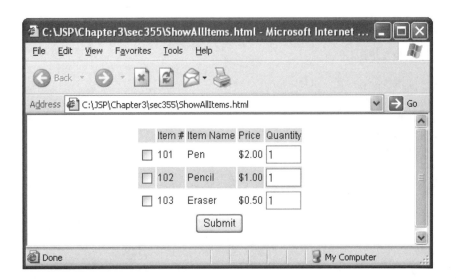

3.6   JavaScript

3.6.1   The Need for JavaScript

Many times users enter invalid data or leave required fields empty before they hit the submit button. This can cause problems when processing the data in the server. For example, if Social Security number is a required field and the user does not enter any value in that field and hits the submit button, the server will not be able to process such "invalid" data. To ensure that the data is valid and all required fields have been entered before the submit button is hit, you can use JavaScript in the HTML pages that runs on the client (browser) to pop up error messages if any data is invalid. JavaScript is a full-fledged topic by itself, and since this book is primarily on learning JSP, we will only be looking at some elementary JavaScript to do form validation. In most cases, it will be assumed that all required data has been properly entered before hitting the submit button.

To see Javascript in action, say that the user goes to Login.html and hits submit without entering the first name. As mentioned earlier, our "valid login" consists of entering nonempty values in the first and last name fields. So if the first name and/or last name is empty, we need to check for that and show an error message to the user to prompt him or her to enter any missing, required fields. In other words, we need to have some mechanism on the client (browser) that validates the form before it is submitted. JavaScript is the language of choice for such client-level validation; it runs inside your browser. Note that once you hit the submit button on a form, it goes to the server, whereas clicking on any other kinds of buttons, checkboxes, text or boxes keeps you on the client's browser only. JavaScript usually consists of one or more functions that process the form fields and validate them.

3.6.2   Where to Place JavaScript Functions

Recall that the <HEAD> tag is meant for putting functions common to the entire page in one place. JavaScript functions need to be written within special <SCRIPT> .. </SCRIPT> tags placed inside the <HEAD> .. </HEAD> tags. Since JavaScript is just one of the several client-level scripting languages, you need to specify to the SCRIPT tag that the scripting language you are using is JavaScript. For this, the <SCRIPT> tag has an attribute called LANGUAGE. To set it to JavaScript, you would say

```
<SCRIPT LANGUAGE="JAVASCRIPT">
. . .
</SCRIPT>
```

3.6.3   JavaScript Object Hierarchy

For referring to the form and its input fields, JavaScript uses a predefined object hierarchy—a set of predefined objects that you can freely use inside your JavaScript without instantiating or defining it. These objects are as follows:

window:	The current Web page that is encapsulated in a predefined object.
document:	A window object has an attribute called document that represents the displayable part of the window.
forms, form:	Each document can have zero or more "form" objects, with each form object representing the HTML form that you define. If you have multiple HTML forms

inside your Web page, you can access them as a set, using another object called "`forms`." (Note the "s" makes it a collection of several forms.) For referring to a specific `form` object in the `forms` collection, you need to specify the `form` name (same as the name attribute used in the `<FORM>` tag).

`elements:`   Each input field on the form represents an "`element`," and all elements put together are referred to as `elements`. You do not normally need to use these objects (`elements` or `element`); you can instead directly refer to each form element by its name. The `elements` object is useful when you want to loop through all form elements.

3.6.4   Using the Dot Operator to Get the Right JavaScript Object

JavaScript objects follow an object hierarchy, so if you want to refer to any predefined object, you simply need to use the dot operator (.) to specify the exact path to get to that object—just as you do in Java. Some examples are shown in the following table.

Object	How you will refer to it in Javascript
window	`window`
document	`window.document`, or simply `document`
forms	`window.document.forms` or simply, `document.forms`
Specific form object (say, form NAME = "main")	`window.document.forms.main`, or simply `document.forms.main`, or even `document.main`
elements (say, form NAME = "main")	`window.document.main.element` or simply, `document.forms.main.elements`
Specific 'element' (say, `<INPUT TYPE = "text" NAME = "firstName">`)	`window.document.main.firstName` or simply, `document.main.firstName`

Let's add a JavaScript function called `validate()` that would check for the form fields (`firstName` and `lastName`) and pop up an "alert" (error) message if either field is empty. An `INPUT` button-type field has an `onclick` attribute that you can set to the JavaScript function name you want to invoke whenever the user clicks on that button. In this case, we want validation to occur at the form level—that is, after all fields on the form have been entered and the user submits the form. The JavaScript function `validate()` will look at each field on the form and make sure the value in each field satisfies the validation rules. So, we will use

```
onclick="return validate()"
```

for the INPUT submit button because we want it to go through the form validating JavaScript function validate() before the form is submitted to the server. If errors are found, we want it to return false. In that case, it will not go ahead to submit the form to the server, but instead, will pop up an error message using the alert statement. Login.html would now look like this:

```
----------------------------------------------------------------------------------
<!-- Begin: Login.html -->
<HTML>
    <HEAD>
        <STYLE>
            .defaultText { font-family:Helvetica,Arial; font-size:10pt; }
        </STYLE>
        <SCRIPT LANGUAGE="JAVASCRIPT">
            function validate()
            {
                if (document.forms.main.firstName.value == "")
                {
                    alert("First Name cannot be empty.");
                    return false;
                }
                else if (document.forms.main.lastName.value == "")
                {
                    alert("Last Name cannot be empty.");
                    return false;
                }
                return true;
            }
        </SCRIPT>
    </HEAD>
    <BODY>
        <FORM NAME="main" ACTION="Welcome.html" METHOD="POST">
            <TABLE>
                <TR CLASS="defaultText">
                    <TD>First name:</TD>
                    <TD><INPUT TYPE="text" NAME="firstName"></INPUT></TD>
                </TR>
                <TR CLASS="defaultText">
                    <TD>Last name:</TD>
                    <TD><INPUT TYPE="text" NAME="lastName"></INPUT></TD>
                </TR>
                <TR>
                    <TD COLSPAN=2 ALIGN="center">
```

```
                    <INPUT TYPE="submit" VALUE="Submit"
                  onclick="return validate()"></INPUT>
                </TD>
              </TR>
            </TABLE>
          </FORM>
      </BODY>
</HTML>
<!-- End: Login.html -->
```

Double-click this file, enter only the first name, leave last name empty, and hit the submit button. It will pop up an error message as follows. Validation prevents you from proceeding further until its rules are met.

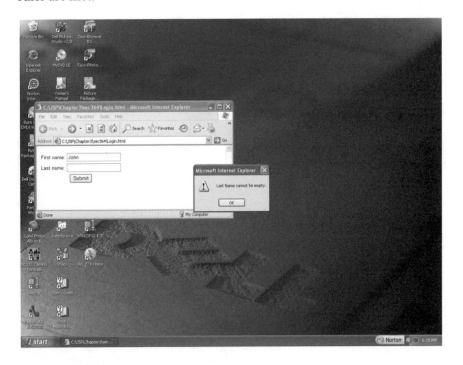

3.7   Summary

In this chapter, you learned how the Internet works and how to write HTML pages and format display using HTML tables and style sheets, how to pass values from one HTML page to another using HTML forms, and how to validate form data using JavaScript. In the next chapter, you will be learning how servlets can be used to process the values sent from HTML forms to create "dynamic" content.

3.8   Chapter Quiz

1. Which of the following is true? (Select all that apply.)

    i. Whenever you type in a Web address in your browser, you are actually requesting a file on a server computer.

    ii. A Web server is a piece of software that runs on the server computer.

    iii. A tag is one or more characters enclosed in angle brackets (< and >) that the browser knows how to interpret and display.

    iv. Every HTML start tag must have a corresponding end tag.

    v. A relative file path is the path relative to the location of the current file in which such a path appears.

    a. All of the above

    b. (i), (ii), and (v) only

    c. (ii) and (iv) only

    d. (i), (ii), (iii), and (v) only

2. Which of the following is true? (Select all that apply.)

    i. HTML tables are useful for formatting and laying out the content, and style sheets are used to make the content more pleasing in appearance.

    ii. A TD tag can never enclose a TABLE tag, but a TABLE tag can always enclose a TD tag.

    iii. A space in HTML is represented as .

    iv. When you use the anchor tag (<A>), the request always goes to the server as a GET.

    v. When you submit an HTML form, it always goes to the URL specified in the form's action as a POST.

    vi. You can have more than one HTML form in a single HTML file.

    a. All of the above

    b. (i) and (iii) only

    c. (i), (ii), (iii), (iv), and (v) only

    d. (i), (iii), (iv), and (vi) only

3. Which of the following is true? (Select all that apply.)

    i. JavaScript runs on the Web server.

    ii. JavaScript is useful for validating HTML form data.

    iii. JavaScript functions are usually placed in a `<SCRIPT>` tag within the `<HEAD>` tag.

    iv. To refer to an input field named `firstName` in an HTML form named `main`, you can say: `document.forms.main.firstName`

  a. All of the above

  b. (i), (ii), and (iv) only

  c. (ii), (iii), and (iv) only

  d. (ii) and (iii) only

4. Say that you have a file called `File1.html` under `C:\JSP\Chapter3` and another file called `File2.html` under `C:\JSP\Chapter3\section31`. Which of the following are valid ways of specifying the `HREF` in the anchor tag in `File1.html`?

    i. `<A HREF="section31/File2.html">Click here</A>`

    ii. `<A HREF="/section31/File2.html">Click here</A>`

    iii. `<A HREF="C:/JSP/Chapter3/section31/File2.html">Click here</A>`

    iv. `<A HREF="../Chapter3/section31/File2.html">Click here</A>`

    v. `<A HREF="./section31/File2.html">Click here</A>`

  a. All of the above

  b. (i), (iii), (iv), and (v) only

  c. (i), (ii), and (iii) only

  d. (i), (iii), and (iv) only

5. What would happen if you entered some value in the `username` field, entered a value of length 3 characters in the `password` field, and hit submit on the following HTML page?

```
<!-- Begin: Login.html -->
<HTML>
    <HEAD>
        <STYLE>
            .defaultText {font-family:Helvetica,Arial; font-size:10pt; }
        </STYLE>
        <SCRIPT LANGUAGE="JAVASCRIPT">
            function validate()
            {
                if (document.main.username.value == "")
```

```
                {
                    alert("Username cannot be empty.");
                    return false;
                }
                else if (document.forms.main.password.value == "")
                {
                    alert("Password cannot be empty.");
                    return false;
                }
                return true;
            }
            function checkLength(obj)
            {
                if (obj.value.length <= 3)
                {
                    alert("Password must be more than 3 characters in length.");
                    return false;
                }
                return true;
            }
        </SCRIPT>
    </HEAD>
    <BODY>
        <FORM NAME="main" ACTION="Welcome.html">
            <TABLE>
                <TR CLASS="defaultText">
                    <TD>User name:</TD>
                    <TD><INPUT TYPE="text" NAME="username"></INPUT></TD>
                </TR>
                <TR CLASS="defaultText">
                    <TD>Password:</TD>
                    <TD>
                        <INPUT TYPE="password" NAME="password"
                                onchange="return checkLength(this)"></INPUT>
                    </TD>
                </TR>
                <TR>
                    <TD COLSPAN=2 ALIGN="center">
                        <INPUT TYPE="submit" VALUE="Submit"
                                onclick="return validate()"></INPUT>
                    </TD>
                </TR>
            </TABLE>
        </FORM>
```

```
        </BODY>
    </HTML>
    <!-- End: Login.html -->
```

a. It will show an alert message "Password must be more than 3 characters in length." but when you click OK on the alert pop-up, it submits the form.

b. It will show an alert message "Password must be more than 3 characters in length." When you click OK on the alert pop-up, it remains on the same page without submitting the form.

c. It will give a JavaScript error because one or more statements inside checkLength() function have invalid syntax.

d. It will give a JavaScript error because the way the checkLength() function is called for onchange event is not right.

3.9   Answers to Quiz

1. The correct answer is (d). All statements except (iv) are true. Option (iv) is false because some HTML tags do not need an end tag (the <BR> tag, for example).

2. The correct answer is (d). All statements except (ii) and (v) are true. Option (ii) is false because a TD tag can enclose another TABLE tag. Option (v) is false because you could specify METHOD="GET" for a form, in which case it would go as a GET instead of a POST.

3. The correct answer is (c). All statements except (i) are true. Option (i) is false because JavaScript runs on the browser, not the Web server.

4. The correct answer is (b). All statements except (ii) are valid. Option (ii) is not valid because putting a slash (/) in the beginning means the root directory, so it would expect a folder called section31 directly under the root directory.

5. The correct answer is (b). It will show an alert message "Password must be more than 3 characters in length." When you click OK on the alert pop-up, it remains on the same page without submitting the form.

3.10   Unsolved Assignments

Assignment 3.1

Objective: To practice the use of cascading style sheets.

Steps:

- Create a new folder called assign31 under C:\JSP\Chapter3. Copy CustomerReport.html from Solved Exercise 3.3 into it.

- Create your own style for each type of row in the customer table, as shown here.

  - The main title (Customer Report) should appear in the following style:

    ```
    -------------------------------------------------
    Style name: headerStyle
    Font: Arial, Helvetica
    Font size: 12 pt
    Font color: #009000
    Font weight: bold
    Font background color: #E0FFE0
    -------------------------------------------------
    ```

  - The subheader (Name Age . . .) should appear in the following style:

    ```
    -------------------------------------------------
    Style name: subHeaderStyle
    Font: Arial, Helvetica
    Font size: 10 pt
    Font color: black
    Font weight: bold
    Font background color: #E0FFFF
    -------------------------------------------------
    ```

  - Odd-numbered data rows in the table should appear in the following style:

    ```
    -------------------------------------------------
    Style name: oddRowStyle
    Font: Arial, Helvetica
    Font size: 10 pt
    Font color: black
    Font background color: #FFEBFF
    -------------------------------------------------
    ```

  - Even-numbered data rows in the table should appear in the following style:

    ```
    -------------------------------------------------
    Style name: evenRowStyle
    Font: Arial, Helvetica
    Font size: 10 pt
    Font color: black
    Font background color: #FFEBDD
    -------------------------------------------------
    ```

- The summary row at the bottom should appear in the following style:

```
------------------------------------------------
Style name: summaryRowStyle
Font: Arial, Helvetica
Font size: 10 pt
Font color: black
Font background color: :#D0D0FF
------------------------------------------------
```

So the page should look like this:

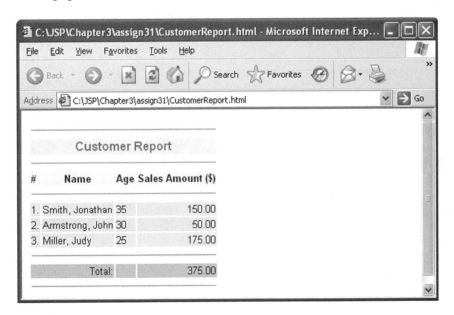

Assignment 3.2

Objective: **To practice relative URL's and passing data across HTML pages using HTML forms.**

Steps:

- Create a new folder: C:\JSP\Chapter3\assign32, with two subfolders under it: one called items (so its path would be C:\JSP\Chapter3\assign32\items), and another called common (so its path would be C:\JSP\Chapter3\assign32\common).

- Copy Login.html from Section 3.6.4 into C:\JSP\Chapter3\assign32, the ShowAllItems.html from Section 3.5.5 into C:\JSP\Chapter3\assign32\items, and Welcome.html from Section 3.5.1 into C:\JSP\Chapter3\assign32\common. Rename Welcome.html as ThankYou.html.

- **Login.html**

  Modify this file so that it shows two INPUT fields called username and password (instead of firstName and lastName). For the username field, use TYPE="text", but for the password field, use TYPE="password" (so when the user types in the password, it does not display the actual characters typed in). Name the form as main. When the user clicks on the submit button (after entering valid values in username and password fields), it should go to ShowAllItems.html under C:\JSP\Chapter3\assign32\items as a POST.

  Form-level validation (use JavaScript):

  - If either username or password is empty, it should show the pop-up error message: Username and password are required.

  - When the user enters a password value of 3 characters or less, it should show the error message: Password must be at least 4 characters.

- **ShowAllItems.html**

  ShowAllItems.html should show a message: Welcome to the Item Order page! at the top in bold font, centered on the page width, followed by a table of available items to offer (same as before). (*Hint:* To center a piece of text in the center of the page, use the <CENTER> tag.) For bold font, create a new style called boldText under the <STYLE> tag.).

  Form-level validation:

  - If the user does not check at least one checkbox and hits submit, a pop-up error message should state: At least one item must be selected. (*Hint:* To test whether a checkbox named x in a form named main is checked, test whether the JavaScript expression document.main.x.checked is equal to true.)

  - When the user selects at least one item and clicks on the submit button on ShowAllItems.html, the form should be submitted (as a POST) so that it goes to the file called ThankYou.html located in C:\JSP\Chapter3\assign32\common.

- **ThankYou.html**

  Should display the message: Thank you for your order! Following this, it should display two links:

  - A link that says: Login should allow the user to go back to the login page.

  - A link that says: "Continue shopping" should take the user to the ShowAllItems.html page.

  - Use your own style sheets to make it look professional.

    Note: You MUST use *relative* file paths throughout this assignment.

  - Submit Login.html, ShowAllItems.html, and ThankYou.html.

A sample interaction is shown here. User hits the Submit button without entering either username or password:

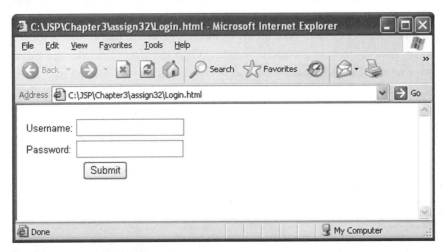

User enters username but no password, and hits Submit button:

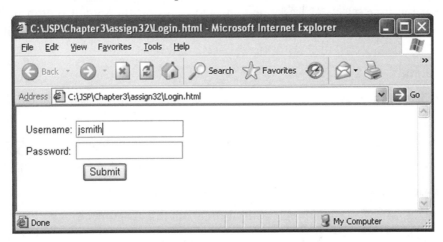

User enters password that is less than 4 characters in length:

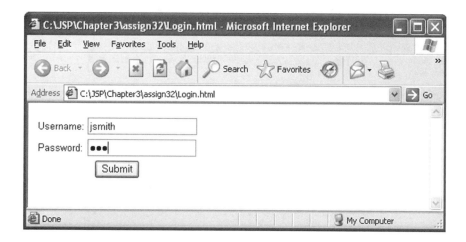

User enters password of 4 characters or more, and hits the Submit button:

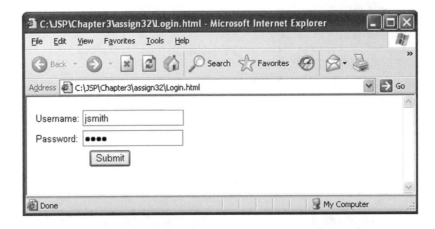

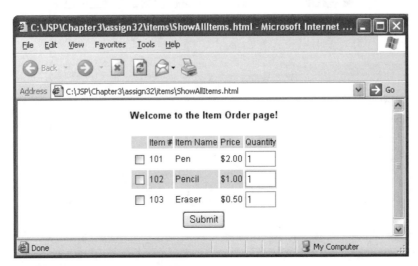

User clicks OK and selects a couple of items, fills in the quantities, and hits the Submit button:

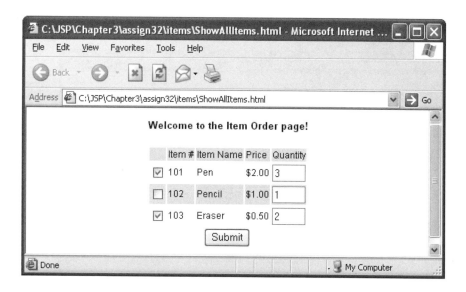

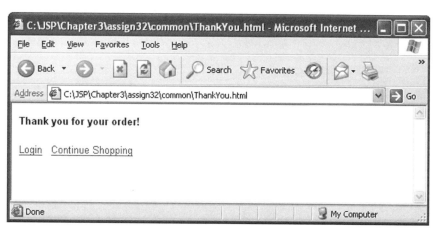

User clicks on Continue Shopping:

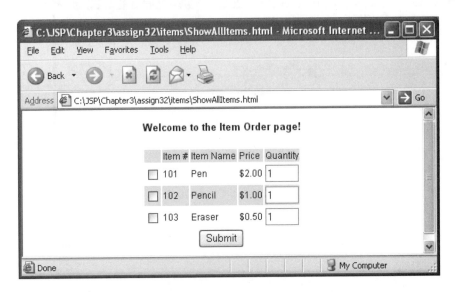

CHAPTER 4

Servlets

Chapter Objectives

- Learn how to create your own servlet class
- Know how to install, configure, and run the Tomcat Web Server
- Study how to create dynamic content using servlets
- Understand what a context and Web application mean
- Become familiar with document base and document root
- Learn what a deployment descriptor is
- Understand how a server configuration file is used
- Study URL patterns for servlets

4.1   Introducing Servlets

HTML forms can take input via their text-boxes, but they cannot process or use that information to create a dynamic response. One way to process input information is to have a **servlet**—a special piece of Java code that can extract information from a request and send the desired response back to the client. As we have seen in the past, the people at Sun seem to have a ready-made solution for every conceivable situation! Yes, for extracting input parameters from the request, they have ready-made packages that can deal with each protocol. For instance, for the HTTP protocol (which is what we have been seeing until now and is the most common—URLs that start with http:// follow the HTTP protocol), Sun has a convenient package called javax.servlet.http that has a useful class called HttpServlet you can use to write your own servlet. Note that the package name starts with javax rather than java—because it is considered an extension to Java. Also note that I said you write your own servlet—you cannot use the HttpServlet class as is since it is abstract. You thus need to define your own servlet class that extends from HttpServlet and customize it for the fields that you have on your form (such as firstName and lastName).

The destination URL on the HTML form that contains the user input fields would now point to your servlet. A servlet is simply a special kind of Java class that has a predefined structure, attributes, and methods, which are called in a specific, predefined sequence every time there is a request for the servlet (the sequence is already predetermined in the HttpServlet parent class). Two of the most important methods in a servlet class are doGet() and doPost(), which are automatically called from the parent HttpServlet class whenever there is a GET/POST type request for the servlet, respectively. These methods are called by the server (via the service() method) to allow a servlet to handle a GET/POST request respectively. If you want your servlet to display custom content, you need to override the doGet() or doPost() method(s) since these get called by the HttpServlet architecture.

Note that javax is part of J2EE or Java EE, and not part of J2SE or Java SE. Appendix D provides a documentation URL for J2EE/Java EE classes. On the Java EE API site, click on javax.servlet.http on the top-left frame, and you will see the HttpServlet class listed in the bottom-left frame. After you click on it, and it will display information about this class. Your HttpServlet subclass must override one of the following methods of HttpServlet class, if custom content is to be displayed:

- doGet() if your servlet supports HTTP GET requests
- doPost() if your servlet supports HTTP POST requests

When you override the doGet() or doPost() method in your servlet class, the server's call to doGet() / doPost() goes directly into your overridden version of the method, so it executes whatever instructions you put in one of those two methods. Recall that an overridden method in a child takes precedence over the one in the parent.

The way you override and use the doGet() and doPost() methods is similar, so I will explain it for the doGet() method as an example. To override the doGet() method, we need to understand its signature, which is defined in the HttpServlet class, as follows:

```
protected void doGet(HttpServletRequest req, HttpServletResponse resp)
            throws ServletException, IOException
```

Notice that it already has an HttpServletRequest parameter called req and an HttpServletResponse parameter called resp. The req parameter represents the current request that is being processed. Earlier we noted that the user-entered input on the HTML form is carried by the request, so all we need is a way of getting that information from the req parameter—and, you guessed it right, you have a ready-made method for that as well! It is called the getParameter() method declared in the HttpServletRequest interface class (actually in the ServletRequest interface that the HttpServletRequest interface extends from). To the getParameter() method, you pass in the name of the input field that you are looking for, and it returns the value entered by the user for that attribute. For example, for getting the user-entered value for <INPUT> field firstName on the HTML form, you would say

```
String firstName = req.getParameter("firstName");
```

and this would return whatever the user entered in the INPUT field named firstName on the immediately preceding HTML form that sent this request. Similarly, req.getParameter("lastName") would return the value entered in an INPUT field named lastName. The value returned by the getParameter() method is always of type String and would contain null if such a parameter does not exist on the request. In our example, we would have the HTML form on Login.html, whose ACTION should now point to our new servlet class, so the immediately preceding HTML form would be the HTML form in Login.html.

Ok—so we got the first and last names from the request, now what? The next thing is to create the dynamic response that would contain the first and last names in it. For this, you already have a handle on the response object—which is same as the resp parameter of type HttpServletResponse in the doGet() method. The HttpServletResponse class has a convenient method called getWriter() that returns an object of type java.io.PrintWriter. You use this object to write whatever HTML you want to be displayed on the client's browser. The method has the signature

```
public java.io.PrintWriter getWriter() throws java.io.IOException
```

Your call to this method in the doGet() may look like this:

```
PrintWriter out = resp.getWriter();
```

The PrintWriter object in the response is similar to the familiar System.out object. In both cases, you use the println() method to print a String; only thing is, the System.out would display the output on the server's console, whereas, the println() method of the PrintWriter object in the response prints it out onto the response itself, which transmits the printed content to the client where it gets displayed as HTML in the browser. Since the client can interpret only plain HTML, you must ensure that whatever String you ask the PrintWriter object to dump is plain HTML, or simply some text that can show up with no problems when enclosed in the <BODY> . . . </BODY> tags.

Let's look at an example of the servlet class in order to understand how this works. Say that you want to create a very simple servlet that simply dumps the text Hello World! onto the browser. Call the servlet HelloWorldServlet, which would look like this:

```java
// ----------- Begin: HelloWorldServlet.java -------------------
import java.io.*;
import javax.servlet.*;
import javax.servlet.http.*;

public class HelloWorldServlet extends HttpServlet
{
    public void doGet (HttpServletRequest req, HttpServletResponse resp)
                throws ServletException, IOException
    {
        PrintWriter out = resp.getWriter();
        out.println("<HTML><BODY>Hello World!</BODY></HTML>");
        out.close();
    }
}
// ----------- End: HelloWorldServlet.java -------------------
```

Save it under a new folder C:\JSP\Chapter4. Since HttpServlet belongs to javax and not java, it will not be present in the JDK you have installed. One of the easiest ways to get the HttpServlet class file is to simply install the Apache Tomcat Web Server, which comes with a servlet-api.jar file that contains HttpServlet.class in it. You then need to change your CLASSPATH to add the directory that contains servlet-api.jar. So let's begin by getting Tomcat first.

4.2   Installing the Tomcat Web Server

1.   Install Tomcat from Appendix F and go to step 4. Otherwise go to

     http://tomcat.apache.org/

     Click on Tomcat 5.x under the Download section on the left. Click on the hyperlink zip under Binary Distributions/Core under the latest release (5.5.20 was used at the time of writing this book; you can use the latest version currently available). When you are asked to open or save, choose Save and save to any folder.

2. Once it is done saving, double-click this zip file, select all files, right-click and choose `Extract` and select the destination as the C: drive. It will extract all files onto a folder called `apache-tomcat-5.5.20` directly under your C: drive. Rename this folder to `Tomcat`.

3. To configure Tomcat, you need to first define an environment variable called `JAVA_HOME` with a value of `C:\JDK` (replace `C:\JDK` with the exact folder/directory where you installed the JDK). Go ahead and define a new environment variable `JAVA_HOME` with this value. (Setting environment variables `PATH` and `CLASSPATH` is explained in Appendix B. You now need to create a new environment variable called `JAVA_HOME` with value `C:\JDK`.)

4. To run Tomcat, open a new command prompt window, change directory to `C:\Tomcat\bin`, and type

   `catalina run <hit Enter>`

   which starts the Tomcat Web Server in a few seconds. The command prompt session would look like this:

To verify that your Tomcat started properly, type in `http://localhost:8080` in your browser's address box. It should show the Tomcat Jakarta page with a message that says you have successfully setup Tomcat, as shown here.

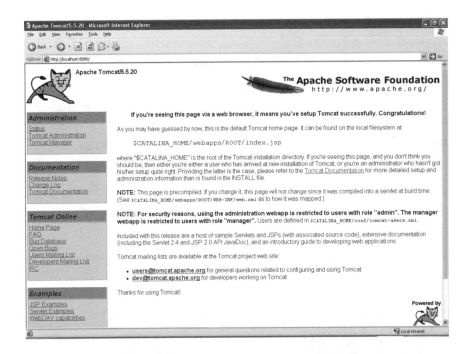

4.3 How Tomcat Worked

Let's understand how Tomcat Web Server worked. The URL you typed was

```
http://localhost:8080
```

As we saw in Chapter 3, the general URL consists of the protocol (`http://` in this example), followed by the host name and by the directory and file name to get. The host name represents the server machine; since you are running Tomcat on your computer, it is the server (or host) and also the client because you have the browser running there as well. So we tested a client-server communication, where both the client and server run on the same machine. (Usually, the generic name to refer to the server running on your own computer is `localhost`.) The host machine actually has several TCP/IP "ports" or channels, each of which can potentially run a different software program in parallel with any others running on the other ports.

By default, Tomcat runs on port 8080. This is preset in the file `server.xml` in `C:\Tomcat\conf`. This file is important because it contains many other default settings that you can change if necessary. (We will look at changing the default behavior in just a moment.) In order for the request to go specifically to the Tomcat server, you had to specify `:8080` after `localhost` in the URL. But where is `localhost` itself defined? It is also defined in the same file, `server.xml`. Open this file in your editor; you will see the following line:

```
<Host name="localhost" appBase="webapps"
    unpackWARs="true" autoDeploy="true"
    xmlValidation="false" xmlNamespaceAware="false">
```

The `server.xml` is an Extensible Markup Language (XML) file, which consists of tags similar to HTML tags. Each tag element opens with an angle bracket (<), followed by the element name, followed by attribute name-value pairs, finally ending with a closing tag that contains the same element name as in the open tag, but is preceded by the forward slash (/). Like HTML tags, XML tags, can nest tags within other tags. In the above line, the XML element name is `Host`, which has an attribute called `name` with a value of `localhost`, another attribute called `appBase` with a value of `webapps`, and so on.

Notice that the closing tag `</Host>` appears many lines below in the same file. In between the open and close `<Host>` tags, it has several other tag elements with their own attribute name-value pairs. All of these "child" tags represent additional information that applies to the "Host" tag. Changing the value of one or more attributes can change the way Tomcat behaves when you start it next time.

XML comments are exactly the same as HTML comments, starting with `<!--` and ending with `-->`.

4.4 General URL Structure

The general URL to access a file on a Tomcat Web Server is as follows:

`<protocol>://<host:port>/<context root>/<directory>/<file>`

We are looking only at HTTP protocols in this book, so the `<protocol>` part is always `http` in our case.

We already looked at the `host:port` part. By default, Tomcat's server root directory, or application base directory (specified by the `appBase` attribute in `server.xml` under `C:\Tomcat\conf`) is `C:\Tomcat\webapps`, so the forward slash following the `host:port` in the URL represents that root directory. Anything after that slash is in reference to the root directory and below. In Chapter 3, we saw that if the directory and file are not specified after the host name in the URL, it looks for a file called `index.html` in the server's root directory. Tomcat has a similar behavior, but it is slightly more extended, which we will see in the next section.

4.5 The Context Root

Following the `host:port`, you need to have a *context root*, followed by the directory path and file name. The directory path needs to be relative to the root directory. If the file resides directly under the root directory, the directory path is simply a forward slash (/). Let's look at each part separately. Tomcat needs something called a *context root*, but what is a *"context"*? If you look at the `C:\Tomcat\webapps` directory, you will see that it has six subfolders:

    balancer

    jsp-examples

    ROOT

```
servlet-examples

tomcat-docs

webdav
```

Each of these directories is a *context* in Tomcat's terminology, or an independent set of files that represent one *web application* that has its own purpose. For example, one Web application may allow you to log in and place orders, whereas another may generate an employee report.

Tomcat allows you to use alias names for the directory path of the actual root directory of each Web application. The mapping between each alias name for a Web application and the actual root directory that it maps to is specified in the server.xml file under C:\Tomcat\conf. So you have six web applications already deployed for you when you install Tomcat. Each of these six directories has its own index.html file. The jsp-examples Web application represents sample code that you can run as long as the Tomcat server is up. To look at what this Web application has to offer, type in

http://localhost:8080/jsp-examples

It should display something like the following screen:

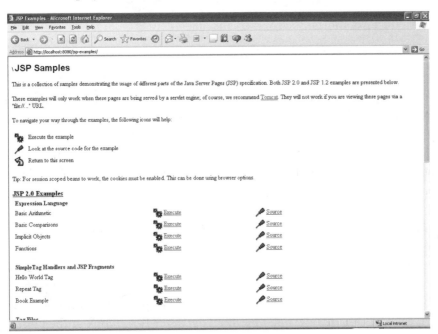

Here, jsp-examples is the context root that follows the host:port part of the URL, so it represents one Web application. This maps to the physical folder called jsp-examples under C:\Tomcat\webapps. If you look under this folder, you will find a file called index.html. That is the one that Tomcat opened and displayed in the browser when you typed in the address as http://localhost:8080/jsp-examples.

The `index.html` file is called a welcome file—a file that is opened when the user requests the Web application root and does not specify a file name.

Another context is `ROOT`, but it behaves somewhat differently. When the context path is absent in the URL, `ROOT` is taken as the default context, so it tries to open the `index.html` (or `index.jsp`) file under the `webapps/ROOT` directory. When you typed in `http://localhost:8080`, it opened the `index.jsp` file under `C:\Tomcat\webapps\ROOT`. Note that `index.jsp` is another valid welcome file (just like `index.html`). The `ROOT` context also behaves differently than other contexts in that the context path is an empty string (`""`), that maps to a `docBase` of `ROOT`, which means you must *not* have any context path following the `host:port` in order to invoke the root context.

To see another context in action, try `tomcat-docs` as follows:

`http://localhost:8080/tomcat-docs`

This opens a different `index.html`—one that resides in `C:\Tomcat\webapps\tomcat-docs`:

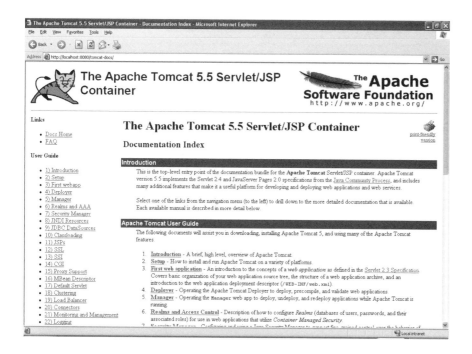

To open a file other than the welcome file under a context, you need to specify the file name if it resides directly under the context root, or its path relative to the context root if it resides in a sub-folder under the context root. As an example, consider the file called `introduction.html` under the `tomcat-docs` context root. To open that file directly, you would type in

`http://localhost:8080/tomcat-docs/introduction.html`

which looks like this:

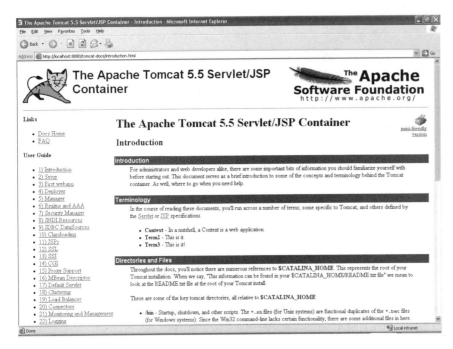

If the file you want to open resides in a subfolder under the context root, then you need to specify its path relative to the context root, after the context root part in the URL. For example, consider the file called check.html under C:\Tomcat\webapps\jsp-examples\checkbox. To open it you would say

http://localhost:8080/jsp-examples/checkbox/check.html

and it would look like this:

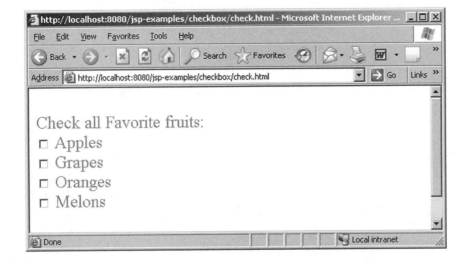

So in general the URL needs to contain host:port, followed by the context root alias, followed by the file name (or path relative to context root + file name).

4.6   The Deployment Descriptor

For any context, by default, when the file name is not specified in the URL, Tomcat is preconfigured to look for a file called index.html in the context's directory under C:\Tomcat\webapps; if found, it returns its contents to the client. In the case of the /jsp-examples context, notice that you did not specify the file name when you said

```
http://localhost:8080/jsp-examples
```

so it took the default for the file name as index.html. If index.html is not found in the context root folder, it looks for a file named index.htm; if that is also absent, it looks for index.jsp in the same directory. Whichever file is found first in that sequence is the one whose contents are displayed in the browser. In other words, when the directory and file are not specified in the URL, Tomcat has a list of files to look for. The file it looks for as a default is called a "welcome file," and the list of default welcome files is specified in the web.xml file under C:\Tomcat\conf directory as follows:

```
<welcome-file-list>
    <welcome-file>index.html</welcome-file>
    <welcome-file>index.htm</welcome-file>
    <welcome-file>index.jsp</welcome-file>
</welcome-file-list>
```

Again, you could change this sequence, say, to put the index.jsp before the others so that it first looks for index.jsp, and not index.html. Note that if it does not find any of the files listed under this tag in the Web root directory, it would give a "Page cannot be displayed" error.

Tomcat uses web.xml, an important configuration file, which is called a *deployment descriptor* file in Tomcat's terminology. The "top-level" web.xml file resides in C:\Tomcat\conf, but you will find other web.xml files in each context's WEB-INF subfolder. Values in the top-level web.xml serve as a default, which get overridden by the ones in the WEB-INF folders of the context, for common tags that reside in both.

To open your custom HTML or JSP files or servlets, you need to create your own context root (recommended) or use one of the six existing context folders under webapps. Before you can create your own context root (also called a Web application), you need to study the general structure of a Web application that Tomcat expects.

4.7   General Web Application Structure

We will be creating our own context roots shortly, but before we do that, we need to become familiar with the general structure that Tomcat requires every context root folder to conform to. The general structure of a context for reference follows. (We will cover some of them as we go, so don't worry about all of it for now.) None of the subfolders shown under the context root (myapp\) is required, but if you want Tomcat to load your custom Java .class files (including servlet .class files), you must have, at a minimum, the WEB-INF subfolder with the classes subfolder under it, and put all your .class files there. Other subfolders are optional, but if present, must contain the kind of files that Tomcat expects in those folders. Shown here are sample file types that could reside in each of these folders:

```
-------------------------------------------------------------------
+ webapps\
    +  myapp\
        -- index.jsp
        -- login.jsp
        -- welcome.html
        -- showallitems.jsp
        +  images\
            -- myimage.jpg
        + META-INF
        + WEB-INF
            -- web.xml
            + classes\
                -- HelloWorldServlet.class
                + sales
                  + reports
                      -- CustomerReport.class
            + lib\
                -- myclasses.jar
                -- struts.jar
            + tlds\
                -- mycustomtags.tld
-------------------------------------------------------------------
```

The classes subfolder in a context is where you put all Java .class files, including your custom servlet classes. Tomcat loads all .class files in that subfolder every time it starts up, but if you recompile any of them after making a change, you need to restart Tomcat so that it picks up the changes, unless the reloadable attribute in the Context element in server.xml is set to "true."

4.8   Getting Plain HTML to Work Via Tomcat

To get your custom HTML/JSP files to display on the browser via Tomcat, you could put them in one of the six existing context directories—but that may be confusing, with your custom files getting mixed with the ones already there. You need to create a new context root to hold your HTML/JSP files and to better organize them. Recall that a context root represents a physical folder that contains all files that a Web application consists of.

As an example, let's try to get the `HelloWorld.html` file to display in the browser, but this time via Tomcat (in other words, using a URL that begins with `http://localhost:8080/`). This can be done in two ways:

- Create a *new* context root folder under Tomcat's `webapps` directory:

  In this approach, you create a new subdirectory under Tomcat's `webapps` directory, and put all your files there, including your own `index.html` (or `index.jsp`) as necessary. All of your files would form a seventh Web application in that case. You can keep adding more Web applications by adding more subdirectories under `webapps`, each a separate set of files meant for a different purpose.

- Create a *new* context root folder outside of Tomcat's `webapps` directory:

  In this approach, you create a working folder wherever you wish, and then modify `server.xml` under `C:\Tomcat\conf` to create a new context root that has a `docBase` value that is the same as your working folder.

Let's look at both options in the next two subsections:

4.8.1 Creating a New Context Root Folder Under Tomcat's webapps Directory

Say that you want to create your own context root folder (say, `myapp`) under Tomcat's `webapps` directory (`C:\Tomcat\webapps`). The hope is that once your own context root is ready, you can place your HTML and JSP files in that folder and access them via Tomcat, provided you convey to Tomcat the path to the context root (relative to Tomcat's `webapps` directory). Contrast this with the fact that you are currently getting Tomcat's `ROOT` context when you specify the URL as:

```
http://localhost:8080/
```

Recall that the / at the end meant Tomcat's `webapps` directory (`C:\Tomcat\webapps`), and `ROOT` was a special context that had an empty string as its context path. So, this URL simply opened the `index.jsp` file under `C:\Tomcat\webapps\ROOT`.

Currently you want to get files in your `myapp` folder located under Tomcat's `webapps` directory. This means you need some way of specifying a relative path to `myapp` from `C:\Tomcat\webapps`. In this simple example, `myapp` is located directly under `webapps`, so its path relative to `webapps` is `myapp`. Go ahead and copy the `HelloWorld.html` file from the beginning of Section 3.2.1 into `C:\Tomcat\webapps\myapp`. You would now expect to type in the URL as:

```
http://localhost:8080/myapp/HelloWorld.html
```

Although it may make sense, the URL wouldn't work this way. Tomcat expects you to specify an alias to the context root path in its `server.xml` file, and use the alias instead of the physical path in the URL. The alias used could be any unique name that differentiates it from other contexts. This requirement may look a bit restrictive at first, but it actually lends a couple of advantages, as follows:

- If your context root is located several folders deep under the webapps directory (in nested sub-folders), then using a short, one-word alias in place of the entire path comes in handy

- Providing an alias for the physical folder path provides an additional layer of security from potential hackers. The URL only exposes the alias, but the client cannot see the real folder path

Say that you want to call your alias in this example myalias, which needs to point to the physical folder C:\Tomcat\webapps\myapp. For Tomcat to map the alias to the physical path, you need to modify the server.xml file under C:\Tomcat\conf.

More specifically, to add your own context root to the Tomcat webapps directory, you need to add a <Context> element under the <Host> element in server.xml. The general syntax of the <Context> element is as follows:

```
<Context path="<aliaspath>" docBase<="path relative to web app root, or absolute path">
        debug="0" reloadable="true" crossContext="true">
```

Here, the path attribute represents the alias for the physical directory for your context root, and the docBase represents the physical directory (relative to the webapps root or absolute path) to look for any index.html (or index.jsp) and also other files in this context (or Web application). So Tomcat allows you to have an arbitrary path name to use as an alias in the URL that may not be the same as a physical folder path, and mapping between the two is contained in the Context element in server.xml.

You could have either a relative or an absolute path for the docBase. (When I say "relative," I mean relative to the Web application root directory.)

To add your own context root inside server.xml, look for the part

```
<Host name="localhost" appBase="webapps"
      unpackWARs="true" autoDeploy="true"
      xmlValidation="false" xmlNamespaceAware="false">
```

Immediately under these lines, add your context for the /myalias path to have a docBase value of myapp, as follows:

```
<Context path="/myalias" docBase="myapp" debug="0"/>
```

Note that docBase="myapp" represents the physical folder name, relative to appBase=C:\Tomcat\webapps (obtained from the <Host> element that this <Context> element is nested under).

Save the file. Anytime server.xml is modified, you need to restart Tomcat so that it picks up the changes. To restart Tomcat, you need to first shut it down. A crude (not recommended) way of shutting it down is to use Ctrl + C keys on the Tomcat console window. You can gracefully shut it down by opening a new command window, going to C:\Tomcat\bin, and then typing in

```
shutdown <hit Enter>
```

The command prompt window would look like this:

You will notice that the Tomcat server shuts down in the original Tomcat command window. Note that you have two separate command prompt windows open at this point: one for Tomcat start-up and the other for shutdown, with the shutdown controlling the start-up one. To start it again, type

`catalina run <hit Enter>`

in the original command window.

Once the server starts, type in the URL

`http://localhost:8080/myalias/HelloWorld.html`

which should show up as shown here.

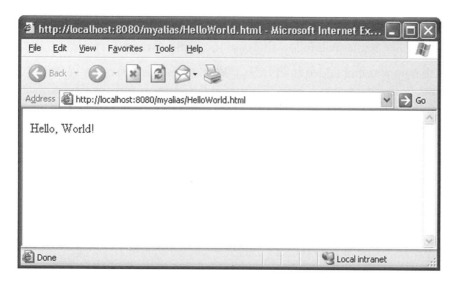

4.8.2   Creating a New Context Root Folder Outside of Tomcat's webapps Directory

We want to talk about creating a new folder outside of Tomcat's webapps and putting HTML files there. This is the approach we will be following in the rest of this book (as opposed to creating under Tomcat's webapps directory). The idea is to be able to refer to all files of a particular chapter at one place and to keep the Tomcat install folder intact as much as possible. Next time you want to install a newer version of Tomcat, the source files and folders you create in this book will remain unaffected. All you need to do is to point the new server.xml to the source folder(s) as necessary. This may not be how it is done in a real corporate programming environment, but helps in organizing files and applications we create in this book and for easier reference later. We have been following a naming convention for folders until now. To better manage folder creation in the rest of the chapters, let's formally state a comprehensive approach that we will use from this point on.

- For every chapter, we will create a new folder under C:\JSP that will hold all files and sub-folders for sections, exercises, and assignments of that chapter. The chapter folder will begin with an uppercase C, and will consist of the word Chapter followed by the chapter number; for example: Chapter4, Chapter5, and so on.

- A section will have a subfolder named with a lowercase s; for example, the subfolder for Section 4.8.2 would be sec482 residing under C:\JSP\Chapter4 and would hold all files for that section (except the ones in solved exercises under that section).

- If you had Solved Exercise 4.8.2, you would create a subfolder called exer482 under C:\JSP\Chapter4, and keep all files of that solved exercise there.

- Finally, if you had Assignment 4.8.2, the subfolder would be called assign482 and reside under C:\JSP\Chapter4.

- Packages and folders (except the chapter's context root) will be named in all lowercase (example: salesdept). File names will follow title case (example: CustomerList.jsp).

- All folder paths that appear embedded in HTML, JSP, or XML files (example: HREF, ACTION attribute of a FORM, document.location in JavaScript) and URLs you type in the browser's address box (example: http://localhost:8080/chapter4/sec482/Test.jsp) will contain a forward slash (/), so will any references to such paths in the text. All other folder paths would have a back-slash (\) — consistent with the way Windows displays folder paths by default.

- We will also create a single web app per chapter, with its context root pointing to the chapter's root folder. The web app will have an alias named with a lowercase c to distinguish from the folder name; for example, for Chapter 4, we will create a <Context> element in server.xml with an alias name /chapter4 and a chapter root folder (docBase) as C:/JSP/Chapter4. This element will be nested under the <Host> element in server.xml under C:\Tomcat\conf. For Chapter 4, the element would look like this:

```
<Context path="/chapter4" docBase="C:/JSP/Chapter4" debug="0"/>
```

- Each chapter's context root would have a WEB-INF subfolder and a classes subfolder under it, where we will be directing all .class files of that chapter during compilation.

- To make the compile command more concise, we will set an environment variable called JSP_OUT with a value equal to WEB-INF\classes folder of the chapter we are in. For example, if we are in Chapter 4, the JSP_OUT environment variable would contain a value of C:\JSP\Chapter4\WEB-INF\classes. You can either:

    - create a permanent environment variable JSP_OUT using Control Panel and keep changing its value as we move from one chapter to the next, or

    - use the SET command to create a JSP_OUT environment variable at the beginning of every new command session.

- In either case, to direct the .class files during compilation, you would use the -d %JSP_OUT% clause in the javac command.

- If your code refers to other classes that reside in package subfolders under WEB-INF\classes, you will need to use the -classpath %JSP_OUT%;%CLASSPATH% option as well (in javac and/or java command, as the case may be) – if CLASSPATH is not empty. Otherwise you would use: -classpath %JSP_OUT% in javac / java.

Ok—back to where we were. We want to display HelloWorld.html via Tomcat, but want to have the context root outside of Tomcat's webapps directory.

To do this, copy HelloWorld.html from C:\Tomcat\webapps\myapp to C:\JSP\Chapter4. Open server.xml and create a "/chapter4" Context element as follows:

```
<Context path="/chapter4" docBase="C:/JSP/Chapter4" debug="0"/>
```

Save the file, restart Tomcat, and type in the URL

```
http://localhost:8080/chapter4/HelloWorld.html
```

It should look exactly the same as before. (The only thing is that it opened the HelloWorld.html under C:\JSP\Chapter4 instead of the one under C:\Tomcat\webapps\myapp.)

4.9 Getting a Custom Servlet to Work Via Tomcat

Now that we have installed Tomcat and feel somewhat comfortable with creating our own contexts, let's get back to our original problem described in Section 4.1—that of compiling HelloWorld-Servlet.java, deploying it, and then accessing it via a URL.

We will look at two ways to compile and deploy the servlet:

- By using the context subfolder myapp you created under webapps
- By using your working folder outside of Tomcat's webapps folder (C;\JSP\Chapter4)

4.9.1   Using the myapp Context Root Folder Under Tomcat's webapps Directory

Since the HelloWorldServlet extends from the HttpServlet class, you need the HttpServlet.class file, which resides in servlet-api.jar that comes with Tomcat. Your C:\Tomcat\common\lib folder should have the servlet-api.jar file. Open this file in WinZip, and you will notice that the HttpServlet.class file resides in it, under a relative path of javax\servlet\http. In order to compile the HelloWorldServlet.java file, you need to add the C:\Tomcat\common\lib\servlet-api.jar to your CLASSPATH, as follows:

```
SET CLASSPATH=%CLASSPATH%;C:\Tomcat\common\lib\servlet-api.jar
```

From the general Web application structure shown earlier, all .class files (including servlet .class files) need to reside under WEB-INF\classes subfolder under your context root. So create a subfolder called WEB-INF under the myapp subfolder and a subfolder called classes under WEB-INF.

Tomcat automatically loads any .class files under every WEB-INF\classes folder in each of its defined contexts (no need to add the WEB-INF\classes folder to the CLASSPATH). The only thing is that every time you modify a .class file, you need to restart Tomcat so that it gets the change.

Compile HelloWorldServlet.java with the -d option:

```
C:\JSP\Chapter4>javac -d C:\Tomcat\webapps\myapp\WEB-INF\classes HelloWorldServlet.java
```

This should create a HelloWorldServlet.class file under C:\Tomcat\webapps\myapp\WEB-INF\classes.

Restart Tomcat so that it loads the servlet .class file.

Deploying the Servlet

You are almost there. One last thing to do before you type in the URL is to uncomment a few lines in the web.xml file under C:\Tomcat\conf. Look for the following lines in that file:

```
----------------------------------------------------------
<!-- The mapping for the invoker servlet -->
<!--
    <servlet-mapping>
        <servlet-name>invoker</servlet-name>
        <url-pattern>/servlet/*</url-pattern>
    </servlet-mapping>
-->
```

In the same file, also look for the lines

```
<!--
    <servlet>
        <servlet-name>invoker</servlet-name>
        <servlet-class>
            org.apache.catalina.servlets.InvokerServlet
        </servlet-class>
        <init-param>
            <param-name>debug</param-name>
            <param-value>0</param-value>
        </init-param>
        <load-on-startup>2</load-on-startup>
    </servlet>
-->
-------------------------------------------------------------
```

Remove the <!-- and --> around both of these elements, then restart Tomcat so it gets the change.

Invoking the Servlet

It is now time to see how to specify the URL to invoke the HelloWorld servlet. As noted earlier, the URL to access a file on the Tomcat server needs to contain host:port, followed by the context path, followed by the directory and file name. In the case of a servlet, the general URL is slightly different, since the goal here is not really to get the content in the servlet .class file itself but instead to get the resulting output from its doGet() or doPost() methods. The general URL for servlets looks like this:

```
<protocol>://<host:port>/<context root>/<servlet url pattern>/<servlet class name>
```

We already looked at the <context root> before, so we will skip that here. Appearing next after the <context root> is the <servlet url pattern>, which represents a text pattern in the URL telling Tomcat that what follows is a servlet. It thus knows how to load it instead of simply opening the content of the file itself. The <servlet url pattern> is the only handle Tomcat has to differentiate between a usual file request and a servlet request. When it knows that what follows is actually a servlet, it looks for the servlet name in the WEB-INF\classes folder under the context root, and invokes the servlet's doGet() or doPost() method as appropriate. The default <servlet url pattern> for servlets is servlet. The <servlet class name> in this example would be HelloWorldServlet—with no file extension.

To summarize, the URL would consist of the following parts:

```
<protocol> = http
<host:port> = localhost:8080
<context root> = myalias
<servlet url pattern> = servlet
<servlet class name> = HelloWorldServlet
```

Type in the complete URL in the browser's address box:

`http://localhost:8080/myalias/servlet/HelloWorldServlet`

This will appear in the browser as shown here.

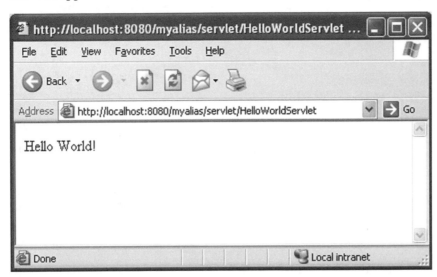

You may be wondering how Tomcat maps the /servlet/ text to indicate that what follows is a servlet. Well, as we have been seeing until now, almost everything is preset in one of Tomcat's xml files. These serve as name-value mappings that are used to control the action in each situation. The answer lies in the lines you uncommented a few moments ago. Open web.xml under C:\Tomcat\conf in your text editor, and look for the part:

```
------------------------------------------------------------------
<servlet-mapping>
    <servlet-name>invoker</servlet-name>
     <url-pattern>/servlet/*</url-pattern>
</servlet-mapping>
------------------------------------------------------------------
```

This represents a mapping between the text /servlet/* (where the asterisk (*) is a wildcard character meaning any text after /servlet/) to a servlet named invoker, which is defined separately in another element in the same file:

```
------------------------------------------------------------------
<servlet>
    <servlet-name>invoker</servlet-name>
        <servlet-class>
```

```
            org.apache.catalina.servlets.InvokerServlet
        </servlet-class>
        <init-param>
            <param-name>debug</param-name>
            <param-value>0</param-value>
        </init-param>
    <load-on-startup>2</load-on-startup>
</servlet>
```

Notice that the `<servlet-name>` tag under `<servlet>` has a value of `invoker` that is exactly the same as the value for `<servlet-name>` tag under `<servlet-mapping>`. This is important for it to work—Tomcat looks for the matching names of `invoker` in both and then executes the `org.apache.-catalina.servlets.InvokerServlet` class that knows how to load the `HelloWorldServlet.class` under `C:\Tomcat\webapps\myapp\WEB-INF\classes`.

Solved Exercise 4.9.1

Objective: To practice dumping HTML content using a servlet.

Steps:

- Create a new folder `exer491` under `C:\JSP\Chapter4`. Copy `HelloWorld.html` from the beginning of Section 3.4, and the `HelloWorldServlet` class from Section 4.1 into it.

- Using `HelloWorld.html` as a guide, modify the `HelloWorldServlet` class so that it dumps exactly the same HTML content that was in `HelloWorld.html`.

Solution:

```java
// ------------ Begin: HelloWorldServlet.java -------------------
import java.io.*;
import javax.servlet.*;
import javax.servlet.http.*;

public class HelloWorldServlet extends HttpServlet
{
    public void doGet (HttpServletRequest req, HttpServletResponse resp)
          throws ServletException, IOException
    {
        PrintWriter out  = resp.getWriter();
        out.println("<HTML><HEAD>");
        out.println("<STYLE>");
        out.println(".myStyle {font-family:Helvetica,Arial; font-size:10pt;
                  color:black; background-color:PINK}");
```

```
        out.println("</STYLE></HEAD>");
        out.println("<BODY>");
        out.println("<TABLE BORDER=1>");
        out.println("<TR CLASS=\"myStyle\">");
        out.println("<TD>Hello</TD><TD>World!</TD>");
        out.println("</TR>");
        out.println("</TABLE>");
        out.println("</BODY></HTML>");
        out.close();
    }
}
// ------------ End: HelloWorldServlet.java -------------------
```

Invoke this servlet using

```
http://localhost:8080/chapter4/servlet/HelloWorldServlet
```

The output should look like this.

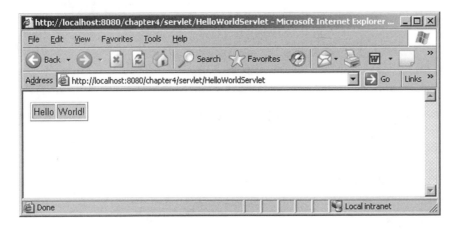

4.9.2   Using a Folder Outside of Tomcat's webapps Directory as Context Root

In Section 4.8.2, we created a /chapter4 context root that points to the C:\JSP\Chapter4 folder and displayed a plain HTML file sitting there. We now reuse that context for the servlet example. In other words, we make the HelloWorldServlet work one more time, but now it should pick up the HelloWorldServlet.class from C:\JSP\Chapter4\WEB-INF\classes folder instead of C:\Tomcat\webapps\myapp\WEB-INF\classes.

First, make sure the JSP_OUT environment variable points to this folder:

```
SET JSP_OUT=C:\JSP\chapter4\WEB-INF\classes
```

and use it in the "-d" option:

`C:\JSP\Chapter4>javac -d %JSP_OUT% HelloWorldServlet.java`

The URL for invoking the servlet would now be as follows:

`http://localhost:8080/chapter4/servlet/HelloWorldServlet`

The output should look like this:

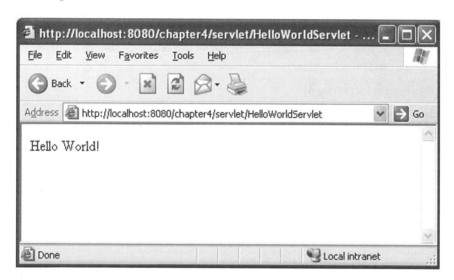

4.10 Form Processing Using a Servlet

We saw how the `doGet()` method works; `doPost()` is exactly identical, except that it gets called when the method type is POST instead of GET. Recall that it is better to have the method type on HTML forms to be POST rather than GET.

We are now in a position to write a servlet that can process HTML form data and return an appropriate response back. Let's reconsider the `Login.html` example where the user enters his or her first and last names in INPUT fields on the HTML form (Section 3.5.3).

Create a new folder `sec410` under `C:\JSP\Chapter4`. Copy `Login.html` and `Welcome.html` from Section 3.5.3 into this new folder. This time, when the user enters first and last names in `Login.html`, it should invoke a servlet that gets the value typed in the two INPUT fields from the request, and send out a dynamic response with the first and last names in it. (For example, `Welcome, John Smith, to the second page!`, where `John` and `Smith` need to be replaced with the actual values entered by the user in the first and last name fields). You will use `Welcome.html` as a guide to develop your new servlet.

Let's call it WelcomeServlet and create it in a new file, WelcomeServlet.java under C:\JSP\ Chapter4\sec410. The form's method is POST, so you will need to implement the doPost() method in the servlet. The request and response are already available as parameters to the doPost() method, whose signature is

```
protected void doPost(HttpServletRequest req,
                      HttpServletResponse resp)
            throws ServletException, IOException
```

As mentioned earlier, to get the values entered by the user on specific fields on the HTML form, you need to use the getParameter() method on the request, sending it the name of the INPUT field. For example, to get the value in the INPUT field with NAME="firstName", use

```
String firstName = req.getParameter("firstName");
```

Getting the last name and any other INPUT field values is similar. Login.html would look like this:

```
-------------------------------------------------
<!-- Begin: Login.html -->
<HTML>
    <BODY>
        <FORM NAME="main" ACTION="../servlet/WelcomeServlet" METHOD="POST">
            First name:<INPUT TYPE=TEXT NAME="firstName"></INPUT><BR>
            Last name:<INPUT TYPE=TEXT NAME="lastName"></INPUT><BR>
            <INPUT TYPE=SUBMIT value="Submit"></INPUT>
        </FORM>
    </BODY>
</HTML>
<!-- End: Login.html -->
-------------------------------------------------
```

Notice that Login.html has the form's action as ../servlet/WelcomeServlet, since Login.html resides in the sec410 folder, which is one level below the context root (C:\JSP\Chapter4).

The WelcomeServlet.java would look like this:

```
-------------------------------------------------
// ----------- Begin: WelcomeServlet.java -------------------
import java.io.*;
import javax.servlet.*;
import javax.servlet.http.*;

public class WelcomeServlet extends HttpServlet
{
    public void doPost ( HttpServletRequest req, HttpServletResponse resp)
```

```
        throws ServletException, IOException
    {
        PrintWriter out  = resp.getWriter();
        String firstName = req.getParameter("firstName");
        String lastName = req.getParameter("lastName");

    out.println("<HTML><BODY>");
    out.print("Welcome, ");
    out.print(firstName + " " + lastName);
    out.println(", to the second page!");
    out.println("</BODY></HTML>");
    out.close();
    }
}
// ------------ End: WelcomeServlet.java ------------------
------------------------------------------------
```

Compile `WelcomeServlet.java` as

`C:\JSP\Chapter4\sec410>javac -d %JSP_OUT% WelcomeServlet.java`

Verify that it created the `WelcomeServlet.class` under `C:\JSP\Chapter4\WEB-INF\classes`. Restart Tomcat, and type in the URL as

`http://localhost:8080/chapter4/sec410/Login.html`

Open `Login.html` in the browser and enter the first and last names:

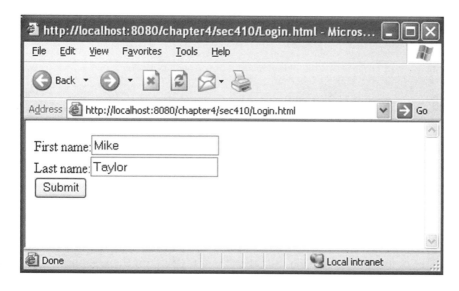

Click on the Submit button. Your screen should look like this:

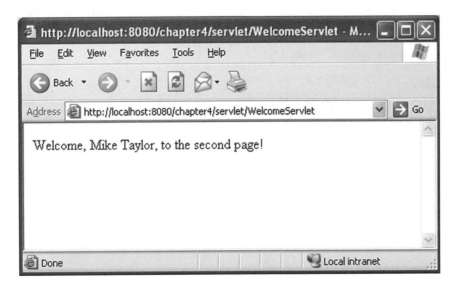

4.11   Summary

In this chapter, you learned how to create your own servlet class that generates dynamic content. You also learned how to install, configure, and run the Tomcat Web Server. You are now familiar with the concepts of contexts, Web applications, document bases, Web application root, deployment descriptors, server configuration files, and URL patterns for servlets.

The next chapter will discuss how to write JavaServer Pages (JSP) that create servlets behind the scenes but look more like HTML, with their own special tags.

4.12   Chapter Quiz

   1. Which of the following is true? (Select all that apply.)

      i. A servlet is a special kind of Java class that can process input entered by the user and return a dynamic response back.

      ii. For HTTP protocol, your servlet must inherit from the HttpServlet class under javax.servlet.http package.

      iii. You must override either the doGet() or doPost() method in your servlet so that it can handle the GET or POST requests respectively.

      iv. The PrintWriter object is obtained via the getWriter() method on the response.

      a. All of the above

   b. (i), (ii), and (iv) only

   c. (ii) and (iv) only

   d. (i), (iii), and (iv) only

2. Which of the following is true? (Select all that apply.)

   i. A Web application is a set of files that work together for a particular purpose.

   ii. In Tomcat terminology, a `context` is the same as a Web application.

   iii. In a `<Context>` element, the `path` attribute contains the alias to the actual directory path specified by the `docBase` attribute.

   iv. A deployment descriptor file (`web.xml`) contains information on servlets and other elements in a Web application, including how they relate to each other.

   a. All of the above

   b. (i), (ii), and (iv) only

   c. (ii) and (iv) only

   d. (i), (ii), and (iii) only

3. Which of the following is true? (Select all that apply.)

   i. A servlet URL pattern is the text you enter in the URL that tells Tomcat that what follows is a servlet.

   ii. The `server.xml` file contains information on the host and the Web application root.

   iii. If you create your own context and want to invoke servlets and/or Java classes in it, you need to have, at a minimum, a `WEB-INF\classes` folder under your context root, and the related `.class` files need to reside under `WEB-INF\classes` (if in default package) or in subfolders below it (if packaged).

   a. All of the above

   b. (i) and (ii) only

   c. (i) and (iii) only

   d. (ii) and (iii) only

4.13   Answers to Quiz

1. The correct answer is (b). All statements except (iii) are true. Option (iii) is false because even if you do not override the `doGet()` or `doPost()` methods, the parent `HttpServlet` class

will be able to handle the requests (although its response would be an empty one). Overriding these methods enables you to get the response you want from the servlet, rather than the default response from the parent.

2. The correct answer is (a). All statements are true.

3. The correct answer is (a). All statements are true.

4.14   Unsolved Assignments

Assignment 4.1

Objective: **To practice dumping HTML content using servlets.**

Steps:

- Create a new folder `assign41` under `C:\JSP\Chapter4`. Copy `CustomerReport.html` from Assignment 3.1, and the `HelloWorldServlet.java` file of Solved Exercise 4.1 into it. Rename `HelloWorldServlet.java` as `CustomerReportServlet.java`.

- Using `CustomerReport.html` as a guide, modify `CustomerReportServlet.java` so that it dumps exactly the same HTML content as in `CustomerReport.html`.

- Compile `CustomerReportServlet.java` using the `-d %JSP_OUT%` option, so that it creates `CustomerReportServlet.class` under `C:\JSP\Chapter4\WEB-INF\classes`.

- Verify that the following URL works correctly, using the new servlet:

  `http://localhost:8080/chapter4/servlet/CustomerReportServlet`

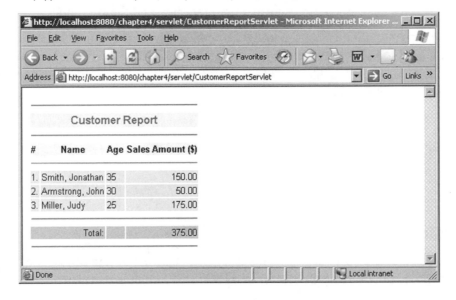

Assignment 4.2

Objective: To practice processing HTML forms using servlets.

Steps:

- Create a new folder `assign42` under `C:\JSP\Chapter4`. Copy `ShowAllItems.html` from Section 3.5.5, and `WelcomeServlet.java` from Section 4.10 into it.

- Rename `WelcomeServlet.java` as `ThankYouServlet.java`. Modify the `doPost()` method so that it displays the order summary based on what the user selected and submitted on `ShowAllItems.html`. For example, if the user checked the box for pencil with a quantity of 3 and the box for eraser with 2 (and left the box for pen unchecked), it should show something like this:

```
Thank you, John Smith, for your order! Summary of your order is:
```

Item #	Item Name	Price ($)	Qty	Value ($)
102	Pencil	1.00	3	3.00
103	Eraser	0.50	2	1.00
Total				$ 4.00

(*Hint:* For a checkbox that is checked, the value on the request is "on," and for one that is unchecked, the value is `null`).

- Modify `ShowAllItems.html` to point its form's action to the new servlet (instead of `ThankYou.html`).

- Use HTML tables to align the values properly into individual cells. Use style sheets to make it look professional.

- Submit `ShowAllItems.html` and `ThankYouServlet.java`.

- Compile the servlet, restart Tomcat, and enter the URL as

  `http://localhost:8080/chapter4/assign42/ShowAllItems.html`
  Select a couple of items, enter the quantity, and hit the Submit button.

  A sample interaction is shown next.

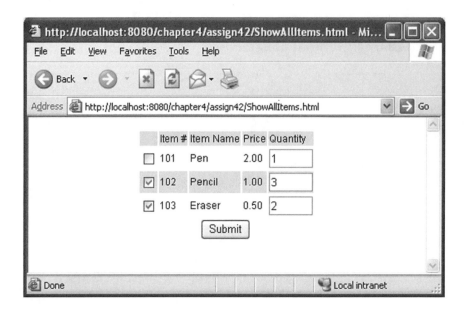

The next screen shows the order summary for the items selected on the previous screen:

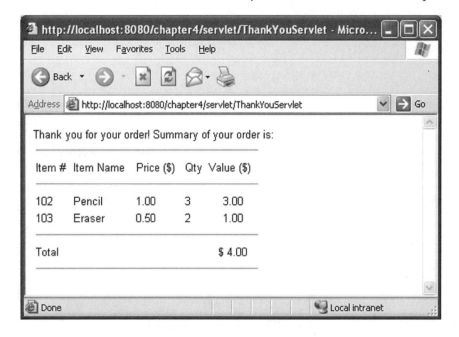

CHAPTER 5

JSP Expressions, Scriptlets, Directives, and Declarations

Chapter Objectives

- Learn how to create "dynamic" content by using JSP

- Understand what JSP expressions are

- Become familiar with what a JSP scriptlet is and how to write one

- Study JSP directives and declarations

5.1   Your First JSP

In Chapter 4, we saw how servlets can create dynamic content in the response sent to the client. They served a useful purpose, but observe that the demarcation between HTML and Java code was kept distinct and separate. Also, we noted that servlets were somewhat restrictive, with code written only within their doGet() or doPost() method(s). In the real world, as projects get more complex, it becomes necessary to create dynamic content at several places on a single Web page.

For example, assume that your Web application has the same overall content but needs to be customized for various clients by putting their logo on the top-right corner of the page. Also assume that the page contains an HTML table and that each client can choose a specific style for the table's data. (One client may want it to show up in Times Roman font with a cyan background, whereas another may want an Arial font with blue background.) So in each <TR> tag of the table, you need to know which client this page is being written for, and that information would most likely reside on the server's database.

This can be done by a single servlet; however, its doGet() or doPost() method needs to include the *entire* HTML content– static and dynamic– that the web page needs to display. You cannot separate the static HTML to reside in an HTML file and include only the dynamic part in the servlet. In other words, sttic and dynamic portions of the web page remain tightly coupled and need to go together in the servlet. Carrying static HTML like this in a servlet is an overhead because any change to the static HTML requires the entire servlet be recompiled and redeployed. This is not very efficient in terms of code development.

Wouldn't it be more convenient if we could somehow write pieces of Java code (meant for the server to process), right where we need it—that is, on the Web page itself, instead of invoking a servlet? So, on the HTML page above, it would be particularly convenient if we could write small pieces of Java code for the part that needs the client's logo and again write another piece of Java code for the part that needs to use a client-specific style sheet. The "piece" of Java code would be similar to the doGet() or doPost() kind of code we wrote earlier.

The Web page's extension will need to change from .html to something else, since an .html page simply gets returned as is to the client with no processing by the server, and if that happens for a page that contains Java code in it, the browser will not be able to decipher the Java part of the page content. This is exactly what a JavaServer Page (JSP) allows you to do: It has a .jsp extension that alerts the server that it may have Java code that needs to be processed, and at the same time, allows the rest of the HTML content to remain intact. The Java code itself is optional; so in theory, you could have a JSP page that consists of plain HTML only. In other words, a JSP consists of Java code (optionally) embedded in HTML, so it pretty much resembles a plain HTML file, with the usual HTML tags, plus special tags that enclose Java code.

Each piece of Java code is enclosed in special tags that alert the server to the embedded Java that needs to be compiled, processed, and converted to equivalent, dynamic HTML content. When the server looks at the embedded Java code, it automatically creates a new servlet behind the scenes, one per JSP, and converts the embedded Java code into equivalent "HTML dumping" code.

Each JSP file would get converted to an equivalent servlet behind the scenes by the server. So even if you have multiple "pieces" of Java code at various places in your JSP, all would be clubbed together into a single servlet. Variables that you create in one piece of Java code would be available in the other piece, since all such variables actually get created within the single _jspService() method that Tomcat would automatically generate for you.

As mentioned earlier, Java code is optional in a JSP. So by definition, any HTML page (with no Java code) that simply has its extension changed from .html to .jsp, would also be a valid JSP page. The only thing is that it will not have any embedded Java code in it and thus will not be "intelligent" and will behave exactly the same as the original HTML page. Let's create the simplest possible JSP by changing the extension from .html to .jsp and see what happens. As stated in Section 4.8.2, you need to first create a folder called Chapter5 under C:\JSP and a <Context> element in server.xml with an alias of /chapter5 that points to that folder. Open server.xml and add the following element under the one for Chapter 4:

```
<Context path="/chapter5" docBase="C:/JSP/Chapter5" debug="0"/>
```

Create WEB-INF\classes subfolders under C:\JSP\chapter5.

Restart Tomcat so that these changes take effect.

Ok—back to writing our simplest possible JSP. Create a new subfolder called sec51 under C:\JSP\chapter5. Copy HelloWorld.html from the beginning of Section 3.2.1 into this folder. Rename HelloWorld.html as HelloWorld.jsp. Type in the URL

```
http://localhost:8080/chapter5/sec51/HelloWorld.jsp
```

It should look like the screen shown on the following page.

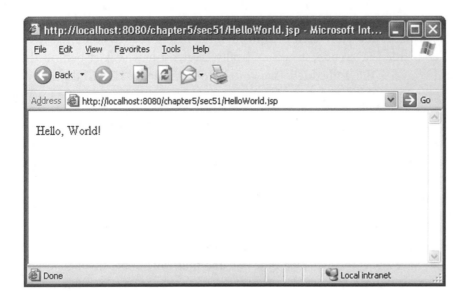

5.1.1 How It Worked

Great! You have just written your first JSP! This seemed to be simple enough, but believe me, Tomcat has put in a lot of effort for this simple action. First, it saw that the request was for a file with a .jsp extension, and so got ready to create an equivalent servlet behind the scenes. For every JSP file that you request, Tomcat actually creates a new .java file at run time with the name derived from the name of your JSP file, and compiles it on its own to create a servlet .class file. It puts all such newly created servlet classes under a "work" folder that, by default, is C:\Tomcat\work\Catalina. Under this, it creates a subfolder for each host. (We currently have only one host called localhost, so you will find a subfolder called localhost.) Next, it has a subfolder for the context alias (chapter5), under which it has folders org\apache\jsp, finally a subfolder called sec51. So for HelloWorld.jsp, you would find the servlet class source file HelloWorld_jsp.java created under C:\Tomcat\work\Catalina\localhost\chapter5\org\apache\jsp\sec51.

Open HelloWorld_jsp.java in your editor; it should contain the following:

```
---------------------------------------------------------------
package org.apache.jsp.sec51;

import javax.servlet.*;
import javax.servlet.http.*;
import javax.servlet.jsp.*;

public final class HelloWorld_jsp
        extends org.apache.jasper.runtime.HttpJspBase
```

```
        implements org.apache.jasper.runtime.JspSourceDependent
{
  private static java.util.Vector _jspx_dependants;

  public java.util.List getDependants() { return _jspx_dependants; }

  public void _jspService(HttpServletRequest request,
                          HttpServletResponse response)
        throws java.io.IOException, ServletException
{
    JspFactory _jspxFactory = null;
    PageContext pageContext = null;
    HttpSession session = null;
    ServletContext application = null;
    ServletConfig config = null;
    JspWriter out = null;
    Object page = this;
    JspWriter _jspx_out = null;
    PageContext _jspx_page_context = null;

    try
    {
      _jspxFactory = JspFactory.getDefaultFactory();
      response.setContentType("text/html");
      pageContext = _jspxFactory.getPageContext(this, request, response,
          null, true, 8192, true);
      _jspx_page_context = pageContext;
      application = pageContext.getServletContext();
      config = pageContext.getServletConfig();
      session = pageContext.getSession();
      out = pageContext.getOut();
      _jspx_out = out;

      out.write("\r\n");
      out.write("<HTML>\r\n");
      out.write("\tHello, World!\r\n");
      out.write("</HTML>\r\n");
      out.write("\r\n");
    }
    catch (Throwable t)
    {
      if (!(t instanceof SkipPageException))
      {
        out = _jspx_out;
```

```
        if (out != null && out.getBufferSize() != 0)
            out.clearBuffer();
        if (_jspx_page_context != null)
            _jspx_page_context.handlePageException(t);
    }
  }
  finally
  {
    if (_jspxFactory != null)
        _jspxFactory.releasePageContext(_jspx_page_context);
  }
 }
}
```

Notice that Tomcat packaged the servlet into a package called org.apache.jsp.sec51, because of which you see the subfolders org\apache\jsp\sec51. The name of the servlet class derived from the name of your JSP file is HelloWorld_jsp. Notice that the servlet extends from org.apache.jasper.runtime.HttpJspBase instead of HttpServlet, which you used in Chapter 4. To see how HttpJspBase looks like, go to the Jasper Javadocs page

http://jakarta.apache.org/tomcat/tomcat-5.5-doc/jasper/docs/api/index.html

and click on org.apache.jasper.runtime in the top-left frame, then on HttpJspBase in the bottom left. In the right frame, you will see that HttpJspBase extends from javax.servlet.http.HttpServlet, so it is, by definition, a valid subclass of HttpServlet. Scroll down a bit, and you will find the service() method. This method is the one that gets called by the framework, which in the case of HttpServlet calls the doGet() or doPost() methods. In the case of HttpJspBase, however, the service() method overrides its parent class version and calls the _jspService() method instead of doGet() or doPost(). The call to _jspService() goes to the _jspService() method in the servlet generated by Tomcat (HelloWorld_jsp.java in our example), where you will find several out.write() statements that dump HTML onto the response. The out object is of type JspWriter which is similar to PrintWriter we saw in Chapter 4; one difference is that it uses out.write() instead of out.println().

5.2   JSP Elements

The simplest JSP page discussed previously simply contained plain HTML. It did not help much because we did not really create any dynamic content using JSP—all we did was to display static HTML. For dynamic content, we need to embed Java code in the JSP. To embed Java code in a JSP, we need to use "special tags" that can be differentiated from the standard HTML tags. The server will thus know that these contain Java code that needs to be compiled, processed, and converted to equivalent HTML that is then sent to the client. The "special tags" are technically called *elements* in JSP parlance. The general syntax of the JSP element is as follows:

```
--------------------------------------------------
<element_tag  attributename1="attribute value1"
              attributename2="attribute value2" .... >
    ....body..
</element_tag>
--------------------------------------------------
```

The part shown by

```
attributename1="attribute value1" attributename2="attribute value2" ....
```

represents a list of attribute name-value pairs that apply to that element_tag. Depending on the element_tag, some of the attributes are required, others are optional; if absent, the attributes take default values. The list of attribute name-value pairs allows us to specify values for specific attributes for a given element_tag.

Elements can in turn be of different types; you need to use the appropriate type of element depending on the purpose. There are five types of elements, as follows:

- JSP expressions
- Scriptlets
- Declarations
- Directives
- Action elements

Out of these, expressions, scriptlets, and declarations are collectively referred to as *scripting elements*. We will look at the action elements in Chapter 8.

5.2.1   JSP Expressions

A good candidate for dynamic content is the first name–last name situation in Section 4.10. But before we take that up, we need to get familiar with some basic JSP terminology. So we will look at a simpler example in this chapter and get back to the "name" example in the next chapter.

One way to embed Java code in JSP is to use a *JSP expression*—a Java expression (*not* a statement) enclosed in the *expression tags* <%= and %>. The Java expression *must* evaluate to a String, because the expression tags simply take the enclosed String and dump it using an out.print() statement. If the expression consists of an object, Java will invoke the toString() method on it from the global superclass Object defined in Object.java. Note the word *expression* here: it is only an expression formed using one or more variables *not* a statement. So the part enclosed between <%= and %> should *not* end in a semicolon.

To see a JSP expression in action, say that you want to display the current date and time whenever someone visits the JSP page (so it should display the *current* time stamp for each visitor). As you know, if you say

```
new java.util.Date(),
```

it generates a Java Date object, and when toString() is called on a Date type object, it returns the String equivalent of the Date object. To display the content of the current Date object as a String, you simply need to enclose the Date object itself in expression tags, so that it will automatically invoke its toString() method and display its String equivalent.

To implement this logic, create a new folder sec521 under C:\JSP\Chapter5, open a text editor, and save the following as CurrentTime.jsp in that folder:

```
-----------------------------------------
<!-- Begin: CurrentTime.jsp -->
<HTML>
    <BODY>
        The current time is: <%= new java.util.Date() %>
    </BODY>
</HTML>
<!-- End: CurrentTime.jsp -->
-----------------------------------------
```

Notice how you embed the Java in the JSP. Since the file has a .jsp extension, the request goes first to your JSP Web server (Tomcat, in this book), which looks for any <%= and %> in your JSP; if found, it evaluates the variables enclosed in such tags and dumps its String equivalent at that position, using an out.print() statement, which is what gets displayed in the client (browser). So in this example, say that the String equivalent of the current new Date() is Sun Jan 14 23:11:15 MST 2007. The Web server will then send the following HTML to the client:

```
-----------------------------------------
<HTML>
    <BODY>
        The current time is: Sun Jan 14 23:11:15 MST 2007
    </BODY>
</HTML>
-----------------------------------------
```

Notice how the part

```
<%= new java.util.Date() %>
```

got replaced with the String

```
"Sun Jan 14 23:11:15 MST 2007"
```

Next time someone requests this JSP, it goes to the JSP Web server again, which evaluates expressions enclosed in any <%= and %> once more, and returns a different HTML (with a new time stamp) to the client. So the response is dynamic, i.e. changes with each request.

Let's go ahead and test our new JSP. Enter the following URL:

```
http://localhost:8080/chapter5/sec521/CurrentTime.jsp
```

and verify that it shows the current time every time you visit the page. It should look like this:

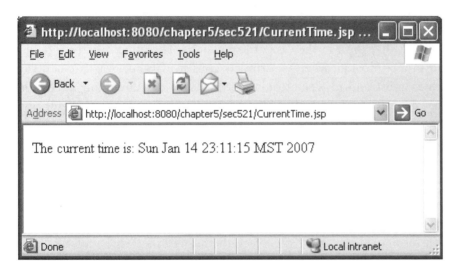

To understand how it worked, go to C:\Tomcat\work\Catalina\localhost\chapter5\org\apache\jsp\ sec521 and open CurrentTime_jsp.java. In the _jspService() method, you will find this:

```
-----------------------------------------------------------
out.write("<!-- Begin: CurrentTime.jsp -->\r\n");
out.write("<HTML>\r\n");
out.write("<BODY>\r\n");
out.write("The current time is: ");
out.print( new java.util.Date() );
out.write("\r\n");
out.write("</BODY>\r\n");
out.write("</HTML>\r\n");
out.write("<!-- End: CurrentTime.jsp -->\r\n");
-----------------------------------------------------------
```

Tomcat converted the expression (<%= new java.util.Date() %>) into an equivalent Java instruction:

```
out.print( new java.util.Date() );
```

You can have one or more expression tags in a single JSP. So if you want dynamic content at two or more places on your JSP, you would simply use a separate expression tag at each place.

5.2.2   Scriptlets

Java expressions are obviously limited in their ability to incorporate complex business logic. They can only dump values of some variable or expression but cannot perform business logic processing that runs into a few lines of code. For that, we need to use *scriptlets*—one or more Java statements enclosed between the special tags <% and %>. Notice the difference between *scriptlets* and *expressions*: *scriptlets* simply enclose Java statements between <% and %>, whereas *expressions* enclose a variable or expression between <%= and %>. So the main difference is the presence of the equal sign (=) after the % in the case of expressions. The other difference is that expressions will not end in a semicolon, whereas scriptlets consist of valid Java statements or instructions, each of which must end in a semicolon. Scriptlets *do not* dump any HTML by themselves (although they could, as we will see in Section 5.3); they are simply a means for processing data or determining the value of some variables needed later in the JSP to display as dynamic HTML content.

To consider an example of scriptlets, let's look at CurrentTime.jsp one more time. Observe that we instantiated a Date type object within expression tags and expected Java to invoke the toString() method on the object so that it complies with the requirement of a String expression in expression tags. Instead of putting all steps into a single expression, we could make it a bit cleaner if we use separate Java statements that instantiate the Date type object, then assign its String equivalent to a String type variable, and finally use the String variable in the expression tag. The statements that create the Date object and get its String equivalent cannot be used in expression tags, since only expressions (and not statements) are allowed in expression tags. Java statements or instructions need to be enclosed in **scriptlet tags** (<% and %>), another type of special tags. The set of instructions along with the scriptlet tags constitute a **scriptlet**. If you use a scriptlet along with expression tags in CurrentTime.jsp, it will look like this:

```
-----------------------------------------
<!-- Begin: CurrentTime.jsp -->
<%
    java.util.Date currentTime = new java.util.Date();
    String strDate = currentTime.toString();
%>
<HTML>
    <BODY>
        The current time is: <%= strDate %>
    </BODY>
```

```
</HTML>
<!-- End: CurrentTime.jsp -->
----------------------------------------
```

Notice that you now have a scriptlet (the part enclosed in <% and %>), and a JSP expression (the part enclosed in <%= and %>). Scriptlets and expressions can coexist in the same JSP.

Let's look at how this works. Create a new folder sec522 under C:\JSP\Chapter5 and save this content as CurrentTime.jsp. Type in the URL as

```
http://localhost:8080/chapter5/sec522/CurrentTime.jsp
```

The following screen will be displayed:

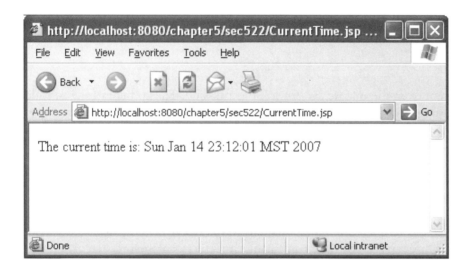

Like expression tags, you can have one or more scriptlets in a single JSP—each spitting out its own dynamic content.

Notice how we use <%= strDate %> as the JSP expression to dump the value of the Java variable str-Date defined inside the scriptlet tags (<% and %>). The Web server would dump values of strDate variable at that exact location in the JSP (i.e., the location of the JSP expression). When the JSP expression part gets compiled into a servlet, the corresponding portion in the _jspService() method would look like this:

```
out.print(strDate);
```

To verify, go to `C:\Tomcat\work\Catalina\localhost\chapter5\org\apache\jsp\sec522` and open Cur-rentTime_jsp.java. In the _jspService() method, you will find the following:

```
-------------------------------------------------------------
out.write("<!-- Begin: CurrentTime.jsp -->\r\n");
java.util.Date currentTime = new java.util.Date();
String strDate = currentTime.toString();
out.write("\r\n");
out.write("<HTML>\r\n");
out.write("<BODY>\r\n");
out.write("The current time is: ");
out.print( strDate );
out.write("\r\n");
out.write("</BODY>\r\n");
out.write("</HTML>\r\n");
out.write("<!-- End: CurrentTime.jsp -->\r\n");
out.write("\r\n");
-------------------------------------------------------------
```

Notice how this is different from the one we saw for a JSP expression. The content of the scriptlet got transmitted as is, from the JSP to its generated servlet class:

```
java.util.Date currentTime = new java.util.Date();
String strDate = currentTime.toString();
```

The expression tag got converted into its equivalent Java instruction:

```
out.print( strDate );
```

The point to note is that the scriptlet content remains intact when it is converted to a servlet, whereas all expression tags are replaced by their equivalent `out.print()` statements.

By using expressions and scriptlets, we have been able to make the page "intelligent," in the sense that we have control on what to dump at specific points on the JSP page.

You can put as many Java instructions as you want inside your JSP as long as all those instructions are enclosed between the scriptlet tags `<%` and `%>`. Whenever the destination URL ends with `.jsp`, the request goes to a JSP Web server that reads Java code enclosed between any scriptlet tags, sets values of variables, which are then dumped as HTML in subsequent embedded JSP expressions, and sends the resulting HTML to the client.

Let's sum up the use of scriptlets and expressions:

- Scriptlets: `<%` and `%>` tags to enclose Java code (for example to define some variables)
- Expressions: `<%=` and `%>`; tags to display Java variable/expression value(s) as HTML.

SOLVED EXERCISES

Solved Exercise 5.2.2 (a)

Objective: To practice the use of scriptlets and expression tags.

Steps:

- Create a new folder `exer522a` under `C:\JSP\Chapter5`. Copy `CurrentTime.jsp` from `C:\JSP\Chapter5\sec522` into this folder.

- Modify `CurrentTime.jsp` such that it displays the current time in a user-friendly format: `MMM dd yyyy hh:mm:ss a`. For example, a Date of "Sun Jan 14 23:13:10 MST 2007" will appear as Jan 14 2007 11:13:10 PM. (*Hint:* For formatting a `java.util.Date` object, you need to use a predefined class called `SimpleDateFormat` under `java.text` package. Use that class to format the date object and to dump the resulting formatted `String` value onto the HTML.)

- Enter the URL as

  `http://localhost:8080/chapter5/exer522a/CurrentTime.jsp`

- The display should now look like this:

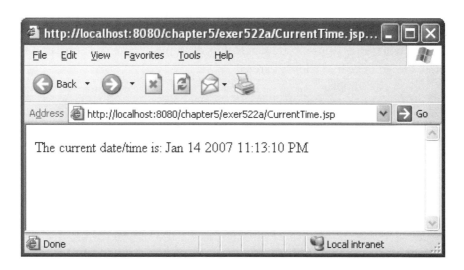

Solution:

```
----------------------------------------------------------------
<!-Begin: CurrentTime.jsp -->
<%
```

```
    java.text.SimpleDateFormat df
        = new java.text.SimpleDateFormat("MMM dd yyyy hh:mm:ss a");
    String strDate = df.format(new java.util.Date());
%>
<HTML>
    <BODY>
        The current date/time is: <%= strDate %>
    </BODY>
</HTML>
<!-- End: CurrentTime.jsp -->
```

Solved Exercise 5.2.2 (b)

Objective: To practice the use of scriptlets and expression tags.

Steps:

- Create a new folder `exer522b` under `C:\JSP\Chapter5`. Copy `CurrentTime.jsp` from `C:\JSP\Chapter5\exer522a` into this folder.

- Modify `CurrentTime.jsp` such that it displays the current data and current time in user-friendly formats: `MMM dd yyyy` and `hh:mm:ss a` respectively, in two separate rows and `TD` cells of an HTML table, with appropriate labels. For example, a date of "Sun Jan 14 23:13:32 MST 2007" should appear as shown here:

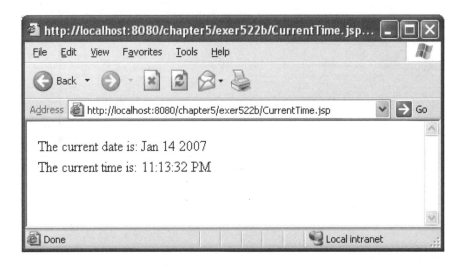

- Enter the following URL:

```
http://localhost:8080/chapter5/exer522b/CurrentTime.jsp
```

Solution:

```
-------------------------------------------------------------------
<!-Begin: CurrentTime.jsp -->
<%
    java.util.Date today = new java.util.Date();
    java.text.SimpleDateFormat dateOnlyFormat
      = new java.text.SimpleDateFormat("MMM dd yyyy hh:mm:ss a");
    String strDateOnly = dateOnlyFormat.format(today);
    java.text.SimpleDateFormat timeOnlyFormat
      = new java.text.SimpleDateFormat("MMM dd yyyy hh:mm:ss a");
    String strTimeOnly = timeOnlyFormat.format(today);
%>
<HTML>
    <BODY>
        <TABLE>
            <TR><TD>The current date is: </TD><TD><%= strDateOnly %></TD></TR>
            <TR><TD>The current time is: </TD><TD><%= strTimeOnly %></TD></TR>
        </TABLE>
    </BODY>
</HTML>
<!-- End: CurrentTime.jsp -->
-------------------------------------------------------------------
```

5.2.3 Directives

You will observe that we used `java.util.Date` in the scriptlet of `CurrentTime.jsp`. In addition, in Solved Exercises 5.2.2 (a) and (b), we also used `java.text.SimpleDateFormat` in the scriptlet of CurrentTime.jsp. The code seems to get cluttered, with every line using a fully qualified data type (such as `java.util.Date` instead of simply `Date`). Obviously, it is much cleaner to have separate import statements for these classes, so that you can refer to those types in your scriptlets without fully qualifying them.

To put import statements in your JSP, you need to enclose them in special tags called *directives*—the tag pair `<%@` and `%>`—at the beginning of the JSP. The general syntax of a directive is as follows:

```
<%@ directive attribute1 = "value1", attribute2 = "value2", ... %>
```

Importing classes is only one use of directives, which are used for other purposes as well. Before we move on to the import example, it would be useful to list the three major types of directives in a JSP:

- page directive
- include directive
- taglib directive

At this point we will focus only on the commonly used page directive here (and omit the include directive since it is not as commonly used). We will look at the taglib directive in Chapter 8, when we study tag libraries.

The page directive must have the tag: <%@ page and %>. One variant of the page directive allows you to import classes into your JSP. For this variant, you must use the import attribute of the page directive, and supply it the list of classes you want to import into your JSP. The classes you want to import need to be *fully qualified* (for example, java.util.Date, not just Date) and separated by commas. The list of classes needs to be enclosed in double-quotes. These import statements resemble those in a normal Java class, but they are slightly different: Instead of ending them with a semicolon, you must specify a list of class names separated by commas.

To see a page directive in action, create a new folder called sec523 under C:\JSP\Chapter5 and copy CurrentTime.jsp from sec522 into it. Modify it to add the page directive for import. Your Current-Time.jsp will now look like this:

```
---------------------------------------------------------
<!-- Begin: CurrentTime.jsp -->
<%@ page import="java.util.Date" %>
<%
    Date currentTime = new Date();
    String strDate = currentTime.toString();
%>
<HTML>
    <BODY>
        The current time is: <%= strDate %>
    </BODY>
</HTML>
<!-- End: CurrentTime.jsp -->
---------------------------------------------------------
```

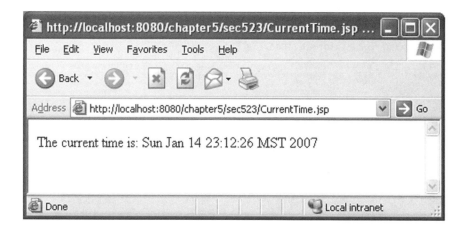

Solved Exercise 5.2.3

Objective: To practice the use of page import directives.

Steps:

- Create a new folder exer523 under C:\JSP\Chapter5. Copy CurrentTime.jsp from C:\JSP\Chapter5\exer522b into this folder.

- Modify CurrentTime.jsp to use a single page import directive for importing java.util.Date and java.text.SimpleDateFormat at the beginning of the JSP. In the scriptlet, use the class names directly (for example, use Date instead of java.util.Date).

- Enter the following URL:

  http://localhost:8080/chapter5/exer523/CurrentTime.jsp

- Verify that it produces exactly the same output as Solved Exercise 5.2.2 (b).

Solution:

```
----------------------------------------------------------------
<!-Begin: CurrentTime.jsp -->
<%@ page import="java.util.Date, java.text.SimpleDateFormat" %>
<%
    Date today = new Date();
    SimpleDateFormat dateOnlyFormat = new SimpleDateFormat ("MMM dd yyyy");
```

```
        String strDateOnly = dateOnlyFormat.format (today);
        SimpleDateFormat timeOnlyFormat = new SimpleDateFormat ("hh:mm:ss a");
        String strTimeOnly = timeOnlyFormat.format (today);
%>
<HTML>
    <BODY>
        <TABLE>
            <TR><TD>The current date is: </TD><TD><%= strDateOnly %></TD></TR>
            <TR><TD>The current time is: </TD><TD><%= strTimeOnly %></TD></TR>
        </TABLE>
    </BODY>
</HTML>
<!-- End: CurrentTime.jsp -->
```

5.2.3.1   Importing Custom Classes into Your JSP

You can also import your custom classes into your JSP in a similar manner. However, you need to know where exactly to place the .class files so that the JSP will pick them up.

Recall what we learned in Section 1.8 on packages: You *cannot* import classes from the default package into a class that belongs to a named (nondefault) package. Since our JSPs get compiled into a servlet that belongs to a named package (org.apache.jsp.X), we need to put our custom classes into named packages, so that we can import them into our JSP using explicit page import directives.

Say that you have a custom class called Customer in a package called myPackage:

```
-------------------------------------------
package myPackage;
public class Customer
{
    private String firstName;
    private String lastName;
    public Customer(String firstName, String lastName)
    {
        setFirstName(firstName);
        setLastName(lastName);
    }
    public void setFirstName(String firstName) { this.firstName = firstName; }
    public String getFirstName() { return firstName; }
    public void setLastName(String lastName) { this.lastName = lastName; }
    public String getLastName() { return lastName; }
}
-------------------------------------------
```

Create a new folder sec5231 under C:\JSP\Chapter5, and save the preceding package as Customer.java in that folder. Change your JSP_OUT environment variable to point to C:\JSP\Chapter5\WEB-INF\classes. Compile Customer.java using the -d %JSP_OUT% option, as follows:

C:\JSP\Chapter5\sec5231>javac -d %JSP_OUT% Customer.java

This should create a package subfolder myPackage under C:\JSP\Chapter5\WEB-INF\classes, with a Customer.class file in it.

Now create a JSP file called ShowCustomer.jsp under C:\JSP\Chapter5\sec5231 that instantiates a Customer type object using the Customer class above. Its content is shown here:

```
---------------------------------------------------------------------------
<!-- Begin: ShowCustomer.jsp -->
<%@ page import="myPackage.Customer" %>
<%
    Customer cst = new Customer("John", "Smith");
    String name = cst.getFirstName() + " " + cst.getLastName();
%>
<HTML>
    <BODY>
        The customer name is: <%= name %>
    </BODY>
</HTML>
<!-- End: ShowCustomer.jsp -->
---------------------------------------------------------------------------
```

Type in the URL

http://localhost:8080/chapter5/sec5231/ShowCustomer.jsp

It should look like this:

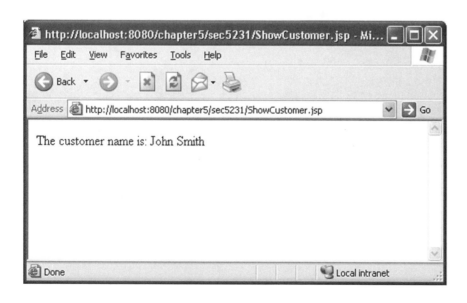

Solved Exercise 5.2.3.1

Objective: To practice the use of packaged custom classes inside a JSP.

Steps:

- Create a new folder called `exer5231` under `C:\JSP\Chapter5`. Copy `Customer.java` from Solved Exercise 1.8.3 in the Java review section of this book and put it in this folder.

- Modify `Customer.java` to name the package as `salesdept` instead of `exer183pkg`. Compile `Customer.java` using -d option of `C:\JSP\Chapter5\WEB-INF\classes`, so that it creates the package subfolder `salesdept` directly under `C:\JSP\Chapter5\WEB-INF\classes`.

- Now write a JSP called `CustomerList.jsp` in the same folder that instantiates and displays the list of three `Customer` objects as in `TestReport.java` of Solved Exercise 1.8.3 (now the only difference is that it should show the same output onto the browser instead of the command prompt).

- Use HTML tables and CSS to format the data being displayed.

- Open the page using the following URL:

  `http://localhost:8080/chapter5/exer5231/CustomerList.jsp`

- The screen should look like this:

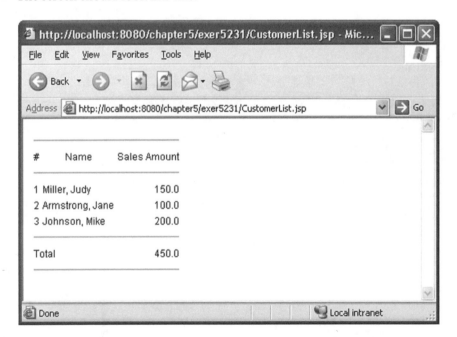

Solution:

```jsp
<!-- Begin: CustomerList.jsp -->
<%@ page import="salesDept.Customer" %>
<%
    Customer[] cst = new Customer[3];
    cst [0] = new Customer("Judy", "Miller", 150.0);
    cst [1] = new Customer("Jane", "Armstrong", 100.0);
    cst [2] = new Customer("Mike", "Johnson", 200.0);
    double totSales = 0.0, salesAmt = 0.0;
%>
<HTML>
    <HEAD>
        <STYLE>
        .defaultText{font-family:Helvetica, Arial;font-size:9pt;}
        </STYLE>
    </HEAD>
    <BODY>
        <TABLE>
            <TR><TD COLSPAN=3><HR></TD></TR>
            <TR CLASS="defaultText">
                <TD>#</TD>
                <TD align=center>Name</TD>
                <TD>Sales Amount</TD></TR>
            <TR><TD COLSPAN=3><HR></TD></TR>
            <%
                for (int i = 0; i < cst.length; i++)
                {
                    salesAmt = cst[i].salesAmount;
                    totSales += salesAmt;
            %>
                <TR CLASS="defaultText">
                    <TD><%= (i+1) %></TD>
                    <TD><%= cst[i].concatName() %></TD>
                    <TD ALIGN="right"><%= salesAmt %></TD>
                </TR>
            <%
                }
            %>
            <TR><TD COLSPAN=3><HR></TD></TR>
            <TR CLASS="defaultText">
                <TD COLSPAN=2>Total</TD>
```

```
                <TD ALIGN="right"><%= totSales %></TD>
            </TR>
            <TR><TD COLSPAN=3><HR></TD></TR>
        </TABLE>
      </BODY>
   </HTML>
   <!-- End: CustomerList.jsp -->
```

5.2.4   JSP Declarations

As mentioned earlier, scriptlets get converted to equivalent Java code that goes into the _jspSer-vice() method of the corresponding servlet class. This means, if you have a lot of Java instructions in your scriptlet, it can soon become unwieldy and difficult to manage. Imagine how restrictive it would be to have a Java class where you are allowed to write code only inside a single method!

There are two ways to organize a large amount of code in a scriptlet:

1. JSP declarations

2. JSP tags (to be discussed in Chapter 8)

JSP declarations are tags that consist of the pair <%! and %>, with one or more Java variable declarations and/or method definitions in between. Declarations allow you to specify whatever attributes and/or methods that you can call from inside your scriptlets or expressions. You can improve your JSP by organizing Java code into more manageable methods. Variables that need to be shared across scriptlets can be declared inside declarations. The following example (which uses a page directive, a declaration, and an expression) illustrates the concept. Copy CurrentTime.jsp from Section 5.2.3 into a new folder: C:\JSP\Chapter5\sec524, and modify it as follows:

```
-------------------------------------------------
<%@ page import="java.util.date" %>
<HTML>
<BODY>
<%!
  Date getDate()
  {
    return new Date();
  }
%>
The current time is: <%= getDate() %>
</BODY>
</HTML>
-------------------------------------------------
```

Another example that shows how you can declare variables and a method in a declaration and use it in scriptlets is shown next. Modify the content of CurrentTime.jsp as follows:

```
--------------------------------------------------
<%@ page import="java.util.Date, java.text.SimpleDateFormat" %>
<%!
    Date today = new Date();
    SimpleDateFormat dateOnlyFormat = new SimpleDateFormat("MMM dd yyyy");
    SimpleDateFormat timeOnlyFormat = new SimpleDateFormat("hh:mm:ss a");
    String getDate(boolean timeOnly)
    {
        if (timeOnly)  return timeOnlyFormat.format(today);
        else return dateOnlyFormat.format(today);
    }
%>
<HTML>
    <BODY>
        <TABLE>
            <TR><TD>The current date is: </TD><TD><%= getDate(false) %></TD></TR>
            <TR><TD>The current time is: </TD><TD><%= getDate(true) %></TD></TR>
        </TABLE>
    </BODY>
</HTML>
--------------------------------------------------
```

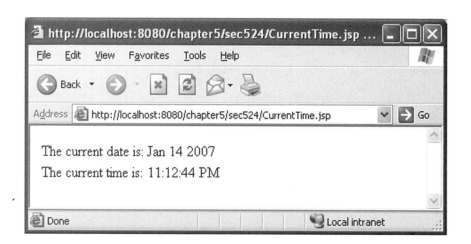

If you open `CurrentTime_jsp.java` under `C:\Tomcat\work\Catalina\localhost\chapter5\org\apache\-jsp\sec524`, you will find the following code in the servlet:

```
------------------------------------------------------------------------------
public final class CurrentTime_jsp
                    extends org.apache.jasper.runtime.HttpJspBase
                    implements org.apache.jasper.runtime.JspSourceDependent
{
    Date today = new Date();
    SimpleDateFormat dateOnlyFormat = new SimpleDateFormat("MMM dd yyyy");
    SimpleDateFormat timeOnlyFormat = new SimpleDateFormat("hh:mm:ss a");

    String getDate(boolean timeOnly)
    {
        if (timeOnly)  return timeOnlyFormat.format(today);
        else return dateOnlyFormat.format(today);
    }
      . . .
    public void _jspService(HttpServletRequest request,
                            HttpServletResponse response)
        throws java.io.IOException, ServletException
    {
        . . .
        out.write("<HTML>\r\n");
        out.write("\t<BODY>\r\n");
        out.write("\t\t<TABLE>\r\n");
        out.write("\t\t\t<TR><TD>The current date is: </TD><TD>");
        out.print( getDate(false) );
        out.write("</TD></TR>\r\n");
        out.write("\t\t\t<TR><TD>The current time is: </TD><TD>");
        out.print( getDate(true) );
        out.write("</TD></TR>\r\n");
        out.write("\t\t</TABLE>\r\n");
        out.write("\t</BODY>\r\n");
        out.write("</HTML>\r\n");
        . . .
}
------------------------------------------------------------------------------
```

As you can see, the content in your declaration went into the very beginning of the servlet class (outside of the _jspService() method), while the HTML dumping code in _jspService() invokes the getDate() method declared as part of the servlet class. Contrast this with scriptlets where variable declarations remained inside _jspService() method. Due to this difference, variables declared inside a declaration are instantiated only once, after the first servlet request. So, if you try to refresh a page, it may not work properly.

Declarations have another major disadvantage in that methods written in a declaration cannot be shared between JSPs. So if more than one JSP needs to use a particular method, the declaration with that method must be repeated in each JSP that needs it. This causes maintenance problems because changes made to a method in one JSP would have to be carried over to the other JSP.

For these reasons, declarations are generally not the preferred approach in JSP. A better alternative is to create your own custom tags, which you will see in Chapter 8.

5.3   Implicit Objects Available in a JSP

In the CurrentTime.jsp example in Section 5.2.1, we dumped the current timestamp using JSP expressions (<%= and %>). Whenever you use a JSP expression, the String value is actually written out to the HTML page by a predefined object available in every JSP called out, of type javax.servlet.jsp.JspWriter. This is similar to the PrintWriter object we saw in Section 4.1.

Instead of using a JSP expression that invokes the out object to write onto the HTML page, we can also use the out object directly inside our scriptlets to get the desired content on the response. In other words, we do not need to declare or instantiate the out object in a JSP. We can simply use it to dump content using out.println() statements.

The out object is one example of a preinstantiated, predeclared object available in JSP. JSP provides other useful, preinstantiated objects that are available in every JSP. You don't have to instantiate or declare them inside your JSP, you can simply refer to them or use them as such. These predefined objects are technically called *implicit objects* in JSP.

Let's rewrite CurrentTime.jsp of Section 5.2.1 using the out object instead of JSP expressions. The new code would look like this:

```
--------------------------------------------------
<!-- Begin: CurrentTime.jsp -->
<HTML>
    <BODY>
        The current time is:
        <%
            out.println(new java.util.Date());
        %>
    </BODY>
</HTML>
<!-- End: CurrentTime.jsp -->
--------------------------------------------------
```

Note that we are using a scriptlet and not a JSP expression, since we use <% and not <%=. Also note that we are using a legitimate Java statement (not an expression), so it must end with a semicolon. This should give exactly the same output as before.

Since you used a scriptlet, you have the flexibility to put more than one Java instruction in it. If you use multiple out.println() statements, you can write a lot of content onto the response. You can even dump regular HTML tags using the out object, so that way you can replace much of the "static" HTML in your page with out.println() statements that achieve the same result.

For example, the preceding CurrentTime.jsp can also be written as follows:

```
--------------------------------------------------
<!-- Begin: CurrentTime.jsp -->
<HTML>
    <%
        out.println("<BODY>");
        out.print("The current time is:");
        out.println(new java.util.Date());
        out.println(</BODY>");
    %>
</HTML>
<!-- End: CurrentTime.jsp -->
--------------------------------------------------
```

Note that you could even have included the <HTML> tag inside the out.println() statements. Deciding exactly what portion should be dumped by the out.println() statements is more of a "developer discretion" issue. Usually out.println() statements are used to dump dynamic content (as opposed to static HTML), but static HTML is also being used here only to show the concept.

Let's consider a more comprehensive example to rewrite Login.html of Section 3.5.3 using the out object in the next solved exercise.

Solved Exercise 5.3

Objective: To learn how to use the out implicit object to dump HTML in a JSP.

Steps:

- Create a new sub-folder called exer53 under C:\JSP\Chapter5. Copy Login.html and Wel-come.html of Section 3.5.3 into this folder.

- Rename Login.html to Login.jsp. Modify Login.jsp so that it dumps the HTML form (i.e., all content within the <BODY ... </BODY> tag) using the out object in a scriptlet. Start Tomcat and run Login.jsp by entering the Web address as

    http://localhost:8080/chapter5/exer53/Login.jsp

- Enter some text in first name/last name and hit submit. Verify that it takes you to the Welcome.html page.

Solution:

```
<!-- Begin: Login.jsp -->
<HTML>
    <BODY>
    <%
        out.println("<FORM NAME=\"main\" ACTION=\"Welcome.html\" METHOD=POST>");
        out.println("First name:<INPUT TYPE=\"text\" NAME=\"firstName\"></INPUT><BR>");
        out.println("Last name:<INPUT TYPE=\"text\" NAME=\"lastName\"></INPUT><BR>");
        out.println("<INPUT TYPE=\"submit\" value=\"Submit\"></INPUT>");
        out.println("</FORM>");
    %>
    </BODY>
</HTML>
<!-- End: Login.jsp -->
```

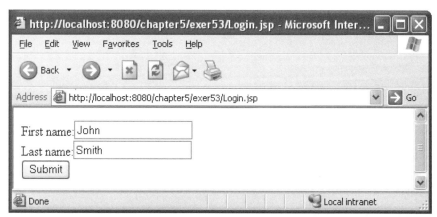

Like the out implicit object, there are a few others that are useful and important; these are listed next. We will talk about the request, response, and session implicit objects in the next chapter when we discuss the processing of HTML forms using JSP.

Object name	Object type
request	javax.servlet.ServletRequest
response	javax.servlet.ServletResponse
pageContext	javax.servlet.jsp.PageContext
out	javax.servlet.jsp.JspWriter
session	javax.servlet.http.HttpSession

5.4   Summary

In this chapter, you learned how to create "dynamic" content by using JSP expressions, scriptlets, directives, and declarations. In the next chapter, you will learn how to use JSP to process HTML form submissions and to manage session-level information.

5.5   Chapter Quiz

1. Which of the following is true? (Select all that apply.)

   i. A JSP expression uses <%= and %>.

   ii. A scriptlet uses <% and %>.

   iii. A declaration uses <%! and %>.

   iv. A directive uses <%@= and %>.

   v. A JSP expression must evaluate to a String.

   a. All of the above

   b. (i), (ii), (iii), and (v) only

   c. (ii), (iii), and (iv) only

   d. (i), (ii), (iii), and (v) only

2. Which of the following is true? (Select all that apply.)

   i. A JSP expression cannot contain a Java instruction; it can contain only a Java expression.

   ii. A scriptlet can contain one or more Java instructions.

   iii. Java code in a declaration goes to the beginning of the servlet class generated, whereas Java code in a scriptlet goes only into the _jspService() method of the servlet.

iv. By using the out object in a scriptlet, you can achieve the same result as in a JSP expression.

v. You do not have to instantiate or declare the out object in your JSP; you can simply begin using it.

a. All of the above

b. (ii), (iii), (iv), and (v) only

c. (ii), (iii), and (v) only

d. (i), (ii), and (iv) only

3. Which of the following is true? (Select all that apply.)

i. Import statements in a JSP can be placed either in a directive or in your scriptlet.

ii. The JSP Web server recompiles the JSP code every time you visit the page.

iii. The JSP Web server recompiles the JSP code every time you modify its contents and save it.

iv. There are several kinds of directives available; the page directive is one of them.

v. There are several kinds of implicit objects available; the out object is one of them.

a. All of the above

b. (i), (ii), (iv), and (v) only

c. (i), (iii), (iv), and (v) only

d. (iii), (iv), and (v) only

4. Which of the following is true? (Select all that apply.)

i. You can have more than one scriptlet in a single JSP file.

ii. You can have more than one JSP expression in a single JSP file.

iii. You can declare a variable in a scriptlet and refer to that variable in another scriptlet downstream in the same JSP.

a. All of the above

b. (i) and (ii) only

c. (i) and (iii) only

d. (ii) and (iii) only

5. Which of the following is true? (Select all that apply.)

i. Every JSP file gets compiled into a servlet.

    ii. A servlet runs on the Web server; it processes a request and sends a response back to the client.

   iii. JSP declarations can contain "methods," just like methods reside in a class.

   iv. A JSP expression uses the out object to dump content onto HTML.

   a. All of the above

   b. (i), (ii), and (iii) only

   c. (i), (iii), and (iv) only

   d. (i), (ii), and (iv) only

5.6 Answers to Quiz

1. The correct answer is (b). All statements except (iv) are true. Option (iv) is false because a directive uses <%@ and %>, not <%@= and %>.

2. The correct answer is (a). All statements are true.

3. The correct answer is (d). All statements except (i) and (ii) are true. Option (i) is false because import statements in a JSP can be placed only in a directive. Option (ii) is false because the JSP Web server does not recompile the JSP code every time you visit the page; it recompiles every time you modify it.

4. The correct answer is (a). All statements are true.

5. The correct answer is (a). All statements are true.

5.7 Unsolved Assignments

Assignment 5.1

Objective: To practice the use of a packaged custom class inside a JSP.

Steps:

- Create a new subfolder called assign51 under C:\JSP\Chapter5. Copy Course.java from Assignment 1.5 (if available) and CustomerList.jsp from Solved Exercise 5.2.3.1 into this folder. If Assignment 1.5 is unavailable, write a new class called Course, based on the instructions in Assignment 1.2 and make it part of a package called computerscience.

- Compile Course.java using the -d option so that it generates the compiled .class file directly under a package subfolder called computerscience under C:\JSP\Chapter5\WEB-

INF\classes. (You will need to use -d %JSP_OUT% in your javac, where JSP_OUT=C:\JSP\Chapter5\WEB-INF\classes).

- Using CustomerList.jsp as a reference, write a new JSP called CourseList.jsp that displays the output as in the following screen-shot. The page should show the list of courses offered when you enter the Web address as

http://localhost:8080/chapter5/assign51/CourseList.jsp

- Submit CourseList.jsp. The screen should look like this:

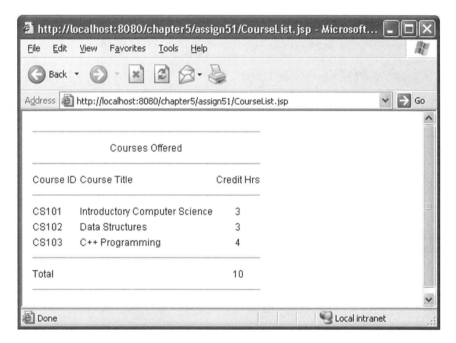

Assignment 5.2

Objective: **To practice the use of out object to dump HTML in a scriptlet**.

Steps:

- Create a new subfolder called assign52 under C:\JSP\Chapter5. Copy ShowAllItems.html from Section 3.5.5 and Welcome.html from Section 3.5.1 into this folder. Rename ShowAllItems.html to ShowAllItems.jsp.

- Modify ShowAllItems.jsp so that it dumps the HTML form and table using the out object in a scriptlet.

- Rename Welcome.html to ThankYou.html. Change the message to: Thank you for the order!

- Open the following URL and verify that it works as expected:

  http://localhost:8080/chapter5/assign52/ShowAllItems.jsp

- Submit ShowAllItems.jsp and ThankYou.html.

A sample interaction is shown here:

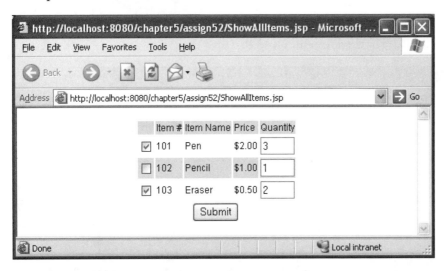

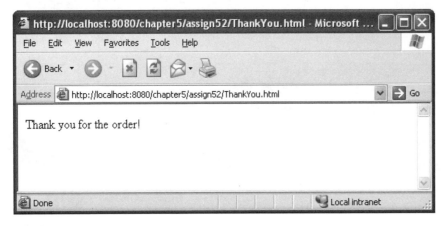

CHAPTER 6

Form Processing and Session Management Using JSPs

Chapter Objectives

- Learn how to use JSPs to process input values on HTML forms to create dynamic content

- Become familiar with what a JSP session object is

- Understand how to use the JSP session object to retain values across multiple levels of JSP pages

6.1 Form Processing Using JSP Expressions and Scriptlets

Ok—we are now in a position to get back to our first name–last name example in Section 4.10. Let's redo it using a JSP instead of a servlet. The form in Login.html had an ACTION value of ../servlet/WelcomeServlet but we need to change that so it goes to a JSP instead of a servlet. Let's call that JSP ProcessLogin.jsp. It will need to get the user-entered values for first and last names and produce an appropriate dynamic response. Create a new folder called Chapter6 under C:\JSP, and a subfolder called sec61 under it. Copy Login.html from Section 4.10 here. Modify the ACTION of the HTML form to "ProcessLogin.jsp" instead of "../servlet/WelcomeServlet", so Login.html would now look like this:

```
-----------------------------------------------------------
<!-- Begin: Login.html -->
<HTML>
    <BODY>
        <FORM NAME="main" ACTION="ProcessLogin.jsp" METHOD="POST">
            First name:<INPUT TYPE=TEXT NAME="firstName"></INPUT><BR>
            Last name:<INPUT TYPE=TEXT NAME="lastName"></INPUT><BR>
            <INPUT TYPE=SUBMIT VALUE="Submit"></INPUT>
        </FORM>
    </BODY>
</HTML>
<!-- End: Login.html -->
-----------------------------------------------------------
```

Inside ProcessLogin.jsp, we need to extract the user-entered values in the INPUT fields of the HTML form on the preceding page. In Section 4.10, we used the getParameter() method on the HttpServletRequest parameter of the doPost() method. In this case, you already have an implicit object called request of type HttpServletRequest that is available for use without instantiating, as discussed in Section 5.3. Similarly, you also have an implicit object called response that is available for use without instantiating. So, to get the INPUT field values, you simply call the getParameter() method on the request implicit object. So ProcessLogin.jsp would look like this:

```
-----------------------------------------------------------
<!-- Begin: ProcessLogin.jsp -->
<HTML>
    <BODY>
        Welcome, <%= request.getParameter("firstName") %>
            <%= request.getParameter("lastName") %>, to the second page!
    </BODY>
</HTML>
<!-- End: ProcessLogin.jsp -->
-----------------------------------------------------------
```

Before you can run your JSP, you need to add a new context root for Chapter 6. Add the following line in C:\Tomcat\conf\server.xml:

```
<Context path="/chapter6" docBase="C:/JSP/Chapter6" debug="0" />
```

Restart Tomcat so that it gets this change. Open Login.html using the following URL:

http://localhost:8080/chapter6/sec61/Login.html

A sample interaction would look like this:

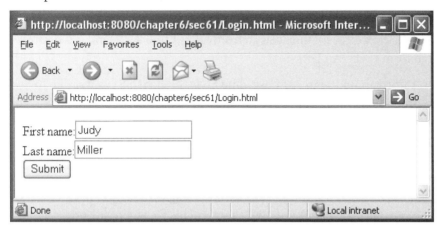

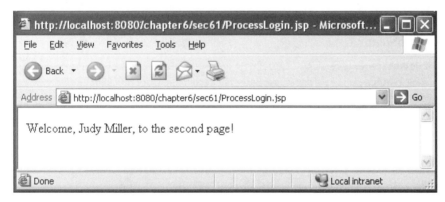

In ProcessLogin.jsp, you can use scriptlets instead of JSP expressions, in which case it would look like this:

```
-----------------------------------------------------------
<!-- Begin: ProcessLogin.jsp -->
<%
    String fName = request.getParameter("firstName");
    String lName = request.getParameter("lastName");
%>
<HTML>
    <BODY>
        Welcome, <%= fName %> <%= lName %>, to the second page!
    </BODY>
</HTML>
<!-- End: ProcessLogin.jsp -->
-----------------------------------------------------------
```

Note that the request object holds values for only one step at a time. In other words, when you are going from Login.jsp to ProcessLogin.jsp, the request object will hold values of INPUT fields defined on Login.jsp. Similarly, if you go from ProcessLogin.jsp to another JSP (say, Final.jsp), and if ProcessLogin.jsp had an HTML form in it, then the request object in Final.jsp would hold INPUT field values of the HTML form on ProcessLogin.jsp but NOT the ones on the HTML form on Login.jsp. The request object is created every time you go from URL-1 to URL-2, and it is destroyed and recreated when you go from URL-2 to URL-3.

Before I continue further, a word about the use of Cascading Style Sheets (CSS) is in order. In Section 4.8.2, I described a comprehensive approach for JSP development that we will follow in this book. Now that we are dealing with HTML forms that contain a lot of labels and text, one more bullet probably needs to be added to the list, about the use of CSS in HTML/JSP pages. In order for our pages to look somewhat professional, we will be using some basic CSS to format the labels and text. While doing so, we do not want to keep adding the styles to each page using the <STYLE> tag. Instead, we will use the <LINK> tag as described in Section 3.4 to point to a single styles.css file that we will create, one per chapter, to store styles for all pages in that chapter. This file will reside under a folder called styles that you will need to create under the context root for each chapter. For chapter 6, go ahead and create a folder called styles under C:\JSP\Chapter6 and create a text file called styles.css under it, with the following content:

```
.defaultText{ font-family:Helvetica,Arial; font-size:10pt; }
.tableEvenRow{ font-family:Helvetica,Arial; font-size:9pt; background-color:#E6E6E6; }
.tableOddRow{ font-family:Helvetica,Arial; font-size:9pt; }
```

You can now refer to this style sheet file in your HTML/JSP using a <LINK> element with an appropriate relative path. For example, a page under C:\JSP\Chapter6\sec61 would use the following under its <HEAD> element:

```
<LINK REL="stylesheet" TYPE="text/css" HREF="../styles/styles.css" />
```

Until now, the HTML form processing that we have seen has been intentionally kept simple to facilitate understanding the concept. We will now look at a solved exercise with more complex HTML form processing and scriptlets; this should give an idea of how corporate JSPs may look in a real-world programming environment.

Solved Exercise 6.1

Objective: To practice the use of scriptlets to process HTML forms.

Steps:

- Create a new folder called exer61 under C:\JSP\Chapter6. Copy Login.html from Section 3.6.4, and ShowAllItems.html from Section 3.5.5 into this folder.

- Rename `ShowAllItems.html` to `ShowAllItems.jsp` and modify it so that its HTML form has the action as `SelectMore.jsp` (instead of `ThankYou.html`).

- Modify `Login.html` so that its form action is `ShowAllItems.jsp` (instead of `Welcome.html`).

- Write a new JSP called `SelectMore.jsp` (start with a copy of `ShowAllItems.jsp` renamed to `Select-More.jsp`) in the same folder, that gets the item(s) selected on `ShowAllItems.jsp` using the `get-Parameter()` method on the `request`, and displays them as already checked. It should show the rest of the items (unselected) as before—unchecked, so that the user can select if necessary. Below the list of items, show a new value that represents the total bill (obtained as the sum of `Item Price X Item Quantity` for all selected items). The total bill should be on a separate row, with the label `Total Bill`, followed by the numeric value of the total bill. Below the `Total Bill` row, there should be two buttons: one labeled `Update` and the other `Checkout` (each of `TYPE="submit"`).

- Do NOT indicate an explicit action value for the HTML form on `SelectMore.jsp`. Instead, write a JavaScript function called `handleButton()`, which takes in the button object as input and uses the `value` attribute on the button to set the form's action as `SelectMore.jsp` (if it is the update button), or `Checkout.jsp` (if it is the checkout button). *Hint:* To set a form's action to `SelectMore.jsp` via JavaScript code, use a statement such as the following:

```
document.forms.main.action = "SelectMore.jsp"
```

A similar statement needs to be used for `Checkout.jsp`. Put that code in a `handleButton()` function and call this function for the `onclick` event of the update and checkout buttons.

- Every time the user hits the update button on `SelectMore.jsp`, the action should go to itself, and reload the new selection(s) along with the ones already selected previously. (So it should show a "cumulative selected items" list, with the remaining items available to select if necessary.) The user can repeat selections on `SelectMore.jsp` any number of times by selecting or unselecting items and hitting the update button. Each time it should show an updated list of items along with a new total bill at the bottom.

- When the user clicks on the checkout button, it should go to `Checkout.jsp` (a new page) that displays a message: `Thank you for your order!` followed by the list of items selected, including each item's number, name, price, and quantity.

- Replace `<STYLE>` tag with `<LINK>` tag in all pages, as described in Section 6.1.

- To test the JSPs, open `Login.html` in your browser using the following URL:

```
http://localhost:8080/chapter6/exer61/Login.html
```

- Enter some text in the first name and last name fields and hit the submit button.

- Verify that it shows `ShowAllItems.jsp` with a list of items that you can check to select. Select one or more items on `ShowAllItems.jsp`, enter the quantity for the selected items, and hit the submit button. Verify that it takes you to the `SelectMore.jsp` page that shows items selected on the previous page as already checked, and it also shows quantity entered on the previous page for those items.

- Submit `Login.html`, `ShowAllItems.jsp`, `SelectMore.jsp`, and `Checkout.jsp`.

- Sample interaction is shown next.

- User enters first and last names, hits the Submit button:

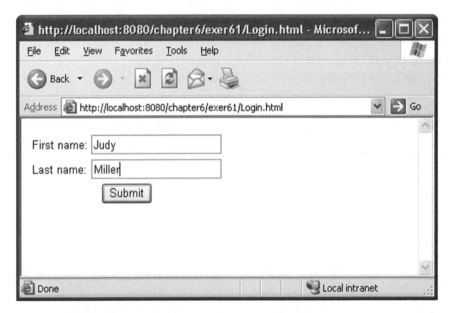

- User makes a couple of selections, hits the Submit button:

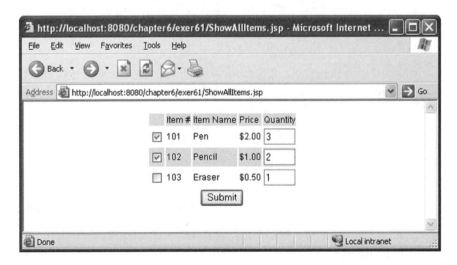

- The next page shows items selected with their quantities. User makes changes to selections, then clicks the Update button:

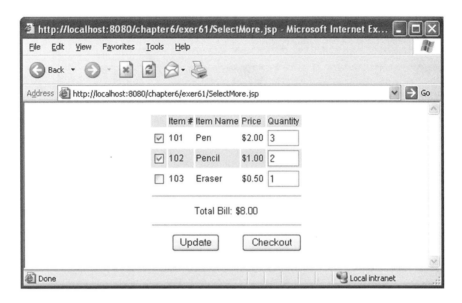

- The page shows a new total. User clicks the Checkout button:

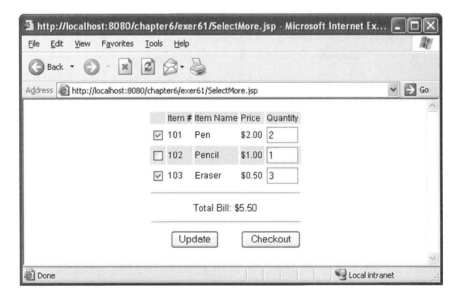

- The next page shows a summary of the user's order:

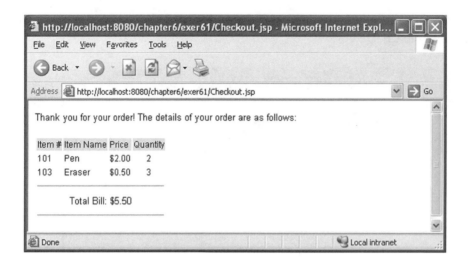

Solution:

```
<!-- Begin: Login.html -->
<HTML>
    <HEAD>
        <LINK REL="stylesheet" TYPE="text/css" HREF="../styles/styles.css"/>
        <SCRIPT LANGUAGE="JAVASCRIPT">
        function validate()
        {
            if (document.forms.main.firstName.value == "")
            {
                alert("First Name cannot be empty.");
                return false;
            }
            else if (document.forms.main.lastName.value == "")
            {
                alert("Last Name cannot be empty.");
                return false;
            }
            return true;
        }
        </SCRIPT>
    </HEAD>
    <BODY>
        <FORM NAME="main" ACTION="ShowAllItems.jsp" METHOD="POST">
            <TABLE>
```

```
                <TR CLASS="defaultText">
                    <TD>First name:</TD>
                    <TD><INPUT TYPE="text" NAME="firstName"></INPUT></TD>
                </TR>
                <TR CLASS="defaultText">
                    <TD>Last name:</TD>
                    <TD><INPUT TYPE="text" NAME="lastName"></INPUT></TD>
                </TR>
                <TR CLASS="defaultText">
                    <TD COLSPAN=2 ALIGN="CENTER">
                    <INPUT TYPE="submit" VALUE="Submit"
                      onclick="return validate()"></INPUT>
                    </TD>
                </TR>
            </TABLE>
        </FORM>
    </BODY>
</HTML>
<!-- End: Login.html -->


<!-- Begin: ShowAllItems.jsp -->
<HTML>
    <HEAD>
        <LINK REL="stylesheet" TYPE="text/css" HREF="../styles/styles.css"/>
    </HEAD>
    <BODY>
        <FORM ACTION="SelectMore.jsp" METHOD="POST">
            <TABLE ALIGN="center">
                <TR CLASS="tableEvenRow">
                    <TD> </TD>
                    <TD>Item #</TD>
                    <TD>Item Name</TD>
                    <TD>Price</TD>
                    <TD>Quantity</TD>
                </TR>
                <TR CLASS="tableOddRow">
                    <TD><INPUT TYPE="checkbox" NAME="penSelect"></INPUT></TD>
                    <TD>101</TD>
                    <TD>Pen</TD>
                    <TD>$2.00</TD>
                    <TD>
                <INPUT TYPE="text" NAME="penQty" SIZE="3" VALUE="1"></INPUT>
            </TD>
                </TR>
                <TR CLASS="tableEvenRow">
```

```html
            <TD><INPUT TYPE="checkbox" NAME="pencilSelect"></INPUT></TD>
            <TD>102</TD>
            <TD>Pencil</TD>
            <TD>$1.00</TD>
            <TD>
        <INPUT TYPE="text" NAME="pencilQty" SIZE="3"  VALUE="1">
        </INPUT>
    </TD>
        </TR>
        <TR CLASS="tableOddRow">
            <TD><INPUT TYPE="checkbox" NAME="eraserSelect"></INPUT></TD>
            <TD>103</TD>
            <TD>Eraser</TD>
            <TD>$0.50</TD>
            <TD>
        <INPUT TYPE="text" NAME="eraserQty" SIZE="3" VALUE="1">
        </INPUT>
    </TD>
        </TR>
        <TR>
            <TD ALIGN="center" COLSPAN=5>
                <INPUT TYPE="submit" NAME="submit" VALUE="Submit"</INPUT>
            </TD>
        </TR>
    </TABLE>
        </FORM>
    </BODY>
</HTML>
<!-- End: ShowAllItems.jsp -->


<!-- Begin: SelectMore.jsp -->
<%@ page import="java.text.DecimalFormat" %>
<%
    boolean bPenSelect = false, bPencilSelect = false, bEraserSelect = false;
    String penQty = "1", pencilQty = "1", eraserQty = "1";
    double totalBill = 0.0;
    String penSelect = request.getParameter("penSelect");
    if (penSelect != null && penSelect.equals("on"))
    {
        bPenSelect = true;
        penQty = request.getParameter("penQty");
        totalBill += Integer.parseInt(penQty) * 2.00;
    }
    String pencilSelect = request.getParameter("pencilSelect");
    if (pencilSelect != null && pencilSelect.equals("on"))
```

```
        {
            bPencilSelect = true;
            pencilQty = request.getParameter("pencilQty");
            totalBill += Integer.parseInt(pencilQty) * 1.00;
        }
        String eraserSelect = request.getParameter("eraserSelect");
        if (eraserSelect != null && eraserSelect.equals("on"))
        {
            bEraserSelect = true;
            eraserQty = request.getParameter("eraserQty");
            totalBill += Integer.parseInt(eraserQty) * 0.50;
        }
        DecimalFormat df = new DecimalFormat("#,##0.00");
%>
<HTML>
    <HEAD>
        <LINK REL="stylesheet" TYPE="text/css" HREF="../styles/styles.css" />
        <SCRIPT>
        function handleCheckout(obj)
        {
            if (obj.value == "Update")
            {
                document.forms.main.action="SelectMore.jsp";
            }
            else if (obj.value == "Checkout")
            {
                document.forms.main.action="Checkout.jsp";
            }
            document.forms.main.submit();
        }
        </SCRIPT>
    </HEAD>
    <BODY>
        <FORM NAME="main" METHOD="POST">
            <TABLE ALIGN="center">
                <TR CLASS="tableEvenRow">
                    <TD> </TD>
                    <TD>Item #</TD>
                    <TD>Item Name</TD>
                    <TD>Price</TD>
                    <TD>Quantity</TD>
                </TR>
                <TR CLASS="tableOddRow">
                    <TD>
                        <INPUT TYPE="checkbox"
```

```
                    NAME="penSelect" <%= (bPenSelect? "CHECKED" : "") %>>
          </INPUT>
       </TD>
       <TD>101</TD>
       <TD>Pen</TD>
       <TD>$2.00</TD>
       <TD>
          <INPUT TYPE="text" NAME="penQty" SIZE="3"
                  VALUE="<%= penQty %>">
          </INPUT>
       </TD>
   </TR>
   <TR CLASS="tableEvenRow">
       <TD>
          <INPUT TYPE="checkbox"
             NAME="pencilSelect" <%= (bPencilSelect? "CHECKED" : "") %>>
          </INPUT>
       </TD>
       <TD>102</TD>
       <TD>Pencil</TD>
       <TD>$1.00</TD>
       <TD>
          <INPUT TYPE="text"
                  NAME="pencilQty" SIZE="3" VALUE="<%= pencilQty %>">
          </INPUT>
       </TD>
   </TR>
   <TR CLASS="tableOddRow">
       <TD>
          <INPUT TYPE="checkbox"
                  NAME="eraserSelect" <%= (bEraserSelect? "CHECKED" : "" ) %>>
          </INPUT>
       </TD>
       <TD>103</TD>
       <TD>Eraser</TD>
       <TD>$0.50</TD>
       <TD>
          <INPUT TYPE="text" NAME="eraserQty" SIZE="3"
                  VALUE="<%= eraserQty %>"> </INPUT>
       </TD>
   </TR>
   <TR>
       <TD COLSPAN=5><HR></TD>
   </TR>
   <TR CLASS="defaultText">
```

```
                    <TD COLSPAN=5 ALIGN="center"> Total Bill: $<%= df.format(totalBill) %></TD>
                </TR>
                <TR>
                    <TD COLSPAN=5><HR></TD>
                </TR>
                <TR>
                    <TD ALIGN="center" COLSPAN=3>
                        <INPUT TYPE="button" NAME="update" VALUE="Update"
                                onclick="handleCheckout (this)">
                        </INPUT>
                    </TD>
                    <TD ALIGN="center" COLSPAN=3>
                        <INPUT TYPE="button" NAME="checkout" VALUE="Checkout"
                                onclick="handleCheckout(this)">
                        </INPUT>
                    </TD>
                </TR>
            </TABLE>
        </FORM>
    </BODY>
</HTML>
<!-- End: SelectMore.jsp -->

<!-- Begin: Checkout.jsp -->
<%
    boolean bPenSelect = false, bPencilSelect = false, bEraserSelect = false;
    String penQty = "1", pencilQty = "1", eraserQty = "1";
    double totalBill = 0.0;
    String penSelect = request.getParameter("penSelect");
    if (penSelect != null && penSelect.equals("on"))
    {
        bPenSelect = true;
        penQty = request.getParameter("penQty");
        totalBill += Integer.parseInt(penQty) * 2.00;
    }
    String pencilSelect = request.getParameter("pencilSelect");
    if (pencilSelect != null && pencilSelect.equals("on"))
    {
        bPencilSelect = true;
        pencilQty = request.getParameter("pencilQty");
        totalBill += Integer.parseInt(pencilQty) * 1.00;
    }
    String eraserSelect = request.getParameter("eraserSelect");
    if (eraserSelect != null && eraserSelect.equals("on"))
    {
```

```
        bEraserSelect = true;
        eraserQty = request.getParameter("eraserQty");
        totalBill += Integer.parseInt(eraserQty) * 0.50;
    }
%>
<HTML>
    <HEAD>
        <LINK REL="stylesheet" TYPE="text/css" HREF="../styles/styles.css" />
    </HEAD>
    <BODY>
        <SPAN CLASS="defaultText"> Thank you for your order!   The details of your order are as
                        follows:</SPAN><br><br>
        <TABLE>
            <TR CLASS="tableEvenRow">
                <TD>Item #</TD>
                <TD>Item Name</TD>
                <TD>Price</TD>
                <TD>Quantity</TD>
            </TR>
            <%
                if (bPenSelect)
                {
            %>
                    <TR CLASS="tableOddRow">
                        <TD>101</TD>
                        <TD>Pen</TD>
                        <TD>$2.00</TD>
                        <TD ALIGN="CENTER"><%= penQty %>     </TD>
                    </TR>
            <%
                }
                if (bPencilSelect)
                {
            %>
                    <TR CLASS="tableEvenRow">
                        <TD>102</TD>
                        <TD>Pencil</TD>
                        <TD>$1.00</TD>
                        <TD ALIGN="CENTER"><%= pencilQty %></TD>
                    </TR>
            <%
                }
                if (bEraserSelect)
                {
            %>
```

```
                    <TR CLASS="tableOddRow">
                    <TD>103</TD>
                        <TD>Eraser</TD>
                        <TD>$0.50</TD>
                        <TD ALIGN="CENTER"><%= eraserQty %></TD>
                    </TR>
            <%
                }
            %>
            <TR>
                    <TD COLSPAN=4><HR></TD>
            </TR>
            <TR CLASS="defaultText">
                    <TD COLSPAN=4 ALIGN="center">
                      Total Bill: $<%= df.format(totalBill) %>
                    </TD>
            </TR>
            <TR>
                    <TD COLSPAN=4><HR></TD>
            </TR>
        </TABLE>
    </BODY>
</HTML>
<!-- End: Checkout.jsp -->
```

6.2   Server-Level Redirection Using `response.sendRedirect()`

In Chapter 3, you saw how we could validate user input by using JavaScript. Sometimes it becomes important to validate at the server-level—i.e., to make sure all incoming data is valid before processing it. That way the business tier is certain the data is correct—independent of the client side scripts that may have inadvertently missed some of the critical validation logic. If data is invalid, the JSP can "redirect" the user back to the appropriate page, using the sendRedirect() method on the response object. Note that sendRedirect() always results in a GET.

For example, say that you want to redirect the user back to the login page if the last name box is empty. Create a new folder sec62 under C:\JSP\Chapter6, and copy Login.html and ProcessLogin.jsp from C:\JSP\Chapter6\sec61 into it. Modify ProcessLogin.jsp so that it does the server-level validation for the last name, as follows:

```
------------------------------------------------------------
<!-- Begin: ProcessLogin.jsp -->
<%
    String fName = request.getParameter("firstName");
    String lName = request.getParameter("lastName");
    if ( lName == null || lName.equals("") )
```

```
        {
            response.sendRedirect("Login.html");
        }
%>
<HTML>
    <BODY>
        Welcome, <%= fName %> <%= lName %>, to the second page!
    </BODY>
</HTML>
<!-- End: ProcessLogin.jsp -->
----------------------------------------------------------
```

Open the following URL:

```
http://localhost:8080/chapter6/sec62/Login.html
```

It should look like this:

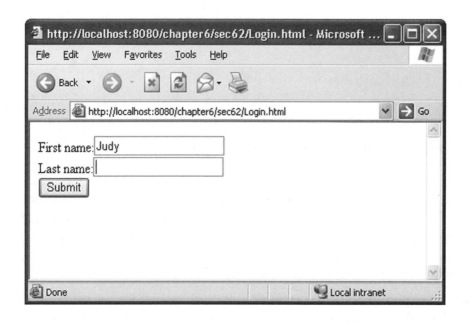

If you leave the last name empty and hit the Submit button, the page gets redirected back to Login.html. The screen would look like the one shown on the following page (after redirection):

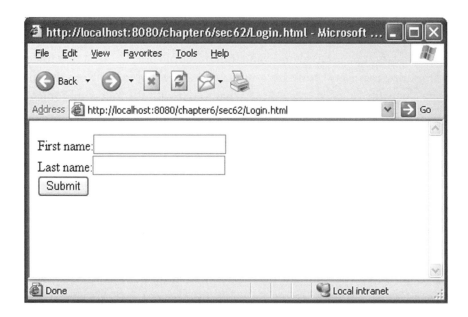

At this stage, if you enter some value in the last name and hit the Submit button, it will take you to ProcessLogin.jsp as before.

6.3 Sessions

Every time you send a request to the server, it treats you as a new user. It does not know that you are the same person who just asked for some other URL a few moments ago. That's how HTTP protocol works—it is called a "stateless protocol" for this reason—but it can be a problem in certain situations.

For example, say that you are logged in and are ordering an item at an online shopping site. When you click on "Add to cart" and proceed to look at some other item, it is critical that the server recognize that you are the same person who wants to continue shopping, and receive one comprehensive bill at the end. As mentioned earlier, the request parameters are valid for only one page downstream—so if you had exactly two pages for the shopping and checkout, then you would be okay using the request parameters, but that is hardly the case in real life! A shopping process usually spans a few pages (more than two), which means that the values entered by the user on the first page are not available on the third page and beyond. Similarly, values entered on the second page will not be available on the fourth page and beyond.

To verify that the request parameters are available only one page down, try this: Say that in the example discussed in Section 6.2, you move the redirection code to another JSP called Validate.jsp, which simply redirects you to the right page based on a validation piece of code. Create a new folder sec63 under C:\JSP\Chapter6. Copy Login.html from Section 6.2 and ProcessLogin.jsp from the end of Section 6.1 into it. Create a new file called Validate.jsp in that folder with the following content:

```
-----------------------------------------------------------
<!-- Begin: Validate.jsp -->
<%
    String fName = request.getParameter("firstName");
    String lName = request.getParameter("lastName");
    if ( lName == null || lName.equals("") )
    {
        response.sendRedirect("Login.html");
    }
      else
    {
        response.sendRedirect("ProcessLogin.jsp");
    }
%>
<!-- End: Validate.jsp -->
-----------------------------------------------------------
```

Modify Login.html so that the form's action is now Validate.jsp instead of ProcessLogin.jsp. Login.html should now look like this:

```
-----------------------------------------------------------
<!-- Begin: Login.html -->
<HTML>
    <BODY>
        <FORM NAME="main" ACTION="Validate.jsp" METHOD="POST">
            First name:<INPUT TYPE=TEXT NAME="firstName"></INPUT><BR>
            Last name:<INPUT TYPE=TEXT NAME="lastName"></INPUT><BR>
            <INPUT TYPE=SUBMIT VALUE="Submit"></INPUT>
        </FORM>
    </BODY>
</HTML>
<!-- End: Login.html -->
-----------------------------------------------------------
```

ProcessLogin.jsp would be same as in Section 6.1.

Open Login.html using:

http://localhost:8080/chapter6/sec63/Login.html

The screen would look like this:

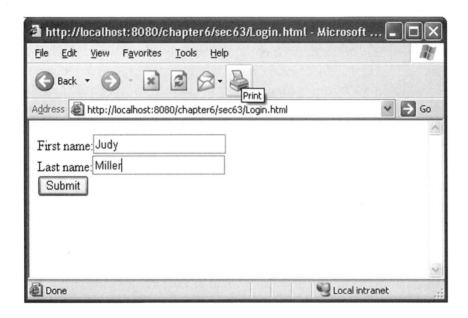

Enter some text in the first and last name fields and hit the Submit button. It will show this screen:

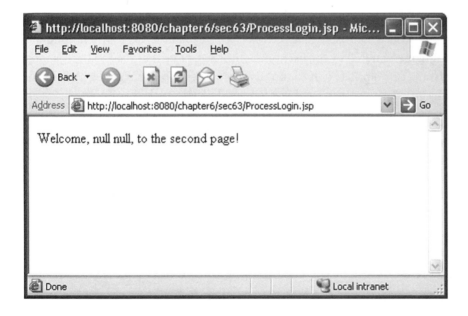

As you can see, it shows "null null" instead of "Judy Miller," because you tried to access parameters on the request that were more than one page in the past (two pages in this case—Validate.jsp and Login.html).

A session, as opposed to a request, is another implicit object available for use in your JSP. The big difference between request and session is that request lives only from one resource request to another, whereas session remains intact from the time the user opens the browser until he or she closes it. In between, the user may have visited several pages, but the session retains values from beginning to end. To retain and extract values entered more than one page in the past, you need to use the session implicit object that is available in every JSP page, just like request and response. The session object is of type HttpSession defined in the javax.servlet.http package, and you can save any number of key-value pairs on it, where the *key* needs to be a String and the *value* could be any valid object (so the value cannot be primitive data such as int, char, and double). It is similar to a HashMap that contains key-value pairs. You can add your own key-value pairs to the session HashMap for later retrieval.

Values put on the session are available across multiple JSP pages, so even if the user goes from URL-1 to URL-2 to URL-3, a value put in the session on URL-1 would be available for access in URL-3. This is a major advantage over the request object that, as we saw earlier, can at most access values from one URL back. Since the session object spans multiple pages, you can conveniently use it to store the fact that a user logged in, and also save his or her first and last name entered on Login.html, for possible later retrieval (perhaps several pages downstream).

Let's say you want to display the user's first and last names on ThankYou.jsp—for example, Thank you, John Smith, for your order! instead of just a generic Thank you for your order! (where John and Smith are the first and last names entered by the user on Login.html). Note that ThankYou.jsp is more than one JSP page away from Login.html, so you cannot use the request object to get first name and last name entered on Login.html. Using a session object is a good idea in such situations.

To understand sessions, consider the example we just saw: Validate.jsp. If ProcessLogin.jsp is going to be able to get the first and last names entered on Login.html, we need to first store the first and last names in the session in Validate.jsp so that we can retrieve them back from the session in ProcessLogin.jsp. The user enters first and last names on Login.html and hits submit, which takes him or her to a second page (Validate.jsp) that reads the first and last names entered on Login.html using the request object, and stores these on the session object, using keys FIRST_NAME and LAST_NAME (you are free to choose any key name, as long as it is unique on the session object). After this, Validate.jsp "redirects" to the third page (ProcessLogin.jsp), which displays the message Welcome, John Smith, to the second page! (using first and last name values from the session object).

Let's follow the process step-by-step. Modify Validate.jsp so that it reads the first and last names from the request, and, if both of these are not null and not empty, stores these values on the session object and calls the sendRedirect() method on the response object passing it the destination as ProcessLogin.jsp. If either the first or the last name is empty, it should call sendRedirect() on response, passing it the destination as Login.html. Modify ProcessLogin.jsp to get the first and last names from the session object and to display a message Welcome, John Smith, to the second page! (where John and Smith need to be replaced with the actual values entered by the user on Login.html).

Validate.jsp would now look like this:

```
-----------------------------------------------------------------
<!-- Begin: Validate.jsp -->
<%
    String fName = request.getParameter("firstName");
    String lName = request.getParameter("lastName");
    if (fName != null && !fName.trim().equals("")
        && lName != null && !lName.trim().equals(""))
    {
        session.setAttribute("FIRST_NAME", fName);
        session.setAttribute("LAST_NAME", lName);
        response.sendRedirect("ProcessLogin.jsp");
    }
    else response.sendRedirect("Login.html");
%>
<!-- End: Validate.jsp -->
-----------------------------------------------------------------
```

Observe how we used the setAttribute() method on the session object, passing it the key-value pair we want to store.

ProcessLogin.jsp would be as follows:

```
-----------------------------------------------------------------
<!-- Begin: ProcessLogin.jsp -->
<HTML>
    <BODY>
        Welcome, <%= (session.getAttribute("FIRST_NAME")
        + " " + session.getAttribute("LAST_NAME")) %>, to the second page!
    </BODY>
</HTML>
<!-- End: ProcessLogin.jsp -->
-----------------------------------------------------------------
```

Notice the getAttribute() method on the session to get back the first and last name values we stored in Validate.jsp.

Open Login.html using the following URL:

```
http://localhost:8080/chapter6/sec63/Login.html
```

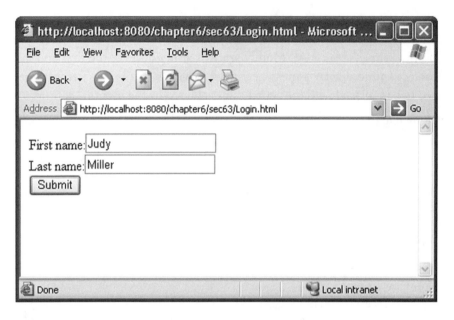

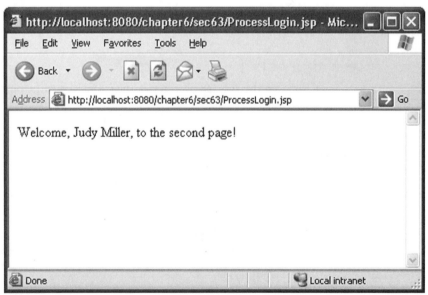

The disadvantage of using sessions is that values can be retained even when you do not want them. So you need to be careful in cleaning up session values when you do not need them. In order to remove a specific key-value pair, use the removeAttribute() method on a session object, passing it the key of the attribute to be removed.

6.4 Summary

In this chapter, you learned how JSP can be used to process input values on HTML forms to create "dynamic" content. You also learned what sessions are and how to use them to retain values across multiple levels of JSP pages. In the next chapter, you will learn about databases, SQL, JDBC, and how to query and manipulate databases from within a JSP.

6.5 Chapter Quiz

1. Which of the following is true? (Select all that apply.)

    i. You must declare and instantiate the request and response objects inside your JSP before you can use them in your code.

    ii. An HTTP request can be either a GET or a POST.

    iii. An HTTP response represents the server's response to the client.

    iv. To access the input field value on an HTML form on a previous page, you use the get-Parameter() method on the request, passing it the input field name.

    v. You can store either a primitive data type or an object as the attribute value in a session.

    a. All of the above

    b. (i), (ii), (iii), and (v) only

    c. (ii), (iii), and (iv) only

    d. (i), (ii), (iii), and (v) only

2. Which of the following is true? (Select all that apply.)

    i. A session retains the value stored across multiple pages.

    ii. A request can retain the parameters from the immediate previous page only.

    iii. The HTTP response usually sends the final content as HTML, irrespective of what the initial request is for.

    iv. The disadvantage of using sessions is that values may be retained even when you do not want them; so you need to be careful by cleaning up session values when you do not need them.

    v. You do not have to instantiate or declare the session object in your JSP; you can simply begin using it.

    a. All of the above

    b. (ii), (iii), (iv), and (v) only

    c. (ii), (iii), and (v) only

    d. (i), (ii), and (iv) only

6.6 Answers to Quiz

1. The correct answer is (c). All statements except (i) and (v) are true. Option (i) is false because you do not have to declare or instantiate the request and response objects inside your JSP. You can simply start using them, since they are implicit objects already defined for you. Option (v) is false because you cannot store a primitive data type as the attribute value in a session.

2. The correct answer is (a). All statements are true.

6.7 Unsolved Assignments

Assignment 6.1

Objective: To practice storing user-entered data in a session and retrieving it later.

Steps:

- Create a new folder called assign61 under C:\JSP\Chapter6. Copy Login.html, SelectMore.jsp, ShowAllItems.jsp, and Checkout.jsp from Solved Exercise 6.1 into this folder. Also copy Validate.jsp from Section 6.3 into this folder.

- Modify Login.html so that the form's action is now Validate.jsp (instead of ShowAllItems.jsp).

- Modify Validate.jsp so that in a successful login (i.e., first name and last name are not empty) it redirects to ShowAllItems.jsp (instead of ProcessLogin.jsp).

- Modify Checkout.jsp so that it displays the first and last names that the user entered on the login page in its message. (*Hint:* Use the session object that stored the first and last names in Validate.jsp.) For example, if the user entered "John" as the first name and "Smith" as the last name on the login page, Checkout.jsp should display the message as

  ```
  Thank you, John Smith, for your order! The details of your order are as follows:
  ```

  followed by the list of items selected, including each item's number, name, price, and quantity (as before).

- Submit Login.html, Validate.jsp, and Checkout.jsp.

  Sample interactions are shown next:

User enters first and last name and hits the Submit button:

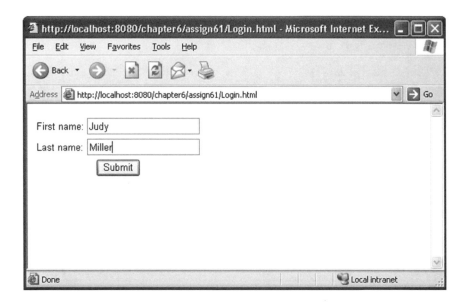

User makes a couple of selections and hits Submit button:

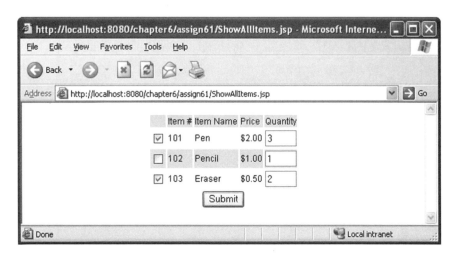

The next page shows items selected with their quantities. User clicks Checkout button:

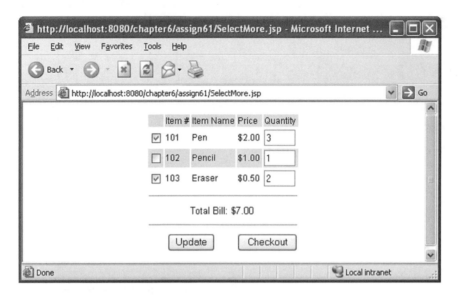

The next page shows a message with the user's first and last name entered on the login page, followed by a summary of the order:

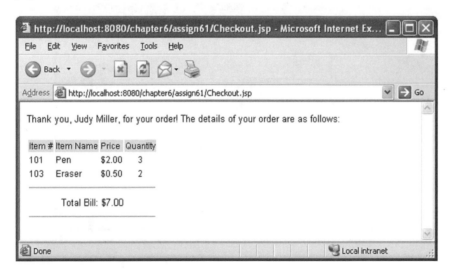

Assignment 6.2

Objective: To learn how to use the HashMap utility class to process user information.

Steps:

- Create a new folder called `assign62` under `C:\JSP\Chapter6`.

- Copy `Login.html` from Assignment 3.2 (if available) and rename it to `Login.jsp`. Change the form's action to `ShowAllItems.jsp` (instead of `ShowAllItems.html`).

- Alternatively (if Assignment 3.2 is not available), copy `Login.html` from Solved Exercise 6.1 and rename it to `Login.jsp`. Modify it to show two `INPUT` fields called `username` and `password` (instead of `firstName` and `lastName`). For the `username` field, use `TYPE="text"`, but for password field, use `TYPE="password"` (so when the user types in the password, it doesn't display the actual characters typed in). Implement the following form-level validation using JavaScript:

  - If either `username` or `password` is empty, it should pop-up an error message: "`Username and password are required`".

  - When user enters a password value of 3 characters or less, it should show an error: "`Password must be at least 4 characters`".

- Copy `Validate.jsp`, `ShowAllItems.jsp`, `SelectMore.jsp`, and `Checkout.jsp` from Assignment 6.1 into this folder.

- Modify `Validate.jsp` as follows:

  - Add a `page` directive to import all classes from the `java.util` package.

  - Instantiate and populate two `HashMap` objects: The first should contain username and password pairs, with the following values:

```
-----------------------------
Username     Password
-----------------------------
jsmith       bluesky
jmiller      clearwater
mtaylor      greentree
-----------------------------
```

The other should contain username and full name pairs with the following values:

```
-----------------------------
Username     Full name
-----------------------------
jsmith       John Smith
jmiller      Judy Miller
mtaylor      Mike Taylor
-----------------------------
```

- Use the `request` object to get the username and password from the login page. To determine whether this username and password combination exists in the first `HashMap`, check if the username entered by the user exists in the key set of the `HashMap`. If it does, look up that username in the username/password `HashMap` and see if its corresponding password is the same as the password entered by the user.

- If the username/password combination is valid, do the following:

  - Using the second `HashMap` (username/full name pairs), get the full name corresponding to the username entered by the user. (*Hint:* Use the `get()` method on the `HashMap` class.)

  - Store the full name of the user in the session (using an appropriate key such as "FULL_NAME"), and redirect the user to `ShowAllItems.jsp`.

- If the username/password combination is not valid, redirect the user back to the login page, sending it a new parameter called `state` with a value of `error` as follows:

  `response.sendRedirect("Login.jsp?state=error");`

  Note that this would invoke `Login.jsp` as a `GET` (as opposed to a `POST`).

- Modify `Login.jsp` to look for this `state` parameter from the `request`. If it contains the value `error`, display an error in red just above the username field, stating `Username/password combination is incorrect. Please try again.` Add a new style in `styles.css` for the red text.

- Modify `Checkout.jsp` to get the full name stored on the session (instead of first and last names separately) and display the "thank you" message as before.

- Submit `Login.jsp`, `Validate.jsp`, `Checkout.jsp`, and `styles.css`. Sample interactions follow.

User enters `jsmith` as a username but password other than `bluesky`, then hits the Submit button:

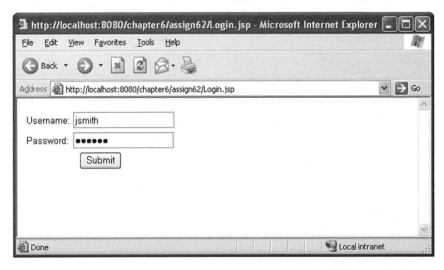

Page shows error message and asks user to try again:

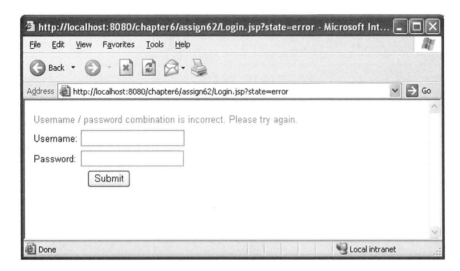

User enters jsmith as username and bluesky as password, and hits the Submit button:

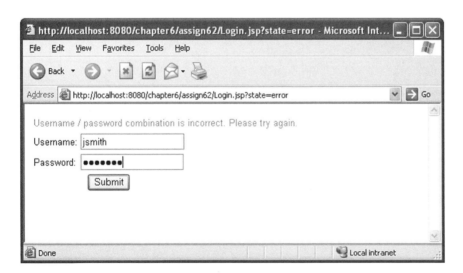

Page shows list of items to choose from. User selects a couple of items, and hits the Submit button:

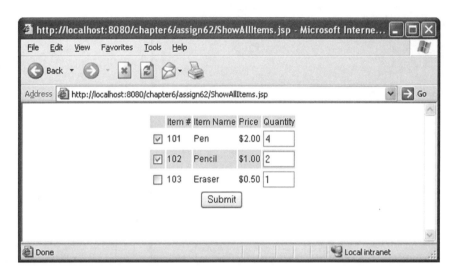

The next page shows items selected with total bill. User clicks the Checkout button:

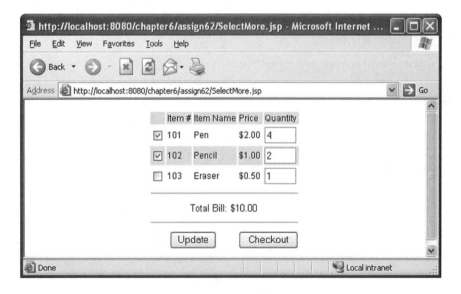

The final screen shows a "thank you" message with first and last names matching the username entered on the login page, followed by a summary of the order:

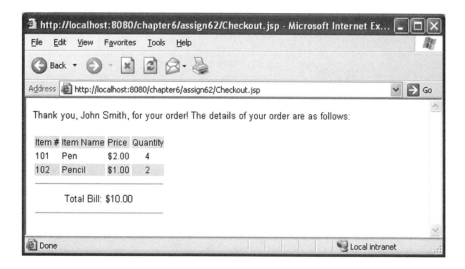

CHAPTER 7

SQL, JDBC, and Writing Database-Driven JSPs

Chapter Objectives

- Learn about Web database programming using Java and JSP

- Understand what SQL is, how to create databases and tables, and how to insert and query for data using a MySQL database

- Become familiar with JDBC drivers and how to use them in connecting to a database via Java code

- Learn how to develop JSPs that connect to a MySQL database

7.1   Database Overview

We are all familiar with using tables and know that a table consists of rows and columns of data. A *database* is a collection of one or more (usually several) tables. In a database context, each row of a table is called a *record*, and the columns in a row constitute *fields*. For example, consider the table of customer data shown here:

Customer ID	First Name	Last Name	Age	Sales Amount
101	John	Smith	35	100.0
102	Judy	Miller	30	150.0
103	Neil	Armstrong	25	200.0

This is a table that has three records, with each record containing five fields (or columns). The first record represents one customer and has a field called "Customer ID" with a value of 101, a field called "First Name" with a value of "John," and so on. Similarly, the second record represents the next customer, and has its own values for the same field names. Note that fields can be of different data types, just like Java data types. In this example, the first and last names are text type data, whereas age is an int type data, and sales amount is a double type data.

In a real-world environment, you would need many such tables to store all of your data. For example, you may have another table called Orders that stores the order information corresponding to customers. All tables can collectively be stored in a database on the server computer.

Let's recap the key concepts discussed here:

- A *database* is a storehouse of data organized into *tables*.
- Each *table* is a set of *records*.
- Each *record* consists of one or more *fields*. The *records* are the same as the rows of the table, and the *fields* represent the columns of the table (which means that each record would have the same number of fields as the number of columns in the table).

7.2   Structured Query Language (SQL)

Many times you may be interested in seeing not the entire content of a table, but only those records that fulfill certain criteria. For example, you may want to find records in the Customer table that have age greater than 30. In a sense, you want to "filter" the data in the Customer table to get a subset of all records. A request for specific data is technically called a "query" in database jargon. The language used to create data and to write queries is called *Structured Query Language (SQL)* (pronounced *sequel*).

There are many vendors of databases—for example, Oracle, Sybase, and MySQL—each of which supports the same SQL language (with slight variations from vendor to vendor, but we can ignore such differences for the moment). So if you learn the SQL language, you can create data and write most of the queries that any database vendor would support. The first step in understanding databases is learning the SQL language. One of the databases (MySQL) is actually free, so go ahead and install it by following instructions in Appendix G.

Once you are done installing, open a new command prompt window, change directory to C:\MySQL\bin (replace C:\MySQL with the exact directory where you installed MySQL), type mysql -u root, and hit Enter. It should come to the *MySQL prompt* (a prompt that looks like mysql>), as shown here:

```
Command Prompt - mysql -u root

C:\>cd MySQL\bin

C:\MySQL\bin>mysql -u root
Welcome to the MySQL monitor.  Commands end with ; or \g.
Your MySQL connection id is 4 to server version: 5.0.27-community-nt

Type 'help;' or '\h' for help. Type '\c' to clear the buffer.

mysql>
```

7.2.1 Essential SQL

You'll be seeing here simple SQL commands that contain only a subset of the full syntax for each command. The idea here is to learn how to connect to a MySQL database from within Java and to use elementary SQL commands. For a comprehensive syntax of these SQL commands, you may want to go to the MySQL reference site:

http://dev.mysql.com/doc/

Click on the "View" link under the "HTML Online" header in the "MySQL Reference Manual" section, and then on "SQL Statement Syntax" on the right.

7.2.1.1 Creating a Database

To create a new database, there is a "create database" command to which you need to provide the name of the database you want to create. Create a database called salesdatabase, by saying:

```
create database salesdatabase; <hit Enter>
```

The session would look like this:

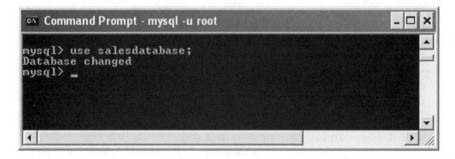

Next time you start MySQL, you can open this database with the use command as follows:

```
mysql> use salesdatabase;
Database changed
```

The session would look like this:

```
Command Prompt - mysql -u root                          _ □ ✕
mysql> use salesdatabase;
Database changed
mysql> _
```

7.2.1.2 Creating a Table

As mentioned earlier, a database is a collection of one or more tables. Create a new table called customer with the five columns ("fields"), by using the create command as follows

```
mysql> create table customer (customer_id int(5) not null primary key, first_name char(10),
last_name char(20), age int(3), sales_amount decimal(6,2));
Query OK, 0 rows affected (0.05 sec)
```

Note that you cannot use spaces in the column names. To make column names more readable, the convention is to use the underscore character (_) to separate parts of the column name, such as first_name.

A few notes on the column spec:

not null   Means the value in that column cannot be empty for any record. If you try to insert a record with an empty value in that column, it will show an error.

primary key	Means the value in that column is unique in the entire table. In other words, every row in the table will have a distinct value in that column. This implies that no two rows will have the same value in that column. If you try to insert rows with the same value in the primary key column, it will error out.
int	Means that these columns (customer_id and age) can contain only integer data, so no character or floating point data would be allowed. If you try to save character or floating point data in a column that is integer, you will get a SQL error.
char	Means that these columns (first_name and last_name) can contain character (text) data. The number in parentheses following the word char shows the maximum number of text characters that the column can take. So, char(10) after first_name would mean that values in the first_name column cannot exceed 10 characters in length. Note that any numeric characters that you save in a char column are treated as textual characters, so if you save 123 into a char column, it would be saved and interpreted as the text string "123" (which is distinct from the number 123).
decimal	Means the column can contain fractional values. (6, 2) means the total field length is 6, out of which 2 places are reserved for the fractional part (digits after the decimal). The integer part can occupy up to 4 digits, so the decimal point itself does not take up any space—its position is implicitly taken to be between the 4th and 5th digits.

Use the show tables command to list all tables in the database.

The session would look like this:

```
Command Prompt - mysql -u root

mysql> use salesdatabase;
Database changed
mysql> create table customer (customer_id int(5) not null primary key,
 first_name char(10), last_name char(20), age int(3), sales_amount dec
imal(6,2));
Query OK, 0 rows affected (0.06 sec)

mysql> show tables;
+-----------------------+
| Tables_in_salesdatabase |
+-----------------------+
| customer              |
+-----------------------+
1 row in set (0.01 sec)

mysql>
```

To verify that it did create a table with the specs you supplied, type in desc customer; and it will spit out the structure of the customer table that it just created, as shown here:

```
Command Prompt - mysql -u root                                    _ □ ×

mysql> desc customer;
+-------------+-------------+------+-----+---------+-------+
| Field       | Type        | Null | Key | Default | Extra |
+-------------+-------------+------+-----+---------+-------+
| customer_id | int(5)      | NO   | PRI |         |       |
| first_name  | char(10)    | YES  |     | NULL    |       |
| last_name   | char(20)    | YES  |     | NULL    |       |
| age         | int(3)      | YES  |     | NULL    |       |
| sales_amount| decimal(6,2)| YES  |     | NULL    |       |
+-------------+-------------+------+-----+---------+-------+
5 rows in set (0.02 sec)

mysql>
```

In the preceding create command, the word int after customer_id and age implies that these columns can contain only integer data, so no character or floating point data would be allowed. If you try to save character or floating point data in a column that is integer, you will get a SQL error. The word char after the first_name and last_name columns implies that these two columns would contain character (text) data. The number in parentheses following the word char shows the maximum number of text characters that the column can take. So, char(10) after first_name would mean that values in the first_name column cannot exceed 10 characters in length. Note that any numeric characters that you save in a char column are treated as textual characters, so if you save 123 into a char column, it would be saved and interpreted as the text string "123" (which is distinct from the number 123).

7.2.1.3 Inserting Data into a Table

To insert data into the customer table, use the insert command as follows:

```
mysql>insert into customer (customer_id, first_name, last_name, age, sales_amount) values (101,
'John', 'Smith', 35, 100.00);
Query OK, 1 row affected (0.03 sec)
```

The command window would look like this:

```
Command Prompt - mysql -u root                                    _ □ ×

mysql> insert into customer (customer_id, first_name, last_name, age, sales_amou
nt) values (101, 'John', 'Smith', 35, 100.0);
Query OK, 1 row affected (0.00 sec)

mysql>
```

7.2.1.4 Querying a Database Using select

To confirm that your data has been inserted correctly into the customer table, use a select query statement as follows:

```
mysql>select * from customer;
```

The session would look like this:

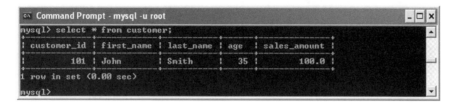

Repeat the insert command with new data to insert the second and third rows:

```
mysql>insert into customer (customer_id, first_name, last_name, age, sales_amount) values (102,
'Judy', 'Miller', 30, 150.0);
Query OK, 1 row affected (0.03 sec)
```

```
mysql>insert into customer (customer_id, first_name, last_name, age, sales_amount) values (103,
'Neil', 'Armstrong', 25, 200.0);
Query OK, 1 row affected (0.03 sec)
```

Now do a select once more, to see all three rows:

```
mysql> select * from customer;
```

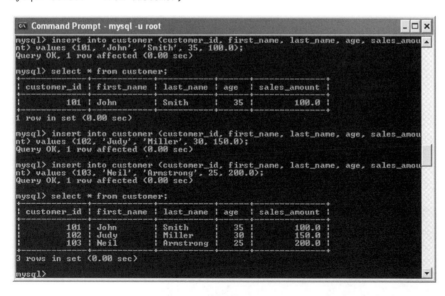

The asterisk (*) that appears in select * from . . . means you are asking it to get all columns from
the table. You can also specify the exact columns that you want to retrieve, for example:

```
mysql> select customer_id, last_name from customer;
```

```
Command Prompt - mysql -u root                              _ □ ×
mysql> select customer_id, last_name from customer;
+-------------+-----------+
| customer_id | last_name |
+-------------+-----------+
|         101 | Smith     |
|         102 | Miller    |
|         103 | Armstrong |
+-------------+-----------+
3 rows in set (0.00 sec)

mysql>
```

You can also put a filter on the records being retrieved, using the where clause in your select. For example, to get customer records that have age greater than or equal to 30, you would say

```
select * from customer where age >= 30;
```

```
Command Prompt - mysql -u root                              _ □ ×
mysql> select * from customer where age >=30;
+-------------+------------+-----------+-----+--------------+
| customer_id | first_name | last_name | age | sales_amount |
+-------------+------------+-----------+-----+--------------+
|         101 | John       | Smith     |  35 |        100.0 |
|         102 | Judy       | Miller    |  30 |        150.0 |
+-------------+------------+-----------+-----+--------------+
2 rows in set (0.00 sec)

mysql>
```

Again, for a full, comprehensive syntax of select, go to the MySQL reference site in Appendix D.

7.2.1.5 Using Aliases for Tables and Columns

Inside the select statement, you can use an alias name for a table and/or for each of the column(s) returned in the query. For example, say that you want to use an alias name of cs for the customer table. Your select may then look like this:

```
mysql> select cs.customer_id, cs.last_name from customer cs;
```

The output would be exactly the same as before:

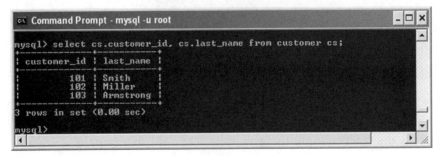

```
Command Prompt - mysql -u root                              _ □ ×
mysql> select cs.customer_id, cs.last_name from customer cs;
+-------------+-----------+
| customer_id | last_name |
+-------------+-----------+
|         101 | Smith     |
|         102 | Miller    |
|         103 | Armstrong |
+-------------+-----------+
3 rows in set (0.00 sec)

mysql>
```

The table alias did not seem to help much here, but we will see how it is useful when doing a table join shortly. Let's not use the table alias until that time.

For a column alias, say that you want to use an alias name of cid for the customer_id column and lname for the last_name column. Your select would now be as follows:

```
mysql> select customer_id as cid, last_name as lname from customer;
```

The SQL output would look something like this:

```
Command Prompt - mysql -u root                                          _ □ ×

mysql> select customer_id as cid, last_name as lname from customer;
+------+-----------+
| cid  | lname     |
+------+-----------+
| 101  | Smith     |
| 102  | Miller    |
| 103  | Armstrong |
+------+-----------+
3 rows in set (0.00 sec)

mysql>
```

Note how the output column headers have changed to use the alias names instead of the original names.

7.2.1.6 Using Library Functions in select

MySQL has some useful library functions that you can use to get derived values from the query. As an example, say that you want to know the maximum value in the age column of the customer table. For this, you can use the max library function as follows:

```
mysql> select max(age) from customer;
```

The output may be as shown here:

```
Command Prompt - mysql -u root                                          _ □ ×

mysql> select max(age) from customer;
+----------+
| max(age) |
+----------+
|       35 |
+----------+
1 row in set (0.00 sec)

mysql>
```

Notice how the column header shows "max(age)". You could combine the use of aliases with library functions. So if you want "max(age)" to show up as "maxAge" instead, your command needs to be as follows:

```
mysql> select max(age) as maxAge from customer;
```

The command session is shown next:

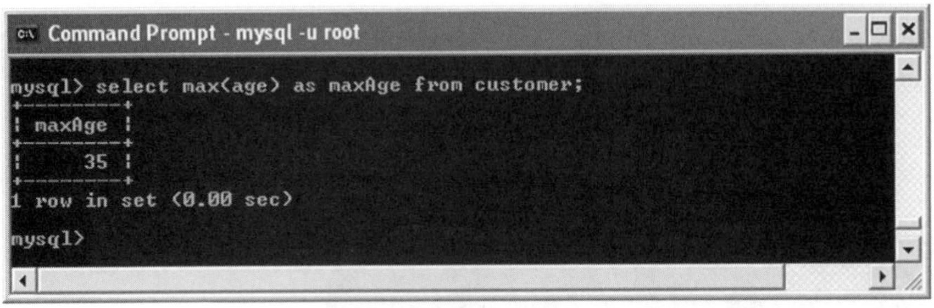

Again, notice that the column header changed to "maxAge".

7.2.1.7 Deleting Records Using delete

The delete command needs to be used to delete one or more records from a table. To delete specific record(s), you need to specify a where condition. For example;

```
mysql> delete from customer where customer_id=103;
```

The command session may look like this:

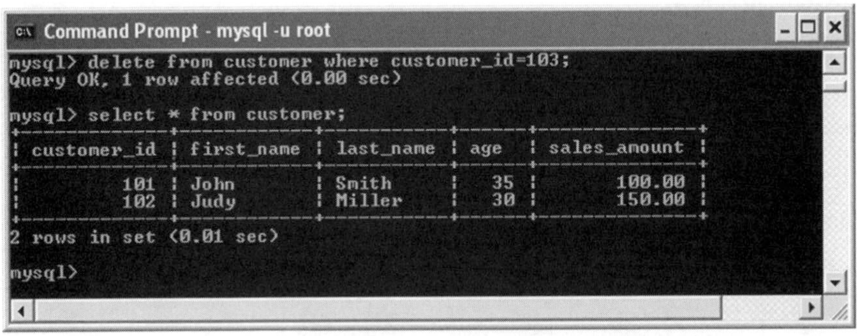

This was only to show the concept; we do want all three records there, so add back the record using insert one more time.

Note that if you do not use the where clause in delete, it will delete *all* records from the table, so you need to be extremely careful with delete!

7.2.1.8 Using the auto_increment Option

As stated earlier, the primary key in a table needs to contain unique values. One way to implement this is to use values starting from 1 for the first record inserted and incrementing by 1 each time a new record is inserted after the first. So you would have values of 1, 2, 3, . . . in the primary key column.

Instead of explicitly inserting the value of the primary key in each insert, you can have MySQL auto-generate and insert it for you, so that you can specify only the rest of the columns in the insert statement. For this, you need to use the auto_increment word next to the name of the column for which you want it to apply. MySQL will automatically begin with a value of 1 for the first insert and increment by 1 for each new insert after the first. Had you used the auto_increment clause for the customer_id column in the customer table, the create statement would have looked something like this:

```
mysql> create table customer (customer_id int(5) not null primary key auto_increment, first_name
char(10), last_name char(20), age int(3), sales_amount decimal(6,2));
Query OK, 0 rows affected (0.05 sec)
```

This is a useful feature but you need to be careful when you are deleting records because the value of the primary key for the next record inserted after a delete may not reuse the primary key of the record deleted, resulting in gaps in the sequence. Also, it seems to have a problem if you want the values to start from a number other than 1. For these reasons, we will not be using the auto_increment clause in this book beyond this point. Instead, we will either explicitly specify the value of the primary key during the insert or use the max function to get the maximum value of the primary key currently in the table, add 1 to it and use the result as the primary key to insert for the next record.

7.2.1.9   Foreign Key

The customer table currently has five columns: customer_id, first_name, last_name, age, and sales_amount. What if you want to add more information about a customer, such as address? You would then need a few more columns in the customer table, such as: address_line1, address_line2, city, state, and zip. What if you need still more information, such as phone number, driving license number, social security number, etc.? The list can go on; as you can see, you would soon end up with an unmanageable number of columns in the customer table.

To solve this problem, bigger tables are broken down into multiple, smaller ones. For example, we could create a new table called address that stores the address information of a customer. One address record is required per customer record, so it is a "one-to-one" relationship. Other tables could have a "one-to-many" relationship, such as one customer could have multiple orders, where orders are stored in a separate order table.

In the address table, if you stored the address information only (address_line1, address_line2, city, state, and zip), there is no way to tell which customer this address information applies to. So you need one more column in the address table and that column needs to be customer_id of the customer table. In other words, every address record will contain a field called customer_id that contains the customer_id of the associated customer record. That way you can "link up" each address record with a corresponding customer record.

To see a foreign key in action, go ahead and create an address table as follows:

```
mysql>create table address (address_id int(5) not null primary key, customer_id int(5) not null,
address_line1 char(30) not null, address_line2 char(30), city char(20) not null, state char(2)
not null, zip int(5) not null);
```

Insert three rows in it as follows:

```
mysql>insert into address (address_id, customer_id, address_line1, city, state, zip) values (1,
101, '1234 Main St', 'Atlanta', 'GA', 10000);
Query OK, 1 row affected (0.03 sec)

mysql>insert into address (address_id, customer_id, address_line1, city, state, zip) values (2,
102, '2000 Miller Ave', 'Boston', 'MA', 20000);
Query OK, 1 row affected (0.03 sec)

mysql>insert into address (address_id, customer_id, address_line1, city, state, zip) values (3,
103, '5000 North Dr', 'Chicago', 'IL', 30000);
Query OK, 1 row affected (0.03 sec)
```

Do a select on address table to ensure the data looks right, as shown here:

7.2.1.10   Inner Join

Breaking down bigger tables into multiple smaller ones has its own repercussions. If you want to look at a customer's first and last name and also address information at the same time, you cannot do it as easily as when you have one combined table. One option is to perform two separate SQL queries: one to get the customer record, note its customer_id and use it to get the related address record, and finally display all required information together.

A cleaner and more concise approach is to use an "inner join" between the customer and address tables. A "join" between two tables creates a Cartesian product of the two tables and returns the matching records from the Cartesian product, based on the match condition specified. Here, the words "Cartesian product" mean a temporary table that takes each record from the customer table, loops through the address table, and attaches the address record at the end—the customer_id in both records may or may not be the same. Since the customer and address tables have three records each, the Cartesian product between the two tables would contain nine records as follows:

customer_id	first_name	last_name	age	sales_amount	address_id	customer_id	address_line1	address_line2	city	state	zip
101	John	Smith	35	100.00	1	101	1234 Main St		Atlanta	GA	10000
101	John	Smith	35	100.00	2	102	2000 Miller Ave		Boston	MA	20000
101	John	Smith	35	100.00	3	103	5000 North Dr		Chicago	IL	30000
102	Judy	Miller	30	150.00	1	101	1234 Main St		Atlanta	GA	10000
102	Judy	Miller	30	150.00	2	102	2000 Miller Ave		Boston	MA	20000
102	Judy	Miller	30	150.00	3	103	5000 North Dr		Chicago	IL	30000
103	Neil	Armstrong	25	200.00	1	101	1234 Main St		Atlanta	GA	10000
103	Neil	Armstrong	25	200.00	2	102	2000 Miller Ave		Boston	MA	20000
103	Neil	Armstrong	25	200.00	3	103	5000 North Dr		Chicago	IL	30000

From this Cartesian product, SQL picks those rows that match the join condition, if specified. Without the join condition, the entire Cartesian product would be returned (which we don't want). The ones we are interested are highlighted in the Cartesian product shown next:

customer_id	first_name	last_name	age	sales_amount	address_id	customer_id	address_line1	address_line2	city	state	zip
101	John	Smith	35	100.00	1	101	1234 Main St		Atlanta	GA	10000
101	John	Smith	35	100.00	2	102	2000 Miller Ave		Boston	MA	20000
101	John	Smith	35	100.00	3	103	5000 North Dr		Chicago	IL	30000
102	Judy	Miller	30	150.00	1	101	1234 Main St		Atlanta	GA	10000
102	Judy	Miller	30	150.00	2	102	2000 Miller Ave		Boston	MA	20000
102	Judy	Miller	30	150.00	3	103	5000 North Dr		Chicago	IL	30000
103	Neil	Armstrong	25	200.00	1	101	1234 Main St		Atlanta	GA	10000
103	Neil	Armstrong	25	200.00	2	102	2000 Miller Ave		Boston	MA	20000
103	Neil	Armstrong	25	200.00	3	103	5000 North Dr		Chicago	IL	30000

Notice that the rows we want have the same customer_id value in both customer and address tables. The join condition in this case would consist of equating the column that is common between the two tables, i.e. customer_id. So your command would look like this:

```
mysql> select * from customer, address where customer.customer_id = address.customer_id;
```

Note how we used the column name preceded by the table name with a dot operator to identify the table to which the column belongs. This would pick only the highlighted rows from the Cartesian product, as follows:

customer_id	first_name	last_name	age	sales_amount	address_id	customer_id	address_line1	address_line2	city	state	zip
101	John	Smith	35	100.00	1	101	1234 Main St		Atlanta	GA	10000
102	Judy	Miller	30	150.00	2	102	2000 Miller Ave		Boston	MA	20000
103	Neil	Armstrong	25	200.00	3	103	5000 North Dr		Chicago	IL	30000

A more concise way to write the SQL query would be to use alias names for the tables. In addition, we want to specify only those columns that we are interested in, say `customer_id`, `first_name`, `last_name`, `address_line1`, `city`, `state`, and `zip`. The SQL statement would be as follows:

```
mysql> select cs.customer_id, cs.first_name, cs.last_name, ad.address_line1,
ad.city, ad.state, ad.zip from customer cs, address ad where cs.customer_id = ad.customer_id;
```

The output may look like this:

```
Command Prompt - mysql -u root

mysql> select cs.customer_id, cs.first_name, cs.last_name, ad.address_line1, ad.city,
ad.state, ad.zip from customer cs, address ad where cs.customer_id = ad.customer_id;
+-------------+------------+-----------+--------------+---------+-------+-------+
| customer_id | first_name | last_name | address_line1 | city    | state | zip   |
+-------------+------------+-----------+--------------+---------+-------+-------+
|         101 | John       | Smith     | 1234 Main St  | Atlanta | GA    | 10000 |
|         102 | Judy       | Miller    | 2000 Miller Ave | Boston | MA    | 20000 |
|         103 | Neil       | Armstrong | 5000 North Dr | Chicago | IL    | 30000 |
+-------------+------------+-----------+--------------+---------+-------+-------+
3 rows in set (0.00 sec)

mysql>
```

The join we used here is called an *inner join*—matching records need to exist in *both* tables. The `customer` and `address` tables have a one-to-one relationship and we assumed that every `customer` record is guaranteed to have an associated `address` record, so we could "connect" the two tables using an inner join.

What if one of the customer records did *not* have an associated `address` record? Let's go ahead and delete the last address record:

```
Command Prompt - mysql -u root

mysql> delete from address where address_id=3;
Query OK, 1 row affected (0.00 sec)

mysql> select * from address;
+------------+-------------+--------------+--------------+---------+-------+-------+
| address_id | customer_id | address_line1 | address_line2 | city    | state | zip   |
+------------+-------------+--------------+--------------+---------+-------+-------+
|          1 |         101 | 1234 Main St  | NULL          | Atlanta | GA    | 10000 |
|          2 |         102 | 2000 Miller Ave | NULL        | Boston  | MA    | 20000 |
+------------+-------------+--------------+--------------+---------+-------+-------+
2 rows in set (0.00 sec)

mysql>
```

The Cartesian product would now look like:

customer_ id	first_ name	last_ name	age	sales_ amount	address_ id	customer_ id	address_line1	address_ line2	city	state	zip
101	John	Smith	35	100.00	1	101	1234 Main St		Atlanta	GA	10000
101	John	Smith	35	100.00	2	102	2000 Miller Ave		Boston	MA	20000
102	Judy	Miller	30	150.00	1	101	1234 Main St		Atlanta	GA	10000
102	Judy	Miller	30	150.00	2	102	2000 Miller Ave		Boston	MA	20000
103	Neil	Armstrong	25	200.00	1	101	1234 Main St		Atlanta	GA	10000
103	Neil	Armstrong	25	200.00	2	102	2000 Miller Ave		Boston	MA	20000

As you can see, it no longer contains a matching record for `customer_id=103`. Rerun the query to see what we get now. You will find that the query returns only two rows (instead of three), as follows:

7.2.1.11   Outer Join

When you deleted an address record, the inner join returned only those records that matched. The query brought back two records instead of three. Makes sense, but sometimes you may want to display *all* customers—irrespective of whether they have address records or not. For the customers that do not have an address record, we may want to show empty or `NULL` values under the address columns. For this, you need to use the other type of join, called an *outer join*. The outer join can in turn be either "left outer join" or "right outer join" depending on which table needs to be retained no matter what (`customer` table in this example). The syntax for the left outer join is:

```
select ... from table1 left [outer] join table2 on <join_condition>
```

The square brackets [] around the word `outer` means it is optional. Try it out:

```
mysql> select cs.customer_id, cs.first_name, cs.last_name, ad.address_line1, ad.city, ad.state,
ad.zip from customer cs left outer join address ad on cs.customer_id = ad.customer_id;
```

The command session is as follows:

Notice how it shows `NULL` in the address fields for the last `customer` which did not have an `address` record.

Ok—the outer join was only to show the concept. We will need all three address records in future exercises, so put it back in using an insert statement.

7.3   Java Database Connectivity (JDBC)

7.3.1   Connecting to a Database from Java

In order to connect to a database, to process SQL queries and to represent the behavior of a database, Java provides a rich collection of predefined classes under its java.sql package. For example, to represent the connection from Java to SQL, it has a class called Connection. Similarly, to represent a result of the select query, it has a class called ResultSet. To execute select, insert, and update statements, it has a separate class called Statement. All of these classes are designed to be independent of the vendor of the actual database we connect to.

In other words, you could be running an Oracle or a MySQL or some other database on the backend, but Java would always expect the database data to be presented to it in the form of java.sql objects, populated with the appropriate data. To comply with this requirement, each database vendor needs to provide some kind of "driver" software that wraps the database data in Java-compatible format. The way Java connects to a database is many times referred to as Java Database Connectivity (JDBC). Let's look at the concept of the JDBC driver in more detail.

7.3.2   The MySQL JDBC Driver

Java is not only platform-independent (which means it can run on any system—from UNIX to Windows to Mac), but also database-vendor-independent. In other words, a Java program that connects to a database would run fine, no matter which database you are using on the "back end." This is achieved by the so-called JDBC driver—a set of classes that each database vendor provides, which contain instructions specific to connecting to a database of that vendor.

So you would have an Oracle JDBC driver provided by Oracle Corporation that, if properly downloaded and set up, would allow you to connect to an Oracle database from within Java code. Similarly, you have a MySQL JDBC driver that MySQL provides, which you need to download and set up before you can connect to a MySQL database from Java. These JDBC drivers make the database call "vendor transparent," by wrapping their objects into ones that Java expects—for example, java.sql.ResultSet and java.sql.Statement. In that sense, they act as a "bridge" between the vendor-specific details of a database and the database-independent Java code, with each database vendor defining what the bridge should contain.

Let's go ahead and download the MySQL JDBC driver and set it up, so that we can connect to it. Follow the installation instructions in Appendix H, and you should be all set for the next section.

7.4   Writing Database-Driven JSPs

Now we are in a position to see how to use java.sql classes to view the data of the customer table via Java. The first step is to instantiate an appropriate Connection object. For any database-related instructions to work, your JSP needs to have the directive

```
<%@ page import="java.sql.*" %>
```

in the beginning (or individual imports for the java.sql classes, such as Statement, Connection, ResultSet). Then, inside a scriptlet, create the Connection object as follows:

```
Class.forName("com.mysql.jdbc.Driver").newInstance();
Connection connection = DriverManager.getConnection(
          "jdbc:mysql://localhost:3306/salesdatabase?user=root&password=");
```

Here, we are explicitly loading a JDBC driver that has the fully qualified name com.mysql.jdbc.Driver. The Class.forName instruction takes the fully qualified name of any class and instantiates a new object using its default constructor. So, this is exactly same as

```
com.mysql.jdbc.Driver driver = new com.mysql.jdbc.Driver();
```

The difference is flexibility: You just provide the String for the fully qualified class name of the driver, and it takes care of the rest.

After the Class.forName instruction, the com.mysql.jdbc.Driver is loaded. When the static method getConnection() is called on the DriverManager of the java.sql package, it will attempt to locate a suitable driver from among those loaded at initialization and those loaded explicitly. Note that, as part of its initialization, the DriverManager class will attempt to load the driver classes referenced in the jdbc.drivers system property. Here we are looking only at explicitly loading the driver.

Note that "3306" is the default "port" on your computer where MySQL runs (just as "8080" is the default port where Tomcat runs). MySQL recognizes a default username of root that has no password. Say that you are interested in simply executing the select statement from within Java, to look at all the three records in the customer table. Create the Statement object, and issue the select query on it, as follows:

```
Statement statement = connection.createStatement();
ResultSet rs = statement.executeQuery("select * from customer");
```

You can think of the ResultSet object, rs, as a collection of HashMaps, one HashMap for each record in the query result. So when your select returns three rows, rs consists of a list of three HashMap objects. To traverse through the result set, you use the next() method on the ResultSet class. To get the value of a specific field (or column) in a row, you use the getInt() (for integer type column), getDouble() (for decimal fraction type column), or getString() (for char or text type column), passing it the exact name of the column that you used when creating the table.

For example, if you want the first name from the result set, you would say

```
rs.getString("first_name")
```

Note that this gets the first_name column value for the *current* row in the result set. In effect, you are doing a get() on the current row's Hashtable, passing it a key of first_name.

At any given time, the ResultSet always points to the *current* row in a set of rows representing the result of the query. To move the ResultSet to point to the next row, you need to use the next() method on the ResultSet class, which moves the current row to the next one. Let's look at an example to understand this better:

```
int customerId = 0, age = 0;
String firstName = "", lastName = "";
double salesAmt = 0.0;
while (rs.next())
{
    customerId = rs.getInt("customer_id");
    salesAmt = rs.getDouble("sales_amount");
    firstName = rs.getString("first_name")
    lastName = rs.getString("last_name")
}
```

We now know how to get values from the result set, but still have not displayed the values from the HTML. That should be pretty straightforward.

Create a new folder Chapter7 under C:\JSP. Before you can run your JSP, you need to add a new context root for Chapter 7. Add the following line in C:\Tomcat\conf\server.xml:

```
<Context path="/chapter7" docBase="C:/JSP/Chapter7" debug="0" />
```

Restart Tomcat so that it gets this change.

Create a new folder called styles under C:\JSP\Chaper7 and copy styles.css from C:\JSP\Chapter6\styles into it.

Create a new JSP called CustomerList.jsp under a new folder, sec74 under C:\JSP\Chapter7, as follows:

```
----------------------------------------------------------------------------------------
<!-- Begin: CustomerList.jsp -->
<%@ page import="java.sql.*,java.text.DecimalFormat" %>
<HTML>
    <HEAD>
        <LINK REL="stylesheet" TYPE="textless" HREF="../styles/styles.css"/>
    </HEAD>
    <BODY>
        <TABLE WIDTH=90%>
            <TR class="defaultText">
                <TD>Customer ID</TD>
```

```
            <TD>First Name</TD>
            <TD>Last Name</TD>
            <TD>Age</TD>
            <TD>Sales Amount</TD>
        </TR>
        <%
            Class.forName("com.mysql.jdbc.Driver").newInstance();
            Connection connection = DriverManager.getConnection(
                "jdbc:mysql://localhost:3306/salesdatabase?user=root&password=");
            Statement statement = connection.createStatement();
            ResultSet rs = statement.executeQuery("select * from customer");
            DecimalFormat df = new DecimalFormat("#,##0.00");

            int customerId = 0, age = 0;
            String firstName = "", lastName = "", strClass = "tableEvenRow";
            double salesAmt = 0.0;

            while (rs.next())
            {
                customerId = rs.getInt("customer_id");
                age = rs.getInt("age");
                salesAmt = rs.getDouble("sales_amount");
                firstName = rs.getString("first_name");
                lastName = rs.getString("last_name");
                // Toggle style class for next row:
                if (strClass.equals("tableEvenRow")) strClass = "tableOddRow";
                else strClass = "tableEvenRow";
        %>
                <TR class="<%= strClass %>">
                    <TD><%= customerId %></TD>
                    <TD><%= firstName %></TD>
                    <TD><%= lastName %></TD>
                    <TD><%= age %></TD>
                    <TD>$<%= df.format(salesAmt) %></TD>
                </TR>
        <%
            }
        %>
        </TABLE>
    </BODY>
</HTML>
<!-- End: CustomerList.jsp -->
```

Open this JSP in your browser with Tomcat and MySQL started, as follows:

`http://localhost:8080/chapter7/sec74/CustomerList.jsp`

You should see the three rows of `customer` table data in your browser window, as shown here:

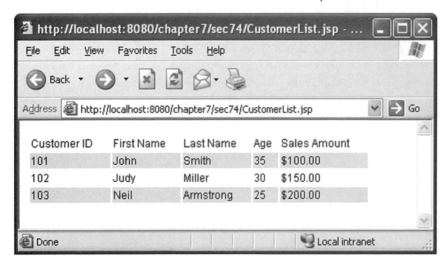

You have just created your first JSP page that connects to a MySQL database!

The only thing is that it currently runs in the Web server running on your computer, so others cannot see it on the Internet. All you need to do now is publish it on the World Wide Web, so that others can see it. Several Web hosts are available out there that host JSP pages with MySQL support at very reasonable rates. They provide step-by-step instructions on how and where to upload your JSP files, and how to administer your MySQL database.

Solved Exercise 7.4 (a)

Objective: To practice using an inner join in a SQL query and display the results via a JSP.

Steps:

- Create a new folder `exer74a` under `C:\JSP\Chapter7`. Copy `CustomerList.jsp` from Section 7.4 into this folder and rename to `AddressListInner.jsp`.

- Make sure you have all three records in the `customer` and `address` tables as in Section 7.2.1.3 and Section 7.2.1.9 respectively.

- Display the contents of the inner join between the `customer` and `address` tables described in Section 7.2.1.10, but this time perform the query inside a scriptlet in `AddressListInner.jsp`, process the results, and show the results in the format shown here:

```
--------------------------------------------------------------------------------
  Customer Id    First Name  Last Name   Address Line 1    City    State    Zip
--------------------------------------------------------------------------------
    101           John        Smith       1234 Main St      Atlanta  GA     10000
    102           Judy        Miller      2000 Miller Ave   Boston   MA     20000
    103           Neil        Armstrong   5000 North Dr     Chicago  IL     30000
--------------------------------------------------------------------------------
```

- Open the URL:

  `http://localhost:8080/chapter7/exer74a/AddressListInner.jsp`

  and verify that it works as expected.

- Submit `AddressListInner.jsp`.

  A sample screenshot follows:

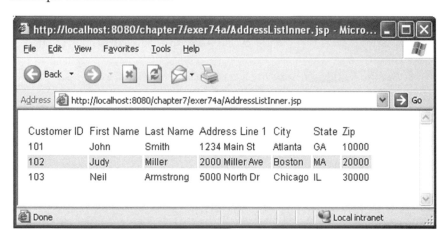

Solution:

```
<!-- Begin: AddressListInner.jsp -->
<%@ page import="java.sql.*" %>
<HTML>
    <HEAD>
        <LINK REL="stylesheet" TYPE="text/css" HREF="../styles/styles.css" />
    </HEAD>
    <BODY>
        <TABLE WIDTH=90%>
            <TR CLASS="defaultText">
                <TD>Customer ID</TD>
                <TD>First Name</TD>
```

```
        <TD>Last Name</TD>
        <TD>Address Line 1</TD>
        <TD>City</TD>
        <TD>State</TD>
        <TD>Zip</TD>
    </TR>
    <%
        Class.forName("com.mysql.jdbc.Driver").newInstance();
        Connection connection =
            DriverManager.getConnection(
                "jdbc:mysql://localhost:3306/salesdatabase?user=root&password=");
        Statement statement = connection.createStatement();
        String sqlGetCustomerAddress
            = "select cs.customer_id, cs.first_name, cs.last_name,";
        sqlGetCustomerAddress += "ad.address_line1, ad.city, ad.state, ad.zip ";
        sqlGetCustomerAddress += "from customer cs, address ad ";
        sqlGetCustomerAddress += "where cs.customer_id = ad.customer_id";

        ResultSet rs = statement.executeQuery(sqlGetCustomerAddress);

        int customerId, zip;
        String firstName, lastName, addressLine1, city, state;
        String strClass = "tableEvenRow";

        while (rs.next())
        {
            customerId = rs.getInt("customer_id");
            firstName = rs.getString("first_name");
            lastName = rs.getString("last_name");
            addressLine1 = rs.getString("address_line1");
            city = rs.getString("city");
            state = rs.getString("state");
            zip = rs.getInt("zip");
            // Toggle style class for next row:
            if (strClass.equals("tableEvenRow")) strClass = "tableOddRow";
            else strClass = "tableEvenRow";
    %>
            <TR CLASS="<%= strClass %>">
                <TD><%= customerId %></TD>
                <TD><%= firstName %></TD>
                <TD><%= lastName %></TD>
```

```
                        <TD><%= addressLine1 %></TD>
                        <TD><%= city %></TD>
                        <TD><%= state %></TD>
                        <TD><%= zip %></TD>
                    </TR>
                <%
                    }
                %>
            </TABLE>
        </BODY>
</HTML>
<!-- End: AddressListInner.jsp -->
```

Solved Exercise 7.4 (b)

Objective: To practice using an outer join in a SQL query and display the results via a JSP.

Steps:

- Create a new folder `exer74b` under `C:\JSP\Chapter7`. Copy `AddressListInner.jsp` from Solved Exercise 7.4(a) into this folder and rename to `AddressListOuter.jsp`.

- Delete the `address` record with `address_id=3`.

- Display the result of the outer join of Section 7.2.1.11, but this time process the query and format the output inside `AddressListOuter.jsp` to look like this:

```
--------------------------------------------------------------------------
Customer Id   First Name  Last Name   Address Line 1    City    State   Zip
--------------------------------------------------------------------------
101           John        Smith       1234  Main St     Atlanta  GA     10000
102           Judy        Miller      2000 Miller Ave   Boston   MA     20000
103           Neil        Armstrong
--------------------------------------------------------------------------
```

- Open the URL:

  `http://localhost:8080/chapter7/exer74b/ AddressListOuter.jsp`

  and verify that it works as expected.

- Submit `AddressListOuter.jsp`.

A sample screenshot follows:

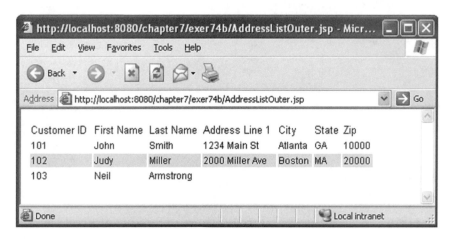

Solution:

```
<!-- Begin: AddressListOuter.jsp -->
<%@ page import="java.sql.*" %>

<HTML>
    <HEAD>
        <LINK REL="stylesheet" TYPE="text/css" HREF="../styles/styles.css" />
    </HEAD>
    <BODY>
      <TABLE WIDTH=90%>
        <TR CLASS="defaultText">
            <TD>Customer ID</TD>
            <TD>First Name</TD>
            <TD>Last Name</TD>
            <TD>Address Line 1</TD>
            <TD>City</TD>
            <TD>State</TD>
            <TD>Zip</TD>
        </TR>
        <%
            Class.forName("com.mysql.jdbc.Driver").newInstance();
            Connection connection =
                DriverManager.getConnection(
                  "jdbc:mysql://localhost:3306/salesdatabase?user=root&password=");
            Statement statement = connection.createStatement();
            String sqlGetCustomerAddress
                = "select cs.customer_id, cs.first_name, cs.last_name, ";
            sqlGetCustomerAddress += "ad.address_line1, ad.city, ad.state, ad.zip ";
```

```
        sqlGetCustomerAddress += "from customer cs left outer join address ad ";
        sqlGetCustomerAddress += "on cs.customer_id = ad.customer_id";

        ResultSet rs = statement.executeQuery(sqlGetCustomerAddress);

        int customerId, zip;
        String firstName, lastName, addressLine1, city, state;
        String strZip, strClass = "tableEvenRow";

        while (rs.next())
        {
            customerId = rs.getInt("customer_id");
            firstName = rs.getString("first_name");
            lastName = rs.getString("last_name");
            addressLine1 = rs.getString("address_line1");
            city = rs.getString("city");
            state = rs.getString("state");
            zip = rs.getInt("zip");
            if (addressLine1 == null) addressLine1 = " ";
            if (city == null) city = " ";
            if (state == null) state = " ";
            if (zip == 0) strZip = " ";
            else strZip = String.valueOf(zip);

            // Toggle style class for next row:
            if (strClass.equals("tableEvenRow")) strClass = "tableOddRow";
            else strClass = "tableEvenRow";
%>
        <TR CLASS="<%= strClass %>">
            <TD><%= customerId %></TD>
            <TD><%= firstName %></TD>
            <TD><%= lastName %></TD>
            <TD><%= addressLine1 %></TD>
            <TD><%= city %></TD>
            <TD><%= state %></TD>
            <TD><%= strZip %></TD>
        </TR>
<%
        }
%>
        </TABLE>
    </BODY>
</HTML>
<!-- End: AddressListOuter.jsp -->
```

In Section 7.2.1, you saw how to manually insert records into the customer table. If you have several customers, this can soon become cumbersome and error prone. Say that you want to make this process more efficient, by providing an HTML form and inserting the data into the customer table via a JSP. We will learn how to do this in the next solved exercise.

Solved Exercise 7.4 (c)

Objective: To learn how to insert data into a database using user-entered information on HTML forms.

Steps:

- Create a new folder exer74c under C:\JSP\Chapter7. Copy the CustomerList.jsp file from Section 7.4 into this folder. Create a new JSP called InputCustomer.jsp that has an HTML form with INPUT fields for the customer's first and last names, age, and sales amount.

- The customer_id value for each new record should be 1 more than the maximum value of customer_id in the customer table, and should be computed behind the scenes by your JSP without asking the user to enter it. For example, if you already have three records in the customer table with customer_id of 101, 102, and 103, the next record that you insert via your HTML form should have a customer_id of 104, and the next one should have 105 and so on.

- In addition to the INPUT fields for name, age, and sales amount, show a "view-only" field on the HTML form that displays the customer_id value that will be used for the new record being created. The user should not be able to edit the customer_id value displayed in this field. The value itself should be obtained by adding 1 to the max customer_id currently in the table. For finding the max value of the customer_id, perform a SQL query on the customer table using the max library function.

- To make an INPUT field as view-only, use the READONLY flag as part of the INPUT tag, for example:

```
<INPUT TYPE = "text" NAME="customerId" READONLY></INPUT>
```

- Add Javascript validation code to ensure that no field is empty at the time of submission.

- The ACTION for the HTML form should be a new JSP called InsertCustomer.jsp that you need to create in the same folder. This JSP will capture all INPUT field information from the HTML form on InputCustomer.jsp and insert into the customer table (one record at a time; for inserting the next customer, the user has to go back to the InputCustomer.jsp page and repeat the process). The CustomerId value to be used for the insert should be obtained as a request parameter from the HTML form on InputCustomer.jsp. On successful insert, it should display a message stating that the insert was successful, and display the data that was just inserted (including the customer ID). Below this, it should show two links:

- Insert next customer: Clicking on this link should take the user back to the InputCustomer.jsp page, ready to accept the next customer's data.

- View customer list: Clicking on this link should take the user to the CustomerList.jsp page, which should show an updated list of customers, with the new one just inserted.

Hint: For inserting data into a database, you will need to use an approach similar to the one used in the select query. Create a Connection and a Statement (no need for a ResultSet, since you are not doing any query), but invoke the executeUpdate() method instead of the executeQuery() method, passing it the insert SQL String.

- Open the following URL:

```
http://localhost:8080/chapter7/exer74c/InputCustomer.jsp
```

and verify that it works as expected.

- Submit InputCustomer.jsp and InsertCustomer.jsp.

A sample session is shown next: The max customer-id in the customer table is currently 103. So the page shows up with a customer-id of 104 for the next customer.

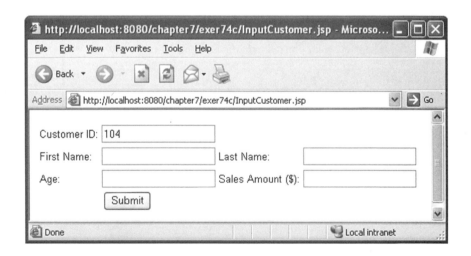

Enter data for the new customer and click the Submit button:

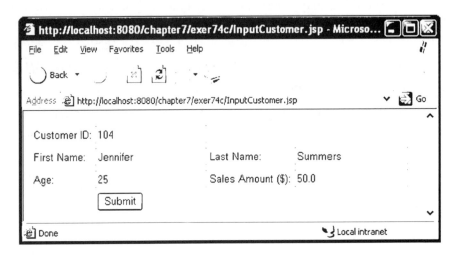

InsertCustomer.jsp inserts a new record in the customer table and shows a summary of the record just inserted:

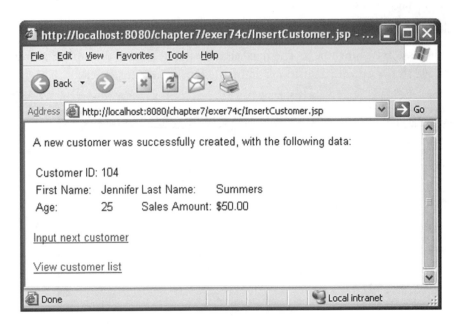

Click on "View customer list" (to verify that the new customer was inserted in the database):

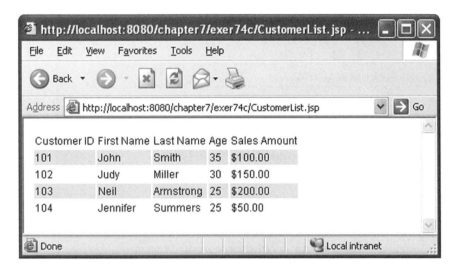

Click on the Back button, then on "Input next customer":

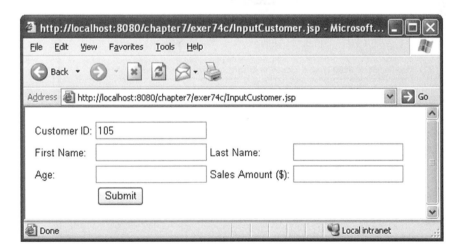

Enter values for the next customer and click the Submit button:

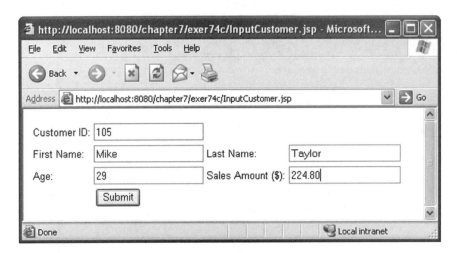

`InsertCustomer.jsp` shows a summary of the record just inserted:

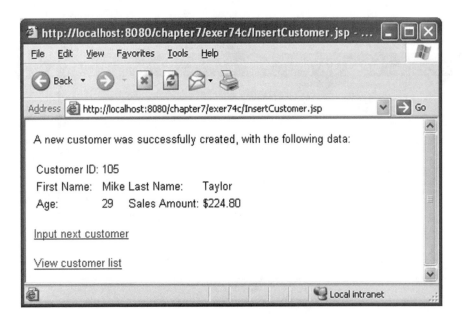

Click on "View customer list":

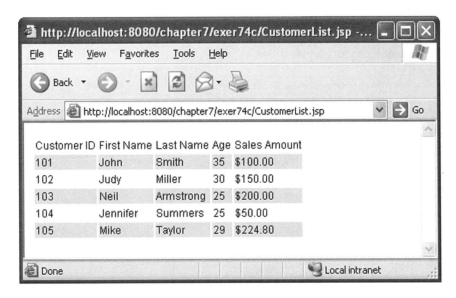

Solution:

```
<!-- Begin: InputCustomer.jsp -->
<%@ page import="java.sql.*" %>
<%
    Class.forName("com.mysql.jdbc.Driver").newInstance();
    Connection connection =
    DriverManager.getConnection(
        "jdbc:mysql://localhost:3306/salesdatabase?user=root&password=");
    Statement statement = connection.createStatement();

    ResultSet rs = statement.executeQuery(
        "SELECT max( customer_id ) as \"maxCustomerId\" FROM customer");
    int maxCustId = 0;
    while (rs.next())
    {
        maxCustId = rs.getInt("maxCustomerId");
    }
%>
<HTML>
    <HEAD>
```

```
<LINK REL="stylesheet" TYPE="text/css" HREF="../styles/styles.css"/>
<SCRIPT LANGUAGE="JAVASCRIPT">
function validate()
{
    if (document.forms.main.firstname.value == "")
    {
        alert("First name cannot be empty.");
        return false;
    }
    else if (document.forms.main.lastname.value == "")
    {
        alert("Last name cannot be empty.");
        return false;
    }
    else if (document.forms.main.age.value == "")
    {
        alert("Age cannot be empty.");
        return false;
    }
    else if (document.forms.main.salesamount.value == "")
    {
        alert("Sales amount cannot be empty.");
        return false;
    }
    return true;
}
</SCRIPT>
</HEAD>
<BODY>
    <FORM NAME="main" ACTION="InsertCustomer.jsp" METHOD="POST">
        <TABLE>
            <TR CLASS="defaultText">
                <TD>Customer ID:</TD>
                <TD>
                    <INPUT type="text" name="customerid"
                           value="<%= String.valueOf(maxCustId + 1) %>" readonly>
                    </INPUT>
                </TD>
                <TD> </TD>
                <TD> </TD>
            </TR>
            <TR CLASS="defaultText">
                <TD>First Name:</TD>
                <TD><INPUT type="text" name="firstname"></INPUT></TD>
                <TD>Last Name:</TD>
```

```
                        <TD><INPUT type="text" name="lastname"></INPUT></TD>
                    </TR>
                    <TR CLASS="defaultText">
                        <TD>Age:</TD>
                        <TD><INPUT type="text" name="age"></INPUT></TD>
                        <TD>Sales Amount:</TD>
                        <TD><INPUT type="text" name="salesamount"></INPUT></TD>
                    </TR>
                    <TR CLASS="defaultText">
                        <TD COLSPAN=2 ALIGN="CENTER">
                            <INPUT type="submit" VALUE="Submit"
                                    onclick="return validate()"></INPUT>
                        </TD>
                    </TR>
                </TABLE>
            </FORM>
        </BODY>
</HTML>
<!-- End: InputCustomer.jsp -->

<!-- Begin: InsertCustomer.jsp -->
<%@ page import="java.sql.*, java.text.DecimalFormat" %>
<%
    Class.forName("com.mysql.jdbc.Driver").newInstance();
    Connection connection =
        DriverManager.getConnection(
            "jdbc:mysql://localhost:3306/salesdatabase?user=root&password=");
    Statement statement = connection.createStatement();
    DecimalFormat df = new DecimalFormat("#,##,0.00");

    String customerId = request.getParameter("customerid");
    String firstName = request.getParameter("firstname");
    String lastName = request.getParameter("lastname");
    String age = request.getParameter("age");
    String salesAmount = request.getParameter("salesamount");

    String sqlInsertCustomer =
        "insert into customer (customer_id, first_name, last_name, age,
            sales_amount) values (" + customerId + ",'" + firstName + "','"
            + lastName + "'," + age + "," + salesAmount + ")";

    statement.executeUpdate(sqlInsertCustomer);
%>
<HTML>
    <HEAD>
```

```
        <LINK REL="stylesheet" TYPE="textless"HREF="../styles/styles.css"/>
    </HEAD>
    <BODY>
    <SPAN CLASS="defaultText">
    A new customer was successfully created with the following data:<BR><BR>
    </SPAN>
        <TABLE>
            <TR CLASS="defaultText">
                <TD>Customer ID:</TD>
                <TD><%= customerId %></TD>
                <TD> </TD>
                <TD> </TD>
            </TR>
            <TR CLASS="defaultText">
                <TD>First Name:</TD>
                <TD><%= firstName %></TD>
                <TD>Last Name:</TD>
                <TD><%= lastName %></TD>
            </TR>
            <TR CLASS="defaultText">
                <TD>Age:</TD>
                <TD><%= age %></TD>
                <TD>Sales Amount:</TD>
                <TD>$<%= df.format(Double.parseDouble(salesAmount)) %></TD>
            </TR>
        </TABLE>
        <SPAN CLASS="defaultText">
            <BR>
              <A HREF="InputCustomer.jsp">Input next customer</A>
              <BR><BR>
              <A HREF="CustomerList.jsp">View customer list</A>
        </SPAN>
    </BODY>
</HTML>
<!-- End: InsertCustomer.jsp -->
```

7.5 Summary

You have covered quite a bit of ground in Web database programming using Java and JSP. You know what SQL is, how to create databases and tables, and how to insert and query for data using a MySQL database. You also learned about JDBC drivers, and how they are useful in connecting to a database via Java code. Finally you developed a working JSP that connects to a MySQL database.

7.6 Chapter Quiz

1. Which of the following is true? (Select all that apply.)

    i. A database is a collection of one or more tables.

    ii. A table is a collection of one or more records.

    iii. A record is a collection of one or more fields.

    iv. A table consists of one or more rows and columns, with each row representing a record, and each column representing a field.

    a. All of the above

    b. (i), (ii), and (iii) only

    c. (ii), (iii), and (iv) only

    d. (i), (ii), and (iv) only

2. Which of the following is true? (Select all that apply.)

    i. SQL stands for structured query language.

    ii. A database query is a request to get a subset of records meeting specified criteria.

    iii. Columns in a table can be of different data types, but each column can hold values of a specified type only.

    iv. A JDBC driver is a set of classes that a database vendor provides to enable Java to connect to a database of that vendor.

    a. All of the above

    b. (i), (iii), and (iv) only

    c. (ii), (iii), and (iv) only

    d. (i), (ii), and (iii) only

3. Which of the following is true? (Select all that apply.)

    i. No two rows of a table can have the same value in a primary key column.

    ii. A Cartesian product between table T1 with m rows and table T2 with n rows would contain $(m \times n)$ rows obtained using every combination of rows from both tables.

    iii. For an inner join, records that satisfy the join condition must exist in both tables.

    iv. For a left outer join, the table on the left in the join clause may or may not have a record that satisfies the join condition.

    v. Say that tables T1 and T2 have a one-to-many relationship. To implement this, you need to include a foreign key in table T2 that is the primary key of table T1.

    a. All of the above

    b. (i), (ii), and (iii) only

    c. (ii), (iv), and (v) only

    d. (i), (ii), (iii), and (v) only

4. Which of the following is true? (Select all that apply.)

    i. To traverse through the result set, you use the `next()` method on the `ResultSet` class.

    ii. A `ResultSet` object can be thought of as a collection of `HashMaps`, one `HashMap` for each record in the query result.

    iii. In order for any database-related instruction to work in your JSP, it needs to have a page directive with `import="java.sql.*` in the beginning (or separate imports for the individual `java.sql` classes, such as `Statement`, `Connection`, and `ResultSet`).

    iv. To get the value of a specific field (or column) in a row, you use the `getInt()` (for integer type column), `getDouble()` (for decimal fraction type column), or `getString()` (for char or text type column), passing it the exact name of the column used when creating the table.

    a. All of the above

    b. (i), (ii), and (iii) only

    c. (ii), (iii), and (iv) only

    d. (i), (ii), and (iv) only

5. Which of the following is true? (Select all that apply.)

    i. To execute a SQL `select` statement, you need to use the `executeQuery()` method on the `Statement` object, passing it the `select` statement as a `String`.

    ii. The `Connection`, `Statement`, and `ResultSet` classes belong to the `java.util` package.

    iii. A JDBC driver makes the database call vendor transparent, by wrapping its objects into those that Java expects—for example, `java.sql.ResultSet` and `java.sql.Statement`.

    iv. The default port on your computer where MySQL runs is `3306`.

   a.   All of the above

   b.   (i), (ii), and (iii) only

   c.   (i), (iii), and (iv) only

   d.   (ii), (iii), and (iv) only

6. Which of the following is true? (Select all that apply.)

   i.   MySQL recognizes a default username of `root` that has no password.

   ii.   `executeUpdate()` cannot be used to insert records; it is used only to update them.

   iii.   To connect to a database from Java, you need to invoke the `getConnection()` method on the `DriverManager` class, passing it the connection `String` that contains the database name, username, and password.

   iv.   The asterisk (`*`) in `select * from` ... means you want all columns from the table retrieved into the result set.

   a.   All of the above

   b.   (i), (iii), and (iv) only

   c.   (i), (ii), and (iii) only

   d.   (i), (ii), and (iv) only

7.7   Answers to Quiz

1. The correct answer is (a). All statements are true.

2. The correct answer is (a). All statements are true.

3. The correct answer is (d). All statements except (iv) are true. Option (iv) is false because in a left outer join, the table on the right (not left) may or may not have records satisfying the join condition.

4. The correct answer is (a). All statements are true.

5. The correct answer is (c). All statements except (ii) are true. Option (ii) is false because the `Connection`, `Statement`, and `ResultSet` classes belong to the `java.sql` package (NOT the `java.util` package).

6. The correct answer is (b). All statements except (ii) are true. Option (ii) is false because `executeUpdate()` is used to insert and update records.

7.8   Unsolved Assignments

Assignment 7.1

Objective: To learn how to retrieve/process data from a MySQL database from inside a JSP.

Steps:

- Copy `Login.jsp`, `Checkout.jsp`, `Validate.jsp`, `SelectMore.jsp`, and `ShowAllItems.jsp` from Assignment 6.2 into a new folder: `C:/JSP/Chapter7/assign71`.

- Instead of storing the username/password and username/full name pairs in `HashMaps`, create a new table in `salesdatabase`, called `user` with the following structure and content:

Column Name	Type	Column Size	Null	Primary Key?
user_id	int	5	not null	Yes
customer_id	int	5	not null	No
username	char	20	not null	No
password	char	20	not null	No

Insert the following data into the `user` table:

user_id	customer_id	username	password
1	101	jsmith	bluesky
2	102	jmiller	clearwater
3	105	mtaylor	greentree

- Note that every customer may not necessarily have a username and password; so it is possible to have a `customer` record without an associated `user` record. In this assignment, assume that only customers with `customer_id` = 101, 102, and 105 have created a username and password in the database.

- Modify `Validate.jsp` to retrieve the data from the `user` and `customer` tables in the database (instead of from `HashMaps`), as follows. Do a `select` SQL query using an inner join between `user` and `customer` tables to get the `user` record with a matching `username` and `password` and the first and last names from the associated `customer` record. The join needs to be done on the `customer_id` column.

- Verify that the JSP works exactly the same as before:

  `http://localhost:8080/chapter7/assign71/Login.jsp`

- Submit a text file containing SQL statements used to create the database and the two tables and to insert data. Also submit Validate.jsp.

After you have created the database tables and inserted data into it, verify that select queries show the content of the tables, as follows:

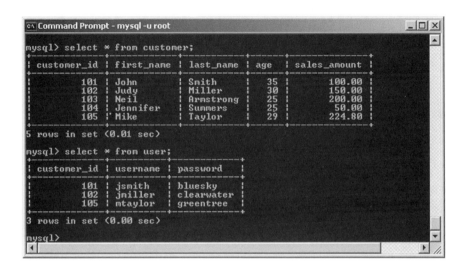

A sample screen interaction is shown next:

User enters jsmith as username, but password other than bluesky and hits the Submit button:

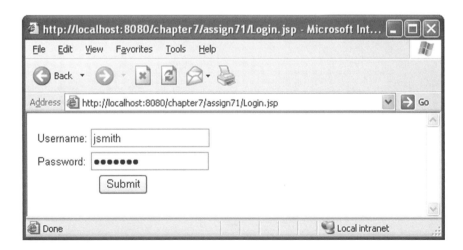

Page shows error message and asks user to try again:

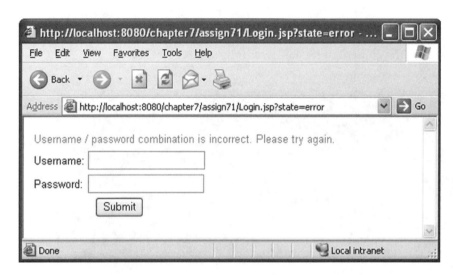

User enters `jsmith` as username and `bluesky` as (correct) password and clicks the Submit button:

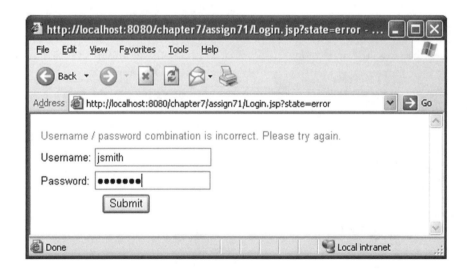

The following page shows up. User selects a couple of items, enters quantity, and clicks the Submit button:

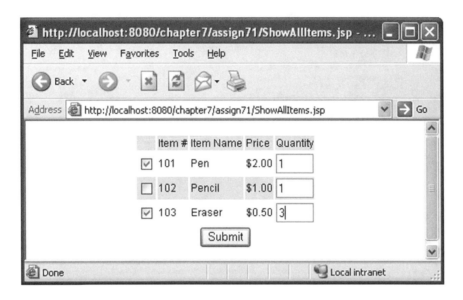

The following page shows up. User clicks the Checkout button:

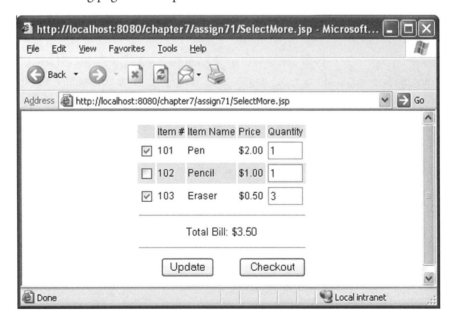

The final screen shows a thank you message with first and last names matching the username entered on the login page, followed by a summary of the order:

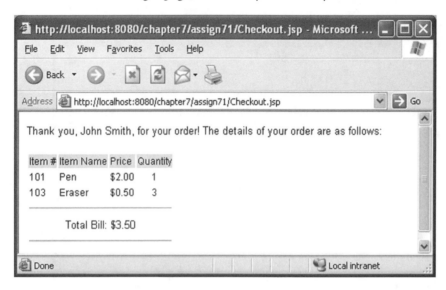

Assignment 7.2

Objective: To practice inserting into/querying a database from inside a JSP.

Steps:

- Copy `Login.jsp`, `Checkout.jsp`, `Validate.jsp`, `SelectMore.jsp`, and `ShowAllItems.jsp` from Assignment 7.1 into a new folder: `C:\JSP\Chapter7\assign72`. Also copy `AddressListOuter.jsp` from Solved Exercise 7.4(b) into this folder.

- Instead of using static HTML for the items on the `ShowAllItems.html` page, create a new table called `item` that contains one record per item available.

  - The `item` table should have the following structure:

Column Name	Type	Column Size	Null?	Primary Key
item_id	int	5	not null	Yes
item_name	char	20	not null	No
item_price	decimal	(6,2)	not null	No

- Insert the following items into the item table:

item_id	item_name	item_price
101	Pen	2.00
102	Pencil	1.00
103	Eraser	0.50

- Create a new table called order_submitted that will contain order information from a customer. It should have the following structure:

Column Name	Type	Column Size	Null?	Primary Key
order_id	int	5	not null	Yes
user_id	int	5	not null	No
submit_date	datetime	-	not null	No

- As each customer places an order, insert a record into the order_submitted table. The insert should be done in Checkout.jsp when the customer clicks on the Checkout button. A customer can have multiple orders; so when the same customer places another order at a later point in time, your JSP should insert a new order_submitted record each time for that customer. The order_id should be one more than the maximum value in the order_submitted table at that point in time (start with order_id = 1 for the first insert). The submit_date field should contain the current date and time stamp. (*Hint:* Use MySQL keyword CURRENT_TIMESTAMP as the value to be inserted in this column.) Get user_id from session, stored in validate.jsp.

- For each record in the order_submitted table, you also need to save information on items and quantities selected as part of the order. To do so, create a new table called order_detail that will contain detailed information for an order, one record per item selected in an order. If an order contains multiple items, this table should have as many records as the number of multiple items for that order. It should have the following structure:

Column Name	Type	Column Size	Null?	Primary Key
order_detail_id	int	5	not null	Yes
order_id	int	5	not null	No
item_id	int	5	not null	No
item_qty	int	5	not null	No

- In Checkout.jsp, after you insert a record into the order_submitted table, also insert records in the order_detail table, with order_id equal to that of the new order_submitted record just inserted. Note that the "order value" of an order can always be computed by doing a query on the order_detail table for that order_id and taking a sum of the products of item price and item quantity for all items. For order_detail_id column, start with a value of 1 for the first insert, incrementing by 1 for each subsequent insert.

- Modify the ShowAllItems.jsp and SelectMore.jsp pages to display the list of items using a select query on the item table (instead of static HTML).

- Rename AddressListOuter.jsp to CustomerUserList.jsp. Inside the scriptlet, do an outer join between the customer and user tables instead of the join between customer and address tables, and display data as shown in the sample screen layout that follows.

```
-----------------------------------------------------------
Customer ID      Customer Name       Username
-----------------------------------------------------------
   101           John Smith          jsmith          View orders
   102           Judy Miller         jmiller
   103           Neil Armstrong
   104           Jennifer Summers
   105           Mike Taylor         mtaylor         View orders
-----------------------------------------------------------
```

Add an extra column at the right as shown, with a link that says "View orders" at the end of a customer's row. That link should show only for those customers that placed at least one order.

To display the data in this manner, do a left outer join between the customer and user tables to ensure that all customers—even those without associated user records—show up. To determine whether to show the "View orders" link for a particular user, do a separate SQL query nested within the first, to get the order_submitted records for a given user. If there is at least one record in that result set, the "View orders" link needs to be shown, otherwise not.

- Clicking on the "View orders" link should take the user to a new page, ViewOrders.jsp as a POST, sending it the user_id of the selected user via an INPUT field of type HIDDEN. The page should display the list of orders for the selected customer. Use an inner join as appropriate. A sample screen layout for this page is as follows:

```
-------------------------------------------------------------------------------
 Customer Id:  101
 User Id:      1
 Username:     jsmith
 Name:         John Smith
-------------------------------------------------------------------------------
 Order ID    Order Value    Submit Date
-------------------------------------------------------------------------------
    1            $5.50         2007-01-14  17:09:32.0      View order details
    2            $4.50         2007-01-15  20:22:33.0      View order details
   ...           ...            ...                           ...
-------------------------------------------------------------------------------
```

- Clicking on the "View order details" link should open a new JSP called ViewOrderDetails.jsp again, as a POST, sending it the order_id of the selected order. This JSP needs to have a field layout as follows:

```
---------------------------------------------
 Customer Id:  1
 User Id:      1
 Username:     jsmith
 Name:         John Smith
 Order Id:     1
 Order Value:  $5.50
 Submit Date:  2007-01-14   17:09:32.0
---------------------------------------------
Order details:
---------------------------------------------
 Item ID     Item Name    Qty   Price   Value
---------------------------------------------
   101         Pen         2    $2.00   $4.00
   103         Eraser      3    $0.50   $1.50
---------------------------------------------
   Total Order Value:            $5.50
---------------------------------------------
```

Again, use an inner join to make the SQL query more efficient.

- After a user places an order, open the CustomerUserList.jsp page in a separate browser as
  http://localhost:8080/chapter7/assign72/CustomerUserList.jsp

- Click on the "View orders" link for that customer, and verify that it shows the correct orders that this customer placed up to that point. Click on the "View order details" link at the end of the orders and verify that it shows the selected items for each order.

- Modify Validate.jsp as necessary to put the user_id in session.

- Submit SQL statements used to create the new tables (item, order_submitted, and order_detail) to insert data in item table, and also submit Validate.jsp, ShowAllItems.jsp, SelectMore.jsp, Checkout.jsp, CustomerUserList.jsp, ViewOrders.jsp, and ViewOrderDetails.jsp.

- A sample interaction is shown next:

User enters jsmith as username and bluesky as (correct) password and clicks the Submit button:

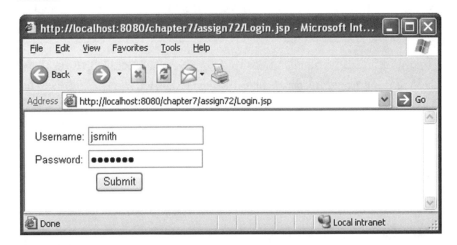

The next page shows a list of items to choose from. User selects a couple of items, enters quantity, and clicks the Submit button:

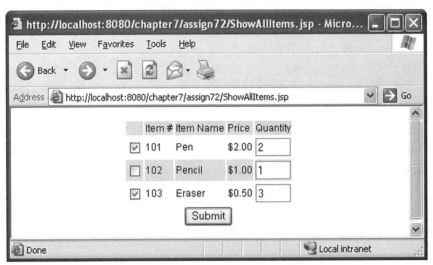

The following page shows the items selected and the total bill. User clicks the Checkout button:

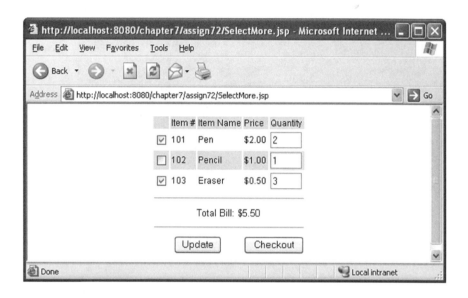

The next screen shows a thank you message with first and last names matching the user-name entered on the login page, followed by a summary of the order:

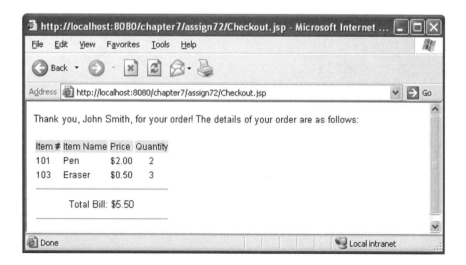

Verify that new records inserted into the order_submitted and order_detail tables:

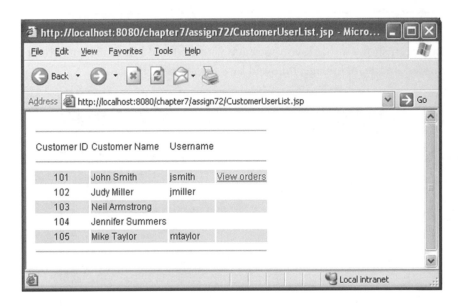

Open CustomerUserList.jsp and verify that the new order shows up for this customer. Click on the "View orders" link:

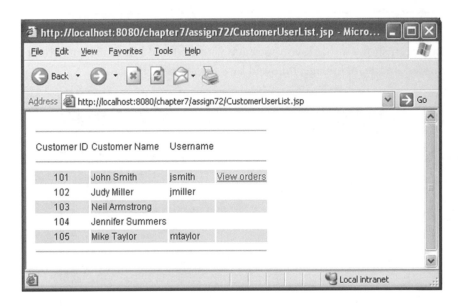

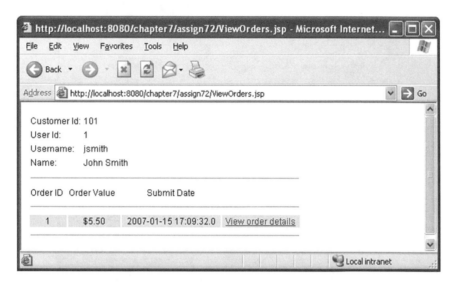

The next page shows the list of items selected in that order:

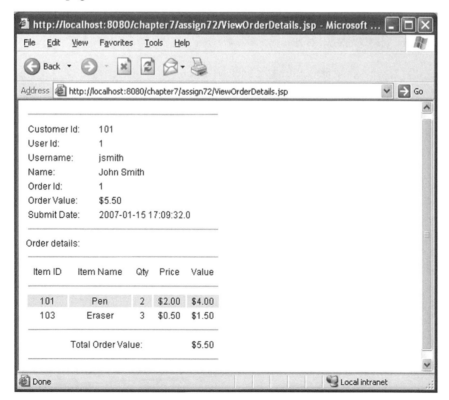

The same user places another order:

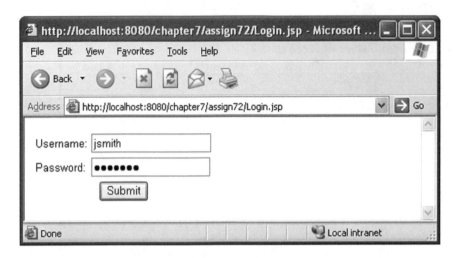

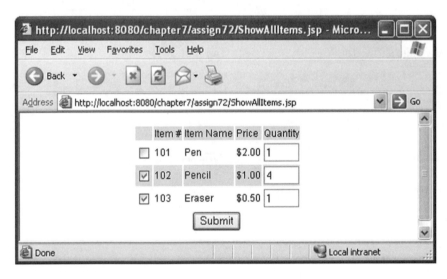

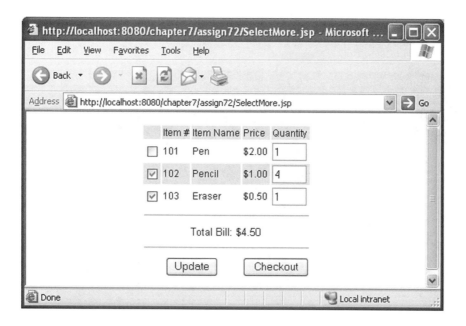

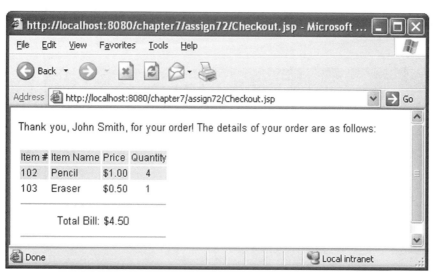

Verify that appropriate records were inserted into the order_submitted and order_detail tables, up to this stage:

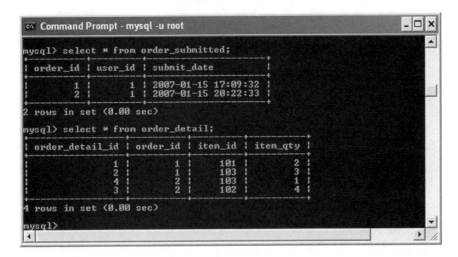

Verify that the new order shows up by looking at CustomerUserList.jsp. Click on the "View orders" link:

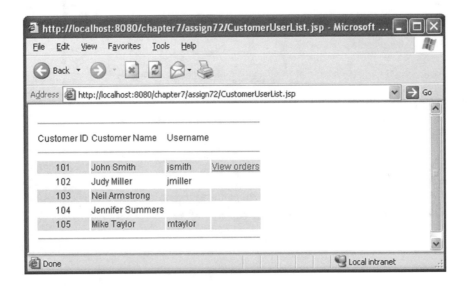

A new order (Order ID = 2) appears below the first one on the order list page:

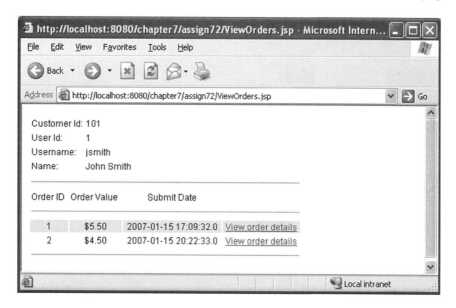

Click on "View order details" next to the new order to see its break-up:

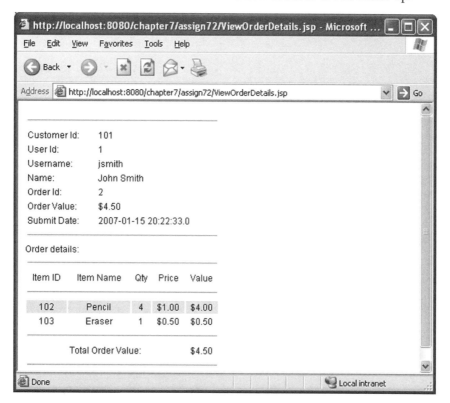

CHAPTER 8

Custom Tags, Tag Libraries, Action Elements, and JavaBeans

Chapter Objectives

- Study the concept of tag libraries and custom tags

- Get familiar with the life cycle and sequence of calls when the JSP contains a custom tag

- See how tags allow us to move major chunks of Java code away from the JSPs and thus help in maintaining the code

- Learn what action elements are, and how they are used in a JSP

- Study the rules for defining a JavaBean and understand how it uses reflection to deduce attribute names from getter and setter method names

- Learn how to specify an attribute in a custom tag and how to set its value via the JSP

- Understand how a JavaBean object and a custom tag can each be used to produce the same end result.

8.1   The Need to Use Custom Tags

You can create a quite professional-looking Web site using the techniques discussed so far. I have actually seen some corporate applications in the real world that are reasonably complex and use only what we learned until now. However, applications can get bigger and bigger with time, and it becomes necessary to organize large amount of Java code in JSPs. Java code can be organized by using declarations that we discussed earlier (Section 5.2.4), but tags are a cleaner and much more powerful way of doing the same thing.

As mentioned earlier, scriptlets can be quite restrictive when it comes to organizing code. It is like saying that all code can reside in a single method of a class, no matter how many lines it goes into. As business logic becomes more complex, it becomes critical to move parts of the Java code into more manageable chunks. Declarations provide one way of doing this, but we still end up having Java code inside the JSP. One downside of this is that the JSP gets compiled only at run time, so it may not be the best option to develop or debug the Java code. Wouldn't it be convenient if we simply develop all the scriptlet content in a separate Java IDE, compile it there, put a special name for that piece of code, put our own special tag in the JSP and specify that its associated Java code is in so-and-so class? It is possible to do so using a *custom tag*.

Custom tags are *new* tags that we create for our Web application, each of which has a unique name and optional attribute-value pairs. The principle is the same as that of HTML tags. Recall that <A> is the anchor tag that has the attribute HREF with some URL as its value; similarly, <TD> is a table cell tag for which you can specify attributes ALIGN with values LEFT, RIGHT, etc. The name of the custom tag needs to associate with an actual Java class file that contains the Java code that every instance of this tag needs to execute. The association between the custom tag name and the Java class needs to be listed in a file that the Web server looks up to find the associated class for each custom tag. Each custom tag must belong to a tag library, which means that you can have several tag libraries, each having an identifying prefix. Each tag library is a collection of several off-the-shelf tags you can use as needed. So, the general syntax of a custom tag is as follows:

```
<library_prefix:tag_name attribute1="value1" attribute2="value2", ... >
  .. body..
</library_prefix:tag_name>
```

Here, the "body" is the part on which we want to perform operations such as formatting. An example of an HTML tag with a body would be the <B> tag:

```
<B>Bold text</B>
```

In this example, the body consists of the words Bold text, which the <B> tag converts to bold font when displaying on the browser.

For tags that do not have a body (which is usually the case for custom tags), this can be written more concisely as

```
<library_prefix:tag_name attribute1="value1" attribute2="value2", ... />
```

8.2 Your First Custom Tag

In Section 5.2.4, we saw how to use declarations to organize code. To understand the concept of a custom tag, we will redo the date-time problem at the beginning of that section but use our custom tag for doing so.

In Section 4.7, we saw how the general structure for a Tomcat Web application looks. That structure shows a folder called tlds under WEB-INF, with a file called mycustomtags.tld in it. Each custom tag needs to belong to a tag library, which consists of a .tld file ("tld" stands for Tag Library Descriptor) and Java class files for all custom tags in the library. The association between the custom tags and their corresponding Java class files needs to be defined in a .tld file under WEB-INF/tlds folder of your Web application. Each custom tag needs to have an associated Java class file that needs to follow a certain structure. When the Web server looks at the custom tag, it finds the associated Java class using the .tld file, and goes to specific methods in that Java class to get the corresponding HTML output for that tag. If you compare a scriptlet with a custom tag, you are simply moving the content of the scriptlet (lines of Java code in the scriptlet) to a separate Java class, replacing the scriptlet with a neat, special "custom" tag in the JSP, and specifying the association between the custom tag and its Java class in a separate .tld file. The result is that the JSP looks cleaner, having only HTML and custom tags, and no explicit Java code. This helps organize large amounts of Java code in the JSP.

As mentioned previously, the Java class that associates with a custom tag needs to follow a certain structure. In its simplest form, it needs to inherit from a predefined class called TagSupport of the javax.servlet.jsp.tagext package. Note that javax is part of J2EE or Java EE, not part of J2SE or Java SE. Open the documentation URL for J2EE/Java EE in Appendix D. Click on javax.servlet.jsp.tagext in the top-left frame and on TagSupport in the bottom-left. You will see that this class has a method called doStartTag() and another called doEndTag(). These two methods get automatically called by the framework when the server encounters the start and end of the custom tag (respectively). In order for your custom Java code to be executed when the server encounters your custom tag in the JSP, you need to put all such custom code in the doStartTag() method of the tag's Java class.

Call the new tag that will display the current date and time currentdatetime. This needs to belong to a tag library, say that it has a prefix datetime. Also, let the Java class associated with this tag be called CurrentDateTimeTag, so you need to create a file called CurrentDateTimeTag.java. Extend CurrentDate-TimeTag from TagSupport and override its doStartTag() method, where you should dump HTML for the current time-stamp. Also, as stated in Section 5.2.3.1, all custom classes that you want to use in your JSP need to be packaged, which means that you will need to package this class as well. Let's call the package datetime. So, the content of your CurrentDateTimeTag class would look like this:

```java
// -------------- Begin: CurrentDateTimeTag.java --------------------------
package datetime;

import java.io.*;
import java.util.*;
import javax.servlet.jsp.*;
import javax.servlet.jsp.tagext.*;

public class CurrentDateTimeTag extends TagSupport
{
    public int doStartTag() throws JspException
    {
        JspWriter out = pageContext.getOut();
        Date today = new Date();
        try
        {
            out.print( today.toString() );
        }
        catch ( IOException ex )
        {
            throw new JspTagException ("CurrentDateTimeTag: " + ex.getMessage() );
        }
        return SKIP_BODY;
    }
}
// -------------- End: CurrentDateTimeTag.java --------------------------
```

Note the pageContext object that is being used here. It was listed in Section 5.3 as one of the implicit objects available in a JSP. However, inside the CurrentDateTag class, we are inside a Java class that inherits from TagSupport, not inside a JSP. If you look at the TagSupport API documentation, you will see that it has a protected attribute called pageContext of type javax.servlet.jsp.PageContext, which contains the same pageContext implicit object available in a JSP (the framework takes care of ensuring that the TagSupport gets the same pageContext into its attribute). The getOut() method on the pageContext returns a JspWriter that you can use to dump whatever HTML you want.

Also observe how the doStartTag() method has a throws JspException clause in its header. JspException is a generic JSP exception that belongs to the javax.servlet.jsp package. For exceptions arising out of JSP tags, one needs to use the JspTagException class, which is a valid subclass of JspException and resides in the same package.

Calling the print() method on the out object can throw an IOException which is not a subclass of JspException. We cannot simply add IOException to the throws clause of doStartTag() since overriding requires the child method to have exactly the same signature as that of the parent (TagSupport). As an alternative, we re-throw the IOException as a JspTagException, sending it a concatenated String using the custom tag name and the IOException's message.

Finally, note the SKIP_BODY part. Every tag has a start, an end, and an optional body. You are currently writing a simple tag with no body, so your doStartTag() must return the SKIP_BODY as the int value returned. The SKIP_BODY is a constant of type int defined in the Tag interface in the javax.servlet.jsp.tagext package. It communicates to the caller of doStartTag() that the body evaluation part needs to be skipped for this tag.

Save CurrentDateTimeTag.java under C:\JSP\Chapter8\sec82. Create a WEB-INF\classes subfolder under C:\JSP\Chapter8. Before compiling it, you need to add the jsp-api.jar available under the C:\Tomcat\common\lib directory to your CLASSPATH, because it contains all tag-related, framework classes:

```
SET CLASSPATH=C:\Tomcat\common\lib\jsp-api.jar;%CLASSPATH%
```

As usual, modify the value of the JSP_OUT environment variable to contain C:\JSP\Chapter8\WEB-INF\classes. Then compile CurrentDateTimeTag.java using the -d option so that the .class file goes directly under the %JSP_OUT% folder:

```
C:\JSP\Chapter8\sec82>javac -d %JSP_OUT% CurrentDateTimeTag.java
```

Ok—you now have the Java class file ready. The next step is to write a tld file that associates the tag with this class.

Create a subfolder called tlds under C:\JSP\Chapter8\WEB-INF and copy jsp2-example-taglib.tld from C:\Tomcat\webapps\jsp-examples\WEB-INF\jsp2 into it. Rename the file to datetime.tld and replace its contents so that it looks like this:

```
------------------------------------------------
<?xml version="1.0" encoding="UTF-8" ?>
<taglib xmlns="http://java.sun.com/xml/ns/j2ee"
   xmlns:xsi="http://www.w3.org/2001/XMLSchema-instance"
   xsi:schemaLocation="http://java.sun.com/xml/ns/j2ee
                  http://java.sun.com/xml/ns/j2ee/web-jsptaglibrary_2_0.xsd"
   version="2.0">
   <tlib-version>1.0</tlib-version>
   <description>Time related custom tags</description>
   <tag>
      <name>currentdatetime</name>
      <tag-class>datetime.CurrentDateTimeTag</tag-class>
```

```
        <body-content>empty</body-content>
    </tag>
</taglib>
------------------------------------------------
```

The meaning of some of the new elements you see above is as follows:

`<name>`:   The name of the custom tag you will be using in your JSP to invoke this cus-
                   tom tag.

`<tag-class>`:   The fully-qualified Java tag class name associated with this custom tag. In this
                   example, the Java class associated with the `currentdatetime` custom tag is `date-
                   time.CurrentDateTimeTag` (where `datetime` is the package name). To find the
                   `.class` file for this, Tomcat will look into the `WEB-INF/classes` folder of your
                   Web application as usual.

`<body-content>`: This attribute has a value of `empty` here because we do not plan to have a body
                   for this simple tag.

Note that only one `<taglib>` element is allowed per `.tld` file. In other words, a single `.tld` file represents one tag library, which may contain one or more custom tags. If you have multiple tag libraries,
the `tlds` folder would contain multiple `.tld` files. The tag library itself has no name, although the
individual tags do have a name. So how does the JSP associate a custom tag usage with a specific tag
library? For this, it expects the physical path to the `.tld` (`/WEB-INF/tlds/datetime.tld`) or its alias path
be specified in the JSP. The remaining steps required before you can use a custom tag in your JSP are
as follows (If using a physical path to the `.tld` in your JSP, steps 1 and 2 can be skipped but we use
an alias path here to learn how it is done):

1. Pick an arbitrary alias you wish to use for your tag library (we will use `/datetime` in the
    current example).

2. Next, associate the alias with a physical path to the `.tld` file that contains the set of tags for
    a tag library. For this, you need to have a `web.xml` file under `WEB-INF` folder of your Web app
    and put a `<taglib>` element nested under the `<web-app>` element. In the current example,
    this element would look as follows:

    ```
    <taglib>
        <taglib-uri>/datetime</taglib-uri>
        <taglib-location>/WEB-INF/tlds/datetime.tld</taglib-location>
    </taglib>
    ```

    The `<taglib-uri>` works in a way that is similar to the alias we saw for the context root; the
    value of the `<taglib-uri>` is an alias that maps to the path of the actual `.tld` file associated
    with that "uri". The path is usually relative to the Web app context root (which is
    `C:\JSP\Chapter8` for this chapter).

To make this change, copy web.xml from C:\Tomcat\conf to C:\JSP\Chapter8\WEB-INF. Remove all content enclosed within the <web-app> .. </web-app> tags and add the above <taglib> .. </taglib> instead. So your web.xml would now have the following content:

```
<?xml version="1.0" encoding="ISO-8859-1"?>
<web-app xmlns="http://java.sun.com/xml/ns/j2ee"
         xmlns:xsi="http://www.w3.org/2001/XMLSchema-instance"
         xsi:schemaLocation="http://java.sun.com/xml/ns/j2ee
                             http://java.sun.com/xml/ns/j2ee/web-app_2_4.xsd"
         version="2.4">
<taglib>
    <taglib-uri>/datetime</taglib-uri>
    <taglib-location>/WEB-INF/tlds/datetime.tld</taglib-location>
</taglib>
</web-app>
```

3. Inside the JSP, add a taglib directive such that its uri attribute contains the physical path to the .tld or its alias created in Step 2 and the prefix attribute contains whatever prefix you wish to use for all tags of that tag library in that JSP (the prefix is required). A prefix is the word you use on the left side of the colon in a tag (example: <prefix:tag>). Within a JSP, you need to use the same prefix for all tags belonging to the same tag library. Using the taglib directive, you could change the prefix from one JSP to another, for the same tag library (although you would not want to do so, as it would be confusing). In the current example, we will use the prefix datetime.

    So your JSP would now look like this:

```
<%@ taglib uri="/datetime" prefix="datetime" %>
<HTML>
    <BODY>
        The current time is: <datetime:currentdatetime/>
    </BODY>
</HTML>
```

    Save this file as CurrentTime.jsp under C:\JSP\Chapter8\sec82. As usual, add a context root for this chapter in C:\Tomcat\conf\server.xml, as follows:

    <Context path="/chapter8" docBase="C:/JSP/Chapter8" debug="0" />

    Restart Tomcat and open the URL:

    http://localhost:8080/chapter8/sec82/CurrentTime.jsp

It should look like this:

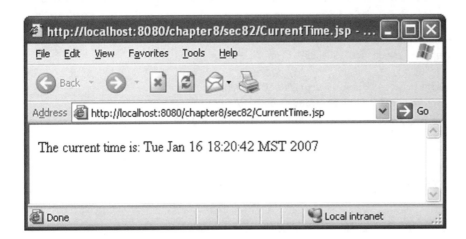

Pretty neat, huh? Figure 8.1 summarizes how the process worked (matching elements are shown in the same color).

The JSP looks very compact now, with no Java code. You can develop the tag class separately in a Java IDE and once it is ready, ship it out as an off-the-shelf component that could be used in any JSP to spit out the current date-time stamp. Think about the power of this approach: You can move several, commonly used scriptlets into custom tag classes, and clean up your JSP by replacing scriptlets with appropriate custom tag(s). Several JSP files spread out across folders or even across applications can reuse the custom tags you create in this way.

Solved Exercise 8.2

Objective: To practice creating custom tag classes and using them in a JSP.

Steps:

- Create a new folder exer82 under `C:\JSP\Chapter8`. Copy `CurrentTime.jsp` and `CurrentDateTimeTag.java` from `C:\JSP\Chapter8\sec82` into this folder. Copy `CurrentDateTimeTag.java` into two new files in the same folder: `CurrentDateTag.java` and `CurrentTimeTag.java`.

- Modify `CurrentDateTag.java` and `CurrentTimeTag.java` to dump the date-only and time-only parts of the current date-time, respectively.

- Modify `datetime.tld` under `C:\JSP\Chapter8\WEB-INF\tlds` to create two new custom tags: `currentdate` and `currenttime`.

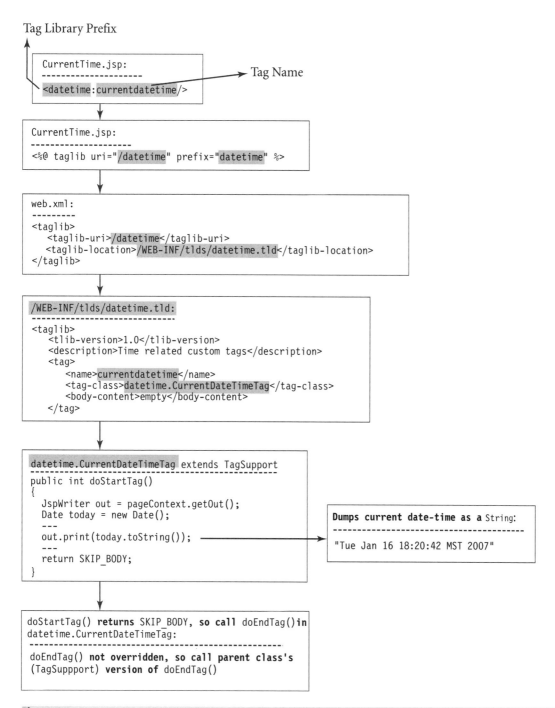

Figure 8.1

How the currentdatetime **Custom Tag Worked**

- Modify CurrentTime.jsp to use these two new custom tags to display the current date and time separately, each with an appropriate label.

- Open the following URL:

  http://localhost:8080/chapter8/exer82/CurrentTime.jsp

  Verify that it shows the date and time separately. It should look like this:

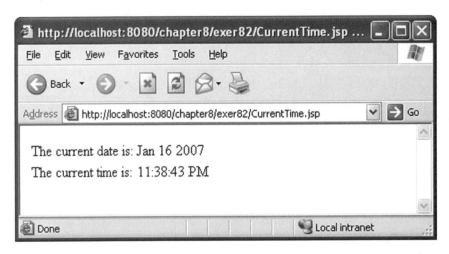

Solution:

```
// -------------- Begin: CurrentDateTag.java --------------------------
package datetime;

import java.io.*;
import java.util.*;
import java.text.SimpleDateFormat;
import javax.servlet.jsp.*;
import javax.servlet.jsp.tagext.*;

public class CurrentDateTag extends TagSupport
{
    public int doStartTag() throws JspException
    {
        JspWriter out = pageContext.getOut();
        Date today = new Date();
        SimpleDateFormat dateOnlyFormat = new SimpleDateFormat("MMM dd yyyy");

        try
```

```
      {
         out.print( dateOnlyFormat.format(today) );
      }
      catch ( IOException ex )
      {
         throw new JspTagException ("CurrentDateTag: " + ex.getMessage() );
      }
      return SKIP_BODY;
   }
}
// -------------- End: CurrentDateTag.java --------------------------


// -------------- Begin: CurrentTimeTag.java --------------------------
package datetime;

import java.io.*;
import java.util.*;
import java.text.SimpleDateFormat;
import javax.servlet.jsp.*;
import javax.servlet.jsp.tagext.*;

public class CurrentTimeTag extends TagSupport
{
   public int doStartTag() throws JspException
   {
      JspWriter out = pageContext.getOut();
      Date today = new Date();
      SimpleDateFormat timeOnlyFormat = new SimpleDateFormat("hh:mm:ss a");

      try
      {
         out.print( timeOnlyFormat.format(today) );
      }
      catch ( IOException ex )
      {
         throw new JspTagException ("CurrentTimeTag: " + ex.getMessage() );
      }
      return SKIP_BODY;
   }
}
// -------------- End: CurrentTimeTag.java --------------------------

datetime.tld:

----------------------------------------------
```

```xml
<?xml version="1.0" encoding="UTF-8" ?>
<taglib xmlns="http://java.sun.com/xml/ns/j2ee"
    xmlns:xsi="http://www.w3.org/2001/XMLSchema-instance"
    xsi:schemaLocation="http://java.sun.com/xml/ns/j2ee
                    http://java.sun.com/xml/ns/j2ee/web-jsptaglibrary_2_0.xsd"
    version="2.0">
    <tlib-version>1.0</tlib-version>
    <description>Time related custom tags</description>
    <tag>
        <name>currentdatetime</name>
        <tag-class>datetime.CurrentDateTimeTag</tag-class>
        <body-content>empty</body-content>
    </tag>
    <tag>
        <name>currentdate</name>
        <tag-class>datetime.CurrentDateTag</tag-class>
        <body-content>empty</body-content>
    </tag>
    <tag>
        <name>currenttime</name>
        <tag-class>datetime.CurrentTimeTag</tag-class>
        <body-content>empty</body-content>
    </tag>
</taglib>
<!-- End: datetime.tld -->

<!-- Begin: CurrentTime.jsp -->
<%@ taglib uri="/datetime" prefix="datetime" %>
<!-- Can use: uri="/WEB-INF/tlds/datetime.tld" instead of: uri="/datetime" -->
<HTML>
    <BODY>
        <TABLE>
            <TR><TD>The current date is: </TD><TD><datetime:currentdate/></TD></TR>
            <TR><TD>The current time is: </TD><TD><datetime:currenttime/></TD></TR>
        </TABLE>
    </BODY>
</HTML>
<!-- End: CurrentTime.jsp -->
```

8.2.1 Getting Request Parameters Inside doStartTag()

Until now, we did not have to worry about request parameters that could affect the way the custom tag dumps output. In the real-world, input supplied on HTML forms may very well determine how the custom tag needs to display the result. For example, say that the user has a checkbox option to specify whether the date only or both date and time need to be displayed. If the box is checked, only the date would be displayed; otherwise both date and time would be displayed. To get the request in a tag class, you need to use the getRequest() method on the pageContext. Recall that pageContext is a protected attribute of TagSupport class, which your custom tag class extends from. This implies that inside doStartTag(), you can simply begin using pageContext without declaring or instantiating it. Let's go ahead and do this to understand it better.

Create a folder called sec821 under C:\JSP\Chapter8 and copy CurrentTime.jsp and CurrentDate-TimeTag.java from C:\JSP\Chapter8\sec82 into it. Create an HTML form in a new file called DateFor-matSelect.html; the form needs to have a checkbox the user can check to specify that only the date needs to be displayed (as opposed to both date and time). On submitting the form, it should go to CurrentTime.jsp where you need to use the currentdatetime custom tag to display the date only or both date and time based on the user's selection on the previous page. For this to work, you need to modify the doStartTag() method in CurrentDateTimeTag.java to call the getRequest() method, which returns the request as a ServletRequest object. Note that ServletRequest belongs to the javax.servlet package and is the parent interface of HttpServletRequest that we are familiar with. Finally use the checkbox input parameter from the request to determine whether the date only or both date and time is to be dumped on the response.

With these changes, DateFormatSelect.html would look like this:

```
-------------------------------------------------
<!-- Begin: DateFormatSelect.html -->
<HTML>
  <BODY>
    <FORM NAME="main" ACTION="CurrentTime.jsp" METHOD="POST">
      <TABLE>
        <TR>
          <TD>Check to display date only:</TD>
          <TD><INPUT TYPE="checkbox" NAME="dateOnly"</INPUT></TD>
        </TR>
        <TR>
          <TD ALIGN="center" COLSPAN=2>
            <INPUT TYPE="submit" VALUE="Submit"/>
          </TD>
        </TR>
      </TABLE>
    </FORM>
  </BODY>
</HTML>
<!-- End: DateFormatSelect.html -->
-------------------------------------------------
```

and `CurrentDateTimeTag.java` would contain the following code:

```
-------------------------------------------------
// -------------- Begin:  CurrentDateTimeTag.java --------------
package datetime;

import java.io.*;
import java.util.*;
import java.text.SimpleDateFormat;
import javax.servlet.*;
import javax.servlet.jsp.*;
import javax.servlet.jsp.tagext.*;

public class CurrentDateTimeTag extends TagSupport
{
    public int doStartTag() throws JspException
    {
        JspWriter out = pageContext.getOut();
        ServletRequest request = pageContext.getRequest();
        Date today = new Date();
        try
        {
            String dateOnly = request.getParameter("dateOnly");
            if (dateOnly != null && dateOnly.equals("on"))
            {
                SimpleDateFormat dateOnlyFormat
                    = new SimpleDateFormat("MMM dd yyyy");
                out.print("Today's date is: " + dateOnlyFormat.format(today));
            }
            else
            {
                out.print("The current time is: " + today.toString());
            }
        }
        catch ( IOException ex )
        {
            throw new JspTagException ("CurrentDateTimeTag: " + ex.getMessage());
        }
        return SKIP_BODY;
    }
}
// -------------- End:  CurrentDateTimeTag.java ---------------------------
-------------------------------------------------
```

Finally, `CurrentTime.jsp` would be as shown here:

```
-----------------------------------------------
<!-- Begin: CurrentTime.jsp -->
<%@ taglib uri="/datetime" prefix="datetime" %>
<HTML>
  <BODY>
      <datetime:currentdatetime/>
  </BODY>
</HTML>
<!-- End: CurrentTime.jsp -->
-----------------------------------------------
```

Open the URL:

`http://localhost:8080/chapter8/sec821/DateFormatSelect.html`

Check the box first, hit the Submit button and verify that it displays only the date. Click on the Back button, uncheck the box, hit the Submit button, and verify that it displays both date and time.

A sample screen interaction is shown next:

The user checks the "date only" checkbox and hits the Submit button:

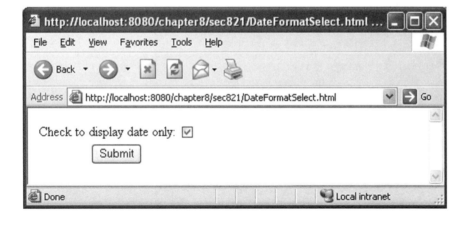

The next page displays the date only using the `currentdatetime` custom tag:

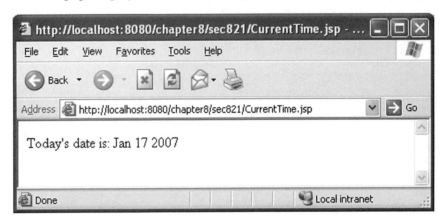

The user clicks the Back button on the browser, unchecks the box, and hits the Submit button:

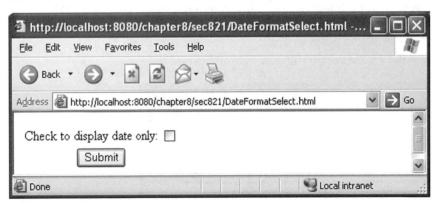

The page displays both date and time:

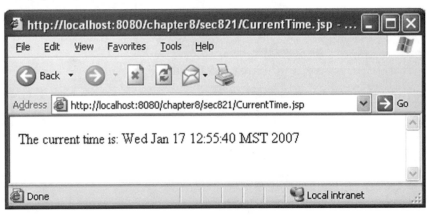

8.2.2 JSP Tag Life Cycle

The doStartTag() is one of the methods called automatically by the TagSupport framework. As mentioned earlier, a custom tag can include a start tag, an end tag, and a body in between. Most custom tags do not need to have a body and must simply extend from TagSupport. However, custom tags that do have a body need to extend from BodyTagSupport instead of TagSupport.

As the name indicates, TagSupport and BodyTagSupport are "support" classes that provide default implementation for some of the required methods and make it transparent to the developer of the custom tag class. The actual requirement for the custom tag class is that it must implement one or more of the following interfaces:

```
javax.servlet.jsp.tagext.Tag

javax.servlet.jsp.tagext.IterationTag

javax.servlet.jsp.tagext.BodyTag
```

Because TagSupport and BodyTagSupport implement these interfaces for you, when you extend from one of them, you just need to concentrate on the specific methods, such as doStartTag(), you want to override. Tags with body must implement the BodyTag interface (or extend BodyTagSupport). Iteration tags are used in a loop (for example, when processing the result set from a database query), and must implement the IterationTag interface. The BodyTag interface extends from the IterationTag interface, which in turn extends from the Tag interface.

There are five important methods in these interfaces:

```
doStartTag()

doInitBody()

doAfterBody()

doEndTag()

release()
```

By default, these methods get called in the sequence shown above (as applicable). The methods doStartTag(), doAfterBody(), and doEndTag() return an integer value that determines whether to skip or to call the methods that are downstream. So the value returned by any of them can change the default sequence. The possible integer values returned by these methods are defined in the Tag, IterationTag, and BodyTag interfaces. The sequence of calls is shown in Figure 8.2.

The use of specific return values has implications as outlined in Table 8.1.

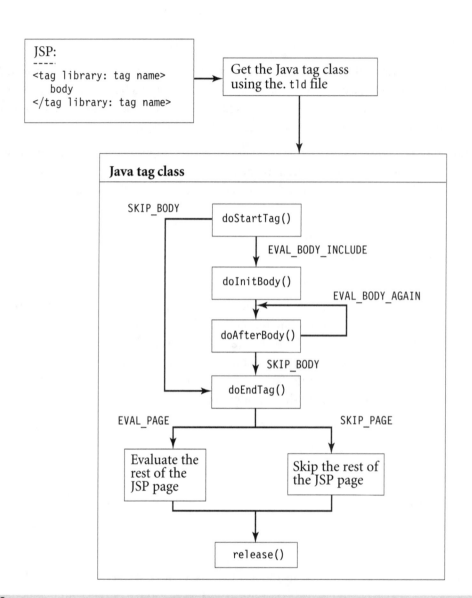

Figure 8.2
JSP Tag Life Cycle

TABLE 8.1   Tag Methods and Return Values

Interface	Method	When called	Return Value	Meaning
Tag	doStartTag()	Called once when the start of the tag is processed. Used for initializing the tag, and usually the complete tag processing (for tags without body).	Tag.SKIP_BODY	Body of the tag must be empty and is skipped
			Tag.EVAL_BODY_INCLUDE	Body of the tag must be present and will be evaluated
			BodyTag.EVAL_BODY_BUFFERED	The body of the tag is output to a buffer in memory which can be processed later.
BodyTag	doInitBody()	Only for tags with body. Called once after doStartTag() but before the body of tag is processed. Used for initializing the tag (in addition to doStartTag()).	void	
IterationTag	doAfterBody()	Only for iteration/body tags. Called after body of tag has been processed but before doEndTag().	IterationTag.EVAL_BODY_AGAIN	doAfterBody() must be called once more
			Tag.SKIP_BODY	End of processing of body of tag.
Tag	doEndTag()	Called once when the end of tag is processed.	Tag.EVAL_PAGE	Evaluate the rest of the page
			Tag.SKIP_PAGE	Skip the rest of the page (after this tag).
Tag	release()	Called once when the tag is finished processing. Used to release unused resources.	void	

8.3   Action Elements and JavaBeans

As promised in Section 5.2, we will look here at another type of JSP element—namely, the action element. Well, now is the time to get familiar with this element, since we will need to use some of its principles in our custom tags beyond this point.

So, what are these elements? **Action elements** are JSP elements that look like HTML tags and have a tag name and list of attribute name-value pairs. The action element takes the list of attribute name-value pairs and passes them on to a Java class associated with the tag name. The Java class is a special class that has access to the `JspWriter` object, which is used to dump HTML that is picked up by the response sent to the client. Each action element has a name. To organize things when several action elements exist, the JSP specification requires that each action element belong to a named group of elements. This group is technically called a tag library, which could be the custom tag library that we just saw or it could be a predefined tag library available for use in your JSP files (just as predefined JDK classes are available for use in your Java class). So, the custom tags we created until now are one type of action element.

The general syntax of an action element is

```
<library_prefix:element_name attribute1="value1" attribute2="value2", ... />
```

Predefined elements include a group called the standard action elements (or simply, standard actions), and the group name assigned to it is `jsp`. In other words, all standard action elements must start with the `<jsp:` suffix. So, what are standard action elements? As the name suggests, they represent the "standard," routine, or most commonly used actions that the JSP needs to perform. For example, you may want to include a whole other JSP at the beginning of your current JSP, so that you do not have to repeat the code here. Or you may want your JSP to simply forward the user to some other JSP, without proceeding further, in which case your current JSP simply acts like a stepping stone to go to the other JSP it is forwarded to. For all of these, there are ready-to-use, predefined elements that you can use in your JSP (so these are *not* custom tags). For including an outside JSP into your current JSP, you use the `<jsp:include>` standard action. For example, your current JSP may have a line such as

```
<jsp:include page="termsandconditions.jsp"/>
```

This will include the entire content of `termsandconditions.jsp` into your current JSP at that point.

In order to forward to another JSP from your current one, you may have a line such as

```
<jsp:forward page="newpage.jsp"/>
```

This has the same effect as `response.sendRedirect()`, which we saw earlier, but avoids the use of explicit Java code in your JSP.

Another standard action element is the `<jsp:useBean>`, which is very important and forms the basis of what we will be learning beyond this point. This element is slightly unusual in the sense that, although it seems to be a predefined tag, it allows you to specify a Java custom class and pass attributes to it, in order to get custom HTML output from it. In that sense, its behavior is similar to that of a custom tag. A **bean** (technically called a **JavaBean**) is simply a Java class that conforms to certain rules or a convention. It is not required to inherit from any class (although it can). The rules for a JavaBean class, listed in the JavaBeans specification, are as follows:

- The class must be `public`, and must provide a no-argument (default) constructor (Java provides one if you don't). This allows applications to dynamically create new instances of your bean, without necessarily knowing ahead of time what Java class name will be used. For example:

```
String className = "salesdept.CustomerBean";
Class beanClass = Class.forName(className);
Object beanInstance = beanClass.newInstance();
```

- As a consequence of having only a no-argument constructor, the bean's properties must be manipulated separately from its instantiation. This is typically achieved via a set of properties or attributes on the bean. The convention for property names is that they start with a lowercase letter, with the rest of the name in title case (example: `dateOnly`).

- Typically, each property needs to have a getter method that returns the property's value and a setter method that modifies it.

- The getter method must not take any parameters and must return an object of the data type of the attribute.

- The setter method must take a single parameter of the same data type as the attribute and have a return type of `void`.

- Although not required, it is strongly recommended that getter and setter methods follow standard naming convention. In other words, the getter method must begin with `get`, followed by the name of the attribute with the first letter in uppercase; similarly, the setter must begin with `set`, followed by the name of the attribute with the first letter in uppercase. For example, for the attribute `firstName`, you need to have a getter method called `getFirstName()` and a setter method called `setFirstName()`. (Note the uppercase F in the getter and setter as opposed to a lowercase f in the attribute name). For `boolean` type attributes, the "get" in a getter needs to be replaced with "`is`". For example, a `boolean` attribute `dateOnly` needs to have a getter method called `isDateOnly()`. The way JavaBean uses getter and setter method names to deduce the attribute name is technically called *reflection*.

- There should not be more than one getter or more than one setter for any property. Overloading is not allowed.

- If a property has both a getter and a setter, the return type of the getter must match the data type accepted by the setter.

- It is not required that every property have a getter and setter. You can have read-only properties that have only a getter; similarly (but less commonly), you can have write-only properties that have only a setter.

- It is not necessary to have a property associated with a getter. For example, you could have a method called getFullName() without the property fullName in the class. The getFullName() in this case needs to simply return an appropriate value back (which may be a derived value from other properties) in order for it to work. Inside the JSP, you can still refer to the property name as fullName, and the framework would use that to inspect the bean class and to figure out which getter method to invoke.

- It is possible to create a JavaBean where the getter and setter do not follow the naming pattern described earlier. That part is beyond the scope of this book, so we will assume that our beans follow the standard naming convention for getters and setters.

To see a JavaBean in action, say that you want to be able to specify an attribute called dateOnly on a JavaBean object; if the value is true, the JSP should display only the date, otherwise it should display the complete date-time stamp.

To do so, you first need to create a custom bean class—call it CurrentDateTimeBean. Create a folder sec83 under C:\JSP\Chapter8 and a file called CurrentDateTimeBean.java in it with the following content:

```
// ------------ Begin: CurrentDateTimeBean.java ----------------------
package datetime;

import java.io.*;
import java.util.*;
import java.text.SimpleDateFormat;

public class CurrentDateTimeBean
{
    private boolean dateOnly;

    public boolean isDateOnly() { return dateOnly; }

    public void setDateOnly( boolean dateOnly ) { this.dateOnly = dateOnly; }

    public String getDate()
    {
        SimpleDateFormat dateOnlyFormat = new SimpleDateFormat("MMM dd yyyy");
```

```
        Date today = new Date();
        if ( dateOnly )
        {
            return dateOnlyFormat.format(today);
        }
        else return today.toString();
    }
}
// ------------ End: CurrentDateTimeBean.java ---------------------
```

Observe how the getter method getDate() does not have an associated class attribute but derives its value using the dateOnly attribute.

To invoke this bean in your JSP, you need to use the <jsp:useBean> standard action element. The general syntax of this element is

```
<jsp:useBean id="bean_name" class="bean_class" scope="bean_scope">
```

Here, the attributes shown have the meaning described in Tables 8.2 and 8.3.

TABLE 8.2   <jsp:useBean> Attributes

Attribute	Meaning
id	This is the name used to identify the bean object inside your JSP. You can use any name for the object, as long as it is unique within the JSP.
class	This is the fully-qualified class name of the bean (including the package).
scope	This refers to the scope in which a bean remains defined. The valid values for the scope are described in Table 8.3.

Table 8.3   Values of <jsp:useBean> scope Attribute

Value of scope	Meaning
page	The bean is in scope only within this page (JSP).
request	The bean is in scope as long as the request is in scope; so the bean is in scope within this page, plus any page to which the request is forwarded to.
session	The bean is in scope for the current session.
application	The bean is in scope throughout the web application

So, to instantiate the CurrentDateTimeBean in the JSP, you would say

```
<jsp:useBean id="datetimebean" class="datetime.CurrentDateTimeBean" scope="page"/>
```

Once you do this, an object called datetimebean of type datetime.CurrentDateTimeBean is available for use beyond that point in the JSP. So you could say something like

```
<%
  if (datetimebean.isDateOnly())
  {
    // .. do something
  }
%>
```

In effect, we have created a "scripting variable" called datetimebean for use inside the JSP. Of course, this was only to show the concept of the bean object; we want to move away from putting explicit Java code in JSP, but it shows how you could use a scripting variable created by <jsp:useBean>.

For getting and setting attributes from or on the bean, you have two standard action elements available: <jsp:getProperty> and <jsp:setProperty>. These are basically the getter and setter you can use on the bean object from within your JSP. So, to get the dateOnly attribute of the datetimebean bean object, you would say

```
<jsp:getProperty name="datetimebean" property="dateOnly"/>
```

The Web server would replace this part (<jsp:getProperty>) with the value of the property dateOnly converted to a String (so it would be replaced with either the String "true" or "false"). The name attribute here corresponds to the id attribute of the <jsp:useBean> element—both of which must contain exactly the same value in order for it to work. To set a property value on the bean, you use the <jsp:setProperty> element as in this example:

```
<jsp:setProperty name="datetimebean" property="dateOnly" value="true"/>
```

The <jsp:setProperty> element can also be enclosed, nested within the <jsp:useBean> element, for example:

```
-----------------------------------------------------------------------------------
<jsp:useBean id="datetimebean" class="datetime.CurrentDateTimeBean" scope="page">
    <jsp:setProperty name="datetimebean" property="dateOnly" value="true"/>
</jsp:useBean>
-----------------------------------------------------------------------------------
```

Ok—you got the bean ready. Next thing to do is to use the bean in your JSP to display the date and time. Copy CurrentTime.jsp from C:\JSP\Chapter8\sec82 to C:\JSP\Chapter8\sec83. Modify it to add a <jsp:useBean> element that creates a scripting variable called datetimebean. Use <jsp:setProperty> action element to set the dateOnly attribute of the bean to true initially, then use the <jsp:getProperty> element to get the bean's date attribute and display on the page. Next, use <jsp:setProperty> element to set the dateOnly attribute to false, and repeat the process to display the complete date-time stamp.

CurrentTime.jsp would look like this:

```
-----------------------------------------------------------------------------------
<!-- Begin: CurrentTime.jsp ----->
<jsp:useBean id="datetimebean" class="datetime.CurrentDateTimeBean" scope="page">
```

```
    <jsp:setProperty name="datetimebean" property="dateOnly" value="true"/>
</jsp:useBean>
<HTML>
  <BODY>
    <TABLE>
       <TR>
          <TD>Today's date is: </TD>
          <TD><jsp:getProperty name="datetimebean" property="date"/></TD>
       </TR>
       <jsp:setProperty name="datetimebean" property="dateOnly" value="false"/>
       <TR>
          <TD>The current time-stamp is: </TD>
          <TD><jsp:getProperty name="datetimebean" property="date"/></TD>
       </TR>
    </TABLE>
  </BODY>
</HTML>
<!-- End: CurrentTime.jsp ----->
-------------------------------------------------------------------------------------
```

Open the following URL:

`http://localhost:8080/chapter8/sec83/CurrentTime.jsp`

It should show up as shown here:

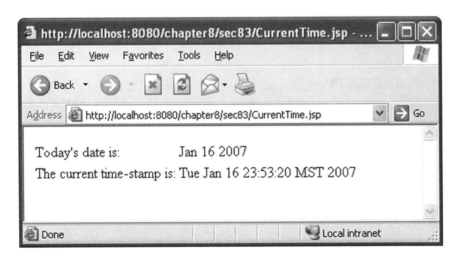

Instead of hard-coding the value of the `dateOnly` property, it can be obtained from a parameter on the request, for example:

```
<jsp:setProperty name="datetimebean" property="dateOnly"
                 value="<%= request.getParameter ("selectDateOnly") %>" />
```

where `selectDateOnly` may be the name of a parameter on an HTML form on the previous page with a value of "true" or "false".

This is a common situation in the real world: You usually get the value from the request and use it to set a property on the bean. This two-step process can be reduced to one step by using an alternative form of the `<jsp:setProperty>` element that allows you to directly specify the parameter name on the request and use it to set the bean's property, as in this example:

```
<jsp:setProperty name="datetimebean" property="dateOnly" param="selectDateOnly"/>
```

Notice how we use the `param` attribute instead of `value`. The request has a parameter called `selectDateOnly` that is used to set the `dateOnly` attribute on the bean. If the request `param` and the bean attribute have the same name (for example, if both are called `dateOnly`), then you can simplify this further by omitting the `param` altogether:

```
<jsp:setProperty name="datetimebean" property="dateOnly"/>
```

In other words, this would set the `dateOnly` attribute on the bean to the value of the `dateOnly` attribute on the request.

Solved Exercise 8.3

> **Objective: To practice using the `<jsp:useBean>`, `<jsp:getProperty>`, and `<jsp:setProperty>` action elements.**

Steps:

- Create an HTML form with INPUT fields for first name and last name (naming these fields `fName` and `lName` respectively). Save the file as `InputCustomer.html` under a new folder `C:\JSP\Chapter8\exer83`.

- Create a bean called `CustomerBean` that has properties for the first and last names (call them `firstName` and `lastName`, and write getters and setters). Also add a method called `getFullName()` that concatenates the first name, a space, and the last name and returns the result as a `String`.

- In `InputCustomer.html`, set the action of the HTML form to a JSP called `CustomerName.jsp`. Inside `CustomerName.jsp`, use the `<jsp:useBean>`, `<jsp:getProperty>`, and `<jsp:setProperty>` standard action elements to display the first and last names entered by the user, followed by a concatenated name.

Solution:

```
<!-- Begin: InputCustomer.html -->
<HTML>
    <BODY>
```

```
            <FORM NAME="main" ACTION="CustomerName.jsp" METHOD="POST">
              <TABLE>
                <TR>
                    <TD COLSPAN=2>Please enter the customer's information:</TD>
                </TR>
                <TR>
                    <TD>First Name:</TD>
                    <TD><INPUT TYPE="text" NAME="fName"/></TD>
                </TR>
                <TR>
                    <TD>Last Name:</TD>
                    <TD><INPUT TYPE="text" NAME="lName"/></TD>
                </TR>
                <TR>
                    <TD ALIGN="center" COLSPAN=2>
                      <INPUT TYPE="submit" VALUE="Submit"/>
                    </TD>
                </TR>
              </TABLE>
            </FORM>
        </BODY>
</HTML>
<!-- End: InputCustomer.html -->

<!-- Begin: CustomerName.jsp -->
<jsp:useBean id="customerbean" class="salesdept.CustomerBean" scope="page"/>
<jsp:setProperty name="customerbean" property="firstName"
                 value="<%= request.getParameter("fName") %>" />
<jsp:setProperty name="customerbean" property="lastName"
                 value="<%= request.getParameter("lName") %>" />
<HTML>
    <BODY>
      <TABLE>
        <TR>
            <TD>First Name:</TD>
            <TD><jsp:getProperty name="customerbean" property="firstName"/></TD>
        </TR>
        <TR>
            <TD>Last Name:</TD>
            <TD><jsp:getProperty name="customerbean" property="lastName"/></TD>
        </TR>
        <TR>
            <TD>Full Name:</TD>
```

```
            <TD><jsp:getProperty name="customerbean" property="fullName"/></TD>
        </TR>
      </TABLE>
    </BODY>
  </HTML>
<!-- End: CustomerName.jsp -->


// ------------ Begin: CustomerBean.java ---------------------
package salesdept;

public class CustomerBean
{
    private String firstName;
    private String lastName;

    public String getFirstName() { return firstName; }
    public String getLastName() { return lastName; }

    public void setFirstName( String firstName ) { this.firstName = firstName; }
    public void setLastName( String lastName ) { this.lastName = lastName; }

    public String getFullName()
    {
        return firstName + " " + lastName;
    }
}
// ------------ End: CustomerBean.java ---------------------
```

Open the following URL:

```
http://localhost:8080/chapter8/exer83/InputCustomer.html
```

A sample interaction is shown next.

The user enters the first and last names, and hits the Submit button.

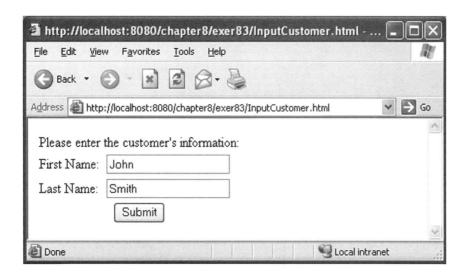

The screen displays the first and last names entered on the previous page, along with a concatenated full name:

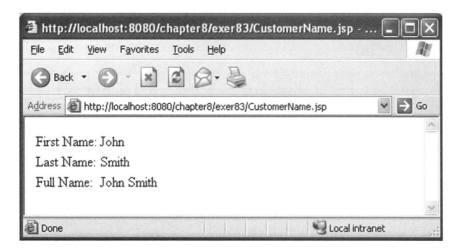

8.4   Passing Attribute Values to Your Custom Tag

Section 5.2 presented the following general syntax of the JSP element:

```
----------------------------------------------------
<element_tag attributename1="attribute value1"
            attributename2="attribute value2" .. >
```

```
        ..body..
</element_tag>
-------------------------------------------------
```

The part shown by

```
attributename1="attribute value1" attributename2="attribute value2" ..
```

represents a list of attribute name-value pairs that apply to the `element_tag`. Depending on the element_tag, some of the attributes are required; others are optional. If absent, the attributes take default values.

A custom tag is one kind of JSP element, where the `element_tag` part consists of (or is replaced with) `library_prefix:tag_name`. Because a custom tag also complies with the general syntax, it too can have an optional list of attribute name-value pairs, with the names representing attributes of the custom tag (much like the attributes of a class). The one we saw in Section 8.2 was the simplest case, where no attributes were specified. Many times, you want to pass some information from the JSP into the custom tag so that it can use those inputs and produce an appropriate output.

To understand custom tags with attributes, let's re-do the example of Section 8.3 using a custom tag instead of a bean. In other words, you need to pass a `boolean` attribute called `dateOnly` to your `currentdatetime` custom tag, so that it should spit out only the date part if that attribute is true, and both date and time in all other cases. The value supplied for this attribute needs to be passed to the custom tag class, `CurrentDateTimeTag`, which should dump the appropriate HTML.

In order for this to work, the `CurrentDateTimeTag` class needs to have a new `boolean` type attribute, say `dateOnly`, and associated getter and setter methods (so it can store the value for later retrieval). The framework can associate the attribute name with the getter and setter methods, provided these methods follow the standard naming convention described in the JavaBean spec of Section 8.3. In other words, for the attribute `dateOnly`, you need to have a getter method called `isDateOnly()` and a setter method called `setDateOnly()`. (Note that the first lowercase letter "d" of the attribute is uppercase "D" in the getter and setter.)

You also need to add the new attribute to the tag definition in the `datetime.tld` file so that your JSP can use it. The relevant part of the `tld` would now look like this:

```
<tag>
    <name>currentdatetime</name>
    <tag-class>datetime.CurrentDateTimeTag</tag-class>
    <body-content>empty</body-content>
    <attribute>
        <name>dateOnly</name>
        <required>true</required>
        <rtexpvalue>true</rtexpvalue>
        <type>boolean</type>
    </attribute>
```

```
</tag>
```

(The highlighting indicates those lines that differ from the ones in Section 8.2.)

The meaning of each of the elements under the `<attribute>` tag is as follows:

`<name>`	Defines the name of the attribute.
`<required>`	Indicates whether the attribute must be provided for this tag (default is `false`).
`<rtexpvalue>`	Indicates whether the attribute is settable using expression tags (`<%= %>`) in the JSP (default is `false`).
`<type>`	Indicates data type of this attribute (usually most attributes are of type `String`, which is the default).

Because you have `<rtexpvalue>` as `true`, you can set this attribute in your JSP by using expression tags, as in this example:

```
<datetime:currentdatetime dateOnly="<%= request.getParameter("dateonly") %>" />
```

Create a new folder called `sec84` under `C:\JSP\Chapter8`. Copy `CurrentDateTimeTag.java` and `Current-Time.jsp` from `C:\JSP\Chapter8\sec82` into this folder. Modify it to add the new attribute and getter/setter, so it would now look like this (with the highlighted portion showing differences with Section 8.2):

```java
// -------------- Begin: CurrentDateTimeTag.java -------------------------
package datetime;

import java.io.*;
import java.util.*;
import java.text.SimpleDateFormat;
import javax.servlet.jsp.*;
import javax.servlet.jsp.tagext.*;

public class CurrentDateTimeTag extends TagSupport
{
    private boolean dateOnly;

    public boolean isDateOnly() { return dateOnly; }

    public void setDateOnly( boolean dateOnly ) { this.dateOnly = dateOnly; }
```

```
public int doStartTag() throws JspException
{
    SimpleDateFormat dateOnlyFormat = new SimpleDateFormat("MMM dd yyyy");

    JspWriter out = pageContext.getOut();
    Date today = new Date();
    try
    {
        if ( dateOnly )
        {
            out.print( dateOnlyFormat.format(today) );
        }
        else out.print( today.toString() );
    }
    catch ( IOException ex )
    {
            throw new JspTagException ("CurrentDateTimeTag: " + ex.getMessage() );
    }
    return SKIP_BODY;
    }
}
// -------------- End:  CurrentDateTimeTag.java --------------------------
```

Modify CurrentTime.jsp to specify this new attribute:

```
<!------ Begin: CurrentTime.jsp ---------------->
<%@ taglib uri="/datetime" prefix="datetime" %>
<HTML>
    <BODY>
        <TABLE>
            <TR>
                <TD>Today's date is: </TD>
                <TD><datetime:currentdatetime dateOnly="true"/></TD>
            </TR>
            <TR>
                <TD>The current time-stamp is: </TD>
                <TD><datetime:currentdatetime dateOnly="false"/></TD>
            </TR>
        </TABLE>
    </BODY>
</HTML>
<!------ End: CurrentTime.jsp ---------------->
```

Open the following URL:

```
http://localhost:8080/chapter8/sec84/CurrentTime.jsp
```

It should look like this:

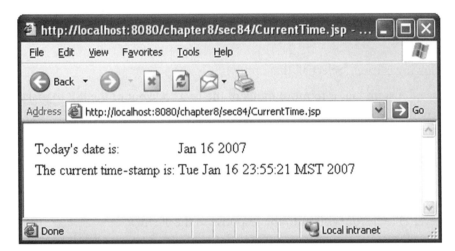

8.5   Summary

In this chapter, we discussed the concept of tag libraries and custom tags, including the life cycle and sequence of calls when the JSP contains a custom tag. We noted that tags allow us to move major chunks of Java code away from the JSP and thus help in maintaining the code. We saw what action elements are, and how they are used in JSPs. We studied the rules for defining a JavaBean and how it uses reflection to deduce attribute names using getters and setters. We also learned how to specify an attribute in a custom tag, and how to set its value via a JSP. Finally, we saw how a JavaBean object and a custom tag can each be used to produce the same end result. In the next chapter, we will look at Struts, a very popular framework of predefined classes and built-in tag libraries we can use in JSPs to streamline the development process.

8.6   Chapter Quiz

1. A JSP uses the custom tag `<datetime:currentdatetime/>`. Here, the part `datetime` represents the

    a.   tag name

    b.   tag library prefix

    c.   tag library descriptor (`tld`) filename

    d.   none of the above

2. In the JSP described in Question 1, the part `currentdatetime` represents the

    a. tag name

    b. tag library prefix

    c. tag library descriptor (tld) filename

    d. tag attribute name

3. Which of the following is true? (Select all that apply.)

    i. The main use of custom tags is to move much of the Java code out of the JSP to make code maintenance cleaner and easier.

    ii. When you use a custom tag in your JSP, the framework always calls the doStartTag() method in your custom tag class, if implemented.

    iii. Inside the doStartTag() method, you can access the JspWriter object from the pageContext object, by calling the getOut() method on pageContext, and use the JspWriter to dump whatever HTML you wish onto the response to the client.

    a. All of the above

    b. (i) and (ii) only

    c. (i) and (iii) only

    d. (ii) and (iii) only

4. Which of the following is true? (Select all that apply.)

    i. Every tag library has a name attribute that cannot be empty

    ii. The <taglib-uri> part of a <taglib> element in web.xml represents the alias path you wish to use for the tag library

    iii. The prefix attribute of a taglib directive in a JSP must be the same as the alias path specified under <taglib-uri> in the <taglib> element of web.xml.

    iv. The uri attribute of a taglib directive in a JSP must match the tag library prefix you use in a custom tag.

    a. All of the above

    b. (ii), (iii), and (iv) only

    c. (i), (iii), and (iv) only

    d. (ii) only

5. Which of the following is true? (Select all that apply.)

    i. A .tld file can contain one or more <taglib> elements, one <taglib> per tag library.

   ii. A custom tag may or may not have a body.

   iii. The `<taglib>` element can appear in both the `.tld` and `web.xml` files, although its nested elements are different

   iv. Inside the `.tld` file, `<rtexpvalue>` part of `<attribute>` element for a custom tag specifies whether you can set the value of this attribute using expression tags.

   a. All of the above

   b. (ii), (iii), and (iv) only

   c. (i), (ii), and (iv) only

   d. (ii) and (iii) only

6. To get the request object inside a custom tag class, you need to use which of the following?

   a. `pageContext.getOut()`

   b. `pageContext.getRequest()`

   c. `session.getRequest()`

   d. `request` is implicitly available in a custom tag class, so you can simply begin using it

7. Which of the following is true? (Select all that apply.)

   i. You can define JSP scripting variables, or objects, using the `<jsp:useBean>` tag.

   ii. You can get and set attributes of a `JavaBean` object using the `<jsp:getProperty>` and `<jsp:setProperty>` tags respectively.

   iii. To name your scripting variable using the `<jsp:useBean>` tag, you need to use the `id` attribute and set its value to the name you wish to use.

   iv. In order for it to work, the `name` attribute value in the `<jsp:useBean>` tag and the `id` attribute value in the `<jsp:getProperty>`/`<jsp:setProperty>` tags must match.

   a. All of the above

   b. (i), (ii), and (iii) only

   c. (i) and (iii) only

   d. (i), (iii), and (iv) only

8. In the `<jsp:useBean>` tag, which attribute do you need to use to specify the name of the `JavaBean` scripting variable you are creating?

   a. `id` attribute

   b. `name` attribute

   c. property attribute

   d. class attribute

9. In the `<jsp:useBean>` tag, which attribute do you need to use to specify the JavaBean class type of the scripting variable?

   a. id attribute

   b. name attribute

   c. type attribute

   d. class attribute

10. When using `<jsp:getProperty>` and `<jsp:setProperty>` tags, you can specify the name of the JavaBean object whose attribute you wish to get or set, by using which attribute of the tag?

   a. id attribute

   b. name attribute

   c. property attribute

   d. class attribute

11. When using `<jsp:getProperty>` and `<jsp:setProperty>` tags, you can specify the attribute of the JavaBean object you wish to get or set by using which attribute of the tag?

   a. id attribute

   b. name attribute

   c. property attribute

   d. class attribute

12. Say that you want to use `<jsp:setProperty>` to set the property of a bean using a request parameter. Which approach(es) can you use in this situation?

   a. Set the value attribute to contain the parameter from the request

   b. Use a param attribute instead of the value attribute and give it the name of the request parameter you are looking for.

   c. If the name of the request parameter is the same as that of the bean property, you can specify only the name/property attributes in `<jsp:setProperty>` and it would set the bean's property from a request parameter that has the same name as that of the bean's property.

   d. Any of the above

8.7 Answers to Quiz

1. The correct answer is (b).

2. The correct answer is (d).

3. The correct answer is (a).

4. The correct answer is (d). All statements except (ii) are false. Statement (i) is false because a tag library does not have a name attribute. Statement (iii) is false because the uri attribute (and not prefix) of a taglib directive in a JSP must be the same as the alias path specified under <taglib-uri> in the <taglib> element of web.xml. Statement (iv) is false because the prefix attribute (and not uri) of a taglib directive in a JSP must match the tag library prefix you use in a custom tag.

5. The correct answer is (b). All statements except (i) are true. Statement (i) is false because a .tld file can only contain exactly one <taglib> element (this means you need one .tld file per tag library).

6. The correct answer is (b). Option (d) is false because the request is not implicitly available in a custom tag class.

7. The correct answer is (b). Statement (iv) is false because the id (not name) attribute value in the <jsp:useBean> tag and the name (not id) attribute value in the <jsp:getProperty>/<jsp:setProperty> tags need to match.

8. The correct answer is (a).

9. The correct answer is (d).

10. The correct answer is (b).

11. The correct answer is (c).

12. The correct answer is (d). Any of the options (a), (b), and (c) is valid.

8.8 Unsolved Assignments

Assignment 8.1

Objective: To practice creating and using custom tags with attributes.

Steps:

- Redo Solved Exercise 8.3, this time creating a custom tag (instead of a bean) to get the same output as before. Create a new folder assign81 under C:\JSP\Chapter8 and copy InputCustomer.html and CustomerName.jsp from exer83 folder into it.

- Call the tag class CustomerTag and put it in a package called salesdept. Save it in a file called CustomerTag.java under C:\JSP\Chapter8\assign81.

- The tag class should have an int attribute called nameType, which can take possible values of 1, 2, or 3. If nameType is 1, the doStartTag() method should dump only the firstName; if it is 2, it should dump only the lastName; and if it is 3, it should dump firstName + a blank space + lastName.

- Create a file called salesdept.tld (under C:\JSP\Chapter8\WEB-INF\tlds) that contains the new tag library with a tag called name that has an attribute called nameType of type int. All tags of this tag library need to use a prefix of customer.

- Modify CustomerName.jsp to use the new custom tag with nameType set to 1, 2, and 3 to display the first name, last name, and full name respectively.

- To test the code, open the following URL:

  http://localhost:8080/chapter8/assign81/InputCustomer.html.

  Enter the first and last names, hit the Submit button, and verify that the output looks the same as in Solved Exercise 8.3.

- Submit CustomerTag.java, salesdept.tld and CustomerName.jsp.

Assignment 8.2

Objective: **To learn to use the param attribute of <jsp:setProperty> action element.**

Steps:

- Redo Solved Exercise 8.3, this time setting the firstName and lastName properties on the bean using the name/property/param attributes of the jsp:setProperty action element (instead of name/property/value attributes).

- Output should be the same as before.

- Submit CustomerName.jsp only.

Assignment 8.3

Objective: **To learn how to avoid using the param and value attributes of <jsp:setProperty> when setting a bean's property from a request that has a parameter with the same name as that of the bean's property.**

Steps:

- Redo Assignment 8.2, this time modifying InputCustomer.html so that it uses the same name for the INPUT fields as the bean properties. (Use firstName and lastName for the names of the INPUT fields on the HTML form.)

- Modify CustomerName.jsp of Assignment 8.2 so that it no longer uses the param attribute, but instead uses only name/property attributes of the jsp:setProperty element.

- Output should be the same as before.

- Submit `InputCustomer.html` and `CustomerName.jsp`.

Assignment 8.4

Objective: **To practice creating a scripting variable via `<jsp:useBean>` and setting its properties using `<jsp:setProperty>`.**

Steps:

- Create a new folder `assign84` under `C:\JSP\Chapter8`. Copy `CurrentDateTimeBean.java` and `CurrentTime.jsp` from Section 8.3 into it.

- Rename `CurrentDateTimeBean.java` as `FlexibleDateTimeBean.java`, and change the class name to `FlexibleDateTimeBean`. Modify `FlexibleDateTimeBean.java` to remove the `dateOnly`-related code. Instead, include an `int` attribute called `dateType` that can take values of 1 (for date only), 2 (for time only), or 3 (for both date and time).

- The date-only format to be used is `MMM dd yyyy`, the time-only format to be used is `hh:mm:ss a`, and the date plus time format to be used is `MMM dd yyyy hh:mm:ss a`.

- Modify `CurrentTime.jsp` to set this new attribute on the bean to 1, 2, and 3 to display the time-stamp in all three formats, with appropriate labels.

- Submit `FlexibleDateTimeBean.java` and `CurrentTime.jsp`. The output may look like this:

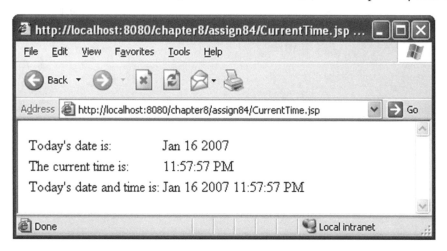

CHAPTER 9

Struts and the Model-View-Controller (MVC) Architecture

Chapter Objectives

- Learn how to use Struts MVC framework classes to streamline the JSP development process.

- Redo some of the previous exercises using Struts.

- See how the use of Struts can make code maintenance more organized, especially if your application size is medium to large, with several JSP files.

9.1   Introduction

We saw how tag libraries and custom tags help us organize Java code by moving it outside of the JSP. This breaks down huge JSP files into much smaller ones that only need to invoke the necessary tags at appropriate places. But we could still have maintenance and organizational issues. Consider the situation where you have a complex Web site that has scores of JSPs, with data sent from one JSP to the next via HTML forms. The sequence and flow of calls amongst the JSPs could cause maintenance problems, although each JSP by itself may be organized. For example, you could have JSP1 that has an HTML form, whose action is JSP2. JSP2 could use the request parameters for accessing the values entered by the user on the HTML form on JSP1, but those values would be retained only as long as the request is available. So, if the user moves on from JSP2 to JSP3, the parameter values of JSP1 are no longer available in JSP3. Earlier we saw how sessions help in storing information across multiple JSP pages, but that approach has its own limitations (mainly maintenance issues) when implementing an application that has several JSP pages. In other words, you have to actively manage the storage of attributes on the session and remove them appropriately. Finally, there may be "standardization" issues with individual developers coding differently, when it comes to processing data from the HTML forms.

Just as JDK provides predefined classes to use in our code, Apache provides a predefined "framework" of classes called Struts that is useful in managing the flow of data among JSPs. For small applications with a handful of JSP files, the use of Struts is not recommended due to the additional overhead involved in conforming to the framework's specifications. On the other hand, for huge corporate applications that contain scores or hundreds of JSP files, with many containing HTML forms and interacting with each other in a complex way (more like a maze!), Struts can make things very streamlined, standardized, and easier to manage. If all developers adhere to the Struts framework, all pages will follow a preset pattern, and it becomes easier to track the flow of data and to maintain the code. You need to keep in mind that Struts is meant to be used mainly in situations where HTML forms are being used and processed.

The Struts framework consists of predefined classes that represent the HTML form and the processing layer. The one that represents the HTML form is called ActionForm and the one for processing the data is called Action. Both of these are defined in the org.apache.struts.action package, so they are available to you only when you download the Struts jar file from http://struts.apache.org, and put it in your CLASSPATH. By default, the ActionForm and Action classes have empty methods that get called in response to specific events by the user (for example, submitting the HTML form). Since the methods are empty, nothing happens in response to such events by default. If you want custom code to execute in response to such events (which you usually do, like getting parameters from the request and storing the user-entered values in the database), you need to create subclasses of the ActionForm and Action classes and override those specific methods that get called in response to specific events.

In other words, you need to create your own classes to represent the following:

- The HTML form
- The processing layer

These two classes need to extend from the Struts framework classes: ActionForm and Action respectively. In order for your custom subclasses to work, you need to do the following:

- Create attributes of the appropriate type in your ActionForm subclass that map to the INPUT fields on your HTML form.
- Override the execute() method in your Action subclass.

The pair of objects instantiated from the ActionForm and Action subclasses is treated as one entity and represents an "*action*" in Struts parlance. This pair represents the flow of data from an HTML form to the processing layer and back to the client (browser), which makes it one round trip. The term **action** here is appropriate because this pair of objects specify the actions to be taken in response to certain events, such as the user submitting an HTML form. The official Struts definition of the term "action" is as follows:

"An *action* is a specially named URL recognized by the Struts framework, which results in forwarding the request to either another URL (which could in turn be another action or a plain JSP)."

For an action to be legitimate, it may or may not have either the ActionForm or Action subclass associated to it. In other words, the action can have either an ActionForm subclass only or an Action subclass only (or both or neither). An action typically has a pair of ActionForm and Action subclasses associated with it, although you can often have only an ActionForm subclass (with no Action subclass) or only an Action subclass (with no ActionForm subclass) associated. An action with neither ActionForm nor Action acts like a pass-through, it simply redirects to the URL without any processing. Do not confuse the terms "action" and "Action subclass"—these two are different.

The ActionForm object represents the request in a way and could be looked upon as such, provided you define attributes in it that map one-for-one to the INPUT fields on the HTML form. For example, if your HTML form has an INPUT field with NAME="firstName", then the ActionForm subclass needs to have an attribute called firstName with a getter [getFirstName()] and a setter [setFirstName()].

In addition to attributes that map one-for-one to INPUT fields on the HTML form, the ActionForm subclass can also contain attributes derived from other attributes (for example, fullName derived from firstName and lastName). In that sense, the ActionForm subclass can be considered a placeholder or a storage area for attributes on the HTML form as well as any derived attributes.

By creating the ActionForm and Action subclass in this way, Struts allows you to pre-process request parameters inside a Java class before forwarding to the destination JSP. The Java class can now be maintained separately from the JSP. Remember that the idea is to move the processing logic from the JSP to Java classes. As long as the request contains the parameters that map to the ActionForm subclass attributes, the Action subclass can process it in a particular way independent of the JSP it gets invoked in. That way, this pair of ActionForm-Action subclasses can be used in any JSP or multiple JSPs and thus code becomes powerful as well as portable.

To request a specific action from the server, Struts requires a new extension, ".do" for URLs. Any URL ending in .do is interpreted by the Web server to be a request for a Struts action. Every .do URL represents one action. Due to this reason, the terms "action" and ".do URL" are equivalent and can be used interchangeably. When using Struts, we need to get away from the concept of requesting a JSP or HTML file; instead, we request an action represented by a URL ending in .do, which in turn would request an appropriate file for you. For example, instead of requesting Login.jsp, you would now request login.do.

When your application consists of several JSPs, you could have several round-trip combinations, each representing one Struts action. If you could short-list the round-trip combinations of interest (i.e. a list of "actions") in some kind of XML file and associate a pair of ActionForm / Action classes for each action, Struts could look up the .do URL request in that file to figure out which ActionForm and Action objects to use for that round trip. Struts actually requires the creation of such an XML file called the **Struts configuration file** and named struts-config.xml, and this file must reside under the WEB-INF folder of your application.

Each action in the Struts configuration file must have an alias path to identify it in the list and that path must be unique among all actions in that file so that there is no ambiguity. The user then refers to a specific action by typing in the alias path of the action, followed by .do as the URL. For example, an action may have an alias path of "/login", which actually means the URL that requests this action needs to be "<web app root>/login.do".

In response to specific events, the framework calls specific methods in specific predefined classes, so if you become familiar with the rules, you need to simply override the specific methods by putting your custom code that you want to execute in response to such events. For example, for every action, the Struts framework will call the execute() method of the Action class. If your Action subclass associated with that action overrides the execute() method of its parent, that code would get executed instead of the one in the parent. Your code in the overridden method usually consists of getting the parameters from the request or from the ActionForm subclass object (i.e., INPUT field values from the HTML form), processing them, and then forwarding to the appropriate URL. That

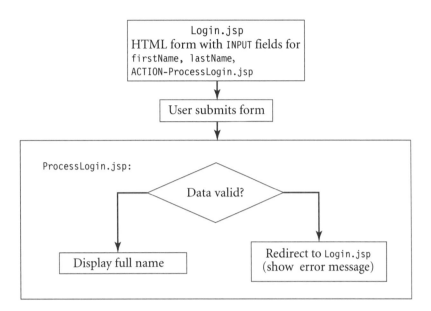

Figure 9.1

Displaying user's name using plain JSPs

way, you can preprocess the incoming information on the request object (if any) from within Java (maybe updating the database in the process), and then decide where to forward the user (could be another .do URL or a plain .jsp). The other .do URL to which you forward would do a similar thing, i.e., process the incoming data and forward to some other URL, and so on. By doing so, we create a network of possible paths that the user can take, and each path is made up of several portions, each portion having a separate ActionForm and/or Action subclass associated with it.

To understand this better, say that we want to redo the example of Section 6.1 using Struts. The old way of doing things would result in the path as shown in Figure 9.1.

Using Struts, it would look as shown in Figure 9.2. (Matching parts are highlighted.)

Note that this shows an overall (conceptual) view of how the process works. In the execute() method, forward is shown as a String only to show the concept, but actually it is of type ActionForward (which will be described later). Specific details will be discussed as we move along through this chapter. Currently you can note that the execute() method returns a different forward ("success" or "error") based

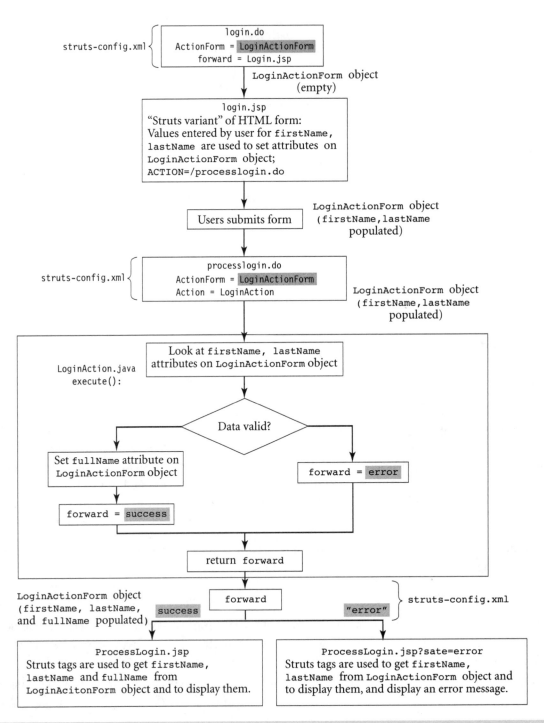

Figure 9.2

Displaying user's name using Struts

on whether the ActionForm object contains valid data, and each of these results in opening a different URL. Also observe how the same ActionForm object is reused between two actions (login.do and processlogin.do). This is necessary because you want the ActionForm object that is populated from login.do to be used for validating data in processlogin.do and forwarding to an appropriate URL. Finally, note that Login.jsp now must use a "Struts variant" HTML form instead of the old <FORM> tag that we used until now, and this is done by using special Struts HTML tags.

When the user enters values in the INPUT fields and submits the form, the ActionForm subclass object's attributes that match these fields automatically take up those values, and this process is handled by the Struts framework. You do not need to put extra code to set these attributes from the request. In other words, once the user submits the form, you can assume that the corresponding ActionForm object's attributes will be populated with values entered by the user.

Inside the execute() method of the Action subclass, you now have another way of getting the parameters from the request. Instead of saying

```
request.getParameter("firstName")
```

you can now say the following inside the execute() method of your Action subclass:

```
LoginActionForm form = (LoginActionForm)actionForm;
String firstName = form.getFirstName();
```

Note that actionForm is a parameter of the execute() method in the Action class. Since the ActionForm object is a kind of wrapper around the request, Struts actually looks at the parameter on the request whenever you invoke a getter on the ActionForm object, so the new approach has the same result as the old code.

Struts is inherently Java-centric, so it expects all user requests for pages to go through Java code first and then to the JSP page, or even to another piece of Java code that eventually ends up in a JSP. Similarly, when the user submits a form, Struts sends the request object to a Java Action class, where the developer can process user input, and then forward to another .do or .jsp URL. If you forward to another .do instead of a JSP, you could have a multilayered processing in Java classes until finally ending up in a JSP.

9.2   The .do URL, Struts Config File, and Action and ActionForm Classes

Struts achieves control over the data flow by introducing a new layer before or after JSP page requests. This "new layer" consists of the .do URLs. We have seen that JSP URLs end in .jsp until now—but a Struts URL needs to be different, if you want it to go through an intermediate layer before going to the JSP. When the Web server encounters a URL that ends with .do, it sends it to the

Struts framework. Note that the .do URLs *do not* represent files like the other URLs we have seen until now. They represent instead a set of actions to be performed when that URL is requested.

Upon receiving the request for a .do URL, the framework looks it up in the *Struts Configuration File* (usually named struts-config.xml), which every Struts application must have under its /WEB-INF directory. The struts-config.xml file specifies a list of possible "actions" (for example, login.do or showdata.do), along with the fully qualified class name of each action's associated Action class and the name of the ActionForm object.

For each action listed in the Struts Configuration File, you need to associate a specific ActionForm and/or Action subclass, so that Struts knows where to go in response to a user's request for that action. This is done via XML attributes for the "action" tag, where you set attributes of each action to the name of the ActionForm and/or Action class. So you need to know what possible XML attributes are available for the action tag.

9.3 Seeing Struts in Action

Let's look at a simple hands-on example to better understand Struts. Say that you have a URL called inputname.do that should show two INPUT fields for first and last name, along with a Submit button as follows:

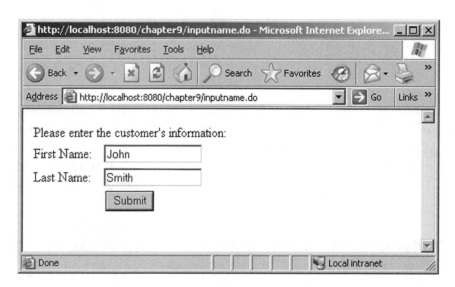

When the user enters the first and last name and hits the Submit button, the following JSP page with the first, last, and full names should appear:

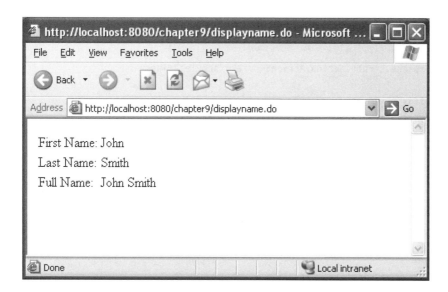

We know how to do this using the plain JSPs, but let's redo it using Struts to get a feel for how it works.

9.3.1   Downloading Struts

You need to first download JAR files that contain the Struts framework classes before you can refer to them in your code. Follow the instructions for downloading Struts in Appendix I.

Before you can continue, you need to add a new context root for Chapter 9. Add the following line in `C:\Tomcat\conf\server.xml`:

```
<Context path="/chapter9" docBase="C:/JSP/Chapter9" debug="0" />
```

9.3.2   Changing the Web Application Deployment Descriptor

The next step in setting up the Web application is to configure the application deployment descriptor (stored in file `WEB-INF\web.xml`) to include all of the Struts components that are required. Copy web.xml from `C:\JSP\Chapter8\WEB-INF` to `C:\JSP\Chapter9\WEB-INF` and modify it so that its content would be as follows:

```
-------------------------------------------------------------------
<?xml version="1.0" encoding="ISO-8859-1"?>
<web-app xmlns="http://java.sun.com/xml/ns/j2ee"
         xmlns:xsi="http://www.w3.org/2001/XMLSchema-instance"
         xsi:schemaLocation="http://java.sun.com/xml/ns/j2ee
                             http://java.sun.com/xml/ns/j2ee/web-app_2_4.xsd"
```

```
        version="2.4">
    <servlet>
        <servlet-name>action</servlet-name>
        <servlet-class>org.apache.struts.action.ActionServlet</servlet-class>
        <init-param>
            <param-name>config</param-name>
            <param-value>/WEB-INF/struts-config.xml</param-value>
        </init-param>
        <load-on-startup>1</load-on-startup>
    </servlet>

    <servlet-mapping>
        <servlet-name>action</servlet-name>
        <url-pattern>*.do</url-pattern>
    </servlet-mapping>
</web-app>
```

Here, we are simply mapping all requests that end with .do to invoke a servlet with an alias name action that maps to the real servlet class org.apache.struts.action.ActionServlet and has a config parameter pointing to your Web app's /WEB-INF/struts-config.xml file.

9.3.3   The Struts Configuration File

The Struts Configuration File serves as a reference that lists the mappings between all possible actions in your Web app to their corresponding ActionForm/Action classes. The ActionServlet object (called the "controller") uses this file to control the flow from one Web page to another as the user clicks on links or buttons. For it to work, each Web application must have an XML file called struts-config.xml that complies with appropriate syntax and content, in its /WEB-INF directory.

The outermost XML element must be <struts-config>. Inside of the <struts-config> element, there are three important elements that are used to describe these actions:

        <form-beans>

        <global-forwards>

        <action-mappings>

We will look at the minimum set for our example. You need to have the <form-beans> and the <action-mappings> tags defined in your struts-config.xml file as a minimum; the <global-forwards> tag is optional.

The <form-beans> Element

The <form-beans> element allows you to declare ActionForm object alias name(s), and the exact ActionForm class(es) they map to. The <form-beans> element (note the plural) can have one or more

<form-bean> elements (note the singular) embedded within itself, each representing an ActionForm alias. For example, say that you want to have an alias with the name of "NameForm" for the ActionForm object of type: salesdept.NameActionForm. The entry in struts-config.xml needs to look like this:

```
<form-beans>
    <form-bean name="NameForm" type="salesdept.NameActionForm" />
</form-beans>
```

The <form-beans> element must be embedded within the overall <struts-config> element.

In other words, this entry says that NameForm is an alias name for the real ActionForm subclass object, which will be of type salesdept.NameActionForm.

The <action-mappings> Element

This section contains your action definitions. You use an <action> element for each of the mappings you would like to define.

The <action> Element

The <action> element describes an ActionMapping object that is to be used to process a request for a specific module-relative URL.

The Concept of Forwards

Each <action> element usually has a set of one or more "forwards" in it, with each forward representing one possible outcome or pathway or resource (typically, a JSP) that is returned by the execute() method in the Action subclass. You can name each forward whatever you want, as long as it is unique within each action. The name of a forward serves as a key for the real ActionForward object that represents the forward in question. The advantage of this approach is that it allows you to change the resource without changing references to it throughout your application.

In the current example, we need two actions as follows:

- One action for opening a JSP with an empty HTML form and associating an ActionForm object to it. When the user enters values in the HTML form's <INPUT> fields, corresponding attributes of the ActionForm object need to get automatically populated with those values. We will call this action inputname.do.

- Until now, we have been using a JSP URL as a form's ACTION attribute. When dealing with Struts, the form's action needs to be another action (.do URL) so that you can process the request parameters in a Struts Action subclass and then forward to the appropriate JSP that simply displays values from the ActionForm object associated with this action. If we use the same `ActionForm` object as the one in the first action, we would be able to get the user-entered values from that action to compute derived values (such as full name using first and last name). We will call this second action `displayname.do`.

The details of attributes available in an `<action>` element are listed in Appendix J. Here we will look at the most important ones to understand the concept.

- The `path` attribute in an `<action>` element is the one that specifies the action path for the `.do` URL. For example, if you want users to use a URL of `login.do`, you need to specify the path in the `<action>` element as "/login". Observe how the `.do` part is removed and a forward-slash (/) is added in front. This is typical—you will find that `.do` URLs appear with and without the `.do` extension in the code or XML files and you need to be careful to know when these are equivalent and when only one of them can be used.

  - The `path` attribute of the `<action>` element in `struts-config.xml` must not use the `.do` extension, otherwise it will not work, so you cannot say: `path` = `"/inputname.do"` under the `<action>` element.

  - In contrast, attributes that represent URLs can use either form (with or without the `.do` extension). For example, an HTML form's `ACTION` attribute could be specified as "/processlogin" or "/processlogin.do" with the same result.

- The `name` attribute in an `<action>` element specifies the name of the `ActionForm` subclass object you want to associate with that action. This must match the `name` attribute of the `<form-bean>` element used to declare the `ActionForm` object type and its name.

- The `scope` attribute specifies the scope or context in which the `ActionForm` object is recognized. The scope could be `request` or `session`, with `session` being the default. Usually you would want to use `request` as the scope to avoid having objects lingering with old or invalid data.

- The `forward` attribute specifies the URL you want this action to open. This is usually a JSP page that has an HTML form with `<INPUT>` fields mapped to the corresponding attributes of the `ActionForm` object of this action.

- Instead of using the `forward` attribute in the `<action>` element, you can also nest one or more `<forward>` elements under the `<action>` element. That way you can specify multiple paths that correspond to various possibilities resulting from processing the form data. As an example, say that you want to forward to the welcome page if data is valid, otherwise you want it to forward back to the login page with an error message. This would result in two separate `<forward>` elements under the one `<action>` element. The `<forward>` element itself has two important attributes: `name` and `path`.

- The name attribute is a key that is used to identify a specific path out of multiple forwards under an <action> element. This must be unique among all forwards for that <action>.

- The path attribute specifies the URL that this forward should open. This is usually a JSP page, but could be another .do URL (action) that may further process the data and finally send to a JSP in its <action> element. Note that if you want to specify another .do URL as the path attribute under the <forward> element, it must contain the .do extension. For example, you could say:

  path = "/processlogin.do"

  but not:

  path = "/processlogin".

  Do not confuse this path attribute with the one under the <action> element—these two are different.

For the inputname.do action, the <action> element would look like this:

```
<action path="/inputname"
        name="NameForm"
        scope="request"
        forward="/sec93/InputName.jsp"/>
```

The reason we use the forward attribute instead of the <forward> nested element is that this action simply opens a single URL in every case. We still want to associate HTML <INPUT> fields to the attributes on an ActionForm object, so we must specify the name attribute to contain the form name declared in the <form-bean> tag for the associated ActionForm subclass (salesdept.NameActionForm).

We will be putting the JSP and Java files of this hands-on example under a folder sec93 under C:\JSP\Chapter9, so go ahead and create that folder if you have not already done so. Observe how the URL in the forward attribute begins with /sec93/, which means all URLs need to be relative to the context root of the current Web app (which is C:\JSP\Chapter9 for this chapter).

For the displayname.do action, the <action> element needs to look like this:

```
<action path="/displayname"
        type="salesdept.DisplayNameAction"
        name="NameForm"
        scope="request">
        <forward name="success"
                 path="/sec93/DisplayName.jsp" />
</action>
```

The reason we use the <forward> element instead of the forward attribute in this action is that we will be adding additional possibilities (forwards) later in this chapter. When using a <forward> element, the execute() method in the Action subclass must have code that returns an ActionForward object for that forward. So for the /displayname action, the execute() method in salesdept.DisplayNameAction must have code that returns an ActionForward object for forward = "success". We will see how this is done in just a moment.

The struts-config.xml file needs to look like this:

```
------------------------------------------------------------
<?xml version="1.0" encoding="ISO-8859-1"?>
<!DOCTYPE struts-config
PUBLIC "-//Apache Software Foundation//DTD Struts Configuration 1.3//EN"
"http://jakarta.apache.org/struts/dtds/struts-config_1_3.dtd">

<struts-config>
    <form-beans>
        <form-bean name="NameForm" type="salesdept.NameActionForm" />
    </form-beans>

    <action-mappings>
        <action path="/inputname"
                name="NameForm"
                scope="request"
                forward="/sec93/InputName.jsp" />

        <action path="/displayname"
                type="salesdept.DisplayNameAction"
                name="NameForm"
                scope="request" >
                <forward name="success"
                        path="/sec93/DisplayName.jsp" />
        </action>
    </action-mappings>
</struts-config>
------------------------------------------------------------
```

Note that the <form-bean> element uses name="NameForm" and type="salesdept.NameActionForm", which means an object called NameForm of type salesdept.NameActionForm needs to be created. The <action> elements that require this ActionForm object must use the same name as in the <form-bean> element in order for it to work. If an ActionForm object is shared between two or more actions, each of those actions must use the same form name. In the preceding struts-config.xml file, you will see that the <form-bean>, and <action> elements for "/inputname" and "/displayname" all use the same form name of "NameForm". Here "/displayname" is the action that gets invoked when the HTML form in "/input-name" is submitted. The two action elements share the same form object because you want the first and last names populated from the first action ("/inputname") to be used to set the full name in the second action ("/displayname"). We will see how this is done as we move along in this section.

It is very important at this stage that you thoroughly understand the meaning of the `<action>` elements and the sequence or flow that each element represents.

As an example, consider the preceding /inputname and /displayname `<action>` elements in struts-config.xml. The flow of calls arising out of these two action elements is depicted in Figure 9.3 (overall) and Figure 9.4 (detailed). (Matching parts are highlighted.)

9.3.4   `ActionForm` and `Action` Subclasses

As discussed previously, we need to first create an `ActionForm` subclass that has attributes representing the INPUT fields on the HTML form. On the preceding HTML form, we can see that it would have two INPUT fields, had it been a plain HTML form: one for the first name, and another for the last name. So, let's create a new `ActionForm` subclass called `NameActionForm` and package it under a new package called salesdept, with two attributes:

```
String firstName;
String lastName;
```

Note that an `ActionForm` class serves as a placeholder not only for request-related parameters (such as those due to INPUT fields on HTML forms), but also for other attributes that may be computed on the fly. For example, if the `ActionForm` has firstName and lastName as attributes, you could add a third attribute called fullName that contains the concatenated first and last names. In other words, it is not necessary that every attribute on the `ActionForm` subclass have a corresponding `<INPUT>` field. So let us add a third attribute for the full name:

```
String fullName;
```

All `ActionForm` objects behave like a JavaBean (which we saw earlier), with similar rules for getting and setting attributes. Our `ActionForm` subclass also needs to follow rules for JavaBean introspection/reflection. So, we will make these attributes private, and add public getter and setter methods. The class would now look like this:

```
------------------------------------------------------------
// ------------  Begin: NameActionForm.java ---------------------
package salesdept;

import javax.servlet.http.*;
import org.apache.struts.action.*;

public class NameActionForm extends ActionForm
```

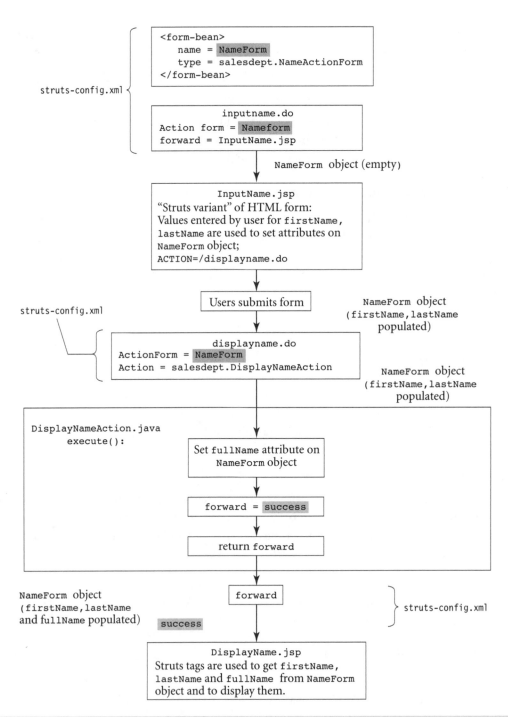

Figure 9.3

Struts Config File and Resulting Data Flow (Overall)

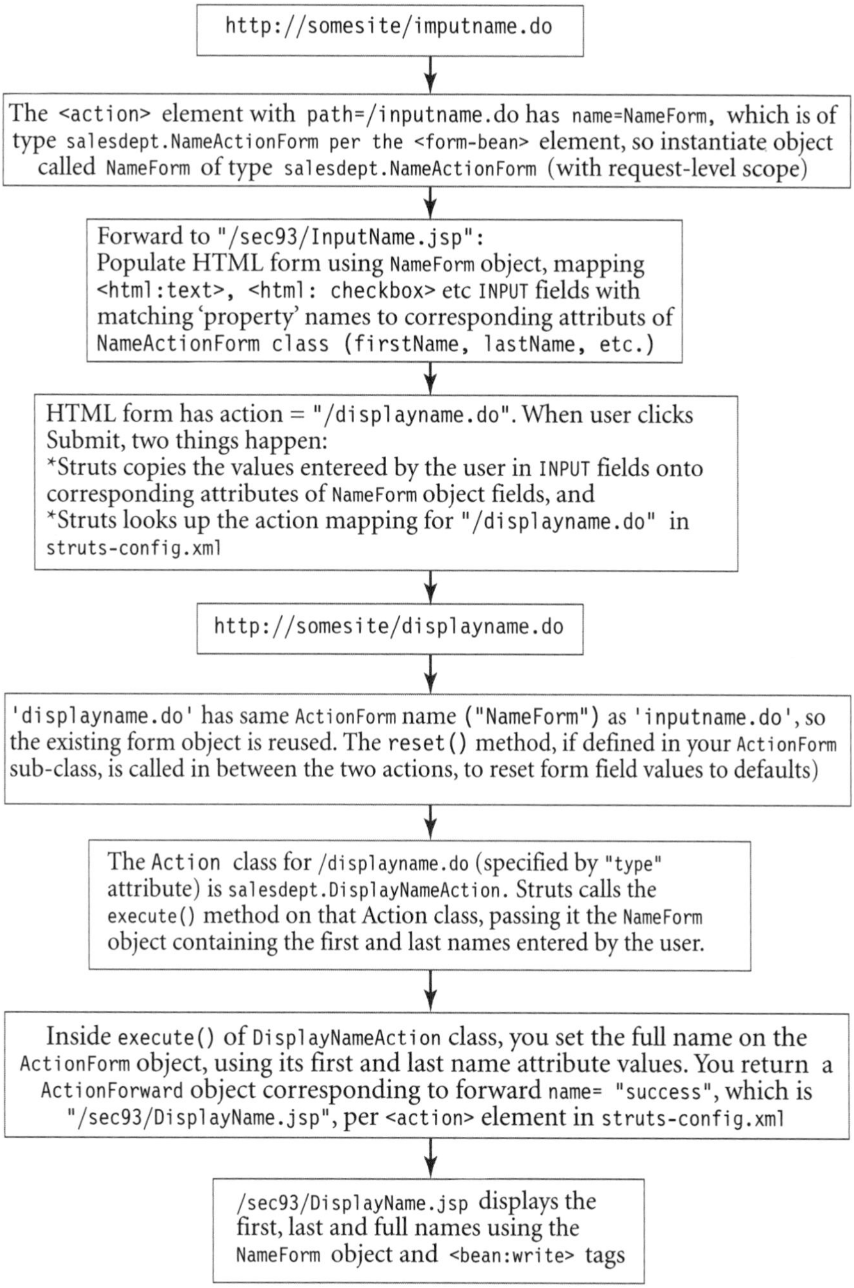

http://somesite/imputname.do

The <action> element with path=/inputname.do has name=NameForm, which is of type salesdept.NameActionForm per the <form-bean> element, so instantiate object called NameForm of type salesdept.NameActionForm (with request-level scope)

Forward to "/sec93/InputName.jsp":
Populate HTML form using NameForm object, mapping <html:text>, <html: checkbox> etc INPUT fields with matching 'property' names to corresponding attributs of NameActionForm class (firstName, lastName, etc.)

HTML form has action = "/displayname.do". When user clicks Submit, two things happen:
*Struts copies the values entereed by the user in INPUT fields onto corresponding attributes of NameForm object fields, and
*Struts looks up the action mapping for "/displayname.do" in struts-config.xml

http://somesite/displayname.do

'displayname.do' has same ActionForm name ("NameForm") as 'inputname.do', so the existing form object is reused. The reset() method, if defined in your ActionForm sub-class, is called in between the two actions, to reset form field values to defaults)

The Action class for /displayname.do (specified by "type" attribute) is salesdept.DisplayNameAction. Struts calls the execute() method on that Action class, passing it the NameForm object containing the first and last names entered by the user.

Inside execute() of DisplayNameAction class, you set the full name on the ActionForm object, using its first and last name attribute values. You return a ActionForward object corresponding to forward name= "success", which is "/sec93/DisplayName.jsp", per <action> element in struts-config.xml

/sec93/DisplayName.jsp displays the first, last and full names using the NameForm object and <bean:write> tags

Figure 9.4

Struts Config File and Resulting Data Flow (Detailed)

```
{
    private String firstName;
    private String lastName;
    private String fullName;

    public String getFirstName() { return firstName; }
    public String getLastName() { return lastName; }
    public String getFullName() { return fullName; }

    public void setFirstName( String firstName )
    {
        this.firstName = firstName;
    }
    public void setLastName( String lastName ) {this.lastName = lastName;}
    public void setFullName()
    {
        fullName = firstName + " " + lastName;
    }
}
// ------------ End: NameActionForm.java ----------------------
----------------------------------------------------------
```

Call the corresponding `Action` subclass `DisplayNameAction`, in which you need to override the execute() method and set the full name attribute on the `ActionForm` object. The code would look like this:

```
----------------------------------------------------------
// ------------ Begin: DisplayNameAction.java ----------------------
package salesdept;

import java.io.*;
import javax.servlet.*;
import javax.servlet.http.*;
import org.apache.struts.action.*;

public class DisplayNameAction extends Action
{
    public ActionForward execute (ActionMapping mapping,
                                  ActionForm  actionForm,
                                  HttpServletRequest request,
                                  HttpServletResponse response)
    {
        NameActionForm form = (NameActionForm)actionForm;
        form.setFullName();
        return mapping.findForward("success");
    }
}
// ------------ End: DisplayNameAction.java ----------------------
----------------------------------------------------------
```

Save these two files under the new folder sec93 under C:\JSP\Chapter9.

9.3.5   How to Use an ActionForm in Your JSP

The ActionForm class represents the request object in a way. So, you need to specify attributes that correspond one-to-one with the INPUT fields on your HTML form. As the user enters values in the INPUT fields, you want the attributes of the ActionForm object that correspond to those fields to also get populated with the user-entered values, behind the scenes. In order for this to happen, your JSP needs to use a special kind of tag in place of the usual <INPUT> tag. The "special" tag belongs to a tag library that comes with Struts, and the tags in that library sound similar to those for HTML forms we have used until now. The Struts tag library's name is html, so you need to prefix all tags from that library with html:. For example, for an <INPUT> field of TYPE="text", the equivalent Struts html tag is: <html:text>. In other words, the old way of specifying a text box would be as follows:

```
<HTML>
    <FORM>
        <INPUT TYPE="text" NAME="firstName"></INPUT>
        . . .
    </FORM>
</HTML>
```

The equivalent Struts html tag library usage would do the same thing as follows:

```
<html:html>
    <html:form>
        <html:text property="firstName" />
        . . .
    </html:form>
</html:html>
```

Note the following line in particular:

```
<html:text property="firstName" />
```

Based on the part: property="firstName", Struts looks for a getter called getFirstName() and a setter called setFirstName(String) in the ActionForm object in context, which is the NameForm object you defined in struts-config.xml. Relevant lines from that file are reproduced here:

```
----------------------------------------
<form-beans>
    <form-bean name="NameForm" type="salesdept.NameActionForm" />
</form-beans>
```

```
<action-mappings type="org.apache.struts.action.ActionMapping">
    <action path="/inputname"
            name="NameForm"
            scope="request"
            forward="/sec93/InputName.jsp"/>
    ...
</action-mappings
--------------------------------------
```

Instead of depending on Struts to use the `ActionForm` object in context, you could be more explicit in specifying the `ActionForm` object to associate the property to, as follows:

`<html:text name="NameForm" property="firstName" />`

The screen would work the same as before. This may not be preferred since changes to the `Action-Form` object name in `struts-config.xml` would require corresponding changes to the JSP. Due to this reason, we will continue with our earlier approach of not specifying the form name in Struts `html` tags.

Note that, for the JSP to recognize the Struts `html` tag, you need to do the following:

- Add the following line at the beginning of the JSP:

  `<%@ taglib uri="/WEB-INF/tlds/struts-html.tld" prefix="html" %>`

- Make sure that you have the `struts-html.tld` file under `WEB-INF\tlds` of your Web app (refer to Appendix I for details on how to get this file).

For `<INPUT>` tag of `TYPE="text"`, if you want to specify the maximum field size to 16 characters, you would say `SIZE=16`. The Struts `<html:text>` tag retains many of the HTML `<INPUT>` tag attributes as is, to the extent possible. So for the `SIZE` attribute, it has an attribute with the same name (`size`). The Struts equivalent of

`<INPUT TYPE="text" NAME="firstName" SIZE=16></INPUT>`

would be

`<html:text property="firstName" size="16" />`

For the Submit button, you have a similar Struts `html` tag `<html:submit>`, which in its simplest form would look like this:

`<html:submit/>`

Call the JSP `InputName.jsp` and save it under `C:\JSP\Chapter9\sec93`. It should look like this:

```
------------------------------------------------------------
<!-- Begin: InputName.jsp -->
<%@ taglib uri="/WEB-INF/tlds/struts-html.tld" prefix="html" %>
```

```
<html:html>
   <BODY>
      <html:form action="/displayname.do">
         <TABLE>
            <TR>
               <TD COLSPAN=2>Please enter the customer's information:</TD>
            </TR>
            <TR>
               <TD>First Name:</TD>
               <TD><html:text property="firstName" size="16"/></TD>
            </TR>
            <TR>
               <TD>Last Name:</TD>
               <TD><html:text property="lastName" size="16"/></TD>
            </TR>
            <TR>
               <TD ALIGN="center" COLSPAN=2><html:submit/></TD>
            </TR>
         </TABLE>
      </html:form>
   </BODY>
</html:html>
<!-- End: InputName.jsp -->
------------------------------------------------------------
```

Notice the form's action is another Struts action: "/displayname.do". It means that when the user submits the form, it will go look up the action mapping for "/displayname" in struts-config.xml, and it would have its own ActionForm and/or Action class associated. Don't confuse the term "HTML form's action" with the "Struts action"—these are different, although somewhat similar in their objectives.

What should the execute() function in that Action subclass do? Well, recall that your objective is to concatenate the user-entered values for first and last name and to display the full name—that's exactly what the action class execute() needs to do. The first and last name are available on the request, but now that you are using the Struts framework, you need to get away from the old style of using the getParameter() method on the request to get individual parameters. Instead, you need to get the corresponding attributes from the ActionForm subclass object.

9.3.6 How and Why to Override the execute() Method in Your Action Subclass

Now that the user-entered values are in the ActionForm's attributes, what happens next? Recall that you need to override the execute() method in the Action subclass, and concatenate the first and last names and set the full name attribute on the `ActionForm` object. The `execute()` method has a parameter that represents the incoming `ActionForm` object; its signature is as follows:

```
public ActionForward execute (ActionMapping mapping,
                              ActionForm actionForm,
                              HttpServletRequest request,
                              HttpServletResponse response)
```

The `actionForm` parameter here would be an instance of the exact `ActionForm` type we associated in the `struts-config-xml` file (which is `salesdept.NameActionForm`). So it has first, last, and full name attributes on it, with first and last names populated but full name empty. To populate the full name, you simply call the `setFullName()` method on it, as follows:

```
NameActionForm form = (NameActionForm)actionForm;
form.setFullName();
```

9.3.7   Getting Request Parameters in Your JSP Using `<bean:write>`

You need to write out the attributes from the `ActionForm` object onto the browser; again, no Java code should appear in the JSPs (Struts philosophy). For writing content onto a page, Struts provides a convenient tag library called `bean` that has a tag called `write` (so the tag would look like: `<bean:write ... />`). A Struts bean is simply a `JavaBean`-compliant object—that is, a set of attributes with getters and setters. The tag has two important attributes:

- `name`: represents the alias name of the `ActionForm` subclass that you specify in `struts-config.xml`.
- `property`: represents the attribute of the HTML form (such as `firstName`, `lastName`).

The `name` attribute needs a bit more elaboration. We used `name` = "NameForm", and this must be the same as the one specified in `struts-config.xml` under the `<form-beans>` tag. So, to write out the `firstName` attribute of the `ActionForm` object with alias name = "NameForm", you would say

```
<bean:write name="NameForm" property="firstName"/>
```

and this would write out the content of the `firstName` attribute of the `NameForm` object (as a `String`) onto the browser page.

To keep things clean, create a separate JSP that displays the first, last, and full names. However, since the `execute()` method has a single `ActionForm` parameter, you need to reuse the `ActionForm` object created under the previous action. By doing so, you can get the first and last names populated on the form in the previous action, and set the full name using these two in the next action. Call the JSP `DisplayName.jsp` and save it under `C:\JSP\Chapter9\sec93` with the following content:

```
---------------------------------------------------------
<!-- Begin: DisplayName.jsp -->
<%@ taglib uri="/WEB-INF/tlds/struts-bean.tld" prefix="bean" %>
<%@ taglib uri="/WEB-INF/tlds/struts-html.tld" prefix="html" %>
<html:html>
```

```
    <BODY>
       <TABLE>
          <TR>
              <TD>First Name:</TD>
              <TD><bean:write name="NameForm" property="firstName"/></TD>
          </TR>
          <TR>
              <TD>Last Name:</TD>
              <TD><bean:write name="NameForm" property="lastName"/></TD>
          </TR>
          <TR>
              <TD>Full Name:</TD>
              <TD><bean:write name="NameForm" property="fullName"/></TD>
          </TR>
       </TABLE>
    </BODY>
</html:html>
<!-- End: DisplayName.jsp -->
-----------------------------------------------------------
```

Notice the `<bean:write>` tag in particular. Struts provides several tag libraries, each with a different prefix. We just saw the Struts `html` tag library and how to use it. The Struts `bean` tag library is another useful library—you use it to get specific attributes from the `ActionForm` object (like parameters corresponding to `INPUT` fields on the HTML form).

9.3.8 Putting It All Together

By now you should have file/folder structure as follows:

```
        C:
        + JSP\
            + Chapter9\
                + sec93\
                    -- InputName.jsp
                    -- DisplayName.jsp
                    -- NameActionForm.java
                    -- DisplayNameAction.java
                + WEB-INF\
                    -- struts-config.xml
                    -- web.xml
                    + classes\
                    + lib\
```

```
               -- commons*.jar
               -- struts-core-1.3.5.jar
               -- struts-taglib-1.3.5.jar
           +  tlds\
               -- struts-html.tld
               -- struts-bean.tld
               -- struts-logic.tld
```

Before you can compile your `Action`/`ActionForm` subclasses and use them in JSPs, you need to add `struts-core-1.3.5.jar` and `servlet-api.jar` to your `CLASSPATH`. So you need to do the following:

`SET CLASSPATH=C:\Tomcat\common\lib\servlet-api.jar; C:\JSP\Chaper9\WEB-INF\lib\struts-core-1.3.5.jar`

Note: You need to replace the preceding `struts-core-1.3.5.jar` with the exact version of the Struts core `.jar` file you downloaded.

Ok—so you are all set to compile and test your code! Change directory to `C:\JSP\Chapter9\sec93`, set environment variable `JSP_OUT=C:\JSP\Chapter9\WEB-INF\classes`, and compile `NameActionForm.java` as follows:

`C:\JSP\Chapter9\sec93>javac -d %JSP_OUT% -classpath %JSP_OUT%;%CLASSPATH% NameActionForm.java`

Repeat for `DisplayNameAction.java`. Restart Tomcat, then open the following URL:

`http://localhost:8080/chapter9/inputname.do`

It should show up as follows:

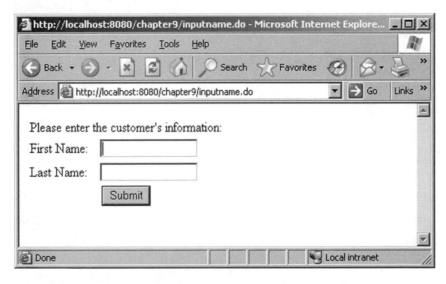

Do a View -> Source, and you will find the following:

```
----------------------------------------------------------------
<!-- Begin: InputName.jsp -->
<html>
   <BODY>
      <form name="NameForm" method="post" action="/chapter9/displayname.do">
         <TABLE>
            <TR>
               <TD COLSPAN=2>Please enter the customer's information:</TD>
            </TR>
            <TR>
               <TD>First Name:</TD>
               <TD>
                  <input type="text" name="firstName" size="16" value=""/>
               </TD>
            </TR>
            <TR>
               <TD>Last Name:</TD>
               <TD>
                  <input type="text" name="lastName" size="16" value=""/>
               </TD>
            </TR>
            <TR>
               <TD ALIGN="CENTER" COLSPAN=2>
                  <input type="submit" value="Submit">
               </TD>
            </TR>
         </TABLE>
      </form>
   </BODY>
</html>
<!-- End: InputName.jsp -->
----------------------------------------------------------------
```

So, everything that finally gets displayed on the browser is still plain HTML (as always). The Struts framework converted all of its special tags in your JSP to equivalent HTML and then sent it to the client. Some things are worth noting here. Comparing the lines we had in the JSP, we see that Input-Name.jsp had the lines that follow:

```
-----------------------------------------------------------------
<html:html>
   <BODY>
      <html:form action="/displayname.do">
         <TABLE>
            <TR>
               <TD COLSPAN=2>Please enter the customer's information:</TD>
            </TR>
            <TR>
               <TD>First Name:</TD>
               <TD><html:text property="firstName" size="16"/></TD>
            </TR>
            . . . .
-----------------------------------------------------------------
```

This converted to the following (in View-> Source):

```
-----------------------------------------------------------------
<html>
   <BODY>
      <form name="NameForm" method="post" action="/chapter9/displayname.do">
         <TABLE>
            <TR>
               <TD COLSPAN=2>Please enter the customer's information:</TD>
            </TR>
            <TR>
               <TD>First Name:</TD>
               <TD>
                  <input type="text" name="firstName" size="16" value=""/>
               </TD>
            </TR>
            . . . .
-----------------------------------------------------------------
```

In other words:

- The `<html:html>` tag converted to a plain `<HTML>` tag.

- The `<html:form action="/displayname.do">` line converted to

  `<form name="NameForm" method="post" action="/chapter9/displayname.do">`

  Note that you do not have to explicitly say `METHOD="POST"` when using the Struts `<html:form>` tag; it automatically adds this part for you.

- The `<html:text property="firstName" size="16"/>` line converted to

  `<input type="text" name="firstName" size="16" value=""/>`

Ok—go ahead and enter the first and last names and hit the Submit button:

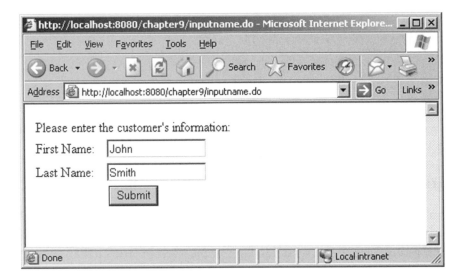

This should take you to the next action `displayname.do`, as shown here:

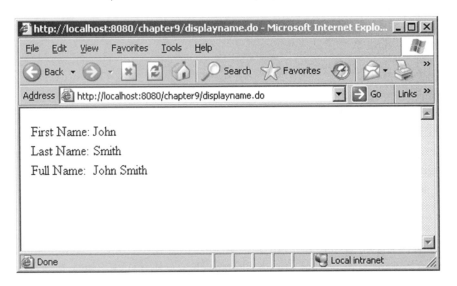

Note that the URL shows up as

```
http://localhost:8080/chapter9/displayname.do
```

If you do a View->Source on this one, you will find that all the `<bean:write>` tags in `DisplayName.jsp` are now replaced with actual values (such as John, Smith, John Smith, etc.). For example, the lines

```
<TD>First Name:</TD>
<TD><bean:write name="NameForm" property="firstName"/></TD>
```

got converted to

```
<TD>First Name:</TD>
<TD>John</TD>
```

Whew! Although that was quite a bit of effort for a simple task, the benefits of Struts become visible for large corporate projects that contain scores or hundreds of JSPs.

9.4   Generalizing Struts—the Model-View-Controller (MVC) Architecture

The Struts framework can be generalized by saying that it consists of three types of objects: *Model*, *View*, and *Controller* (in short, called the *MVC architecture*). Let's look at these new terms. The JSP and the `ActionForm` object together form the presentation layer or the **View** in Struts parlance; similarly, the processing layer (i.e., the `Action` object) is called a **Model**. A **Controller** represents the servlet; so it is an object that knows what, when, and how to send or retrieve data and how to manage it. Struts has a special servlet class called `ActionServlet` that has some Struts-specific features in it. The **Controller** manages the data flow between the View and the Model. In other words, the View encapsulates the presentation tier, the Model contains the business logic, and the Controller is a servlet that controls the flow of data.

The Struts' official Web site offers the following summary of MVC architecture:

> In the MVC design pattern, application flow is mediated by a central Controller. The Controller delegates requests—in our case, HTTP requests—to an appropriate handler. The handlers are tied to a Model, and each handler acts as an adapter between the request and the Model. The Model represents, or encapsulates, an application's business logic or state. Control is usually then forwarded back through the Controller to the appropriate View. The forwarding can be determined by consulting a set of mappings, usually loaded from a database or configuration file.

9.4.1   Model

The Model portion of an MVC-based system can often be divided into two major subsystems: the **internal state** of the system and the **actions** that can be taken to change that state. The `Action` class under the `org.apache.struts.action` package represents a superclass for all Models in your application. Actions encapsulate calls to business logic classes, interpret the outcome, and ultimately dispatch control to the appropriate View component to create the response. For custom states and/or actions, you need to create your own Model subclasses from the Action class.

9.4.2   View

The View portion of a Struts-based application consists of the JSP, together with any presentation-tier Java classes (such as ActionForm classes). The ActionForm class in the org.apache.struts.action package is a superclass for all View-related Java code—in other words, code that captures and validates input supplied by the user. Again, for custom form elements and validation, you need to write your own subclass extending from the ActionForm class. The Struts custom tag libraries provide direct support for the View layer of a MVC application.

9.4.3   Controller

The *Controller* portion of the application is focused on receiving requests from the client (typically a user running a Web browser), deciding what business logic function is to be performed, and then delegating responsibility for producing the next phase of the user interface to an appropriate View component. In Struts, the primary component of the Controller is a servlet of class ActionServlet. This servlet is configured by defining a set of ActionMappings. An ActionMapping defines a path that is matched against the request URL of the incoming request and usually specifies the fully qualified class name of an Action class.

The MVC architecture can be summed up as shown in Figure 9.5.

9.5   Basic Form Validation Using Struts

In the same way that you removed Java code from the JSP as much as possible, it is a good idea to minimize the use of JavaScript and move such form validation and error checking to Struts' Java classes. Struts provides attributes in its <action> elements that allow you to do some basic validation. For example, say that in the HTML form being used in this chapter, both first and last names are required before hitting the Submit button. In other words, you need to check if the first or last name is empty; if so, you need to display an appropriate error message.

In JavaScript the alert function was used to pop up an error message. But pop-ups are not always considered the best way of displaying error messages. The Struts approach is to display them on the browser window itself—for example, at the top of the HTML form, or at specific points on the form where the data is missing. So if a user leaves the last name blank and hits the Submit button, an error message would appear as follows:

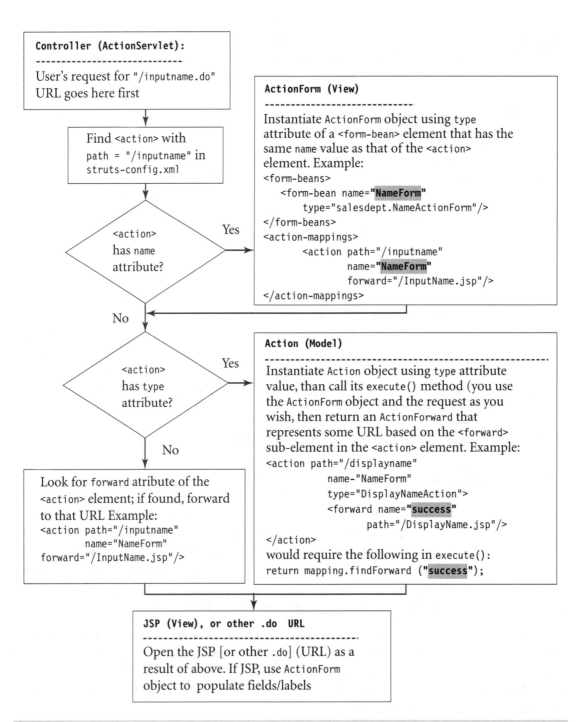

Figure 9.5

The Model-View-Controller (MVC) Architecture

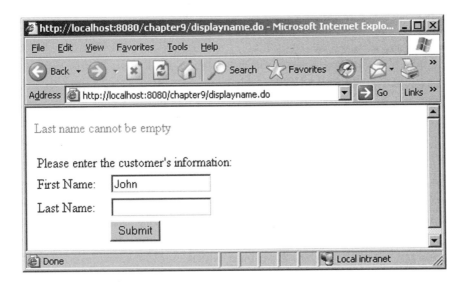

The error message can also be made to appear beside the last name field, as follows:

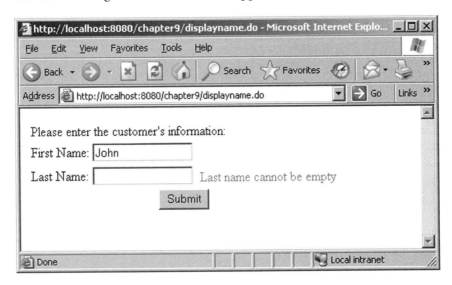

So, how do you do this in Struts? Well, there are two ways you can do this:

- implement the `validate()` method in your `ActionForm` subclass, or
- add error validation in your `Action` subclass.

Let's look at each of them.

9.5.1   Validation Using the `validate()` Method of `ActionForm` Subclass

If you look at the `<action>` element attributes in Appendix J, you will notice an attribute called `val-idate` that has a default value of `true`. This means we had this `validate=true` all along but it never validated anything for us. The reason is, we did not implement the `validate()` method in our `ActionForm` subclass (the default implementation in the `ActionForm` parent class does not do anything). The `validate()` method in the `ActionForm` subclass allows you to add a list of one or more error messages, based on missing or empty attributes on the `ActionForm` object. This list of error messages can then be displayed in your JSP by using the `<html:errors>` tag.

When the `ActionForm` subclass has the `validate()` method implemented, there is one more thing you need to keep in mind: the corresponding `<action>` element(s) in `struts-config.xml` that use(s) that `ActionForm` class must have an additional `input` attribute defined. The `input` attribute specifies the URL (`jsp` page or other action) that you want the control to go to when the validation fails. In this case, you want the control to remain on the `InputName.jsp` page, which should display the error messages at the top of the form. Finally, you need to make sure that the action that first shows up and displays the empty form has the `validate` set to `false`. If it does not, it will keep showing the error messages even when the form displays empty fields the first time in. The form's action (`/display-name`) is the one that needs to have `validate` set to `true` (or omitted, since `true` is the default); it would then direct the flow to the `InputName.jsp` page, along with a nonempty `ActionErrors` list object if there are errors. So, our `<action>` elements would now look like this:

```
<action path="/Inputname"
        name="NameForm"
        validate="false"
        scope="request"
        forward="/sec93/InputName.jsp"/>


<action path="/displayname"
        type="salesdept.DisplayNameAction"
        name="NameForm"
        input="/sec93/InputName.jsp"
        scope="request">
        <forward name="success"
                 path="/sec93/DisplayName.jsp" />
</action>
```

The `InputName.jsp` needs to add an `<html:errors/>` tag, so it would look like this:

```
<!-- Begin: InputName.jsp -->
<%@ taglib uri="/WEB-INF/tlds/struts-html.tld" prefix="html" %>
```

```
<html:html>
    <BODY>
        <FONT COLOR=red><html:errors/></FONT>
        <html:form action="/displayname.do">
            <TABLE>
                <TR>
                    <TD COLSPAN=2>Please enter the customer's information:</TD>
                </TR>
                <TR>
                    <TD>First Name:</TD>
                    <TD><html:text property="firstName" size="16"/></TD>
                </TR>
                <TR>
                    <TD>Last Name:</TD>
                    <TD><html:text property="lastName" size="16"/></TD>
                </TR>
                <TR>
                    <TD ALIGN="center" COLSPAN=2><html:submit/></TD>
                </TR>
            </TABLE>
        </html:form>
    </BODY>
</html:html>
<!-- End: InputName.jsp -->
```

The validate() method needs to be implemented in the NameActionForm class, and it needs to look like this:

```
public ActionErrors validate( ActionMapping mapping,
                              HttpServletRequest request )
{
    ActionErrors errors = null;

    if ( firstName == null || firstName.trim().equals("") )
    {
        if ( errors == null ) errors = new ActionErrors();
        errors.add("firstName", new ActionMessage("firstNameError"));
    }
    if ( lastName == null || lastName.trim().equals("") )
    {
        if ( errors == null ) errors = new ActionErrors();
        errors.add("lastName", new ActionMessage("lastNameError"));
    }
```

```
    return errors;
}
```

The line

```
errors.add("firstName", new ActionMessage("firstNameError"));
```

needs a bit of explanation. Before looking at what it is trying to do, you need to understand the concept of resource bundles.

9.5.1.1   Resource Bundles and Internationalization

Web pages have a significant amount of static text (i.e., text that does not change with time) such as labels and error messages, all usually written in English. But what would you do if your application needs to show up in a different language, say French? One way is to write a Java tag class that stores all the English labels in your entire application, as well as their translations in specific languages, and that is be able to spit out the translated label or error message for you. Struts provides a mechanism in its framework so you don't have to write such a special tag class. It calls all labels and error messages taken together as *resources*. A *resource bundle* is an object that can map the original label or error message by a key and get its translation in whatever language is requested. The concept or process is called *internationalization*. Again, Struts has predefined off-the-shelf framework classes that handle all such translations for you. All you need to do is to create a "properties file" (a file that has a .properties extension) that contains all possible labels and error messages, one per language. So, for example, you may create a properties file called ErrorMessages.properties that will contain key-value pairs, the values comprising of all error messages that you have in the entire Web application, in English, and another called ErrorMessages_fr_FR.properties that contains the same keys, but values would be the French equivalents of the ones in English. Here fr and FR are standard codes for language (French) and country (France).

An example would make this clearer. Say that when the last name field is empty and the user hits the Submit button, you want to show the error message: Last name cannot be empty. Similarly, when the first name is empty, you want to show a message: First name cannot be empty. You create a file called ErrorMessages.properties with the following content:

```
firstNameError=First name cannot be empty
lastNameError=Last name cannot be empty
```

and save it under the WEB-INF\classes folder of your Web app. Next, you modify struts-config.xml to add the following as a nested entry directly under the <struts-config> element.

```
<message-resources parameter="ErrorMessages"/>
```

(Note that ErrorMessages here is the name of the .properties file without its extension.)

Also note that firstNameError and lastNameError are keys for retrieving the corresponding messages First name cannot be empty and Last name cannot be empty respectively. So we have two key-value pairs in this properties file.

An ActionMessage class is yet another Struts framework class; it encapsulates or represents a single message. To display the list of error message(s) on your JSP, you need to create an instance of the ActionMessage class, one per error message, and add it to the ActionErrors object that your validate() method in ActionForm class needs to return. So the part

```
new ActionMessage("firstNameError")
```

that you see in validate() method of NameActionForm class means you are creating a single ActionMessage object that represents the error First name cannot be empty, and firstNameError is the key in the properties file that maps to the actual value (First name cannot be empty). The key firstNameError needs to match the one used in the .properties file (otherwise it will not work).

The full line that adds the ActionMessage object to the ActionErrors list object, errors, is

```
errors.add("firstName", new ActionMessage("firstNameError"));
```

Notice the use of the key firstName here. It is the key by which you can retrieve this specific Action-Message object from the ActionErrors list object, and place it at an appropriate place on the JSP as necessary.

Don't confuse the two keys used in the same line:

- One is firstNameError, which is the key in the properties file that maps to the actual value.
- The other is firstName, which is the key by which you can retrieve this specific ActionMessage object from the ActionErrors list object.

Go ahead and compile this change:

```
C:\JSP\Chapter9\sec93>javac -d %JSP_OUT% -classpath %JSP_OUT%;%CLASSPATH% NameActionForm.java
```

Restart Tomcat, and open the page as before:

```
http://localhost:8080/chapter9/inputname.do
```

Enter the first name, leave the last name empty, and hit the Submit button. You should see the error message in light gray as shown here:

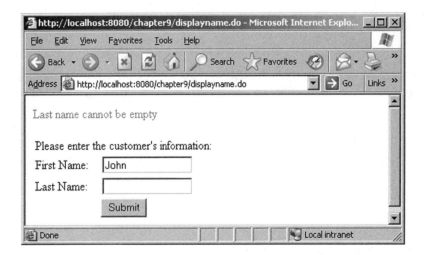

A couple of notes:

- If the validation results in more than one error message, `<html:errors/>` displays them on one continuous line instead of displaying each message on a separate line. You do not want this; you want each error message to display on a separate line. To do so, you need to add the HTML `<BR>` tag at the end of each message in the `.properties` file as follows:

  `firstNameError=First name cannot be empty<BR>`

  `lastNameError=Last name cannot be empty<BR>`

  Embedding HTML tags in `.properties` files like this may not be the best approach. An alternative is to use the `<html:messages/>` tag, which can display the error messages on separate lines without using the `<BR>` tag in the `.properties` file. Its usage would look something like this:

  `<html:messages id="msg">`

  `    <li><bean:write name="msg"/></li>`

  `</html:messages>`

  Replace `<html:errors/>` in the JSP with these lines and verify that it displays error messages on individual lines. Here `<li>` is an HTML tag for "list item." (Details of this tag are available at the HTML reference site in Appendix D.) The decision to use `<html:messages/>` instead of `<html:errors/>` is left to the developer.

- The `parameter` attribute in the `<message-resources>` tag in `struts-config.xml` represents the fully-qualified name of the `.properties` file (without the `.properties` extension), relative to the `WEB-INF\classes` folder of the Web app. In the current example, the file name under `WEB-INF\classes` was `ErrorMessages.properties`, so you used `parameter="ErrorMessages"` as follows:

  `<message-resources parameter="ErrorMessages" />`

To better organize .properties files, you could create subfolders under WEB-INF\classes and put .properties files there. For example, say that you create a folder called resources under WEB-INF\classes and put ErrorMessages.properties there. The parameter attribute in the <message-resources> tag now needs to have a value of resources.ErrorMessages instead of ErrorMessages, so it needs to look like this:

```
<message-resources parameter="resources.ErrorMessages" />
```

- You named the file ErrorMessages.properties but the actual standard is to include the two character abbreviation for language and country. So if this .properties file is meant for English language labels or messages for U.S. users, it needs to be named ErrorMessages_en_US.properties. Currently ErrorMessages.properties worked fine because a filename with neither language nor country abbreviation is the default that the resource bundle uses when it does not find one with those abbreviations.

To change the error display so that it shows up beside the field that is empty, change InputName.jsp to put the <html:errors> tag beside each INPUT field, and use the property attribute (which maps to the key that was used when adding errors to the ActionErrors object in the ActionForm class), as follows:

```
------------------------------------------------------------
<!-- Begin: InputName.jsp -->
<%@ taglib uri="/WEB-INF/tlds/struts-html.tld" prefix="html" %>

<html:html>
    <BODY>
        <html:form action="/displayname.do">
            <TABLE>
                <TR>
                    <TD COLSPAN=2>Please enter the customer's information:</TD>
                </TR>
                <TR>
                    <TD>First Name:</TD>
                    <TD><html:text property="firstName" size="16"/>  
                        <FONT COLOR=red>
                            <html:errors property="firstName"/>
                        </FONT>
                    </TD>
                </TR>
                <TR>
                    <TD>Last Name:</TD>
                    <TD><html:text property="lastName" size="16"/>  
                        <FONT COLOR=red>
                            <html:errors property="lastName"/>
                        </FONT>
                    </TD>
                </TR>
                <TR>
                    <TD ALIGN="center" COLSPAN=2><html:submit/></TD>
```

```
            </TR>
         </TABLE>
      </html:form>
   </BODY>
</html:html>
<!-- End: InputName.jsp -->
------------------------------------------------------------
```

It should now appear as shown here:

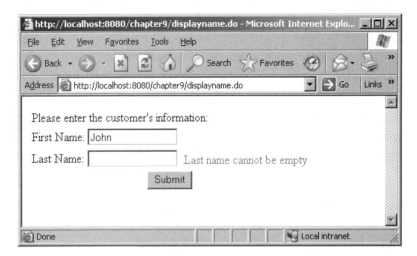

Note that <html:errors/> shows the error messages only if the list is not empty. If the list is empty, nothing shows up due to <html:errors/>.

If you want the error messages to show up in French, you would create a file called ErrorMessages_fr_FR.properties that contains the same keys, but values would be the French equivalents of the ones in English. So its content would be something like this:

```
firstNameError=French translation of: First name cannot be empty
lastNameError=French translation of: Last name cannot be empty
```

Here the values need to be French translations of the English ones. When a French user logs on, Struts can figure out the user's language based on a Locale object (of type java.util.Locale) that it creates behind the scenes, and loads the ErrorMessages_fr_FR.properties instead of the ErrorMessages.properties, so that all error messages show up in French. The way Struts loads the Locale object based on the user's language is beyond the scope of this book. For our purposes here, it is sufficient to understand the overall concept of resource bundles and internationalization.

9.5.2   Validation Using execute() Method of Action Subclass

Instead of implementing the validate() method in the NameActionForm class, you could add the validation to the DisplayNameAction class's execute() method, and add a new forward to the <action> element, to which the action class forwards if form data is invalid. Let's call the new forward `inputError`, so the `<action>` elements in `struts-config.xml` would look like this:

```
<action path="/inputname"
        name="NameForm"
        scope="request"
        forward="/sec93/InputName.jsp"/>

<action path="/displayname"
        type="salesdept.DisplayNameAction"
        name="NameForm"
        scope="request">
        <forward name="success"
                path="/sec93/DisplayName.jsp" />
        <forward name="inputError"
                path="/sec93/InputName.jsp" />
</action>
```

(Notice how we remove the `input` attribute from `displayname`, instead we add a new `forward` named "inputError." Also note that we removed the `validate` attribute from `inputname`.)

The `DisplayNameAction` class would now look like this:

```
// ------------ Begin: DisplayNameAction.java ----------------------
package salesdept;

import java.io.*;
import javax.servlet.*;
import javax.servlet.http.*;
import org.apache.struts.action.*;

public class DisplayNameAction extends Action
{
    public ActionForward execute (ActionMapping mapping,
                                  ActionForm actionForm,
                                  HttpServletRequest request,
                                  HttpServletResponse response )
    {
        ActionMessages messages = null;
        NameActionForm form = (NameActionForm)actionForm;
        String firstName = form.getFirstName();
        String lastName = form.getLastName();

        if ( firstName == null || firstName.trim().equals("") ||
             lastName == null || lastName.trim().equals("") )
        {
            messages = new ActionMessages();
            if ( firstName == null || firstName.trim().equals("") )
```

```
              {
                  messages.add("firstName", new ActionMessage("firstNameError"));
              }
              if ( lastName == null || lastName.trim().equals("") )
              {
                  messages.add("lastName", new ActionMessage("lastNameError"));
              }
          }
          else
          {
              form.setFullName();
              return mapping.findForward("success");
          }
          if ( messages != null )
          {
              saveErrors(request, messages);
          }
          return mapping.findForward("inputError");
      }
}
// ----------- End: DisplayNameAction.java ----------------------
```

Comment out the `validate()` method in the `NameActionForm` class, and compile both `NameActionForm` and `DisplayNameAction` with these changes. Make sure you do the resource bundle part described in Section 9.5.1.1 (that's common to both approaches). Restart Tomcat, open the URL as before, and verify that it behaves exactly the same as before (Section 9.5.1).

9.6 Defining New Scripting Variables Using `<bean:define>`

In Section 9.3.7, we saw one use of the `<bean>` tag library—that of rendering a particular attribute from a `bean`. The other use of this tag library is to define a new bean on the fly. You can then reuse that bean elsewhere in your JSP to set/get attributes as necessary.

The official Struts site has the following statement on the `<bean>` tag library:

> The "`struts-bean`" tag library contains JSP custom tags useful in defining new beans (in any desired scope) from a variety of possible sources, as well as a tag to render a particular bean (or bean property) to the output response.

In Chapter 8, we saw something similar when we talked about the `<jsp:useBean>`, `<jsp:getProperty>`, and `<jsp:setProperty>` tags. There we created a bean object and gave it an identifying name using the `id` attribute of the `jsp:useBean` tag. The concept of using the `id` attribute to identify bean objects is going to be very useful beyond this point, so make sure you feel comfortable using it.

The Struts `bean` tag library has a tag similar to the `jsp:useBean` tag; it is called the `define` tag. The `define` tag too has an `id` attribute that you use to give an identifying name to the bean (you do so when you are creating a new bean on the fly). The beauty of using the Struts `bean` tag is that you do not need to explicitly create a Java class for the bean, because it represents a single attribute from the original bean. The use of the term "bean" for everything is a bit confusing, but hopefully we will learn to live with it.

The `<bean:define>` tag represents a simple Java attribute (such as `String`, `int`, `double`, etc.), whereas the `jsp:useBean` tag was for a full-fledged `JavaBean` class that may have several attributes in it. Note that primitive types such as `int`, `double` are wrapped into their appropriate Java wrapper class, so `int` would get stored as `java.lang.Integer`, and so on. So the Struts `bean:define` actually creates a scripting variable that has a page scope; and you can refer to it/use it anywhere in the current JSP.

To see the `<bean:define>` in action, say that you want to store the `firstName` attribute of the `ActionForm` object into a new bean called `myBean` (of type `String`). You would do so using the line

```
<bean:define id="myBean" name="NameForm" property="firstName"/>
```

in your `DisplayName.jsp`. At a later point on the JSP, you can display the content of the bean you just created, using the `<bean:write>` tag as before, but this time you will not specify the `property` attribute, since the new bean itself is an attribute (`firstName`) from the `ActionForm` object. So later in the JSP, if you want to dump the content of this bean, you would say

```
<bean:write name="myBean"/>
```

The full JSP would look as follows (with the bolded portion showing the part that is different here compared to the earlier version):

```
----------------------------------------------------------
<!-- Begin: DisplayName.jsp -->
<%@ taglib uri="/WEB-INF/tlds/struts-bean.tld" prefix="bean" %>
<%@ taglib uri="/WEB-INF/tlds/struts-html.tld" prefix="html" %>
<html:html>
    <BODY>
        <TABLE>
            <TR>
                <TD>First Name:</TD>
                <TD><bean:write name="NameForm" property="firstName"/></TD>
            </TR>
            <TR>
                <TD>Last Name:</TD>
                <TD><bean:write name="NameForm" property="lastName"/></TD>
            </TR>
            <TR>
                <TD>Full Name:</TD>
                <TD><bean:write name="NameForm" property="fullName"/></TD>
            </TR>
        </TABLE>
```

```
      <bean:define id="myBean" name="NameForm" property="firstName"/>

      <TABLE>
        <TR>
          <TD>Testing new bean.. first name is:</TD>
          <TD><bean:write name="myBean"/></TD>
        </TR>
      </TABLE>
    </BODY>
</html:html>
<!-- End: DisplayName.jsp -->
```

This would appear as shown here:

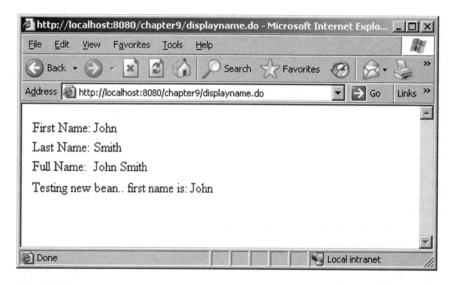

9.7 Looping Through a Result Set Using `<logic:iterate>`

We could get a simple JSP to work—one that concatenates the first and last name entered by the user. As you know, real-world applications are far more complex. Many times, we need to loop through a result set and display data one at a time (as we did in Section 7.4). For this, you need a temporary scripting variable ("bean") in each iteration, so that you can get the bean's appropriate property and display it. For example, say that you want to redo the customer list example we saw in Section 7.4, but this time using Struts (which means, no Java in the JSP). As you loop through the result set of customers, each row represents one customer, and can be thought of as one bean with the customer's attributes (first name, last name, age, etc). In each iteration of the loop, if you had a temporary bean that takes on the current customer's attributes, you could use it to display the customer's data and repeat the process for all customers. Struts provides a convenient tag for this purpose, the iterate tag, defined in its logic Tag Library. So you would use it as <logic:iterate> (we will see the details in just a moment).

We need to represent the customer's attributes at two stages: the first is when the SQL query is run, to build a list of customer objects that we store on the request, and the other is the ActionForm sub-class that takes the attributes from each customer object to convert to "displayable" format for the JSP. We have been using the second one until now. For the SQL part, we need a JavaBean class, for which we can reuse the one in Solved Exercise 8.3 (CustomerBean.java). Create a new folder sec97 under C:\JSP\Chapter9 and copy CustomerBean.java from C:\JSP\Chapter8\exer83 into this folder. Since each object of this class will represent one row from the customer table in the database, it is a good idea to rename it CustomerDBObject.java. The class inside it also needs to be renamed Customer-DBObject. It needs to look like this:

```java
// ------------ Begin: CustomerDBObject.java ----------------------
package salesdept;
public class CustomerDBObject
{
    private int customerId;
    private String firstName;
    private String lastName;
    private int age;
    private double salesAmount;

    public int getCustomerId() { return customerId; }
    public String getFirstName() { return firstName; }
    public String getLastName() { return lastName; }
    public int getAge() { return age; }
    public double getSalesAmount() { return salesAmount; }
    public String getFullName() { return firstName + " " + lastName; }

    public void setCustomerId( int customerId ) {this.customerId = customerId;}
    public void setFirstName( String firstName ) {this.firstName = firstName;}
    public void setLastName( String lastName ) { this.lastName = lastName; }
    public void setAge( int age ) { this.age = age; }
    public void setSalesAmount( double salesAmount )
    {
        this.salesAmount = salesAmount;
    }
}
// ------------ End: CustomerDBObject.java ----------------------
```

Notice how we have attributes that map one-to-one with the columns of the customer table in the database. In addition, we have additional getters such as getFullName() that define new attributes on the fly, based on combinations of other attributes, firstName and lastName. Because the getter exists this way, the JSP can invoke the `fullName` attribute like any other attribute, although the `fullName` is not explicitly declared as one of the class attributes.

In Section 7.4, we had the Java code for getting the database connection sitting in the JSP. Now that we do not want to have any Java code in the JSP, we need to move all that logic to a separate Java class—let's call it `CustomerDBProcess` and store it in `CustomerDBProcess.java` under `C:\JSP\Chapter9\sec97`. It will have a getter method for getting a list of `CustomerDBObject` objects, based on a SQL query, and will look like this:

```
----------------------------------------------------------------------------
// ------------ Begin: CustomerDBProcess.java ----------------------
package salesdept;
import java.util.List;
import java.util.ArrayList;
import java.sql.*;
public class CustomerDBProcess
{
   private ResultSet rs;
   private Statement statement;

   // Constructor
   public CustomerDBProcess() throws ClassNotFoundException,
                                   InstantiationException,
                                   IllegalAccessException,
                                   SQLException
   {
     Class.forName("com.mysql.jdbc.Driver").newInstance();
     Connection connection = DriverManager.getConnection(
          "jdbc:mysql://localhost:3306/salesdatabase?user=root&password=");
     statement = connection.createStatement();
     rs = null;
   }

   // Get all customers' data
   public List<CustomerDBObject> getCustomerList() throws SQLException
   {
     List<CustomerDBObject> custList = null;

     rs = statement.executeQuery("select * from customer");

     while (rs.next())
     {
         CustomerDBObject cust = new CustomerDBObject();
         cust.setCustomerId (rs.getInt("customer_id"));
         cust.setAge(rs.getInt("age"));
```

```
            cust.setSalesAmount(rs.getDouble("sales_amount"));
            cust.setFirstName(rs.getString("first_name"));
            cust.setLastName(rs.getString("last_name"));
            if (custList == null) custList = new ArrayList<CustomerDBObject>();
            custList.add(cust);
        }
        return custList;
    }
}
// ------------ End: CustomerDBProcess.java ----------------------
-----------------------------------------------------------------------------------
```

Create a new action class called DisplayCustomerListAction and save it as DisplayCustomerListAction.java under the sec97 folder. It needs to call the getCustomerList() function of CustomerDBProcess class and set an attribute on the request to store the list object. Let's store it under the key customerList on the request. The contents of this class would be as follows:

```
-----------------------------------------------------------------------------------
// ------------ Begin: DisplayCustomerListAction.java ----------------------
package salesdept;
import java.io.*;
import java.util.List;
import java.util.ArrayList;
import java.sql.*;
import javax.servlet.*;
import javax.servlet.http.*;
import org.apache.struts.action.*;

public class DisplayCustomerListAction extends Action
{
    public ActionForward execute (ActionMapping mapping,
                                  ActionForm actionForm,
                                  HttpServletRequest request,
                                  HttpServletResponse response )
    throws ClassNotFoundException, InstantiationException, IllegalAccessException, SQLException
    {
        CustomerDBProcess custDBProcess = new CustomerDBProcess();
        List custList = custDBProcess.getCustomerList();
        request.setAttribute("customerList", custList);

        return mapping.findForward("success");
    }
}
// ------------ End: DisplayCustomerListAction.java ----------------------
-----------------------------------------------------------------------------------
```

Also copy CustomerList.jsp from C:\JSP\Chapter7\sec74 into the sec97 folder. Modify it to use the <logic:iterate> tag, with id="customer", where customer represents the current customer in the customerList bean. Also, create a new folder called styles under C:\JSP\Chapter9 and copy styles.css from C:\JSP\Chapter7\styles into it. Finally, copy the MySQL JDBC Driver .jar from Chapter 7 WEB-INF\lib folder to C:\JSP\Chapter9\WEB-INF\lib. (The bolded portion shows those parts that differ from Section 7.4).

```
<!-- Begin: CustomerList.jsp -->
<%@ taglib uri="/WEB-INF/tlds/struts-bean.tld" prefix="bean" %>
<%@ taglib uri="/WEB-INF/tlds/struts-html.tld" prefix="html" %>
<%@ taglib uri="/WEB-INF/tlds/struts-logic.tld" prefix="logic" %>
<HTML>
   <HEAD>
     <LINK REL="stylesheet" TYPE="text/css" HREF="../styles/styles.css" />
   </HEAD>
   <BODY>
     <TABLE>
       <TR CLASS="defaultText">
          <TD>Customer ID</TD>
          <TD>First Name</TD>
          <TD>Last Name</TD>
          <TD>Age</TD>
          <TD>Sales Amount</TD>
       </TR>
       <logic:iterate id="customer" name="customerList">
          <TR>
             <TD><bean:write name="customer" property="customerId"/></TD>
             <TD><bean:write name="customer" property="firstName"/></TD>
             <TD><bean:write name="customer" property="lastName"/></TD>
             <TD><bean:write name="customer" property="age"/></TD>
             <TD><bean:write name="customer" property="salesAmount"/></TD>
          </TR>
       </logic:iterate>
     </TABLE>
   </BODY>
</HTML>
<!-- End: CustomerList.jsp -->
```

Finally, modify the struts-config.xml file to add a new <action> element for displaying the customer list—let's call it customerlist. The new <action> entry would look like this:

```
<action path="/customerlist"
        type="salesdept.DisplayCustomerListAction"
```

```
        scope="request">
        <forward name="success"
                path="/sec97/CustomerList.jsp" />
</action>
```

Compile all Java code, restart Tomcat, and enter the URL as

`http://localhost:8080/chapter9/customerlist.do`

You should see the page as shown here:

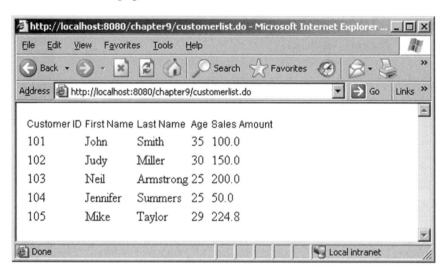

Notice how the dynamic style sheet is not implemented for the table rows. Earlier, we used a script-let to toggle the style for even and odd rows. But now our rule is: "No Java in JSP." One way to apply the style to the rows is to add a new attribute to the `CustomerDBObject` class. (Recall that it is simply a placeholder for attributes, getters, and setters, whether those attributes belong to the database table or not.) Let's go ahead and add a new attribute called `rowClass` of type `String`. (The bolded portion shows the part that differs from the earlier version.)

```
// ------------ Begin: CustomerDBObject.java ----------------------
package salesdept;
public class CustomerDBObject
{
    private int customerId;
    private String firstName;
    private String lastName;
    private int age;
    private double salesAmount;
    private String rowClass; // CSS style class for current customer
```

```
public int getCustomerId() { return customerId; }
public String getFirstName() { return firstName; }
public String getLastName() { return lastName; }
public int getAge() { return age; }
public double getSalesAmount() { return salesAmount; }
public String getFullName() { return firstName + " " + lastName; }
public String getRowClass() { return rowClass; }

public void setCustomerId( int customerId ) {this.customerId = customerId;}
public void setFirstName( String firstName ) {this.firstName = firstName;}
public void setLastName( String lastName ) { this.lastName = lastName; }
public void setAge( int age ) { this.age = age; }
public void setSalesAmount( double salesAmount )
{
    this.salesAmount = salesAmount; }
}
public void setRowClass( String rowClass ) { this.rowClass = rowClass; }

// ------------ End: CustomerDBObject.java ---------------------
```

Now change the getCustomerList() method in CustomerDBProcess class to toggle this attribute in each iteration as shown here:

```
// Get all customers' data
public List<CustomerDBObject> getCustomerList() throws SQLException
{
    List<CustomerDBObject> custList = null;

    rs = statement.executeQuery("select * from customer");
    String rowClass = "tableEvenRow";

    while (rs.next())
    {
        CustomerDBObject cust = new CustomerDBObject();
        cust.setCustomerId (rs.getInt("customer_id"));
        cust.setAge(rs.getInt("age"));
        cust.setSalesAmount(rs.getDouble("sales_amount"));
        cust.setFirstName(rs.getString("first_name"));
        cust.setLastName(rs.getString("last_name"));
        // Toggle the CSS style sheet class
        if (rowClass.equals("tableEvenRow"))
        {
            rowClass = "tableOddRow";
        }
```

```
        else
        {
            rowClass = "tableEvenRow";
        }
        cust.setRowClass(rowClass);
        if (custList == null) custList = new ArrayList<CustomerDBObject>();
        custList.add(cust);
    }
    return custList;
}
```

Change the CustomerList.jsp in order to use the current value of the rowClass attribute:

```
<!-- Begin: CustomerList.jsp -->
<%@ taglib uri="/WEB-INF/tlds/struts-bean.tld" prefix="bean" %>
<%@ taglib uri="/WEB-INF/tlds/struts-html.tld" prefix="html" %>
<%@ taglib uri="/WEB-INF/tlds/struts-logic.tld" prefix="logic" %>
<HTML>
  <HEAD>
    <LINK REL="stylesheet" TYPE="text/css" HREF="../styles/styles.css" />
  </HEAD>
  <BODY>
    <TABLE>
      <TR CLASS="defaultText">
        <TD>Customer ID</TD>
        <TD>First Name</TD>
        <TD>Last Name</TD>
        <TD>Age</TD>
        <TD>Sales Amount</TD>
      </TR>
      <logic:iterate id="customer" name="customerList">
        <TR CLASS="<bean:write name="customer" property="rowClass"/>">
          <TD><bean:write name="customer" property="customerId"/></TD>
          <TD><bean:write name="customer" property="firstName"/></TD>
          <TD><bean:write name="customer" property="lastName"/></TD>
          <TD><bean:write name="customer" property="age"/></TD>
          <TD><bean:write name="customer" property="salesAmount"/></TD>
        </TR>
      </logic:iterate>
    </TABLE>
  </BODY>
</HTML>
<!-- End: CustomerList.jsp -->
```

Compile all Java code and restart Tomcat. You should now see the change shown here:

Solved Exercise 9.7

Objective: To learn how to develop a Struts-based application that inserts data into a database using user-entered information on HTML forms.

Steps:

- In Solved Exercise 7.4(c), we saw how we can insert records into the customer table via the JDBC driver in a JSP scriptlet. Let's redo the same example using Struts.

- Create a new folder exer97 under C:\JSP\Chapter9. Copy the InputName.jsp and CustomerDBProcess.java files from C:\JSP\Chapter9\sec93 and C:\JSP\Chapter9\sec97 respectively into this folder. Rename InputName.jsp to CustomerInfo.jsp. This JSP will represent a combination of the InputCustomer.jsp and InsertCustomer.jsp pages of Solved Exercise 7.4(c). It will behave differently based on a new mode attribute on the request, which needs to be set in the appropriate Action class:

  - If mode=input, the JSP should show the INPUT text fields for Customer ID (read-only), first name, last name, age, and sales amount. (Make it look identical to the way InputCustomer.jsp showed up in Solved Exercise 7.4(c)). Change the form action to a new action insertcustomer.do (instead of displayname.do).

  - If mode=displayonly, the JSP should show up the same as InsertCustomer.jsp of Solved Exercise 7.4(c). In other words, instead of INPUT text fields and a submit button, it needs to have display-only fields showing the customer record just inserted, along with links to insert the next customer and to view the current customer list. (Note that, for the customer list link, you can reuse the customerlist.do action you created earlier.)

(*Hint:* Use the <logic:equal> element in the JSP to decide which part shows up, based on the mode attribute on the request. For details of available attributes for this tag, please refer to the Struts API URL in Appendix D.)

- Copy NameActionForm.java from C:\JSP\Chapter9\sec93 into this folder. Rename it CustomerInfoActionForm.java and modify it to add the new attributes (customerId, age, and salesAmount).

  - Note that if you declare the age as int type, and salesAmount as double, these default to 0 and 0.0 respectively, so the JSP would show these fields with default values of 0 and 0.0—which may not look good. To fix this, declare these two attributes as String, and set them to empty String in the reset() method you need to now implement in the CustomerInfoActionForm class. Also note that when the user clicks on the "Input next customer" link and does not implement the reset() method, the form will show values from the previous customer inserted, so the user needs to set *all* fields to empty strings in the reset() method.

  - Because all input fields are required, implement the validate() method to return errors if one or more of these fields is empty (or if either age or salesAmount is 0). Instead of displaying the relevant error in front of each field, display a list of error messages using the <html:errors> tag, with each message on a new line. (*Hint:* You need to use the <br> tag at the end of each error message in the .properties file, so that individual error messages show up on different lines.)

- Modify CustomerDBProcess.java to add two new methods: one called getMaxCustomerId() that queries the customer table and returns the max customer_id value in the table, and another called addCustomer() that takes a CustomerDBObject object as input, and inserts it into the database. Note that you can reuse the CustomerDBObject class you created earlier, so there is no need to copy or reimplement it.

- Create a new Action subclass called InputCustomerAction. Implement its execute() method where you should call the getMaxCustomerId() method of CustomerDBProcess, add 1 to it, and set the form's customerId attribute equal to the sum. The rest of the form attributes need to be left empty, since this action is meant for accepting a new customer's information. (Note that all input fields should show up empty the first time this JSP shows up.) Also set an attribute called mode on the request, with a value of input.

- Create a new <action> element called inputcustomer in struts-config.xml that has the Action class as InputCustomerAction and the JSP as CustomerInfo.jsp.

- Create a new Action class called InsertCustomerAction. Implement its execute() method to instantiate a new CustomerDBObject object and populate it with all attributes from the form (customerId, first name, last name, age, and salesAmount). Call the addCustomer() method of the CustomerDBProcess class, passing it the CustomerDBObject object just created. Also set an attribute called mode on the request, with a value equal to displayonly.

- Create a new `<action>` element called `insertcustomer` in `struts-config.xml` that has the `Action` class as `InsertCustomerAction` and forwards to `success` that takes the user to `CustomerInfo.jsp`.

- Verify that it works as expected, by using the following URL:

  `http://localhost:8080/chapter9/inputcustomer.do`.

- Submit `struts-config.xml`, `CustomerInfoActionForm.java`, `ErrorMessages.properties`, `Customer-DBProcess.java`, `InputCustomerAction.java`, `InsertCustomerAction.java`, and `CustomerInfo.jsp`.

  A sample interaction is shown next (assuming max `customer_id` in the customer table is 105):

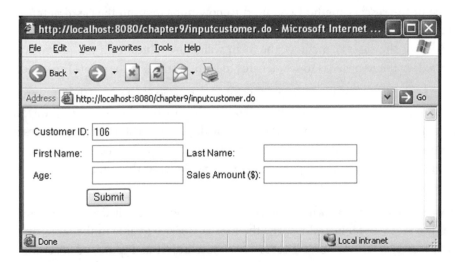

Enter values in all fields, and hit the Submit button:

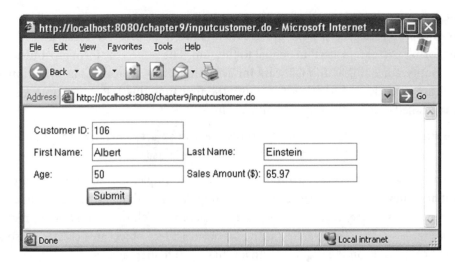

It should take you to the following page:

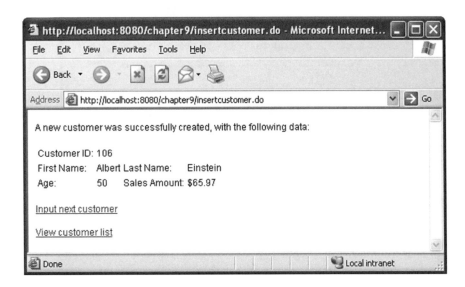

Click on "Input next customer" and make sure it does not carry values from the previous customer:

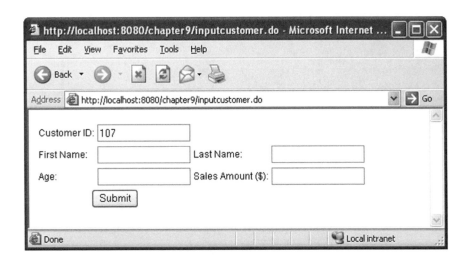

This time, check that the validation works fine. Enter values in the first name and sales amount fields, but leave the last name and age fields empty, and hit the Submit button.

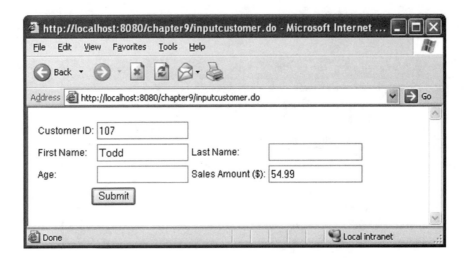

You should see the following screen:

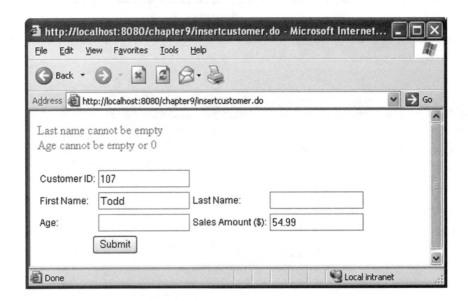

Enter the missing values, and hit the Submit button. The following screen appears.

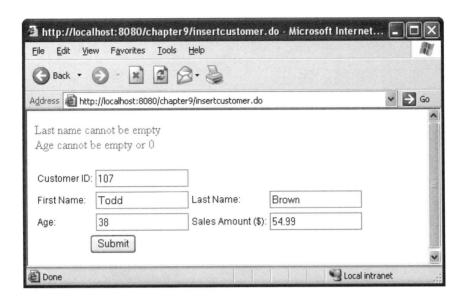

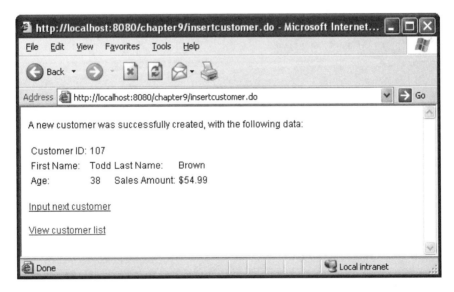

Click on "View customer list" to ensure that the two new records have been added, as shown on the following screen.

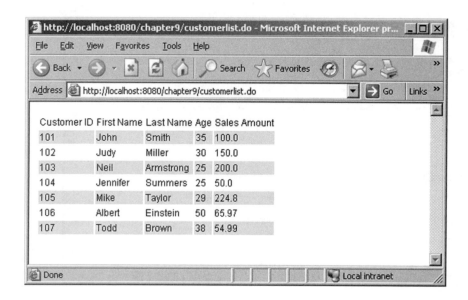

Solution:

`struts-config.xml` (relevant part only):

```
--------------------------------------------------------------------------------
<form-beans>
   ...
   <form-bean name="CustomerInfoForm" type="salesdept.CustomerInfoActionForm" />
</form-beans>

<action-mappings>
...
   <action path="/inputcustomer"
           name="CustomerInfoForm"
           type="salesdept.InputCustomerAction"
           validate="false">
               <forward name="success" path="/exer97/CustomerInfo.jsp" />
   </action>

   <action path="/insertcustomer"
           name="CustomerInfoForm"
           type="salesdept.InsertCustomerAction"
           validate="true"
           input="/exer97/CustomerInfo.jsp">
               <forward name="success" path="/exer97/CustomerInfo.jsp" />
   </action>
</action-mappings>
--------------------------------------------------------------------------------
```

```java
// ------------   Begin: CustomerInfoActionForm.java ----------------------
package salesdept;

import javax.servlet.http.*;
import org.apache.struts.action.*;

public class CustomerInfoActionForm extends ActionForm
{
    private int customerId;
    private String firstName;
    private String lastName;
    private String fullName;
    private String age;
    private String salesAmount;

    public int getCustomerId() { return customerId; }
    public String getFirstName() { return firstName; }
    public String getLastName() { return lastName; }
    public String getFullName() { return fullName; }
    public String getAge() { return age; }
    public String getSalesAmount() { return salesAmount; }

    public void setCustomerId( int customerId )
    {
        this.customerId = customerId;
    }
    public void setFirstName( String firstName )
    {
        this.firstName = firstName;
    }
    public void setLastName( String lastName ) { this.lastName = lastName; }
    public void setFullName()
    {
        fullName = firstName + " " + lastName;
    }
    public void setAge( String age ) { this.age = age; }
    public void setSalesAmount( String salesAmount )
    {
        this.salesAmount = salesAmount;
    }

    public void reset(ActionMapping mapping, HttpServletRequest request)
    {
        firstName = "";
        lastName = "";
        fullName = "";
        age = "";
        salesAmount = "";
    }
```

```java
    public ActionErrors validate( ActionMapping mapping,
                                  HttpServletRequest request)
    {
        ActionErrors errors = null;

        if ( firstName == null || firstName.trim().equals("") )
        {
            if ( errors == null ) errors = new ActionErrors();
            errors.add("firstName", new ActionMessage("firstNameError"));
        }
        if ( lastName == null || lastName.trim().equals("") )
        {
            if ( errors == null ) errors = new ActionErrors();
            errors.add("lastName", new ActionMessage("lastNameError"));
        }
        if ( age == null || age.trim().equals("") ||
             Integer.valueOf(age) == 0 )
        {
            if ( errors == null ) errors = new ActionErrors();
            errors.add("age", new ActionMessage("ageError"));
        }
        if ( salesAmount == null || salesAmount.trim().equals("") ||
             Double.valueOf(salesAmount) == 0 )
        {
            if ( errors == null ) errors = new ActionErrors();
            errors.add("salesAmount", new ActionMessage("salesAmountError"));
        }
        request.setAttribute("mode", "input");

        return errors;
    }
}
// ------------ End: CustomerInfoActionForm.java ----------------------

# -------------------- Begin: ErrorMessage.properties -----------------
firstNameError=First name cannot be empty<br>
lastNameError=Last name cannot be empty<br>
ageError=Age cannot be empty or 0<br>
salesAmountError=Sales amount cannot be empty or 0<br>
# -------------------- End: ErrorMessage.properties --------------------
```

CustomerDBProcess.java (relevant part only):

```java
// ------------ Begin: CustomerDBProcess.java ----------------------
package salesdept;
```

```java
import java.util.List;
import java.util.ArrayList;
import java.sql.*;

public class CustomerDBProcess
{
    ...

    // Get max customer_id from customer table
    public int getMaxCustomerId() throws SQLException
    {
        rs = statement.executeQuery("select max(customer_id) from customer");

        while (rs.next())
        {
            return rs.getInt("max(customer_id)");
        }
        return 0;
    }

    // Insert a customer record
    public void addCustomer(CustomerDBObject cust) throws SQLException
    {
        String sqlInsertCustomer
          = "insert into customer (customer_id, first_name, last_name, age, sales_amount)";
     sqlInsertCustomer += "values (" + cust.getCustomerId() + ",'" +
                                cust.getFirstName() + "','" + cust.getLastName()+ "'," +
                                cust.getAge() + "," + cust.getSalesAmount() + ")";

        statement.executeUpdate(sqlInsertCustomer);
    }
}
// ------------ End: CustomerDBProcess.java ----------------------

// ------------ Begin: InputCustomerAction .java ----------------------
package salesdept;

import java.io.*;
import java.util.List;
import java.util.ArrayList;
import java.sql.*;

import javax.servlet.*;
import javax.servlet.http.*;
```

```java
import org.apache.struts.action.*;

public class InputCustomerAction  extends Action
{
    public ActionForward execute ( ActionMapping mapping,
                                    ActionForm actionForm,
                                    HttpServletRequest request,
                                    HttpServletResponse response )
    throws ClassNotFoundException, InstantiationException, IllegalAccessException, SQLException
    {
        CustomerInfoActionForm form = (CustomerInfoActionForm)actionForm;

        CustomerDBProcess custDBProcess = new CustomerDBProcess();

        int maxCustId = custDBProcess.getMaxCustomerId();

        form.setCustomerId(maxCustId+1);

        request.setAttribute("mode", "input");

        return mapping.findForward("success");
    }
}
// ------------ End: InputCustomerAction .java ----------------------

// ------------ Begin: InsertCustomerAction .java ----------------------
package salesdept;

import java.io.*;
import java.util.List;
import java.util.ArrayList;
import java.sql.*;

import javax.servlet.*;
import javax.servlet.http.*;
import org.apache.struts.action.*;

public class InsertCustomerAction  extends Action
{
    public ActionForward execute ( ActionMapping mapping,
                                    ActionForm actionForm,
                                    HttpServletRequest request,
                                    HttpServletResponse response )
    throws ClassNotFoundException, InstantiationException, IllegalAccessException, SQLException
    {
        CustomerInfoActionForm form = (CustomerInfoActionForm)actionForm;
```

```java
        CustomerDBProcess custDBProcess = new CustomerDBProcess();

        CustomerDBObject custDBObj = new CustomerDBObject();

        custDBObj.setCustomerId(form.getCustomerId());
        custDBObj.setFirstName(form.getFirstName());
        custDBObj.setLastName(form.getLastName());
        custDBObj.setAge(Integer.parseInt(form.getAge()));
        custDBObj.setSalesAmount(Double.parseDouble(form.getSalesAmount()));

        custDBProcess.addCustomer(custDBObj);

        request.setAttribute("mode", "displayonly");

        return mapping.findForward("success");
    }
}
// ------------ End: InsertCustomerAction .java ---------------------
```

```jsp
-------------------------------------------------------------------------------------------
<!-- Begin: CustomerInfo.jsp -->
<%@ taglib uri="/WEB-INF/tlds/struts-bean.tld" prefix="bean" %>
<%@ taglib uri="/WEB-INF/tlds/struts-html.tld" prefix="html" %>
<%@ taglib uri="/WEB-INF/tlds/struts-logic.tld" prefix="logic" %>

<HTML>
    <HEAD>
        <LINK REL="stylesheet"TYPE="text/css" HREF="../styles/styles.css/>
    </HEAD>
    <BODY>
        <logic:equal name="mode" value="input">
            <FONT COLOR=red><html:errors/></FONT>
            <html:form action="/insertcustomer.do">
                <TABLE>
                    <TR CLASS="defaultText">
                        <TD>Customer ID:</TD>
                        <TD>
                            <html:text property="customerId"
                                       size="16" readonly="true"/>
                        </TD>
                        <TD> </TD>
                        <TD> </TD>
                    </TR>
```

```
            <TR CLASS="defaultText">
                <TD>First Name:</TD>
                <TD><html:text property="firstName" size="16"/></TD>
                <TD>Last Name:</TD>
                <TD><html:text property="lastName" size="16"/></TD>
            </TR>
            <TR CLASS="defaultText">
                <TD>Age:</TD>
                <TD><html:text property="age" size="16"/></TD>
                <TD>Sales Amount ($):</TD>
                <TD>
                        <html:text property="salesAmount" size="16"/>
                </TD>
            </TR>
            <TR>
                <TD COLSPAN=2 ALIGN="center"><html:submit/></TD>
            </TR>
        </TABLE>
    </html:form>
</logic:equal>

<logic:equal name="mode" value="displayonly">
    <SPAN CLASS="defaultText">A new customer was successfully created, with the
                        following data:<BR><BR>
    </SPAN>
    <TABLE>
        <TR CLASS="defaultText">
            <TD>Customer ID:</TD>
            <TD>
                <bean:write name="CustomerInfoForm" property="customerId"/>
            </TD>
            <TD> </TD>
            <TD> </TD>
        </TR>
        <TR CLASS="defaultText">
            <TD>First Name:</TD>
            <TD><bean:write name="CustomerInfoForm" property="firstName"/></TD>
            <TD>Last Name:</TD>
            <TD><bean:write name="CustomerInfoForm" property="lastName"/></TD>
    </TR>
    <TR CLASS="defaultText">
    <TD>Age:</TD>
        <TD><bean:write name="CustomerInfoForm" property="age"/></TD>
        <TD>Sales Amount:</TD>
        <TD>$<bean:write name="CustomerInfoForm" property="salesAmount"/></TD>
```

```
        </TR>
      </TABLE>
      <SPAN CLASS="defaultText"><BR>
        <A HREF="inputcustomer.do">Input next customer</A><BR><BR>
        <A HREF="customerlist.do">View customer list</A>
      </SPAN>
    </logic:equal>
  </BODY>
</HTML>
<!-- End: CustomerInfo.jsp -->
```

9.8 Summary

In this chapter, we learned how to use Struts MVC framework classes to streamline our JSP development process. We verified that we could redo our previous exercises using Struts. The use of Struts can make code maintenance more organized, especially if your application size is medium to large, with several JSPs.

9.9 Chapter Quiz

1. Which of the following is true? (Select all that apply).

    i. The *.do URL pattern is mapped in web.xml.

    ii. Each .do URL in your application must be defined in the Struts Config file.

    iii. The use of Action and ActionForm for a .do URL is optional. You can have a .do action mapping with neither name (ActionForm) nor type (Action) attribute.

    iv. In an action mapping, if the validate attribute is true, you must include an input attribute.

    a. All of the above

    b. (i), (ii), and (iii) only

    c. (ii), (iii), and (iv) only

    d. (i), (ii), and (iv) only

2. Which of the following is true? (Select all that apply).

    i. The validate() method in the ActionForm class can be used to put validation logic when the form is submitted.

    ii. Properties files contain properties of ActionForm objects.

    iii. A resource bundle is an object that can get messages and labels in an appropriate language, based on the user's locale.

    iv. The ActionForm subclass that you create must contain only attributes that have a corresponding INPUT field on the HTML form.

    a. All of the above

    b. (i), (ii), and (iii) only

    c. (i) and (iii) only

    d. (i), (iii), and (iv) only

3. The ActionForm object associated with a .do action mapping in struts-config.xml can be known by looking at which attribute of the <action> element?

    a. path attribute

    b. name attribute

    c. type attribute

    d. input attribute

4. The Action object associated with a .do action mapping in struts-config.xml can be known by looking at which attribute of the <action> element?

    a. path attribute

    b. name attribute

    c. type attribute

    d. input attribute

5. When the user enters a .do URL on the Web browser, Struts looks for which attribute of <action> elements in struts-config.xml to see if there is a match with what the user requested?

    a. path attribute

    b. name attribute

    c. type attribute

    d. input attribute

6. The URL that will be opened when validate fails on the ActionForm object is given by which attribute of the <action> element?

    a. path attribute

    b. name attribute

c. `type attribute`

d. `input attribute`

7. Say that you have `inputcustomer.do` action mapping in your `struts-config.xml`, with an `ActionForm` and `Action` class associated with it, as shown here:

```
----------------------------------------------------------------------

    <form-beans>

        <form-bean name="CustomerInfoForm" type="salesdept.CustomerInfoActionForm" />

    </form-beans>

    <action-mappings>

        <action path="/inputcustomer"

                name="CustomerInfoForm"

                type="salesdept.InputCustomerAction"

                <forward name="success" path="/CustomerInfo.jsp" />

        </action>

    </action-mappings>

----------------------------------------------------------------------
```

When the user requests this resource, which of the following sequence of calls is correct?

a. The JSP is evaluated first, and based on the Struts tags in it, the `CustomerInfoActionForm` object is instantiated and then `InputCustomerAction` class's `execute()` method is called.

b. The `CustomerInfoActionForm` object is instantiated first, then the `execute()` method of the `InputCustomerAction` class is called, and finally the `ActionForward` returned by it is used to decide which JSP (or other .do action) to invoke.

c. The `execute()` method of the `InputCustomerAction` class is called first, then the `Action-Form` object is instantiated, and finally the JSP is rendered.

d. None of the above.

9.10 Answers to Quiz

1. The correct answer is (a). All statements are true.

2. The correct answer is (c). Option (ii) is false because properties files contain key-value pairs representing messages and labels to be displayed to the user. Option (iv) is false because `ActionForm` objects can contain attributes other than those that map to INPUT fields on the HTML form.

3. The correct answer is (b).

4. The correct answer is (c).

5. The correct answer is (a).

6. The correct answer is (d).

7. The correct answer is (b).

9.11 Unsolved Assignments

Assignment 9.1

Objective: **To learn how to develop a Struts-based application for updating data in a MySQL database.**

Steps:

- Redo the customer list example in Section 9.7, but this time, add a new hyperlink called Edit at the end of each customer row. It should look like this:

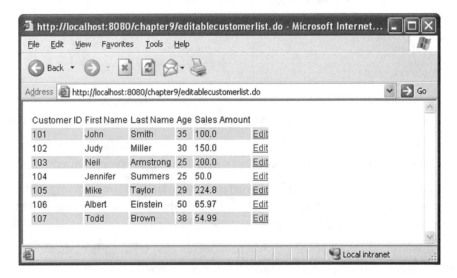

- When users click on the Edit link, it should open a new action editcustomer.do that has a new Action class called EditCustomerAction and a new JSP called EditCustomer.jsp associated with it. Reuse the old DisplayCustomerListAction and CustomerInfoActionForm classes—which means there is no need to rewrite them. Also, reuse the old CustomerDBProcess class but add new public methods to it, with the following signatures:

```
void updateCustomer(CustomerDBObject cust)
CustomerDBObject getCustomer(int custId)
```

- Write a new JSP called EditableCustomerList.jsp that shows the customer list with the new Edit hyperlinks. The action for each hyperlink should be the new action mapping editcustomer.do, passing it the param of customer_id. *Hint:* Use the <html:link> element. For the exact attributes of this element, you may want to look at the Struts API link in Appendix D (the HTML Taglib Guide in particular).

- The EditCustomerAction class should take the customer id sent as a parameter via the <html:link> element, call the getCustomer() method of CustomerDBProcess class, and copy fields one-by-one to the form. It should then display EditCustomer.jsp with the fields populated for the selected customer. (The customer id field should show the value but remain read-only as before.) When the user makes changes to one or more fields and hits the Submit button, it should go to a new action, updatecustomer.do with UpdateCustomerAction class that calls the updateCustomer() method of CustomerDBProcess class, updates the appropriate customer record in the database, and then takes the user back to the editable customer list screen. (The screen should now show the modified values for the customer just edited.)

- Note: No Java allowed in any JSP—use Struts tags as required.

- For the exact syntax of the SQL update statement, please refer to the MySQL documentation URL listed in Appendix D.

- Submit the modified struts-config.xml, CustomerDBProcess.java, EditableCustomerList.jsp, EditCustomerAction.java, EditCustomer.jsp, and UpdateCustomerAction.java.

- The following URL needs to be used to test the assignment:

  http://localhost:8080/chapter9/editablecustomerlist.do

A sample interaction is shown next.

The list of customers shows up with the Edit link in front of each. Click on the link for the customer you wish to edit:

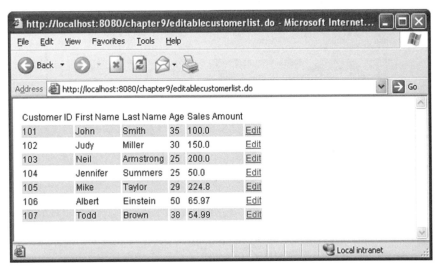

The following page displays current data for that customer:

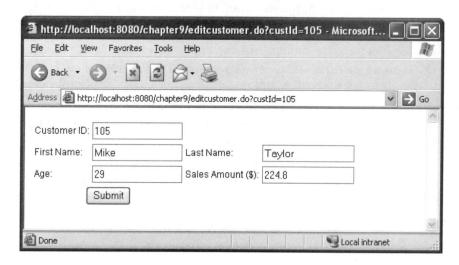

Enter new values in one or more fields, and hit the Submit button:

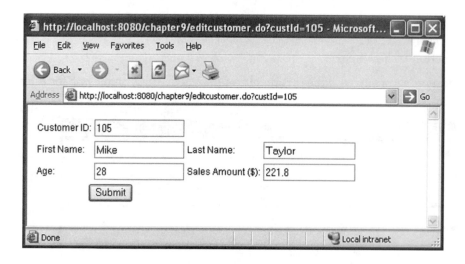

This will take the user to the editable customer list, showing the modified values for the customer just edited:

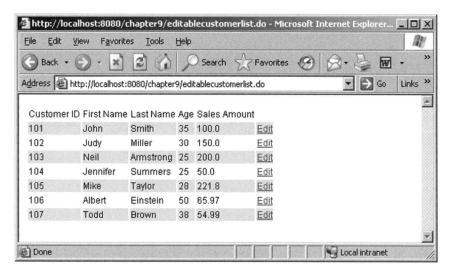

APPENDIX A

Installing the JDK

The instructions below are for downloading and installing the J2SE(=JDK) 6 version, which was the latest available as of writing this book. The exact filenames are specific to that version of JDK. You can consider a more current version, in which case you need to replace "JDK 6" with the exact version you use.

1. Create a new folder called JDK under the C: drive.

2. Open the following URL:

   ```
   http://java.sun.com/javase/downloads/index.jsp
   ```

3. Click on the "Download" link under "JDK 6." It will show the following page:

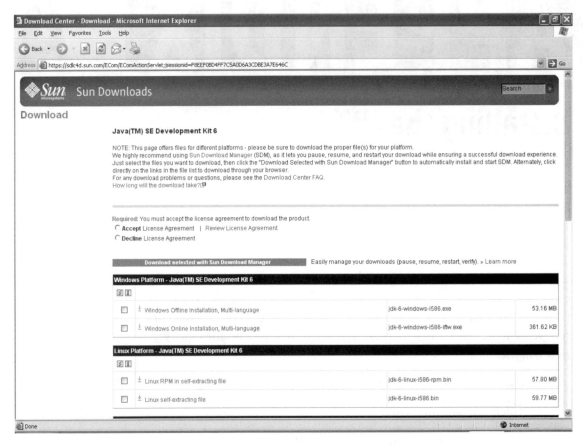

4. Click on the Accept radio button. Then click on the link that says "Windows Offline Installation, Multi-language" on the left of jdk-6-windows-i586.exe, under the section "Windows Platform - Java(TM) SE Development Kit 6."

5. A window will pop up, asking if you want to Run, Save, or Cancel. Click Save, specify any folder to save the file, and click OK. (It will take a few minutes to save the file.)

6.   Once it is done saving, double-click the saved .exe file in Windows Explorer. It will ask you to Run or Cancel; choose Run. It will then ask you to either Accept or Decline the terms of the license agreement:

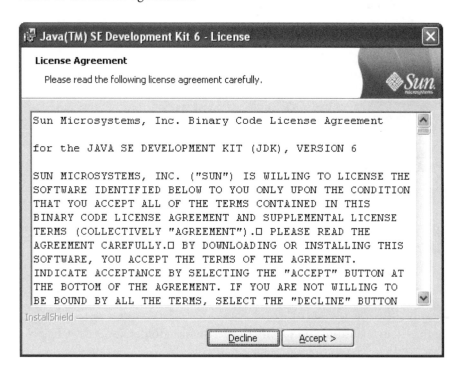

7.   Click Accept. It will display the following window:

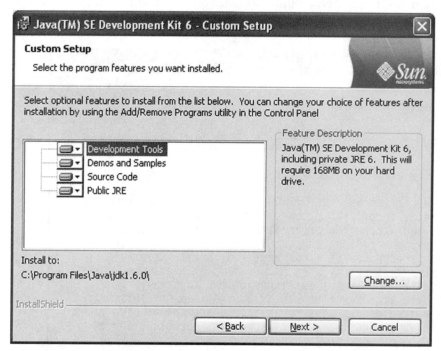

8.   Click on the Change button, and specify the destination folder as C:\JDK. Click Next.

9. This will install the JDK on your machine. (This will take a few minutes.) During the install, it will pop up another window:

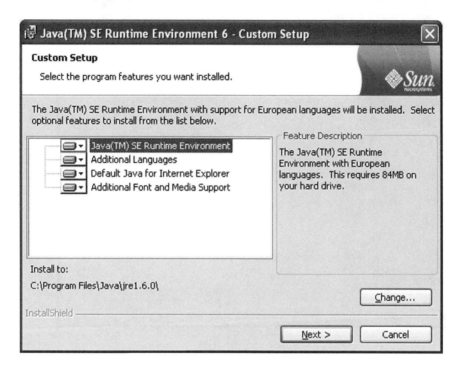

10. Click Next. After a few moments, the installation will be complete:

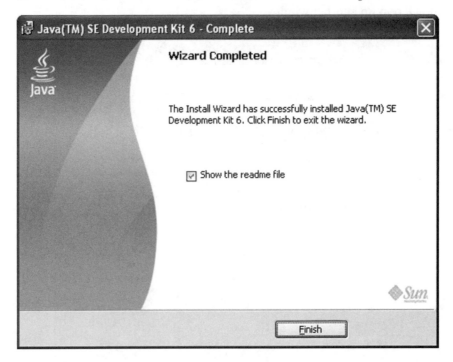

APPENDIX B

Setting Environment Variables

B.1 Compiling and Running Java Programs

After installing the JDK, the next logical step is to run a sample Java program on your computer. The sample program you will be running is called HelloWorld. This program prints out the words "Hello, World!" on your computer's screen every time you run it.

Recall that a program consists of multiple instructions that need to follow certain rules (syntax) in order to work properly. Before you can "run" a program, you need to first make sure your instructions follow certain rules or syntax. Checking the syntax in a program is technically called *compiling* a program. The JDK that you just downloaded has a specific file that can check the syntax for you. This file is javac.exe that you will find under your C:\JDK\bin folder. Files with an .exe extension are called *executable files.* An executable file is in a "ready-to-run" condition. That is why it is called "executable"—all you need to do is supply it with certain input that it expects, and it will produce the output it is designed to generate. Specifying an executable file's extension (.exe) is optional; so you can simply say javac instead of javac.exe.

Before you can run a program, you need to compile it—i.e., check for any syntax errors. The javac.exe file under C:\JDK\bin has been provided by Sun to look for syntax errors in Java program files whose names you supply as input, and to generate a list of syntax errors, if any. If no errors are found, the javac command will not say so, nor will it show any errors. (That is the desired state, which means you can go ahead and execute the program using the java command.)

If javac does find errors, it will display the line numbers along with a brief description of the error. You need to then go back to the program file, correct the errors, save the file, and then try to compile it again. You repeat this until there are no compile errors shown. A successful compile (no errors) creates a new file with the same name as the source file but with an extension of .class in that folder. So compiling HelloWorld.java should produce a file called HelloWorld.class in the same folder. The .class file is then used to execute (run) the program. For running the program, Sun provides another executable file called java.exe that you will find in your C:\JDK\bin folder.

Executable programs (such as javac.exe and java.exe) are run at a "command prompt." What does a command prompt look like? To see it in action, click on Start->All Programs->Accessories->Command Prompt. It should look like this:

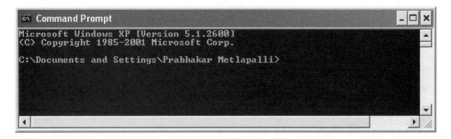

Note that the name will be replaced with your name and that the default directory will be shown as C:\Documents and Settings\<user_name>.

The command prompt window will be a frequently used tool throughout this book, so make sure you feel comfortable using it before proceeding further.

You will create the source file in C:\JSP\Chapter1. By default, the javac.exe compiler expects the source file (.java) to reside in the current folder (i.e., the one from which you issue the javac command). So for compiling the HelloWorld.java program file sitting in C:\JSP\Chapter1, you need to first point to C:\JSP\Chapter1. For this, open a command prompt window and make it point to the C:\JSP\Chapter1 folder using the cd (change directory) command. The command prompt session will look like this:

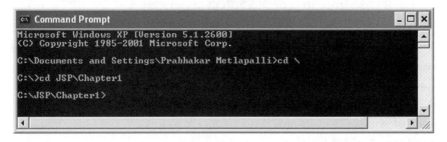

The javac.exe and java.exe executable commands can then be run from this folder, for compiling and running the HelloWorld program.

B.2   The PATH Environment Variable

Note that you would be compiling the HelloWorld program from the C:\JSP\Chapter1 folder, but the javac.exe file sits in a different folder (C:\JDK\bin). You cannot directly type in the javac.exe command from the C:\JSP\Chapter1 folder, because the computer does not know that it needs to look for the javac.exe file in the C:\JDK\bin folder, unless you tell it so. Whenever you issue an executable command (such as javac.exe and java.exe), the computer looks for that executable file in a predefined list of folder names. This list of folders is stored in a special variable ("environment variable") called PATH.

Every computer has an environment variable called PATH that is already configured to contain a list of one or more folder names (with paths). A variable is something that can store different data; its data value can change with time (hence it is called "variable"). A variable needs to have a name so that you can identify or refer to that variable later. In sum, a variable has a name and a value; the value can change with time. Variables such as PATH are called "environment variables." These are recognized in the entire computer and so are available for every program that you run. In addition, their values do not depend on what folder you are pointing to.

The exact value with which your computer's PATH is preconfigured depends on what programs are already installed on it. (Many programs change the PATH during the installation process.) For example, your computer may already have the PATH set to a value of C:\WINDOWS;C:\WINDOWS\COMMAND. Observe how the value of PATH consists of two folder names (actually two folder paths): C:\WINDOWS, and C:\WINDOWS\COMMAND separated by a semi-colon (;).

There is a convenient command called the ECHO command that you can use to find out what your computer's PATH already contains. To issue this command, you need to open a command prompt window. (It does not matter what folder it is pointing to; remember that environment variables are available everywhere on your computer.) Type in: ECHO %PATH% and hit Enter. Your command prompt session may look like this (assuming you are pointing to C:\WINDOWS):

```
C:\WINDOWS>ECHO %PATH% (press Enter key)
```

Here you are asking the value of the environment variable called PATH to be displayed. Note that the % signs before and after the variable name mean that you want the value of the PATH variable to be displayed, not just the word PATH by itself. When you press the Enter key, it displays the output of the ECHO command—namely, the value of the PATH variable you requested. So your command prompt session may look like this:

```
C:\WINDOWS>ECHO %PATH% (press Enter key)
```

`C:\WINDOWS;C:\WINDOWS\COMMAND`

Notice how the value of PATH is displayed on the next line (the line below the one where you typed in the command). Also observe how individual folder paths are separated by semicolons.

Since your .exe files (javac.exe and java.exe) reside under C:\JDK\BIN, which will not be part of your current PATH, you need to change the PATH so that it contains C:\JDK\BIN as well. That way next time you say javac or java, it knows to look into C:\JDK\BIN as well. To change or set values of environment variables on your computer, you need to use either of the following:

- The SET command (temporary set—valid only for that command session).
- The Control Panel (permanent set—valid in any command session; it remains valid unless you manually change it again via Control Panel).

I recommend that the value of PATH be changed permanently (it can be done so that it will not adversely affect other programs you may have installed on your machine and use the same PATH. Simply add the new folder name at the end of the current PATH, so that it is last in precedence.)

B.2.1   Setting the PATH temporarily

Let's begin by setting PATH temporarily to understand how it works. You can either set the PATH to contain C:\JDK\BIN, or add to the current value of PATH (if you want to use the value of the current PATH). Both approaches would work for this book. For a temporary set, it does not really matter; but for a permanent set, adding to PATH is the preferred approach, so that other programs will not be affected. I describe both approaches to show the concept.

To set PATH to C:\JDK\BIN, simply type in

`SET PATH=C:\JDK\BIN (hit Enter)`

(*Note:* In the SET command, no spaces are allowed before or after the equal sign, semicolon, back-slash, and percent signs.) Note also that you need to press the Enter key after the end of every command; so I will not mention this henceforth and it will be implied that you need to do this.

Your command session will look like this:

Note that it does NOT matter which folder you are pointing to. Here you are pointing to the C:\WIN-DOWS folder, but you could as well be pointing to any other folder, and set the environment variable—with the same result. Environment variables are not per folder, but per command session (temporary set) or multiple command sessions (permanent set, which will be described in just a moment).

Instead of setting PATH to contain only C:\JDK\BIN, if you want to add C:\JDK\BIN to your current PATH, type in

SET PATH=C:\JDK\BIN;%PATH%

The command session would look like this:

Here, %PATH% means the existing value of PATH, and you are saying that the new value of PATH should be C:\JDK\BIN followed by whatever is contained in the current (existing) PATH variable. So if your current PATH contains, say, C:\WINDOWS;C:\WINDOWS\COMMAND, you are saying it should now contain C:\JDK\BIN;C:\WINDOWS;C:\WINDOWS\COMMAND. Note that a semicolon is used to separate folder paths in the list.

To confirm that it did make the change, issue an ECHO %PATH% command again. It should display the new value with C:\JDK\BIN in it, and your command session should look like the following window.

Note that this sets the new value only on a temporary basis; the new value is lost the moment you close the command window (and goes back to the old value after that). You want the new value to remain permanent, so that you do not have to type in the SET command every time you open a command window. This option is discussed next.

B.2.2 Setting the PATH Permanently

- If you are using Windows 95/98, do the following:

  - Open C:\Autoexec.bat in Notepad, then type in the following line at its end:

    SET PATH=C:\JDK\BIN

  - Or, if you want to retain the current PATH, type in

    SET PATH=C:\JDK\BIN;%PATH%

  - Save the file, and restart your machine.

- If you are using Windows NT/2000/XP, do the following:

  - Open Control Panel ->System, ->Environment tab (Win NT), or Advanced tab (Win XP) and choose Environment Variables, then look for PATH in the System Variables, and change it to add C:\JDK\BIN; in the beginning. So if it is currently showing a value as

    C:\WINDOWS;C:\WINDOWS\COMMAND

    add C:\JDK\BIN; at the beginning so it shows a value as

    C:\JDK\BIN;C:\WINDOWS;C:\WINDOWS\COMMAND

  - Open a new command prompt window and issue an ECHO %PATH% command to confirm that it did add C:\JDK\BIN in it.

B.3   The CLASSPATH Environment Variable

When running HelloWorld, what should you do if you get an error such as the following?

```
Exception in thread "main" java.lang.NoClassDefFoundError: HelloWorld
```

The error states that Java is unable to locate the HelloWorld.class file (which it needs to execute the HelloWorld program). To fix it, you need to specify the list of folders Java needs to look into, for any .class files required to run a program. There are two ways to do this:

- Use a "-classpath <list_of_folder_paths>" option in your java command, where <list_of_folder_paths> needs to be replaced with a list of one or more folder paths where you want Java to look for any required .class files. As usual, folder paths in the list need to be separated by semicolons. This needs to be done every time you use the java command, each time providing the appropriate list of folder paths containing the required .class files.

- Define an environment variable called CLASSPATH (or modify its value if it is already defined), so that it contains the full path of the folder that contains the HelloWorld.class file. This is a one-time change; Java is preconfigured to look in the CLASSPATH environment variable for .class files, whenever an explicit –classpath option is not used in the java command. Using –classpath temporarily overrides the value of CLASSPATH; in other words, the list of folders specified after –classpath would be used (if available), instead of the ones in the CLASSPATH environment variable.

B.3.1   Use of –classpath

Using –classpath <list_of_folder_paths> in your java command, you can specify the list of folders that you want Java to look into for any .class files required to run the program.

As an example, let's say you want Java to look into your current folder (from where you issue the java command) for .class files (HelloWorld.class) when running the HelloWorld program. The current folder is represented by a period (.). So your session would look like this:

Here's another example: Say that you want Java to look in C:\Temp for .class files, in addition to the current folder (first to look in the current folder, if not found there, then to look in C:\Temp). In this case, your session would look like this:

```
C:\JSP\Chapter1>java -classpath .;C;\Temp HelloWorld
Hello, World!

C:\JSP\Chapter1>_
```

If you do not use an explicit -classpath option, it would depend solely on whether (and how) an environment variable called CLASSPATH is defined on your machine.

B.3.2 Use of the CLASSPATH Environment Variable

CLASSPATH is an environment variable that contains a list of one or more folder names that contain necessary .class files. By default, Java is preconfigured to use the CLASSPATH environment variable (if defined) to figure out where to look for .class files when running Java programs. Issue an ECHO %CLASSPATH% command from a command window to see what it contains (if already defined). For this, open a command prompt window and use an ECHO command as follows (the % signs before and after the CLASSPATH mean that you want its value, not the word CLASSPATH, to be displayed).

C:\>ECHO %CLASSPATH%

Again, it does not matter which folder you are pointing to. (You could be pointing to C:\WINDOWS, or any other folder, instead of C:\.)

If it shows a message such as: ECHO is On (which is the default message if the value is undefined), or simply %CLASSPATH%, it means CLASSPATH is undefined on your machine.

If it is defined, it would show the contents of the CLASSPATH variable, as shown here:

```
C:\>ECHO %CLASSPATH%
C:\WINDOWS;C:\TEMP

C:\>
```

There are three subcases here. For the HelloWorld exercise, you do not need to make any change if subcase (I) or (II) applies to you.

(I)   If CLASSPATH is undefined on your machine and you do not use an explicit -classpath option, java.exe is preconfigured to look into the current folder. In the HelloWorld exercise, we assume that you run the program from the same folder that contains the HelloWorld.class file, so you do not need to either use a -classpath option or to set the CLASSPATH to contain the period (current folder) if CLASSPATH is undefined.

(II) If CLASSPATH is already defined on your machine (before this book) and *does* include the period (.) in it, you would be fine running the command without using the -classpath option or modifying the CLASSPATH. In this case, the ECHO %CLASSPATH% command may look something like this:

Observe that you do have a period (.) in this case, so this would be fine and you can run the java command without a -classpath option and without modifying the CLASSPATH. In either case (I) or (II), you use the java command supplying only the filename:

```
C:\JSP\Chapter1>java HelloWorld
Hello, World!
C:\JSP\Chapter1>_
```

(III) If CLASSPATH is already defined on your machine (before this book) and does *not* include the period (.) in it, java.exe uses that CLASSPATH implicitly if you do not use an explicit -classpath option in your java command. So in that case, it would never look into the current folder but would look only in the folders specified in the current CLASSPATH variable. This would result in an exception error message similar to the one shown at the beginning of Section B.3 because Java cannot find the required .class file using the list of folders in CLASSPATH.

The ECHO %CLASSPATH% command may thus look like this:

```
Command Prompt                                           _ □ ×
C:\WINDOWS>ECHO %CLASSPATH%
C:\WINDOWS;C:\TEMP

C:\WINDOWS>_
```

Observe that you do not have a period (.) in the CLASSPATH.

In this case, you have two options:

- If you want to leave your CLASSPATH as is, use the explicit -classpath option every time in the java command as explained in Section B.3.1 (that always overrides whatever is contained in CLASSPATH).

- Change the CLASSPATH variable either permanently (recommended) or temporarily, to include the period (.) in it. The period (.) represents the current folder (from where you are running the java command). Again, like the PATH environment variable, you can either change it temporarily using the SET command (valid for that command session only), or make it a permanent change using the Control Panel (valid in any command session, until you change it again via the Control Panel). To change CLASSPATH, follow the instructions similar to setting the PATH variable. So for a temporary change, it may look like this:

SET CLASSPATH=.;%CLASSPATH%

This means you are asking the period (.) to come in front (to take highest precedence), before the ones already defined in the current CLASSPATH. The command session is shown here:

```
Command Prompt                                           _ □ ×
C:\WINDOWS>SET CLASSPATH=.;%CLASSPATH%

C:\WINDOWS>_
```

For a permanent change, open Control Panel->System->Advanced->Environment Variables, look for any CLASSPATH environment variable; if found, click the Edit button, and add a period and a semicolon (.;) in front of it, as shown here:

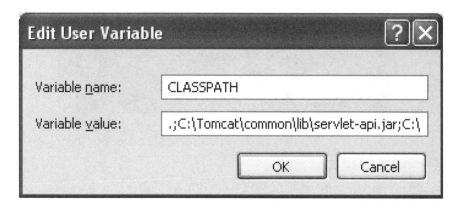

Click OK to make the change.

If no CLASSPATH environment variable is found, create one by clicking on the New button, and set its value to ".." as shown here:

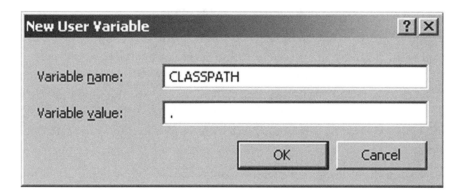

After this change, open a new command prompt window, and use the java command supplying only the filename, as in case (I) or (II):

Or you could even combine both the −classpath and CLASSPATH, as shown in the following window.

```
Command Prompt                                          _ □ ×

C:\JSP\Chapter1>java -classpath %CLASSPATH% HelloWorld
Hello, World!

C:\JSP\Chapter1>_
```

B.3.3 CLASSPATH versus PATH

The CLASSPATH variable is *not* the same as PATH. PATH tells your computer where to look for .exe files when you issue specific commands at the DOS prompt, whereas CLASSPATH tells it where to look for .class files (the ones that get created when you compile a .java file). The procedure described previously for setting the PATH variable temporarily or permanently applies for setting the CLASSPATH variable as well (in fact this applies for setting any environment variable).

B.3.4 CLASSPATH in javac Versus CLASSPATH in java command

You can use an explicit -classpath option in either the javac or the java command, but in each case it would have a different meaning. If you use it in the javac command, it would mean that Java should look for *other* .class files in the list of folders specified after -classpath, as necessary. For example, if your Test.java file refers to another class called Sample in its code, and if the Sample.class file exists in a folder other than the folder that is intended to hold Test.class, then you need to specify the file path of Sample.class explicitly in the javac command using the -classpath option when compiling Test.java.

When running a program using java, the -classpath option would indicate the list of folders that Java should look for—the .class files needed to run your Java program (such as Test.class).

APPENDIX C

Operator-Precedence Table

For easy reference, the precedence levels of various operators in Java are presented in the following table. Do NOT attempt to memorize these. All the possible operators are listed here only as a reference. The text will discuss only those that are the most important.

The operators in each group (or row) have the same precedence level; if multiple operators of the same group are present in an expression, values are evaluated according to the associativity mentioned for that group. The groups appearing in the beginning have a higher precedence than the ones following them; higher precedence implies that the group will be evaluated before groups with a lower precedence.

Operator Precedence Group	Associativity
(), [], ., postfix ++, postfix −	left
unary +, unary -, prefix ++, prefix −	right
(type), new	left
*, /, %	left
+, -	left
<<, >>, >>>	left
<, <=, >, >=,instanceof	left
==, !=	left
&	left
^	left
|	left
&&	left
||	left
?:	left
=, +=, -=, *=,/=, %=, <<=, >>=, >>>=, &=, |=, ^=	right

APPENDIX D

Book Support Site and API Documentation Links

1. Book Support Site (also includes online Java refresher courses):

   http://javaonline.org

   Click on "JSP Book Support" link.

2. HTML/CSS API:

   http://www.htmlref.com

   Related link (for hexadecimal color combinations):

   http://www.yvg.com/twrs/RGBConverter.html

3. JDK/J2SE API:

   http://java.sun.com/javase/reference/api.jsp

   Click on the link under "Core API Docs" for the JDK version you installed.

   In this book, JDK 6 was used and the corresponding API link is as follows:

   http://java.sun.com/javase/6/docs/api/

4. J2EE API:

   http://java.sun.com/javaee/reference/

   Then click on the link that says "Java EE 5 SDK API Specifications" (or whatever latest Java EE version it shows under "API Specifications").

5. Servlet/JSP API:

    `http://tomcat.apache.org`

    Click on "Tomcat 5.5" link under Documentation

    Click on "JSP API Javadocs" or "Servlet API Javadocs" (as required) under the Reference section, or on "Jasper Javadocs" under the section titled "Apache Tomcat Developers."

6. MySQL Reference:

    `http://dev.mysql.com/doc/`

    Click on the "View" link under the "HTML Online" header in the "MySQL Reference Manual" section, and then on "SQL Statement Syntax" on the right.

7. Struts API:

    `http://struts.apache.org`

    Click on the link under Documentation for the Struts version you downloaded.

    For Struts 1.3.5 that was used in this book, the following URL gives details of the API specification:

    `http://struts.apache.org/1.3.5/apidocs/index.html`

APPENDIX E

Installing WinZip

Open the following URL:

`http://www.winzip.com/ddchomea.htm`

Download the free trial and follow the instructions to install.

Since it is free for a limited time, I recommend that you also download the following at this time (each of which requires use of WinZip):

- Tomcat (instructions in Appendix F)
- MySQL (instructions in Appendix G)
- MySQL JDBC driver (instructions in Appendix H)
- Struts (instructions in Appendix I)

APPENDIX F

Installing Tomcat

Note: This book uses Tomcat version 5.5.20, so the instructions that follow apply to that version. You can consider a more current version in which case you need to replace 5.5.20 with the exact version you use. For any reason, if things do not work out with a more current version, you can always fall back on this specific version that has been verified to work.

1. Open the following URL:

   `http://tomcat.apache.org/`

2. Click on "Tomcat 5.x" under the Download section on the left. Click on the hyper-link "zip" under Binary Distributions/Core under the latest release. It will ask you to open or save, choose Save and save to any folder.

3. Once it is done saving, double-click this zip file, select all files, right-click and choose extract and select the destination as the C: drive. It will extract all files onto a folder called 'apache-tomcat-5.5.20' directly under your C: drive. Rename this folder Tomcat (so you now have C:\Tomcat).

4. To configure Tomcat, you need to first define an environment variable called JAVA_HOME with a value of C:\JDK (replace C:\JDK with the exact folder/directory where you installed the JDK). Go ahead and define a new environment variable JAVA_HOME with this value. Setting environment variables PATH and CLASSPATH is explained in Appendix B. You now need to create a new environment variable called JAVA_HOME with value C:\JDK.

APPENDIX G

Installing and Using MySQL

G.1 Installing MySQL

Note: This book uses MySQL version 5.0.27, so the instructions that follow apply to that version. You can consider a more current version in which case you need to replace 5.0.27 with the exact version you use. For any reason, if things do not work out with a more current version, you can always fall back on this specific version that has been verified to work.

1. Go to the MySQL download site:

    `http://dev.mysql.com/downloads/`

    Click on the Download link under "MySQL Community Server." At the time of writing this book, it showed MySQL 5.0 Community Server as the Generally Available (GA) Release.

2. Go to the "Windows downloads" section and click on "Download" in front of "Without installer (unzip in C:\)." It will pop up a window that asks you if you want to Open or Save. Choose Save, and save the file to any folder.

    Once it is done saving, open the zip file in WinZip, select all files, and right click and choose Extract and specify the destination as C:\. This step created a new folder called `mysql-5.0.27-win32` under the C: drive. Rename the `mysql-5.0.27-win32` folder to `MySQL` (so you now have C:\MySQL).

3. Create a file called my.ini under the Windows Root directory. To find this directory on your machine, open a command prompt window and type: echo %WINDIR%. It will show you something like C:\WINDOWS, which is the Windows Root directory on your machine. The command session may look like this:

The content of the my.ini file should be

[mysqld]

set basedir to your installation path

basedir=C:/MySQL

set datadir to the location of your data directory

datadir=C:/MySQL/data

4. The subsequent instructions are for Windows XP; for other platforms, you may want to visit

    http://dev.mysql.com/doc/refman/5.0/en/windows-install-archive.html

    Open a new command prompt window (Start->All Programs->Accessories->Command Prompt). Change directory (cd) to C:\MySQL\bin.

    At this point, you have two options:

    - Install MySQL as a Windows Service, so that it starts every time you start Windows (which needs admin privilege).

    - If you do not have such a privilege, you can start it one time using the command prompt.

    Let's look at both approaches.

G.1.1 Installing MySQL as a Windows Service

At the C:\MySQL\bin> prompt, type: mysqld-nt --install (hit Enter). This will add the MySQL to the list of services.

To start the MySQL service, if using 98/NT/2000/XP, go to Control Panel, click on Services (98/NT), or "Administrative Tools -> Services" (2000/XP), then double-click on MySQL. Click on the Start button, and also ensure that the "Automatic" mode is selected under "Startup type." Hit OK; you should see the word "Started" in front of MySQL in the list of services.

It should look like this:

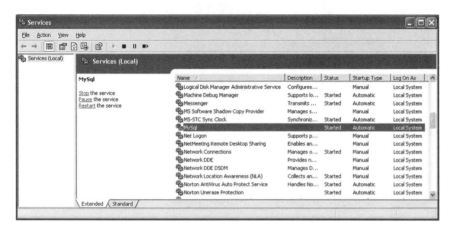

G.1.2   Installing MySQL as a One-Time Service

At the C:\MySQL\bin> prompt, type: mysqld-nt --console (hit Enter). This will show a log of actions it performs as it brings up the MySQL service. The command session may look like this:

This means the MySQL service has started successfully, using the current command prompt window. Let it run in the background. In other words, do NOT close this command prompt window.

G.2   Using MySQL

To begin using MySQL, you should open a new command prompt window, go to C:\MySQL\bin, then type: mysql –u root (hit Enter). Here, the –u root part means you want to login to MySQL with username = root, which needs no password. This should take you to the mysql> prompt as shown here, from which you can type any of the MySQL commands as necessary. The command session may look like this:

G.3   Gracefully Shutting Down the MySQL Service

With the MySQL service running in the original command prompt window, open a new command prompt window, go to C:\MySQL\bin, and type: mysqladmin -u root shutdown (hit Enter); it should shut down the MySQL service gracefully in the original window; these two windows would look something like this:

G.4   Uninstalling the MySQL Service

First shutdown the service (either using the mysqladmin command or the Control Panel -> Administrative Tools -> Services -> MySQL -> (right click) Properties -> Stop.

Next, open a command prompt window, go to C:\MySQL\bin and type: mysqld-nt --remove (hit Enter). This will uninstall the MySQL service. You can now reinstall MySQL if you wish (maybe to get a later version).

APPENDIX H

Downloading the MySQL JDBC Driver

Note: This book uses MySQL JDBC driver version 5.0.4, so the instructions that follow apply to that version. You can consider a more current version in which case you need to replace 5.0.4 with the exact version you use. For any reason, if things do not work out with a more current version, you can always fall back on this specific version that has been verified to work.

1. Go to the MySQL download site:

   `http://dev.mysql.com/downloads/`

2. Click on: Connectors, then on: Connector/J. Click on "Download" in front of "Source and Binaries (zip)".

3. A window will pop up asking whether you want to Open or Save the file. Choose Save, and save it in any folder. Open the file using WinZip. Select all files, do a right-click, choose Extract, and specify the C: drive as the destination. This will create a folder called `mysql-connector-java-5.0.4` under the C: drive, and this folder will contain a file called `mysql-connector-java-5.0.4-bin.jar`.

4. If you have not already created the Chapter 7 folders, create the following folder structure:

   ```
   C:
   + JSP\
       + Chapter7\
           + WEB-INF\
               + lib\
   ```

5. Copy the `mysql-connector-java-5.0.4-bin.jar` file from `C:\mysql-connector-java-5.0.4` to `C:\JSP\Chapter7\WEB-INF\lib`.

APPENDIX I

Downloading Struts

Note: This book uses Struts version 1.3.5, so the instructions that follow apply to that version. You can consider a more current version in which case you need to replace 1.3.5 with the exact version you use. For any reason, if things do not work out with a more current version, you can always fall back on this specific version that has been verified to work.

1. Open the following URL:

   ```
   http://struts.apache.org
   ```

2. Click on the zip file under Full Distribution and save it to any location. Open the file using WinZip. Select all files and extract to the C: drive. This creates a folder called `struts-1.3.5` under the C: drive. If you have not already created the Chapter 9 folders, create the following folder structure:

   ```
   C:
   + JSP\
      + Chapter9\
        + WEB-INF\
           + classes\
           + lib\
           + tlds\
   ```

3. Copy the following .jar files from `C:\struts-1.3.5\lib` to `C:\JSP\Chapter9\WEB-INF\lib`:

    - `commons*.jar` (all .jar files that begin with "commons")

    - `struts-core-1.3.5.jar`

    - `struts-taglib-1.3.5.jar`

4. Open `struts-taglib-1.3.5.jar` using WinZip, then extract the following .tld files to any folder:

    - `struts-bean.tld`

    - `struts-html.tld`

    - `struts-logic.tld`

    Now copy these three files to `C:\JSP\Chapter9\WEB-INF\tlds`.

APPENDIX J

Struts Configuration File and Tag Libraries

J.1 The Struts Configuration File

How does the controller servlet learn about the mappings you want? It would be possible (but tedious) to write a small Java class that simply instantiated new `ActionMapping` instances, and called all of the appropriate setter methods. To make this process easier, Struts uses the Jakarta Commons Digester component to parse an XML-based description of the desired mappings and create the appropriate objects initialized to the appropriate default values.

The developer's responsibility is to create an XML file named `struts-config.xml` and place it in the `WEB-INF` directory of an application.

We have been using the term "Web application" until now, but the term "module" is used in this appendix and needs some elaboration. In order to better organize and manage a Web application, it can be split into smaller modules; in that case, each module must have its own Struts configuration file. This means that multiple Struts configuration files need to be created, one per module, and placed under the `WEB-INF` folder of the Web application. If the Web app is not split in this manner, it would consist of a single module that is identical to the entire Web app. In that case, the terms "Web app" and "module" would mean the same thing and would be equivalent.

The outermost XML element must be `<struts-config>`. Inside of the `<struts-config>` element, there are three important elements that are used to describe actions:

```
<form-beans>
<global-forwards>
<action-mappings>
```

J.1.1   The `<form-beans>` Element

This section contains definitions of form beans—descriptors that are used to create `ActionForm` instances at runtime. You use a `<form-bean>` element (note the singular) for each form bean. The `<form-beans>` element (note the plural) describes the set of form bean descriptors for a module.

Attribute	Meaning
name	A unique identifier for this bean, which will be used to reference it in corresponding action mappings. Usually, this is also the name of the request or session attribute under which this form bean will be stored.
type	The fully qualified Java class name of the `ActionForm` subclass to use with this form bean.

The `<form-bean>` Element

The `<form-bean>` element describes a particular form bean, which is a JavaBean that extends from the `org.apache.struts.action.ActionForm` class. The attributes shown here are defined:

Attribute	Meaning
className	The configuration bean for this form bean object. If specified, the object must be a subclass of the default configuration bean `org.apache.struts.config.FormBeanConfig`.
name	The unique identifier for this form bean. Referenced by the `<action>` element to specify which form bean to use with its request.
type	The fully qualified Java class name of the `ActionForm` subclass to use with this form bean.

J.1.2   The `<global-forwards>` Element

The `<global-forwards>` element describes a set of `ActionForward` objects (`org.apache.struts. action.ActionForward`) that are available to all `Action` objects as a return value. The individual Action-

`Forwards` are configured through nested `<forward>` elements. An `<action>` element may override a global forward by defining a local `<forward>` of the same name.

The global-forwards section is used to create logical name mappings for commonly used presentation pages. Forwards are instances of the `ActionForward` class returned from an `execute()` method of an `ActionForm`. These map logical names to specific resources (typically JSPs), allowing you to change the resource without changing references to it throughout your application. You use a `<forward>` element for each forward definition, which has the following important attributes:

Attribute	Meaning
name	The logical name for this forward. This is used in the `execute()` method of your `ActionForm` to forward to the next appropriate resource; an example would be `homepage`.
path	The context relative path to the resource; an example would be `/index.jsp or /index.do`.
redirect	True or false (default): Whether the `ActionServlet` should redirect to the resource instead of forward. A `redirect = true` means it would send the request as a GET, so INPUT field values on the HTML form on the source page are not accessible on the destination page. You normally want this to be `false`.

Local `<forward>` Elements

The local `<forward>` elements nested within the `<action>` elements are optional but very useful.

J.1.3   The `<action-mappings>` Element

This section contains your action definitions. You use an `<action>` element for each of the mappings you would like to define. Most `<action>` elements will define at least the attributes shown in the following table.

Attribute	Meaning
name	The name of your `<form-bean>` element to use with this action.
path	The application context-relative path to the action.
type	The fully qualified `java` classname of your `Action` class.

The `<action>` Element

The `<action>` element describes an ActionMapping object that is to be used to process a request for a specific module-relative URL. The following are the important and commonly used attributes:

Attribute	Description	Required/Optional	Default Values
path	The module-relative path of the submitted request, starting with a forward slash (/) character, and without the filename extension if extension mapping is used. *Note:* Do not include a period in your path name because it will look like a filename extension and cause your Action to not be located.		
type	The fully qualified Java class name of the Action subclass (org.apache.struts.action.Action) that will process requests for this action mapping. Not valid if either the "forward" or "include" attribute is specified. Exactly one out of "forward," "include," or "type" must be specified.		
name	Name of the form bean, if any, that is associated with this action mapping.		
scope	The context ("request" or "session") that is used to access an ActionForm bean, if any.	Optional if "name" is specified; otherwise it is not valid.	session
forward	Module-relative path of the servlet or other resource that will process this request, instead of the Action class specified by "type." The path WILL NOT be processed through the "forwardPattern" attribute that is configured on the "controller" element for this module.	Exactly one of "forward," "include," or "type" must be specified.	
input	Module-relative path of the action or other resource to which control should be returned if a validation error is encountered.	Valid only when "name" is specified. Required if "name" is specified and the input bean returns validation errors. Optional if "name" is specified and the input bean does not return validation errors.	

Attribute	Description	Required/Optional	Default Values
validate	Set to "true" if the validate method of the Action-Form bean should be called prior to calling the Action object for this action mapping, or set to "false" if you do not want the validate method called.		true

J.2   Configuring the `ActionServlet` Instance

Add a `<servlet>` entry defining the action servlet itself, along with the appropriate initialization parameters. Such an entry should be nested under the `<web-app>` element in web.xml and might look like this:

```
<servlet>
    <servlet-name>action</servlet-name>
    <servlet-class>org.apache.struts.action.ActionServlet</servlet-class>
    <init-param>
        <param-name>config</param-name>
        <param-value>/WEB-INF/struts-config.xml</param-value>
    </init-param>
    <load-on-startup>1</load-on-startup>
</servlet>
```

The following table describes an important and commonly used initialization parameter supported by the action servlet under the `<servlet>` tag—namely, the parameter called `config`. Other parameters are optional and take defaults that are OK. (You can find details of all parameters in the `Javadocs` for the `ActionServlet` class. Refer to Appendix D for the Struts API URL.) Square brackets describe the default values that are assumed if you do not provide a value for that initialization parameter.

Initialization Parameter	Meaning
config	Context-relative path to the XML resource containing the configuration information for the default module. This may also be a comma-delimited list of configuration files. Each file is loaded in turn, and its objects are appended to the internal data structure. [/WEB-INF/struts-config.xml]. **WARNING:** If you define an object of the same name in more than one configuration file, the last one loaded quietly wins.

J.3   Internationalization, Properties Files, and Resource Bundles

Properties files and resource bundles are designed for localization and will render the best available text labels and error messages for a user's locale.

The Struts framework and its custom tag libraries were designed from the ground up to support the internationalization features built into the Java platform. All the field labels and messages can be retrieved from a message resource. To provide messages for another language, simply add another properties file to the resource bundle.

Internationalism aside, other benefits to the message resources approach are consistent labeling between forms and the ability to review all labels and messages from a central location.

Struts has built in support for internationalization. You can define one or more <message-resources> elements for your Web application; modules can define their own resource bundles. Different bundles can be used simultaneously in your application; the "key" attribute is used to specify the desired bundle. The <message-resources> element must nest directly under the <struts-config> element in struts-config.xml. The meaning of various attributes in the <message-resources> element is as follows:

Attribute	Required/Optional	Meaning
className	optional	Classname of configuration bean. [org.apache.struts.config.MessageResourcesConfig]
factory	optional	Classname of MessageResourcesFactory. [org.apache.struts.util.PropertyMessageResourcesFactory]
key	optional	ServletContext attribute key to store this bundle. [org.apache.struts.action.MESSAGE]
null	optional	Set to false to display missing resource keys in your application—for example, *???keyname???* instead of null [true]
parameter	required	Name of the resource bundle. This must be the same as the fully-qualified name of the .properties file. For example, if you have ErrorMessages.properties under the WEB-INF\classes\resources folder, then parameter value must be resources.ErrorMessages.

The next three sections in this appendix summarize the use of important tags from the Struts bean, logic, and html tag libraries. For a comprehensive listing and detailed information on all tags in these tag libraries (including examples), please refer the Struts API URL in Appendix D.

J.4   The Struts bean Tag Library

Struts <bean> tags are useful in defining new beans (in any scope) from a variety of possible sources, and also contain tags to render a particular bean (or bean property) to the output response.

Tag	Use
message	Render an internationalized message string to the response.
resource	Load a Web application resource and make it available as a bean.
define	Define a scripting variable based on the value(s) of the specified bean property.
write	Render the value of the specified bean property to the current JspWriter.

J.5   The Struts logic Tag Library

The Struts logic tag library contains tags that are useful in managing conditional generation of output text looping over object collections for repetitive generation of output text and application flow management.

Tag	Use
present	Generate the nested body content of this tag if the specified value is present in this request.
notPresent	Generate the nested body content of this tag if the specified value is not present in this request.
empty	Evaluate the nested body content of this tag if the requested variable is either null or an empty string.
equal	Evaluate the nested body content of this tag if the requested variable is equal to the specified value.
iterate	Repeat the nested body content of this tag over a specified collection.
greaterThan	Evaluate the nested body content of this tag if the requested variable is greater than the specified value.
greaterEqual	Evaluate the nested body content of this tag if the requested variable is greater than or equal to the specified value.
lessEqual	Evaluate the nested body content of this tag if the requested variable is less than or equal to the specified value.
lessThan	Evaluate the nested body content of this tag if the requested variable is less than the specified value.
notEmpty	Evaluate the nested body content of this tag if the requested variable is neither null, nor an empty String, nor an empty java.util.Collection (tested by the isEmpty() method on the java.util.Collection interface).

Tag	Use
`notEqual`	Evaluate the nested body content of this tag if the requested variable is not equal to the specified value.
`redirect`	Render an HTTP Redirect

J.6   The Struts `html` Tag Library

Tag	Use
`base`	Render an HTML `<base>` element
`button`	Render a button input field
`cancel`	Render a cancel button
`checkbox`	Render a checkbox input field
`errors`	Conditionally display a set of accumulated error messages
`file`	Render a file select input field
`form`	Define an input form
`frame`	Render an HTML frame element
`hidden`	Render a hidden field
`html`	Render an HTML `<html>` element
`image`	Render an input tag of type "image"
`img`	Render an HTML `<img>` tag
`javascript`	Render JavaScript validation based on the validation rules loaded by the `ValidatorPlugIn`
`link`	Render an HTML anchor or hyperlink
`messages`	Conditionally display a set of accumulated messages
`multibox`	Render a checkbox input field
`option`	Render a select option
`options`	Render a collection of select options
`optionsCollection`	Render a collection of select options
`password`	Render a password input field

Tag	Use
radio	Render a radio button input field
reset	Render a reset button input field
rewrite	Render a URL
select	Render a select element
submit	Render a submit button
text	Render an input field of type text
textarea	Render a \<textarea>
xhtml	Render HTML tags as XHTML

Index